The Roman Empire
and the
Indian Ocean

For my parents
William John McLaughlin
and Elizabeth Terry McLaughlin

The Roman Empire and the Indian Ocean

The Ancient World Economy and the Kingdoms of Africa, Arabia and India

Raoul McLaughlin

Pen & Sword
MARITIME

First published in Great Britain in 2014
and reprinted in this format in 2018 by
PEN & SWORD MARITIME
An imprint of Pen & Sword Books Ltd
Yorkshire – Philadelphia

ISBN 978-1-52673-807-3

Typeset by Concept, Huddersfield, West Yorkshire, HD4 5JL.
Printed and bound in England by CPI Group (UK) Ltd, Croydon, CR0 4YY.

Pen & Sword Books Ltd incorporates the imprints of Atlas, Archaeology, Aviation,
Discovery, Family History, Fiction, History, Maritime, Military, Military Classics,
Politics, Select, Transport, True Crime, Air World, Frontline Publishing,
Leo Cooper, Remember When, Seaforth Publishing, The Praetorian Press,
Wharncliffe Local History, Wharncliffe Transport, Wharncliffe True Crime and
White Owl.

For a complete list of Pen & Sword titles please contact
PEN & SWORD BOOKS LTD
47 Church Street, Barnsley, South Yorkshire, S70 2AS, England
E-mail: enquiries@pen-and-sword.co.uk
Website: www.pen-and-sword.co.uk
or
PEN & SWORD BOOKS
1950 Lawrence Rd, Havertown, PA 19083, USA
E-mail: uspen-and-sword@casematepublishers.com
Website: www.penandswordbooks.com

Contents

List of Plates

Acknowledgements

I was educated at Lagan College in Belfast, the first cross-community integrated school to be established in Northern Ireland. The college was founded to offer young people of all cultural backgrounds an education free from the divisions of race, religion or social class. I owe a lot to my school, its staff and principal at that time, Dr Brian Lambkin.

I attended Queen's University Belfast for an undergraduate degree in Archaeology and Ancient History and the early stages of my doctoral research was financed by the Northern Ireland Department of Education and Learning. I am grateful to Doctor John Curran and Professor David Whitehead for giving me the opportunity to teach tutorial classes in Republican Roman and Classical Greek history at Queen's.

After finishing my doctorate in 2006, I completed and published my monograph, *Rome and the Distant East: Trade Routes to the Ancient Lands of India, Arabia and China* (2010). Turning my doctoral research into a book and the completion of further volumes has meant financial hardship. This book is therefore dedicated to my immediate family, my parents William and Elizabeth McLaughlin, my brother Leon and my sister Thayna, all of whom gave me their support and encouragement.

Raoul McLaughlin
Belfast
September 2013

Abbreviations

C.I.L. = *Corpus Inscriptionum Latinarum.*
C.I.S. = *Corpus Inscriptionum Semiticarum.*
F.H.N. = *Fontes Historiae Nubiorum.*
I.L.S. = *Inscriptiones Latinae Selectae.*
O.G.I.S. = *Orientis Graeci Inscriptiones Selectae.*
Periplus = *The Periplus of the Erythraean Sea.*
P. *Vindob.* G. 40822 (*Papyri Vindobonensis Graecus*) = The 'Muziris Papyrus'.
R.E.S. = *Répertoire d'épigraphie Semitique.*

Ancient Figures and Modern Estimates

Roman currency
- 4 brass sesterces = 1 silver denarius.
- 25 silver denarii = 1 gold aureus.

- 1 day's labour: 1 silver denarius.
- 1 month's earnings: 1 gold aureus.
- 1 Roman pound (*libra*) = 12 ounces or 329 grams.

- Greek silver talent: 24,000 sesterces.
- Greek silver drachma: 1 denarius or 4 sesterces.
- Greek silver talent: 6,000 drachma (denarii).

- Egyptian silver talent: 6,000 sesterces.
- Egyptian silver drachma: 1 sesterce.
- Tetradrachm: 1 denarius (4 sesterces).

Mediterranean shipments
- Citizens in Rome eligible for the government grain dole: 200,000 men.[1]
- Size of grain dole: 88,000 tons.[2]
- Contribution of Egypt: 29,000 tons.[3]

Cost of a Legion = 11 million sesterces
- 5,000 Legionaries paid 900 sesterces annually = 4.5 million.[4]
- 5,000 Auxiliaries paid 750 sesterces annually = 3.75 million.[5]
- 54 Centurions (each paid 13,500); 4 Centurions First Cohort, *Primi Ordines* (paid 27,000); Senior Centurion – *Primus Pilus* (54,000); 5 Tribunes (45,000); Legion Legate (61,000) = 1 million sesterces.[6]
- Discharge bonuses (*praemia*) paid after 25 years service: *c.*120 legionaries per year granted 12,000 sesterces = 1.4 million plus 1.1 million sesterces bonus for auxiliaries.[7]
- Plus additional cost of junior and auxiliary officers, cavalry pay (900 sesterces per horseman), purchase of cavalry horses (deposit cost: 500 sesterces) and pack animals.[8] Animal feed perhaps received through local taxes.[9]
- Cost of food and clothing was deducted from troop pay.[10] But some soldiers were able to accumulate significant funds in their military accounts.[11]

Roman Military (300,000 professional soldiers)
- Augustan era (27 BC–AD 14): 28 Legions reduced to 25 after the Varus disaster (AD 9).[12]

- First-Second century AD: 27–30 Legions in service (150,000 Legionaries supported by 150,000 Auxiliaries).[13]

Modern estimates for Roman State spending (1,000 million sesterces per annum)[14]

- Military: Legions and Auxiliaries, Praetorian Guard in Rome and Roman navy = 640+ million sesterces.
- Civilian Employees = 75 million sesterces.
- Imperial hand-outs including *donatives* (occasional cash gifts to soldiers) = 44 million sesterces.
- Imperial building projects = 60 million sesterces.
- Emperor's Household and imperial gifts = 50–100 million sesterces.

Ancient Greek and Roman Authors

484 BC–425 BC: Lifetime of the Greek writer Herodotus, author of the first classical history.

60 BC–30 BC: The Greek historian Diodorus Siculus writes his universal history.

70 BC–19 BC: Lifetime of the Roman poet Virgil.

20 BC–AD 24: The Greek geographer Strabo writes and revises his *Geography*.

65 BC–8 BC: Lifetime of the Latin poet Horace.

50 BC–AD 15: Lifetime of the Latin poet Propertius who wrote eulogies.

43 BC–AD 18: Lifetime of Ovid, a Roman poet who composed important works on the theme of love and seduction.

AD 14: The first Roman Emperor Augustus dies and his achievements are published in an inscription called the *Res Gestae*.

AD 14–AD 37: A wealthy Roman named Apicius becomes famous for his banquets. His name is attached to a collection of household recipes.

AD 27–AD 66: Lifetime of Petronius, a Roman courtier who wrote a story called the *Satyricon*.

AD 50: An anonymous Greek merchant writes the *Periplus of the Erythraean Sea*, describing Roman trade voyages around and across the Indian Ocean.

AD 77: Pliny the Elder, Roman governor and advisor to the Emperor Vespasian, publishes his encyclopedic *Natural History*.

AD 40–AD 102: Lifetime of the Roman poet Martial who composed a large collection of Latin epigrams.

AD 45–AD 96: Lifetime of Statius, a Latin poet who composed works commenting on Roman society and promoting patrons.

AD 55–AD 138: Lifetime of Juvenal, a Latin poet who composed a collection of satires.

AD 61–AD 112: Lifetime of Pliny the Younger, a Roman magistrate who wrote and published a series of letters to colleagues and superiors, including the Emperor Trajan.

AD 56–AD 117: Lifetime of Tacitus, a Latin senator and leading historian.

AD 46–AD 119: A Greek historian named Plutarch writes a series of moralistic biographies of famous Greek and Roman generals and statesmen.

AD 119: An imperial secretary named Suetonius published a biography of early Roman Emperors.

AD 150: An Alexandrian mathematician named Claudius Ptolemy publishes a world Geography containing detailed coordinates for the construction of maps.

AD 129–AD 200: Lifetime of the renowned Greek doctor Galen, who wrote numerous medical texts.

AD 205–AD 229: A Roman Consul named Dio Cassius writes a Greek history of the Roman Empire from its earliest times to his own era.

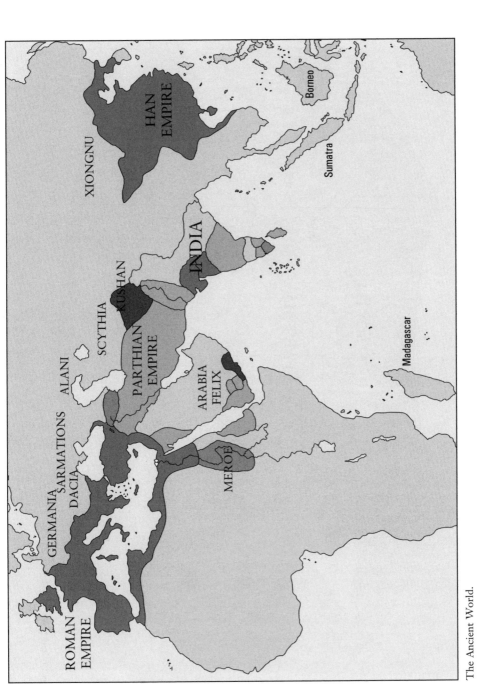

The Ancient World.

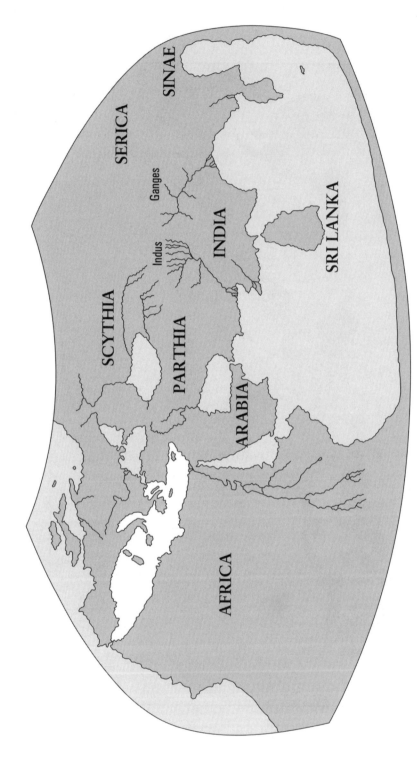

Claudius Ptolemy's World Map (AD 150).

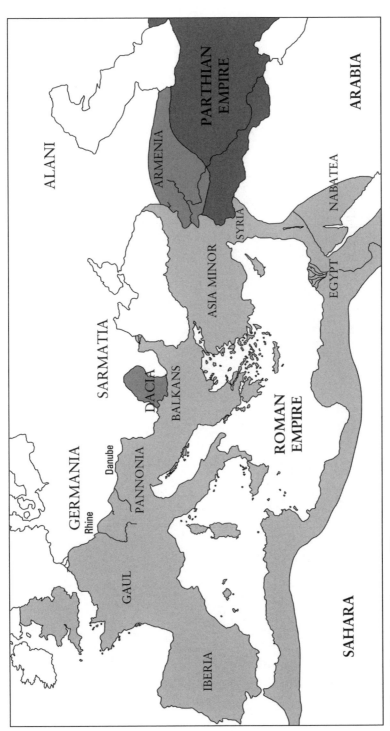

The Roman Empire (second century AD).

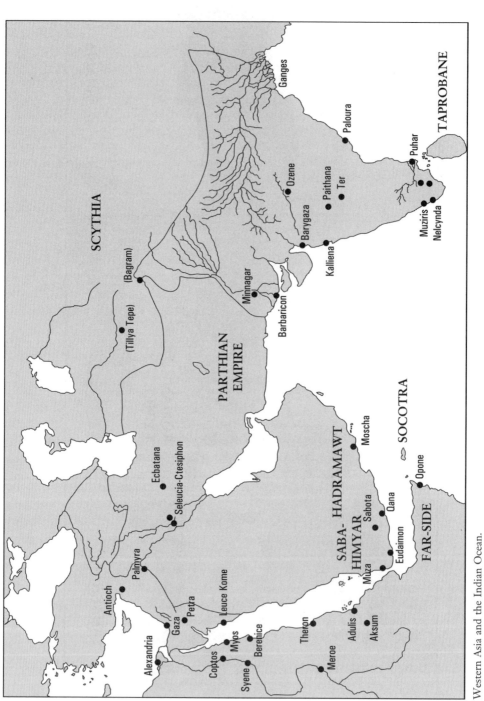

Western Asia and the Indian Ocean.

Introduction:
The Ancient Economy

This book sets out to bring the Ancient World Economy to widespread attention. It focusses on ancient evidence without the influence of modern precepts, ideology, or theory-based economic models. The book presents the case for an ancient world economy and gives a perspective to eastern trade by discussing better known phenomena such as the Roman grain dole. Information is based on the relevant source testimony and archaeological remains from the main civilisations involved in the Ancient Economy. These explain the condition of the Roman Empire and reveal what imperial authorities knew about State revenues and the value of international trade.

This book deals with a fundamental question – how did the Roman Empire function and in particular, how did it pay for its military costs? The answer requires a wider view than that presented by most Classical Historians who confine their studies to the Mediterranean and the western part of Europe. Roman contacts with eastern civilisations have been judged to be outside the scope of Classical Ancient History and therefore beyond productive scholarly consideration. But the Roman Empire belonged to an ancient world economy that stretched thousands of miles across the Indian Ocean and significant commercial contacts linked Roman subjects with their distant counterparts in east Africa, southern Arabia and the kingdoms of ancient India. These trade exchanges are confirmed by source testimony from many different cultures and verified by numerous archaeological finds.

Preoccupied by contemporary issues, past generations of Classical Historians have dismissed the significance of ancient India and China. The last Classical Historian to write a book on Indo-Roman commerce was a Cambridge based scholar named E.H. Warmington. Born in the nineteenth century, Warmington published *The Commerce between the Roman Empire and India* in 1927 at a time when India, Somalia, the Sudan and Aden (in Yemen) were part of the British Empire. Current debate on the Roman economy preserves a complex legacy of past fixations, including mid-twentieth century reactions to the Soviet Union (a centralised socialist state-economy) and the issue of whether Rome was 'market orientated' or 'capitalist' drew relevance from Cold War concerns (1947–1991). However, some of the underlying assumptions defining modern study are still grounded in much older traditions, including nineteenth-century concepts of social class, race and colonialism.

Current historians often use modern theory-based models as a shortcut to identify and explain processes and qualify select ancient evidence. Most current discussions of the Roman economy are a reaction to debate-led theories and generally support, or criticise, pre-set thesis statements. Debate is focussed on semantics and on defining abstract features such as 'market growth' or 'economic prosperity'. A careful re-examination of ancient evidence reveals the authentic Roman economy and this can be done without modern pretexts, or the use of current models as a foil for debate. The sources suggest that the movement of world resources through international commerce was a vital element in the success of Imperial Rome.

The Romans were well aware that their Mediterranean Empire was not the only powerful regime in the ancient world and there were other prominent powers in the east that matched their administration. Some Latin poets publicised ideas of a globalised Roman authority, but their views were far from reality.[1] Anyone in a Roman crowd moving through a commercial district could see evidence of a wider ancient world in the fashions worn by rich patrons, the incense burnt at religious altars, or the spices that flavoured many Mediterranean meals. This is the ancient world described and evidenced by the ancient sources and this book explains how these distant contacts provided Rome with the revenues it needed to finance its army and sustain its Empire, thereby enabling the *Pax Romana* (Roman Peace and good-order).

The Romans knew about India, but were unaware of the Far East until the first century BC when silk began to reach the Mediterranean by way of the Parthian Empire which ruled ancient Iran. There were thousands of miles of steppe-land and desert between Rome and China and the presence of intervening regimes, such as Parthia, prevented contact and limited the flow of information. The Parthians understood the profits to be made by controlling overland trade and therefore denied Roman subjects access to the caravan routes that led across Iran.[2]

The final Civil War of the Roman Republic was fought in 31 BC, when the Roman general Octavian, adopted son of Julius Caesar, declared war on the Egyptian Queen Cleopatra and her consort Mark Antony. Cleopatra ruled the rich Ptolemaic Kingdom of Egypt and Mark Antony commanded the Roman Legions of the eastern Mediterranean. Together they planned to defeat Octavian with a rapid seaborne campaign, then seize Rome and take power in Italy. The decisive sea battle was fought at Actium in western Greece. During the engagement, when the galleys commanded by Mark Antony seemed to be losing, Cleopatra suddenly turned her fleet about and fled. In desperation Antony followed Cleopatra back to the Egyptian capital Alexandria and so lost the battle. Anthony's eastern Legions deserted him and the victorious Octavian readied his army to capture Egypt and put an end to the reign of the Ptolemaic Queen Cleopatra.

The world changed when Rome annexed Egypt and gained access to the Red Sea shipping-lanes that led into the Indian Ocean. Within a decade, there were over a hundred Roman ships sailing to India and the Mediterranean markets were suddenly inundated with goods from across the eastern world.[3] These imports included products such as incense, spices, gemstones and silks. The Roman Empire imposed a quarter-rate import tax known as the *tetarte* on these commodities and as trade increased, the *tetarte* began to generate enormous new revenues for the imperial regime. It is estimated that by the first century AD, foreign trade was supplying Roman government with perhaps a third of the income it required to finance the entire Empire.[4]

The Emperor Augustus used these new revenues to fund the first full-time professional army created by any ancient regime.[5] This military institution was both unique and crucial to the long-term security and success of Roman civilisation. It was a career-based military force structured around the Roman Legions and their auxiliary support. At its height, the Roman Empire employed 300,000 professional soldiers to defend its vulnerable frontiers and maintain order amongst subject nations. But this army depended upon the finance that was obtained from taxes imposed on international business. Consequently, the fortunes of the Roman Empire were inextricably linked to world trade and in particular, to the eastern economies of India and China.

CHAPTER ONE

Revenue and the Roman Economy

Roman authorities were well informed about the revenues that sustained their Empire. For example, during the Republican period Cicero listed the information that a senator ought to possess concerning the interests of the Roman State. This included, 'how many soldiers the Roman Republic has, what are its financial resources, what allies it has, who are its friends and what subjects have to pay tax'.[1] Many of these details were known by members of the Roman ruling class comprising *senators* and *equites*.

The Roman elite also recorded and circulated financial information within their own writings. In his last book on Roman History the Greek author Appian promised to consider 'the size of the Roman army, the tribute that they collect from each province, what they spend on naval garrisons, and other things of that nature'.[2] Unfortunately this work has not survived and few modern historians now recognise the significance of the extant ancient testimony that does describe Roman finances.

Some of the more astute Emperors appointed men who had demonstrated a good understanding of provincial finances to high office. For example, the Emperor Hadrian selected Antoninus Pius to be his successor because he displayed an array of interests and noble qualities, which included a thorough knowledge of State business. It was said that Antoninus 'knew the budgets of all the provinces and their sources of revenue extremely well'.[3] When the Emperor Augustus was gravely ill in 23 BC he gave a senator named Piso a 'list of the military and the public revenues written in a book'.[4]

A staff of administrative slaves and freedmen worked for the imperial regime in order to manage provincial finances and keep track of the different revenues and expenses. The Emperor operated his own imperial treasury called the *fiscus* which was managed by an official known as a *rationibus*. The court poet Statius describes the responsibilities of the *rationibus*, 'to him alone have been entrusted the records of the revered treasury, the riches received from all peoples, revenues that have come from the entire world'. The *rationibus* kept income accounts and had to track expenditure. As Statius explains, 'he balances income against major expenses – such as how much will be needed to maintain the demands of the Roman military in every region'.[5]

Newly appointed Roman governors brought some of their own staff to the provinces and these men worked alongside the existing administration. Most governors therefore had good knowledge of the revenues and expenses involved in the provinces they managed and this information was freely exchanged between their colleagues in Rome who had served in various regions of the Empire during their own careers.[6] Official information about provincial revenues could be assembled into a comprehensive report and on the discretion of the Emperor these accounts were made widely available to the Roman elite. Unfortunately, most medieval scholars were not interested in preserving documents that contained mainly financial information; so much of this data is no longer available. But the surviving sources do mention several occasions when an imperial budget was circulated amongst the Roman governing class.

At his death in AD 14, the Emperor Augustus left a document in his Will that described the overall revenues and expenses of the Roman Empire. He also left instructions that this financial information was to be read out in front of the Senate to inform the ruling class about the fiscal condition of the Roman State. Suetonius reveals that the document gave an account of: 'how many soldiers there were in service and where they were; how much money there was in the central Roman treasury and the provincial treasuries; how much were the outstanding revenues and where they could be located'. Tacitus provides further details on the same incident stating that 'the document contained a description of the resources of the State, the number of citizens and allies under arms, information on the fleets, subject kingdoms, provinces, taxes both direct and indirect, necessary expenses and customary bounties.'[7] Suetonius refers to the administration that managed this financial data. Augustus stated that his representatives would 'supply the names of freedmen and slave-secretaries who could provide accounts on demand regarding each of the categories of expenditure'.[8]

The Emperor Caligula published an imperial budget at the onset of his reign (AD 37–41). In it he made a commitment to deposed client princes by restoring their former realms and repaying them the revenues that had been extracted from their territories when the Emperor Tiberius was in power. Suetonius reports: 'any king who Caligula restored to his throne was awarded the arrears of taxes and revenue that had accumulated since his disposition. This included Antiochus of Commagene who got a refund of a million gold pieces from the treasury.'[9] This initiative indicates that the Roman State kept financial records stretching back over several decades and these archives were available for official consultation if it proved necessary.

In certain parts of the Empire the collection of some Roman taxes was granted to private companies in return for a fee paid to the State. Precise details about these arrangements were not generally made public since many of the profit-making companies included members of the governing class. There was a change in policy during the reign of Nero when Tacitus reports that 'the Emperor issued an edict that the regulations about every branch of the public revenue should be published including details which had previously been withheld'. These details revealed how much provincial income came from the sale of tax-collecting contracts and 'arrangements were made to ensure an exact correspondence between the amount of income and required spending'.[10]

Knowledge of Trade

Roman authorities knew about the scale and value of eastern trade because it was part of the tax system that sustained their Empire. International trade had to pass through designated custom posts and all exports and imports were subject to fixed-rate taxes. Source evidence suggests that total trade figures were available, along with specific totals for certain commodities such as coin or bullion.[11]

In the case of Indo-Roman trade, members of imperial government such as Pliny the Elder could easily obtain information about bullion exports from Roman tax records collected at Coptos. All goods sent to the Egyptian Red Sea ports had to pass through this single custom station and separate officials were tasked with assessing different commodities.[12] Trade ventures were also timed according to seasonal schedules, so goods intended for export to India would generally have to pass through custom stations during certain identifiable periods. For example, cargoes headed for India were loaded before July and goods destined for the nearest ports in East Africa would pass through the custom stations in July and August to facilitate sailings in September.[13] Roman officials who knew the amount of revenue gained from customs tax could easily estimate the overall value of any particular export. Frontier customs taxes were set at a quarter-value, so the collected revenue multiplied by four would suggest the scale of trade to those who wanted to know the figures.[14]

In the case of exports from Egypt, the Romans probably allowed private business to bid for the right to collect certain government imposed customs taxes. Acquiring a contract was a competitive process and the winning company had to outbid rival businesses in order to gain the commission. The successful company had to keep the bid beneath the value that the tax might produce and by this means cover their costs, yet still make sufficient profit from the collection rights. Any tax collected beyond the bid amount could be kept by the private company, so there were often good opportunities for profit. These contracts gave Roman authorities an indication of trade levels, especially if particular companies bid to collect taxes on specific exports such as bullion, or fabrics.

The export amounts suggested by tax records would have been confirmed by businessmen who had dealings with central Roman government. These included Annius Ploclamus who ran an eastern trade business and had a freedman associate manage his contract to collect Red Sea taxes (AD 50).[15] This freedman discovered a new route to Sri Lanka and returned with a team of Sinhalese ambassadors. Annius Ploclamus may have accompanied this embassy to meet the Emperor Claudius, with his freedman probably serving as translator for the visiting envoys. During these proceedings the Emperor and his advisers would have had an opportunity to question Annius and his freedmen about the scale and value of Indo-Roman trade. Later members of the Anni family are evidenced in Puteoli, including another Annius Ploclamus who served as a *decuriones* (town magistrate) in AD 187 and an L. Annius, the son of Annius Numisianus, who was honoured with a public statue.[16]

A further example indicates the contacts that could occur between important businessmen and senior members of Roman government. Josephus mentions a prominent Jewish businessman named Tiberius Julius Alexander (Major) who was an *alabarch* in charge of collecting import taxes at Alexandria.[17] This income made Tiberius Alexander extremely influential and he is probably the 'Alexander' mentioned in the *New Testament* when the Apostles Peter and John began their ministry in Jerusalem after the Crucifixion.[18] Josephus reports that Alexander paid for gold-plated decorations to embellish the nine gates that led into the Jewish Temple complex in Jerusalem.[19] Sometime before AD 35 Alexander also lent the Jewish prince Herod Agrippa 200,000 Greek drachmas to repay his debts in Rome, with 30,000 handed over in Alexandria and another 170,000 to be collected in Puteoli.[20] Subsequently, he arranged for his youngest son Marcus to marry the daughter of Herod Agrippa in a union that would combine business finances with royal lineage.[21]

Alexander also assisted the imperial family and when Antonia, the mother of Claudius, wanted someone to oversee her Egyptian properties she chose Alexander to manage these affairs.[22] In AD 38, Tiberius Alexander joined a political delegation to Rome led by his brother the Jewish philosopher Philo. The Emperor Caligula detained Tiberius Alexander in Rome as a political hostage in order to guarantee compliance amongst the Jewish community in Alexandria. He was not released until Claudius became emperor in AD 41.[23]

Tiberius Alexander used his profits to give his eldest son a political career in imperial service and to establish his younger son Marcus as a leading businessman. Beginning in AD 37, transport receipts from the *Nicanor Archive* reveal that Marcus had commercial agents at Coptos and in the main Red Sea ports. In Myos Hormos he used a free agent named Saturneinos and a slave managed his business at Berenice.[24] Marcus was sending ships to India and trading along the sea-lanes described in the merchant handbook called the *Periplus of the Erythaean Sea*. During this period his elder brother Tiberius Julius Alexander (Junior) held office as a Roman administrator in the Thebaid district of southern Egypt, which included Coptos.[25] Marcus died sometime before AD 44, as his widow remarried that year.[26] By AD 66, his brother Tiberius Alexander Junior was serving as the governor of Egypt and during the Roman civil war of AD 69 supported the general Vespasian in his bid to become emperor.[27] When Vespasian was victorious, Tiberius Alexander became one of the most influential people in the Empire. He was part of Vespasian's inner circle of advisors, but he also had family members involved in the eastern trade business. Tiberius Alexander could therefore confirm details about the scale and value of international commerce, including the amount of bullion carried aboard Roman vessels bound for India. Tiberius Alexander ended his military career as Prefect of the Praetorian Guard and his statue was erected in the Roman forum to honour his achievements.[28]

Other leading members of Roman government spent their early careers in the frontier provinces and would have learned about foreign trade from these experiences. A responsible Roman governor would have toured his province to inspect the outlying garrisons and investigate issues on the frontier.[29] For example, Strabo received figures for the size of the Roman fleet sailing to India while he was on a tour with the Roman governor Aelius Gallus. Gallus was on a journey from Alexandria through Coptos to the cities of Syene and Philae on the frontier between Egypt and Nubia.[30] It would have been a simple matter to question a trusted Roman businessman and enquire how much bullion was typically carried aboard vessels sailing to different eastern destinations.

Roman authorities could have gained information about the scale of Arabian trade at Coptos, Leuke Kome, or Gaza. The *Periplus* reports that there was a Roman customs post at the Nabataean port of Leuke Kome and this garrison was commanded by a centurion to ensure that all quarter-taxes were paid in full.[31] Pliny also mentions 'our customs agents' at the Mediterranean port of Gaza and he was able to give precise figures for the amount of tax taken in non-Roman territory. He reports that 688 denarii were collected per camel-load by foreign agents on the Incense Trail between southern Arabia and Nabataea.[32] This indicates that precise figures were available for taxes that included regions beyond Roman control. Imperial officials would have known how many camels were arriving at Gaza, how much revenue this trade raised in customs tax and how much Roman bullion was being expended to sustain this commerce.

Roman authorities knew about the amount of incense being produced in southern Arabia and this information would have come from traders and foreign envoys.[33] By the first century AD the Hadramawt Kingdom was managing the main frankincense groves as a royal monopoly and the Qataban realm was collecting a quarter-tithe on all myrrh produced in its territories.[34] Both regimes therefore had good knowledge about the scale of incense production in their territory and were able to convey these details to the Roman government. Pliny and the author of the *Periplus* suggest that Arabian kings sent frequent embassies to the Roman Emperors and these officials could confirm the value of the incense trade.[35]

Roman authorities could also have calculated the value of Arabian trade by estimating how much incense was produced in southern Arabia. The Roman elite devoted their attention to vineyards, so the idea of estimating production from areas under cultivation was a familiar concept.[36] Pliny repeats well-known figures about the size of the incense-growing territories in southern Arabia and the number of families tasked with cultivating these plots.[37] Leading Roman authorities could have estimated frankincense production from these details.

The Roman System: The Republican Period
During the Republican period, the Roman regime operated an army raised mainly by citizen levies. The Romans and their Italian allies recruited and trained a body of soldiers drawn from their large citizen populations. As Rome expanded, it raised revenue by imposing war indemnities on the defeated foreign powers and demanding regular tribute from subject regions.

Conquest was a profitable venture for Roman commanders and their troops, who could capture booty and seize foreign resources. But when a region was conquered, the Roman State had to assume the long-term costs of regional administration and the expense of defending that particular territory. This was an expensive process and often, in the long-term, the cost of a region was barely covered by its regular revenues.

Between 66 and 63 BC, the Roman general Pompey Magnus campaigned in the eastern Mediterranean and added substantial new territories to the Republic. These included Bithynia et Pontus and Cilicia in Asia Minor, most of Syria and the island of Crete. He also accepted further regions into Roman control as protectorates, including the Kingdom of Judea. In 61 BC, Pompey staged an elaborate Triumph in Rome to display the wealth of these newly subdued territories. Amongst the exhibits, Pompey paraded information about the revenues his conquests would provide for the enlarged Roman Empire. Plutarch reports that, 'it was shown on written tablets that the new taxes Pompey added to the State came to 50 million denarii and the Republic now received revenues of 85 million denarii'.[38] This meant that Pompey had increased the Roman revenues from 200 million to 340 million sesterces per annum.

In this period, the Ptolemaic Kingdom was the last major Greek regime to retain power in the eastern Mediterranean. By 80 BC, the Ptolemaic regime was confined to ancient Egypt where it received revenues worth about 300 million sesterces from a highly prosperous, well-ordered kingdom. Details of the Ptolemaic revenues are given by the Greek geographer Strabo who spent time in both Alexandria and Rome during the Augustan period. Strabo also consulted legal and political speeches given by prominent Republican statesmen who were contemporaries of Pompey and King Ptolemy XII Auletes (80–51 BC). Strabo reports, 'Cicero tells us about the revenues of Egypt in a certain speech. He states that Auletes, who was the father of Cleopatra, received annual revenue of 12,500 talents'.[39] In Roman currency this was equivalent to about 75 million silver denarii, or 300 million sesterces.

Asia Minor, the Near East and Egypt were ancient urbanised territories that had been part of sophisticated and well-organised kingdoms for thousands of years. Consequently, they had pre-existing well-developed monetary economies that were capable of producing large cash revenues on a regular basis. By contrast most of northern Europe was rich in agricultural produce, but had few centralised civic institutions such as towns, or mints able to produce and circulate extensive currencies. Julius Caesar added a large territory to the Roman Empire when he conquered greater Gaul (58–50 BC), but the region provided only moderate income for the Roman Republic. Suetonius reports that 'when Caesar reduced the defeated parts of Gaul to the status of a province he imposed upon them a yearly tribute of 40 million sesterces'.[40] This is a seventh of what Egypt provided for their Ptolemaic Kings.

During the late Republic, Asia Minor (Anatolia) was possibly the only Roman territory that, after paying its own costs, was still able to forward substantial revenues to the central government in Rome. In a law court speech, Cicero explains that 'the revenues of the other provinces are such that we can scarcely derive enough from them for their own protection'. Asia Minor was an exception because it exported more valuable goods than other subject territories. This was because it had rich soil, a wide variety of crops and a large amount of land given over to pasture. As Cicero explains, 'due to multitude of its exports, Asia is greatly superior to all other countries'.[41] Cicero confirms this situation in a political speech delivered in 63 BC. In it he calls Roman Asia 'the most beautiful estate belonging to the Roman people – the main source of our riches, our chief ornament in time of peace, our chief source of supply in time of war, the foundation of our revenues'.[42]

When the Roman general Mark Antony took the eastern Mediterranean as his share of the divided Empire, he made an alliance with the Ptolemaic Queen, Cleopatra VIII. Together they used the Ptolemaic revenues to fund an expensive war against the Parthian Empire which ruled ancient Persia (40–33 BC). During this period, increased taxes damaged Egyptian businesses and the regime neglected important elements of Egypt's economic infrastructure, including the canals necessary for irrigation and transport.[43] When Octavian conquered Egypt in 30 BC, it was reported that this new province could only provide revenues of about 40 million sesterces per annum. Velleius sums up the situation when he writes that Octavian 'made Egypt tributary, thereby contributing nearly as much revenue to the treasury as Caesar had brought in from the Gauls'.[44]

The inclusion of Egypt into the Roman Empire brought the total imperial revenues to about 420 million sesterces per annum. This included the Republican provinces (340 million), Caesar's Gaul (40 million) and newly conquered Egypt (40 million sesterces). But this income alone was not enough to sustain the enlarged Empire and provide the funds needed to meet its long-term military costs. Octavian (Augustus) therefore convened a conference with his closest advisors to debate the future of the Roman State. He was told by his leading general Agrippa 'you will need to procure a large supply of money from all available sources, because our present revenues are not sufficient to support the troops and our other expenses'.[45] The best solution for this revenue deficit seemed to be further conquests and plans were therefore made to seize the Sabaean Kingdom of southern Arabia and invade the Parthian Empire.[46]

By this period the Sabaean Kingdom was producing over 40 million sesterces worth of incense per annum.[47] The nation also had stockpiles of precious metals that could be used to subsidise the Roman regime and postpone the approaching financial crisis. Strabo was an associate of the Roman general Aelius Gallus who the Emperor ordered to 'gain authority over these Arabs, or subjugate them'. Strabo explains that 'the Emperor's plans were based on well-established reports that the Arabs are very wealthy because they sell aromatics and extremely valuable gemstones for gold and silver. But they never offer the wealth they receive from this trade to outsiders.'[48] However, when the invasion failed, the imperial regime was forced to seek other revenue sources to pay for its long-term expenses.

The Cost of Empire

Modern scholars have calculated the costs of the Roman Empire based on its military expenses and other outlays. Army pay, military numbers and other items of State spending have all been analysed and estimated to create figures for the Roman State 'budget'.[49] These estimates also indicate the income of the Empire, since the regime must have had sufficient revenues to pay its regular expenses.

But the problem of how and where these revenues were acquired is harder to clarify.

It seems that compared with other ancient regimes Rome did not impose large amounts of tribute on its subject populations. In 167 BC, the Romans imposed an annual tribute on the conquered kingdom of Macedonia. Plutarch reports: 'Macedonia was restored to its people. Their cities were permitted freedom and independence and in return they were to pay the Romans 100 talents (2.4 million sesterces) in tribute, a sum less than half of what they used to pay to their kings'.[50] Similar policies were enacted during the Imperial era and Tacitus explains that when the Kingdom of Cappadocia was made a province in AD 17, 'royal tributes were reduced to encourage hope that Roman rule would be lenient'.[51]

Tribute levels imposed by the Roman State probably remained relatively stable over long periods of time. Strabo reports that after Marcus Metellus conquered the Celtiberians he placed an annual tribute of 14 million sesterces on Spain (143 BC). A century later Spain was able to provide funds worth 18 million sesterces to the faction that opposed Julius Caesar during the Civil War that began in 49 BC.[52]

During the Imperial period the Romans collected regular census reports from subject provinces that contained details about population size and private wealth. Roman government used these details to allocate where and how regional tribute was to be collected. Tribute was seen as an act of political submission and many communities resented paying any tax to a foreign power, even when the tribute taken was minimal. Augustus imposed three censuses on Greater Gaul between 27 BC and AD 14.[53] Many Gauls would have resented this State intrusion and the census taken in 12 BC provoked a regional uprising.[54]

The tribute that the Romans imposed on their eastern conquests seems to have been comparatively low and probably not subject to regular increases. Herodotus provides tribute figures for the Persian Empire in the fifth century BC. He reports that western Anatolia gave the Persian King Darius 1,170 Attic talents per annum (equivalent to 28 million sesterces).[55] During the second century AD, the Roman province of Asia included most of this territory and collected a similar amount of tribute.[56] This suggests that Rome did not demand large sums or substantially increase tribute payments imposed on its subject territories.

Cicero writes that in the Republican period Asia Minor was the only region to provide Rome with worthwhile surplus revenues and most provinces of the Roman Empire could barely meet their own protection costs.[57] Furthermore, the revenues forwarded to central government in Rome were relatively small. During the Civil War of 43 BC, the *quaestor* (lieutenant governor) in charge of the Roman province of Asia delivered 2 million sesterces to the Republican commander Brutus. Plutarch explains 'he gave him 500,000 drachmas which was the money that he was delivering to Italy'.[58] This situation seems to have continued during the Imperial period when the Emperors were in power. In most Roman provinces locally produced revenues were used up by regional costs and only a small token amount of surplus wealth was forwarded to Rome as a symbolic act of compliance.

In the Imperial period there were almost forty Roman provinces and most sent less than 4 million sesterces to central government as part of their annual tribute. This situation is confirmed by Seneca who reports that the Emperor Caligula spent 10 million sesterces on a single banquet, representing the 'tribute-money from three provinces'.[59] When Caligula restored the small Kingdom of Commagene in Asia Minor, he repaid its ruler 1 million aurei (100 million sesterces). This was the amount that the Roman regime had collected from the region as tribute in the course of twenty years.[60] The figure suggests that a prosperous and well-urbanised territory might only produce about 5 million sesterces of surplus revenue per annum. The idea that most provinces provided limited revenue could explain other measures. In AD 67, the Emperor Nero made all of Greece exempt from direct Roman taxes to celebrate his tour of the leading Greek festivals.[61] The Roman system was able to support this scheme because Greece was not a heavily garrisoned region and probably sent only small amounts of revenue to Rome.

The Roman ethos promoted the idea of public spending on buildings and grandiose displays to benefit, or entertain, large numbers of people. This meant that Roman governors were encouraged to spend most of their excess revenues on improving their province. Any surplus funds were spent on expensive acts of State benevolence, including regional building initiatives. Little of this surplus was ultimately transported to central government in Rome and most regional revenues were used for the benefit of local citizens and subjects. Philostratus describes how all the revenues raised in the Roman province of Asia were spent on a single project to benefit one city. They were used for the construction of an aqueduct that took several years to complete and cost 28 million sesterces.[62] This policy of spending local surplus would have been sufficient to manage the Empire, except that some Roman provinces could not meet their own long-term costs and therefore were governed at a loss.

Deficit regions were a problem for the late Roman Republic and certain European provinces had to be subsidised from treasury funds. Cicero describes events in 57 BC when Calpurnius Piso was made governor of Macedonia with the support of his son-in-law Julius Caesar. Piso was granted funds by the Roman treasury to finance his governorship, but Cicero accused him of keeping the money for personal gain. In court he claimed, 'the treasury gave you 18 million sesterces as governor of your province, but you left this money in Rome to be lent out at interest'.[63]

Deficit Regions

The ancient evidence indicates that most of the Empire's revenue deficit territories were in northern Europe. Northern Europe may have been well populated and rich in agricultural produce and natural materials, but before the Roman conquest, urban development had been limited. The Celts and the Germans did not live in rich kingdoms similar to the long-established urbanised civilisations existing in the Near East and India. Their economies were not currency-centred and did not have the benefit of tax-systems developed over many centuries to produce easily transferable cash revenues for centralised government. This was a serious problem for the Roman State, as large garrisons were needed to hold and defend the frontier territories of northern Europe and these regions could not support their military cost with locally raised taxes. The Roman State therefore sent large amounts of money into these regions in the form of army pay. This military money attracted merchants and supported the businesses that kept garrisons supplied with essential goods and services.

The provinces with revenue shortfalls became a long-term problem as Appian confirms in his *Roman History*, written about AD 150. Appian explains, 'the Romans lose money on some of their subject nations, but they are ashamed to set them aside, even though they are detrimental'.[64] Some of these deficit territories were necessary for frontier defence and others provided corridors for contact between crucial regions. Some had been places where ambition or honour had taken Roman interests, then committed their forces to long-term occupation.

Defence was an important issue as between 113 and 101 BC the Roman Empire withstood a large-scale invasion of Germanic peoples called the Cimbri and the Teutones, who had migrated through Gaul towards Italy. This invasion was the mass movement of thousands of refugee families supported by a vast horde of warriors who threatened to overrun the Italian peninsula and permanently occupy Roman territory. The crisis was averted by a Roman general named Gaius Marius who was proclaimed 'Third Founder of Rome' because he preserved Roman possession of the land.[65]

Julius Caesar used the subsequent Roman fear of Germanic invasion to justify his conquest of Gaul. Caesar advised: 'it would be dangerous to the Roman people if the Germans should become accustomed to cross the Rhine. What if a great mass of them entered Gaul? After possessing Gaul, these wild and savage men will not restrain themselves. They will enter our province (Transalpine Gaul) and march into Italy, just as the Cimbri and Teutones attempted'.[66] His solution was to subjugate Gaul to prevent the region falling under Germanic control (58–50 BC).

His successor the Emperor Augustus thought that the part of Germany that lay between the Rhine and the Elbe was a viable conquest. After two decades of campaigning, the region seemed pacified (12 BC–AD 6). But in AD 9 there was an uprising among German tribes who annihilated three Roman Legions as they marched through the dense Teutoburg Forest. After this defeat, Roman forces withdrew back to the Rhine frontiers and Greater Germany was left to its native peoples.

Other conquests ordered by the Emperor Augustus did succeed. Celtic Pannonia was added to the Empire so that the Danube became a defensible frontier and the land routes between Italy and Greece were properly safeguarded. But the loss of Germany shocked Augustus and convinced him that further conquests were unwise. Suetonius reports that Augustus 'thought that taking large risks with the chance of small gain was like fishing with a golden hook. If lost, the value of the hook was greater than any catch.'[67] In his will Augustus warned his successor Tiberius that 'the Empire should be confined to its present limits' and there is evidence that during this era the Roman State was struggling to pay its military costs.[68] In AD 14 the Rhine and Danube legions threatened to revolt due to reduced pay and the claim that veteran troops were not receiving their expected discharge payments.[69]

The situation in Gaul can be used to suggest the scale of the Roman deficit problem. When Suetonius writes about the conquest of Greater Gaul he describes a vast territory that produced only moderate amounts of revenue for Rome (40 million sesterces). By the first century AD, Greater Gaul was split into five separate provinces which included two narrow frontier zones called Germania Superior and Germania Inferior. In total there were eight Legions stationed near the Rhine frontiers which would have cost the Roman State over 80 million sesterces per annum to maintain.[70] Gaul could not have paid for these Legions if the central Gallic provinces were only contributing revenues of about 40 million sesterces per annum. Rome probably increased provincial taxes during the early Imperial period, but it is unlikely that the regime was able to double the Gallic revenues in order to meet regional expense costs. Appian confirms that parts of the Empire still operated at a loss in the second century AD, so it is apparent that Rome had not rectified its deficit problems.

Tacitus offers an insight into the Roman mind-set and its response to the deficit provinces. During the Roman civil war of AD 69 there was a revolt in the northern Rhineland territories (modern Belgium) when German auxiliaries known as Batavians staged a regional uprising with the support of the local Gallic population. When the Roman army crushed the rebellion, the Gauls were singled out for severe condemnation. A Roman commander addressed them: 'you have often provoked us, yet we have imposed upon you by right of conquest only one demand: that you pay the costs of keeping the peace here. For the tranquillity of nations cannot be preserved without armies; armies cannot exist without pay; pay cannot be furnished without tribute.' He added, 'perhaps you think that you yourselves can equip armies to repel the Germans and the Britons for less tribute than you pay us?' The answer was no – as 'Gaul always had its petty kingdoms and internal wars' and without the Empire paying money into the region for its defence, then 'there would be nothing but discord in its future'.[71]

The Roman armies posted on the Rhine frontier guaranteed the security and prosperity of Gaul. Towns and cities developed, craft industries appeared, agricultural productivity was increased by new farming techniques and the population grew. When Josephus explains the importance of Gaul to the Empire he describes how 'the prosperity of the Gauls grows from their soil and enables them to inundate the whole world with their goods. This is because they submit to being the milch cow of Rome.'[72] However, this trade provided Roman government with little direct revenue, because custom-taxes between Roman provinces (*portoria*) were set at a comparatively low value (one-fortieth).[73]

The Case of Britain
In the Augustan period the Roman Empire had high defence costs and limited surplus revenues, so the invasion of Britain seemed a remote prospect. Strabo

thought that Britain would never be added to the Empire because its population was not a threat to Roman territory. Writing before AD 14 he explains, 'the Romans could have held Britain, but they scorned the opportunity because they saw that there was nothing to fear from the Britons. They are not strong enough to cross over and attack us.'[74]

Another reason to leave Britain as a free territory was the low revenues expected from its conquest and occupation. These were predicted to be less than the expense of stationing a Legion on the island (about 11 million sesterces).[75] Trade between the provinces produced relatively little revenue for the Roman State, but the situation was different for cross-border commerce. This was because the Roman regime collected quarter-rate taxes on all goods crossing the imperial frontiers. In the Augustan era, trade between Gaul and Britain must have been worth over 44 million sesterces a year since Rome collected at least 11 million sesterces from taxing this commerce. Strabo calculated that 'at present more revenue is derived from the custom duties imposed on their commerce than the tribute could bring in, given the expense of the garrison needed to guard the island and to collect revenues from it'.[76]

When the Emperor Claudius launched the Roman conquest of Britain in AD 43 he was motivated by ideas of honour and prestige.[77] But once southern Britain became Roman territory, the quarter-rate frontier tax was replaced by a standard one-fortieth *portorium*. Revenues on cross channel-trade would have fallen to about a million sesterces and income from the new province must have been less than that from Gaul (40 million sesterces collected from a larger territory). Writing a century after the Romans began their conquest of Britain, Appian reports: 'the Romans have taken possession of the larger and better part of the island. They do not care for the remainder because even the part they do hold is not profitable.'[78] Tacitus describes how Nero thought of abandoning Britain during the Boudican Revolt of AD 61, but 'changed his purpose only because he was ashamed to seem as denigrating the glory of Claudius'.[79]

Ancient evidence indicates the scale of the Roman investment in Britain. Diodorus describes Alexandria in the first century BC when the city was 'the prime city of the civilized world and far ahead of all other cities in terms of its extent, elegance, riches and luxury'. He reports that 'when we were in Egypt, those who kept the census returns of the population said that there were more than 300,000 free residents in Alexandria. The Ptolemaic King received more than 6,000 talents from the place.'[80] This is equivalent to approximately 36 million sesterces and nearly the amount needed to pay for the annual cost of three Roman Legions (33 million sesterces). In the first century AD the Roman Empire deployed three or four Legions in Britain at any given time. These had to be supported by regional taxes supplemented by central government funds.[81] Revenue comparable to the tax-wealth of Alexandria, one of the largest and richest cities in the entire empire, was therefore being paid into Roman Britain. The result was rapid and substantial urbanization as cities developed in a previously rural landscape. But overall, the conquest and occupation of Britain placed further stress on imperial finances in return for few strategic gains.

The situation in Britain demonstrates another important aspect of the Roman system. In the Augustan era cross-channel trade raised revenue equal to a quarter of the income obtained from occupied Gaul. Furthermore, frontier tax was a revenue source that required only a relatively small investment of troops to manage. This has relevance for the eastern frontier where Roman merchants were trading with large urbanised kingdoms that produced numerous unique and expensive commodities.

Roman Revenue Wealth
The evidence suggests that once their internal costs had been paid, most Roman provinces sent very little cash revenue to Rome. But the Empire had other ways to profit from its conquered territories. During the Imperial period the main gold and silver mines in Europe were brought under government control and large amounts of new bullion passed directly into the Roman treasuries. This bullion was minted into new coin and sent to the deficit provinces to pay for military wages in the frontier regions. Ancient evidence suggests that by the late first century AD, bullion production provided Rome with between 120 and 200 million sesterces per annum. This was about a sixth of the revenue that the Roman Empire needed to meet its basic costs (1,000 million sesterces per annum).[82]

There were gold mines in Gaul and the Eastern Desert of Egypt, but the main bullion sources for the Roman regime were in the Iberian Peninsula (modern Spain and Portugal). Pliny the Elder served as procurator in Hispania Tarraconensis, so he had good knowledge of bullion production in Iberia (AD 72–4).[83] Some of the most productive silver mines available to Rome were in southern Spain where work had begun in the third century BC by the Carthaginians. Pliny describes how a site named Baebcio 'provided Hannibal with 300 pounds of silver a day as tunnelling was extended a mile and a half into the mountain'.[84] Strabo records that in the second century BC the mines near Carthago Nova 'covered an area four hundred *stades* in circuit (44 miles); employed 40,000 workers and contributed 25,000 drachmas (100,000 sesterces) to the Roman treasury per day'.[85] These figures suggests silver production of about 36 million sesterces per annum, but output during the first century AD was probably smaller as the underground deposits became harder to access.

Roman gold mining operations were highly productive during the first century AD and Pliny gives figures for Iberian output in this period. He reports that Iberia produced up to 20,000 pounds of gold a year which is equivalent to 800,000 aurei or 80 million sesterces.[86] This was enough to pay the annual cost of more than seven legions, or almost the entire army stationed on the Rhine frontiers. Bullion income was therefore an important part of the imperial finances and it helped the Empire to maintain its deficit regions. Gold from Iberia was a long-term, reliable income source and as Pliny comments, 'no other part of the world has offered such a continuous production of gold for so many centuries'.[87]

Sometimes there were short-lived, but highly lucrative, bullion strikes in relatively underdeveloped parts of the Empire such as Dalmatia (modern Croatia).

Pliny describes how, 'recently in Dalmatia when Nero was Emperor, a metal seam was discovered near the surface that yielded fifty pounds of gold a day'.[88] This represents a bonus of about 70 million sesterces per annum that suddenly enriched government finances. This probably explains how Nero was able to pay an extra 60 million sesterces a year into the State treasury, the *aerarium*.[89] The *aerarium* was managed by the Senate and received many of its finances from the old Republican provinces.

Gold output from the Dalmatian mines would have declined as the most accessible deposits were stripped from the surface and specialist miners began underground exploration. However, these mines were still a major source of revenue in AD 93 when Statius lists Iberian and Dalmatian gold as one of the main incomes received by the imperial treasury (the Emperor's *fiscus*).[90] It is significant that Statius does not mention silver mines as a major state-resource, so by this period the Roman regime was probably receiving comparatively limited quantities of new silver bullion.

In the early second century AD, the Emperor Trajan led Roman Legions across the Danube to conquer the mountainous Transylvanian Kingdom of Dacia. Dacia possessed gold mines that possibly compensated for any long-term decline in output from Iberian and Dalmatian sites. Modern scholars have estimated coin production in the Roman Empire by counting the number of dies used to strike new coins. By the time of the Emperor Hadrian (AD 117–138), the Roman mint was producing a probable 16 million denarii and 1.1 million aurei per year. This is equivalent to 64 million sesterces worth of silver and 110 million sesterces worth of gold.[91] However, most of this silver was possibly collected from older coinage melted down for reissue.

Rome could sustain its military provinces as long as this high-value bullion income continued without interruption. This bullion created prosperity within Roman territories, but it was also needed to replace the wealth lost from the Empire through large-scale eastern commerce, particularly through trade with India.

The Roman System: The Imperial era
The early Roman Empire was successful because a large part of its State income came from taxing international commerce. During the Imperial period, Roman rule was structured around the military and the main expense incurred by the imperial government was the cost of the army. Most provinces paid very little tribute to central government and the expense of Empire was met by newly mined bullion and frontier customs taxes imposed on international trade. By the first century AD, the value of eastern imports entering the Empire via the Indian Ocean was more than 1,000 million sesterces per annum and this commerce raised more than 250 million sesterces in tax revenue for the Roman government.[92]

In the ancient world, merchants made money by trafficking distinct craft goods, or shipping unique regional products. The Mediterranean territories grew similar basic crops due to their comparable climate and this limited the prospects for trade. As Pliny observes, 'wine and roses, myrtle leaves and olive oil, are products that belong to almost all our countries in common'.[93] But most spices and incense could not be grown productively in the Mediterranean. As Pliny explains, 'the cinnamon shrub is not strong enough to be grown in Syria and delicate *amomum* and nard plants cannot survive travel out of India, even by sea to Arabia'. Some eastern plants could be grown in Italy, but they did not thrive or bear fruit. Pliny explains that 'the climate is unrelenting. The pepper-vine will live in Italy, the cassia-plant can grow in northern climates and incense-trees have been known to survive in Lydia. But we do not have the sunshine to ripen their fruit or make their resin productive.'[94]

Eastern trade was significant because of the enormous quantity and variety of unique products that Africa, Arabia and Asia could supply to the Roman Empire. These were commodities grown in particular environments, or gathered from rare localised resources. Pliny confirms how Rome was dependent on eastern imports for its consumer fashions. He describes an expensive popular perfume called the 'Royal Unguent' because the recipe was taken from a formula used by Parthian kings. There were more than twenty eastern ingredients in this perfume including cinnamon, spikenard root and myrrh. Pliny observed that: 'none of the components of this scent are grown in Italy, the world conqueror. None are even grown in the whole of Europe, with the exception of only two substances.'[95]

Rome imposed a quarter-rate customs tax on all foreign goods crossing the imperial frontiers known as the *tetarte*. In Egypt this meant that Alexandrian merchants paid the imperial government a costly dividend to transfer eastern merchandise from the Red Sea to the Mediterranean. These goods were taxed as soon as they entered Roman authority, so merchants could not evade the high dues that government agents levied on this economic activity. Merchants paid the tax at the frontier, but they could recoup this expense with profits made by selling these goods at high prices to affluent consumers throughout the Mediterranean. During the Imperial period competitive spending on eastern goods became synonymous with fashion and status throughout Roman territory and people from across the Empire with surplus money to spend would willingly pay for attractive foreign commodities. Rome therefore presided over a system where people with wealth voluntarily paid high prices for the privilege of owning foreign products and this enriched the State.

The income from international trade provided the first Emperor Augustus with the funds he required to instigate important reforms to the Roman military. At the start of his reign, Augustus needed to end the cycle of civil wars that had characterised Roman politics during the previous fifty years (88–30 BC). He believed that the best way to achieve this aim was to de-politicise the army by separating the mass of Roman citizens from the responsibility of military service. Dio explains the argument given by Agrippa, 'if we permit all the men of military age to have weapons and to practise warfare, they will always be a source of sedition and civil wars'. The solution was to replace the citizen levies with a permanent army of full-time professional soldiers. These soldiers would be recruited 'from the citizens, the subject nations, and the allies'.[96]

The new army was based around the existing Legions, but employed full-time soldiers who received regular pay and other financial benefits from the State. Each region of the Empire was assigned the forces required to maintain its security and the new army was planned accordingly. Agrippa explained, 'the reason for a standing army is this: we are distant from the frontiers of our Empire and on every side enemies live near our borders. So, at critical times, we cannot depend upon expeditionary forces.'[97] Dio describes how the Emperor assessed and set tribute levels in the established Roman provinces, 'he instituted various required reforms, made donations of money to some regions, while at the same time commanding others to contribute an amount in excess of the previous tribute'.[98]

When Octavian (Augustus) defeated Antony in 30 BC, there were up to fifty Roman Legions in existence, constituting up to 500,000 troops. Augustus reduced this figure to just twenty-eight Legions consisting of about 300,000 full-time soldiers with auxillary support.[99] The size and pay of this army was planned according to set State revenues.[100] Enormous sums were then spent demobilizing the surplus troops who expected land, or cash bonuses, to support their return to civilian life.

There is good evidence for the size of the Roman Legions and the auxiliary units that gave them support on the battlefield. This information can be combined with evidence for military pay to suggest the overall cost of the Roman army. Modern scholars who have made these calculations suggest that during the Augustan era the Roman army cost the Empire about 640 million sesterces a year. In this period, total spending by the Roman State has been estimated at 1,000 million sesterces per annum, taking into consideration administration costs, building expenses and other outlays.[101] As long as international commerce thrived, the Roman Empire could meet these high-level military costs.

International commerce offered Roman government a way to indirectly tax the surplus wealth that was generated across their empire. Roman subjects did not pay this tax imposition unless they could afford to buy eastern goods, so impoverished people living on basic subsistence did not have tax forced upon them. Instead, affluent people paid highly for their consumerism and their spending contributed to the finances that the Roman government used to support a professional army. A secure and prosperous Mediterranean in turn bolstered international commerce and increased the trade revenues collected by the Roman government.

In the Roman Empire, merchants performed a function that in other regimes was managed by a complex and costly range of tax officials and State agents. Firstly, traders who dealt in eastern goods sought out prosperous communities in the Roman Empire who had surplus disposable wealth. Merchants acquired this wealth by selling people commodities that had already been heavily taxed by the State. Secondly, by regularly paying its frontier legions with high-value coin, the Roman Empire incentivised the trade systems that furnished the army with many of the essential supplies they required for their operations. Merchants voluntarily took on this responsibility because of the profits that could be gained. In both respects, private individuals operating commercial businesses provided much of the essential economic infrastructure that Rome required to manage its empire.

This system also allowed Roman government to minimise the intrusive tax burdens it imposed on its provincial subjects. In many areas the Romans left the collection of local taxes to the indigenous elite who had been in power before the Roman conquest. These were exactly the class of people who, in places like Britain and Judea, would be most likely to organise any native opposition to Rome. This approach encouraged co-operation with Rome and undermined possible resistance against the Empire. Many conquered peoples might have felt humiliated by foreign interference in their countries, but by ancient standards the Roman Empire did not generally impose oppressive measures on those who willingly submitted to their authority.

This incentive-based system had further benefits for Rome as it allowed the Empire to prosper with only a minimal level of State infrastructure. For example, control over several crucial custom points in Egypt and the Arabian frontier, with only a small investment of military personnel, provided the Empire with up to a third of its required revenues. Added to this were the millions of sesterces in bullion extracted from imperial mines and paid directly into the army as newly minted cash. Neither of these operations required large numbers of civilian State employees who needed to be paid substantial amounts to perform intricate, empire-wide, bureaucratic tasks. Rome could maintain a minimal bureaucracy and therefore ensure that its essential administrative expenses were focussed on an effective military infrastructure. By minimalizing its civilian bureaucracy, the Empire also reduced the potential for the corruption and tax abuses that these organisations could engender. The Roman State had therefore found a successful way to gain profit from international business through market consumerism.

But this also made imperial Rome vulnerable to events that might occur far beyond the direct control of their Empire and its armies. For example, when Arab settlers in Somalia angered local people, the Africans started a forest fire that burned the cinnamon groves.[102] The fall in cinnamon output would have caused a significant loss to tax-based Roman frontier revenues. The Romans tried to protect their foreign interests and expanded their control over the Indian Ocean trade networks by placing a military station at the Farasan Islands. This outpost in Yemen gave the Roman Empire command over traffic passing into and across the Red Sea. But Rome could not hope to control events in places such as India, the main source of the international commerce that financed their Empire.

CHAPTER TWO

Roman Prosperity

When Octavian (Augustus) defeated Queen Cleopatra he obtained an enormous fortune from the capture of Ptolemaic treasures. Dio confirms that 'great quantities of treasure were found in Alexandria because Cleopatra had seized practically all the offerings from even the holiest shrines and this helped the Romans enlarge their spoils'. Furthermore, all the richest people in the conquered territory had two-thirds of their wealth confiscated.[1] As a consequence, unprecedented amounts of bullion were brought back to Rome and distributed amongst the citizen population. Augustus used these funds to supplement State spending and reward Roman citizens with generous grants, both as a way to meet political obligations and to buy popular support. The wealth greatly enriched Roman society and caused a sudden and unexpected increase in international commerce.

Dio reports that in one of these pay-outs, 'Augustus gave gifts to the soldiers and distributed 400 sesterces to every Roman citizen'.[2] This was the equivalent of 100 silver denarii per citizen, which was more than a labourer could earn in three months. The money was considered to be a political privilege, so it reached Roman citizens from all classes and at all financial levels. The result was a consumer boom as many people spent their newly acquired bonus wealth on non-essential goods. Sellers also realised that they could ask for higher-prices now that consumers had greater available cash to spend on products.

The economic effects of this distribution are well documented in the surviving sources. Paulus Orosius reports that 'when Octavian conquered Alexandria, by far the richest and greatest of all cities, its wealth so enhanced Rome that the abundance of money raised the value of property and other saleable goods to double their previous levels'.[3] Suetonius explains that 'Augustus brought the treasures of the Ptolemies to Rome for his Alexandrian triumph and so much cash passed into private hands that the interest rate on loans dropped sharply, while real estate values soared'.[4] Dio confirms, 'such a vast an amount of money circulated through all parts of Rome that the price of goods rose and loans for which the borrower had been glad to pay 12 per cent, could now be had for one third that rate'.[5]

These higher prices attracted many foreign merchants to Rome in pursuit of profit as the increased wealth entering circulation made it easier to borrow money at lower interest rates. The profits funded ventures east to secure further unique products to sell to customers in the enriched imperial capital. All these events coincided with Rome gaining control over the Egyptian Red Sea ports and the sea-lanes that led to ancient India. When Strabo journeyed up the Nile with the Roman governor of Egypt, he heard direct reports about this dramatic increase in eastern trade. After only a few years of Roman rule the number of ships sailing from Egypt to India had increased from less than 20 to at least 120 vessels.[6] This was an unexpected development for the Empire and it provided important new revenues for the imperial regime.

The Profits of Egypt

During the Late Republic, Roman revenues were about 380 million sesterces per annum.[7] By the Imperial period the Empire was divided into approximately forty provinces. This suggests that many provinces could generate about 10 million sesterces of revenue per annum.[8] However, in most provinces after local expenses were paid less than a third of regional revenues were sent to Rome.[9]

A Roman legal document called the *Muziris Papyrus* confirms how imperial customs agents taxed incoming eastern cargoes. The document records how a ship called the *Hermapollon* returned from a trade venture to Tamil India carrying over 9 million sesterces worth of eastern goods. State-officials collected about 2.2 million sesterces worth of tax on this single cargo.[10] The entire merchant fleet of 120 ships was probably importing over a billion sesterces of Indian cargo per annum.[11]

A quarter-rate *tetarte* tax on Indian imports worth 1,000 million sesterces would have raised annual revenues worth 250 million sesterces for the Roman regime. However, many of these goods would be taxed again when they were exported from Alexandria to Rome or other Mediterranean cities. A single Mediterranean *portoria* tax (one-fortieth) on goods worth 1,000 million sesterces would have produced further revenues worth perhaps 25 million sesterces per annum.[12] This meant that Roman authorities imposed a double tax on Egypt's trade with India. Strabo confirms that 'large fleets are sent as far as India and the extremities of Africa and the most valuable cargoes are brought to Egypt. From Egypt they are sent forth again to all other regions and as a consequence, double duties are collected on both imports and exports'.[13] Together the one-fortieth *portoria* and the quarter-rate *tetarte* tax could have raised 275 million sesterces for the Roman State.[14]

Added to this figure was the quarter-rate customs-tax collected on Roman goods exported to the distant east. Pliny reports that Rome exported over 100 million sesterces of bullion to India, Arabia and China, but this wealth probably passed through different customs stations in separate regions (Egypt: Coptos, Palestine: Gaza and Arabia: Leuke Kome).[15] It is possible that total Roman exports from Egypt to India, including goods and bullion, were valued at more than 100 million sesterces and produced more than 25 million sesterces of revenue. This is because Han texts suggest a tenfold price difference between Roman exports to India (100 million sesterces) and Indian imports (1,000 million sesterces).[16]

By 20 BC, Augustus was receiving income from Egypt that was larger than the revenues that King Ptolemy XII Auletes had derived from the same region in 80 BC. Strabo explains: 'even though Auletes administered his kingdom in a wasteful and careless way, he received annual revenues of 12,500 talents (300 million sesterces). So consider what the present revenues must be, now that

Egypt is under diligent management and commerce with India and Africa has been increased to such a great extent.'[17] Revenues from the Republican Empire were about 380 million sesterces, so the restoration of Egypt increased the imperial income to more than 700 million sesterces per annum.[18] Therefore, during the Augustan era, Egypt was providing up to half the income needed to finance the entire Roman Empire.

Trade with India allowed the Romans to double the amount of revenue they received from Egypt and by the mid-first century AD the province was producing annual revenues worth 600 million sesterces.[19] This is confirmed by Josephus who describes how King Herod Agrippa tried to discourage his people from rebelling against Rome (AD 66). Agrippa reminded the Jews how rich and powerful the Roman Empire had become after subduing Egypt. He reportedly said: 'look at Roman power in our nearest neighbour Egypt. Egypt reaches to Ethiopia and Arabia Felix (Yemen) and it is the port for India.' Agrippa told his people, 'Egypt has a powerful incentive to revolt because of Alexandria, a city of great size, population and wealth. Alexandria is three-and-a-half miles long and over a mile wide. It pays Rome every month more tribute than you pay in a year and sends Rome enough grain for four months of the year.'[20] Josephus reports that the Jewish Kingdom ruled by Herod Agrippa produced revenues of about 48 million sesterces per annum, so every year Egypt was probably sending more than 570 million sesterces to Rome.[21]

The growth in eastern trade explains how the Roman government received a sudden boost to its revenues during the reign of the Emperor Tiberius (AD 14–37). When Tiberius died he left 2,700 million (2.7 billion) sesterces in the imperial treasury, which is almost three times the amount the State required to pay its annual costs.[22] To have obtained these funds, the Roman government must have been receiving a revenue surplus worth more than 110 million sesterces per annum.[23] The early Empire operated with minimal surplus revenues and as a result Augustus warned his successors not to undertake further conquests.[24] But by the time of Tiberius, trade had transformed Roman opportunities to expand their empire and in AD 43 Claudius could afford the conquest of Britain, adding another deficit region to the imperial domains.

The Emperor Domitian (AD 81–96) raised army pay by a third and this increased Roman military spending by over 200 million sesterces a year.[25] The initiative was possible because eastern trade was producing large amounts of new revenue for the Roman regime. By this period, Egypt was generating at least 600 million sesterces per annum, or about two-thirds of the revenue Rome needed to pay for its Empire. There were only two legions stationed in Egypt, so military costs in the region were low and most Egyptian revenue could be sent directly to Rome.[26] The other provinces that comprised the Empire were generating at least 380 million sesterces a year, but most of these funds were being used locally on defence or other regional projects. This meant that Egypt gave Rome the funds it needed to balance the finance of its deficit regions. In effect, Egypt was paying for the Empire and Egyptian revenues were probably the only large scale transfer of provincial taxes directly to Rome.

Egypt had its own regional currency and Roman government transferred revenues from Alexandria to Rome in standard imperial coin. Alexandrian merchants brought imperial coin profits back to Egypt and this ensured that a sufficient store of money was available in Alexandria to pay future imperial revenues. Strabo describes the cargo imbalance between the two territories by reporting that 'the exports from Alexandria are larger than the imports. Anyone can judge this by seeing the merchant vessels at either Alexandria or Puteoli (the port of Rome). Observe how the ships on arrival are heavy and vessels on departure are much lighter.'[27]

The Romans understood the connection between Egyptian trade revenues and imperial income. Tacitus describes an incident late in the life of Augustus when the Emperor's ship was sailing past the bay of Puteoli. An Alexandrian freighter on its way to Rome approached the imperial vessel to salute the ageing Emperor. The merchant crew and passengers who had donned white garments and dressed in garlands began burning celebratory incense. Tacitus records that they 'lavished good wishes and the highest praise on the Emperor, saying that he had given them their livelihood. They sailed the seas because of him and because of him they enjoyed their freedom and their fortunes.' Augustus watched this display with pleasure and 'gave forty gold pieces to each one of them. But he made them swear that they would spend their money on goods from Alexandria.'[28] The Emperor appreciated that anyone who purchased incense and other eastern products was paying into a tax system that ultimately enriched the Roman government.

During this period, custody of Egypt meant control over the bulk of imperial revenues and possession of a third of the grain dole needed to feed the city of Rome. Augustus and his successors realised the revenue potential of Egypt and understood that access to this powerful resource had to be restricted. The Emperors therefore placed severe political limitations on Alexandria and its local administrators. The governor of Egypt held equestrian rank and no senators were permitted to visit the province. No Alexandrian could become a senator and the leading citizens of the city were forbidden to convene any administrative council.[29] The Emperor could not afford to have any challenger or separatist movement originate in Egypt to disturb imperial finances and threaten food shortages in Rome.

During the Roman civil war of AD 69 Vespasian calculated that since he 'held Egypt which controlled the grain supply of Italy and possessed the revenues of the richest provinces, the army of Vitellius could be forced to surrender by lack of pay and food'.[30] His supporter Mucianus repeatedly asserted that money 'was the sinews of war'.[31] Any permanent loss of Egypt and its eastern trade could ultimately mean the financial collapse of the entire Roman Empire.

Surplus Income and the Grain Dole

The Roman Empire was committed to large-scale schemes intended to reward and benefit its citizens. One example was the grain dole (*annona*) introduced by politicians in the Late Republic as a way of securing support from the citizen assemblies who took the lead in electing officials and ratifying State policy. The *annona* was enacted for political reasons, but many Romans believed the practice was warranted; as Florus explains, 'what could be more just than a people in need maintained from their own treasury?'[32] The scheme was continued in the Imperial period when Augustus guaranteed that 200,000 adult male citizens in Rome received a regular grain dole from the State.[33] Leading historians suggest the practice also benefited many wealthy Romans, as low-income people in the city could afford to purchase the wine and olive oil produced on large villa estates.[34]

Juvenal considered how the Roman people had once allocated military commands in overseas conflicts, but in his own time they were preoccupied with the issues of food costs and public entertainments, or 'bread and circuses'.[35] The Emperors were also committed to expensive public building programs in Rome and hired large numbers of unskilled workers. Pay from these schemes further subsidised the common people and allowed them to meet the cost of living in the capital. Suetonius reports an incident when an engineer offered Vespasian the use of a machine that could reduce the size of the city workforce needed to move heavy columns. The Emperor 'gave the engineer a large reward for his invention, but refused to use it, saying: "I must feed my common poor"'.[36]

Roman government paid private merchants to ship state-owned stocks of grain from the provinces to Rome. This incentivised commerce since the merchants who took these contacts were guaranteed earnings in Rome, even if market conditions proved unfavourable for other deals. Philostratus describes how many low-level merchants operated ships that 'roamed the seas searching for some market that is badly stocked where they can sell and buy'.[37] The grain-dole ensured that Rome was a destination visited on many of these ventures.

By guaranteeing food supplies for those who lived in the capital, the dole system allowed Rome to develop a larger urban-population than any other ancient city. The Han Empire of ancient China had a population equivalent to the Roman Empire, but its capital Luoyang was home to approximately 500,000 people.[38] By contrast, during the height of its Empire in the first century AD, Rome had up to a million inhabitants. This urban population was not equalled in Europe until the onset of the Industrial Revolution and the rapid growth of the city of London in the early nineteenth century.[39]

The grain dole was not a means-tested provision so even those with sufficient income were granted this benefit. Each citizen regularly received a grain parcel that could be made into a quantity of bread which was more than enough to feed an adult male throughout the year. Any surplus would have gone to feeding family members, or providing for other dependants, including household slaves. The grain allowance was offered to 200,000 male citizens, but it was so generous that it probably supplied enough bread to feed 400,000 people including women, children and slaves.[40] For many households the money that would have been spent on basic grain could go towards affordable incense, spices and other minor luxuries. Therefore, by subsidising thousands of its citizens, the Roman State indirectly fostered centralised market commerce.

Modern scholars have calculated that the Roman Emperors needed at least 88,000 tons of grain a year to maintain the dole for approximately 200,000 male citizens in Rome.[41] Most of the grain sent to the Roman capital came from estates in North Africa that were either owned by the State, or subject to a government tithe that seized a large share of their output for shipment to Rome.[42] Egypt was an important grain producer because the floodwaters of the Nile carried rich soil deposits from the Sudan that replenished, as well as irrigated, the vast field systems lining the river. Ancient sources suggest that Egypt provided up to a third of the grain supply that fed Rome. Josephus reports that every year Alexandria 'sends Rome enough grain for four months'.[43] This represents at least 29,000 tons of grain shipped from Alexandria to Rome to sustain the government dole. In terms of monetary value, 29,000 tons of grain would have been worth at least 8 million sesterces in Egypt and 16 million sesterces in Rome, had the entire stock been bought and sold at market prices.[44]

The Roman State paid private merchants to ship the grain dole to the main ports that supplied Rome. The grain was then transferred into large government warehouses for safekeeping until distribution could be arranged. In the summer months it took only a few days to sail from North Africa to Italy and ships loaded with grain took advantage of predictable good weather.[45] But the voyage from Alexandria to Rome was a more difficult crossing and would take several weeks to accomplish.[46] There was also a possibility of bad weather during the voyage and several stopping-points might have to be made along the route if the ship encountered rough conditions.

A passage from the Christian *New Testament* indicates the hazards involved when sailing from Egypt to Italy. In AD 60, the Apostle Paul was sent to stand trial in Rome and placed aboard an Alexandrian grain ship. The vessel was sailing in late summer or early autumn, and Paul warned his guards, 'I can see that this voyage is going to end in hurt and damage to the cargo, the ship and our lives'.[47] But the centurion in charge of the prisoners was convinced by the ship's owner and captain that the voyage was safe. Paul was correct and the ship was wrecked by a storm off the island of Malta. The crew survived and when spring came they continued their voyage aboard another Alexandrian ship that had been forced to shelter at Malta during the winter season. This ship had also taken a chance on a late summer sailing, but had escaped destruction by finding a safe winter harbour on Malta. Paul was delivered to Rome where he was arrested and placed under armed guard. He continued his ministry by writing letters of encouragement to newly established Christian communities.

Roman Government offered various incentives to guarantee grain shipments to the city of Rome, including exemption from certain civic taxes. Furthermore, anyone who would manage a transport vessel on the grain-run for six years was offered citizenship and social privileges.[48] The *Digest of Roman Law* confirms that 'exemption from public employments is granted to those who have constructed ships destined for the transport of provisions to the Roman people. These ships should have a capacity of at least 50,000 *modii* (350 tons), or several, each with a capacity at least than 10,000 *modii* (70 tons).'[49] Mediterranean merchants had no system to insure their cargoes against shipwreck, but the Emperor Claudius gave grain-shippers 'the certainty of profit by assuming the expense of any loss that they might suffer from storms'.[50] Ships that offloaded grain cargoes in Rome either took on ballast, or loaded wares that might fetch some profit back in eastern Mediterranean markets.[51]

Nonetheless, many people in Rome had to purchase grain from private merchants to feed themselves and their families.[52] If market prices were considered too high, then Roman government could intervene by offering surplus State stocks at appropriate prices, or buying private supplies to re-sell at lower rates. Pliny the Younger explains that 'longstanding obligations are met and provincials are not burdened by new impositions. The treasury buys what needs to be bought, with prices agreed between buyer and seller, so that there is plenty in Rome without causing starvation in other places.'[53]

When there were protests about grain prices in Rome, the Emperor Tiberius 'fixed a definite price to be paid by the buyer and guaranteed the seller a subsidy of two sesterces per measure'.[54] After the Great Fire of Rome (AD 64) the Emperor Nero lowered the grain price to 3 sesterces per *modius* to assist the population.[55] These subsidies and interventions encouraged and ensured private grain shipments to the capital.

Ships on the normal trade run from Alexandria to Rome could complete several voyages during the summer months and most of these ships probably ranged in size from 70 to 400 tons.[56] An Egyptian papyrus provides a short register of nine ships arriving at Alexandria which belonged to a single businessman. The document records the tonnage of five ships at between 50 and 80 tons, a 230 ton vessel and an empty grain freighter from Ostia registered at 410 tons.[57]

A few specialist grain-freighters were equipped to carry more than 1,000 tons of cargo and Lucian describes one of these giant vessels which was named after the Egyptian goddess Isis. The captain of the *Isis* was forced to find winter harbour at the Athenian port of Piraeus when his ship was caught out by bad weather on a late voyage. Ships as large as the *Isis* could only dock at main harbours, whereas smaller vessels had more opportunities to stop and trade with intervening ports between Alexandria and Rome. The *Isis* became a temporary visitor attraction at Piraeus because of its extraordinary size and ornate design. Lucian reports that the ship was 180 feet long with a beam 45 feet wide. Its cargo hold was 44 feet deep which suggests a cargo capacity of up to 1,100 tons.[58]

Modern scholars have focused their studies on the grain supply to Rome because it is considered one of the largest economic processes that occurred in the Roman Empire. The grain trade also provides some basic evidence for the scale of the Roman economy. The grain dole delivered from Egypt to Rome can be conceptualised in many different ways, but the simplest approach is to visualise 100 vessels making two voyages per year, each with a grain cargo weighing 150 tons. This offers an important perspective to the scale and significance of Roman trade with the distant east.

Another important point about trade within the Roman Empire is that internal customs taxes (*portorium*) were generally low. Merchants shipping cargo between the provinces had to pay tax rates that were often set at about one-fortieth, or less than 3 per cent of the value of their goods. Furthermore, Italy was exempt from these port taxes as a special privilege designed to encourage incoming trade.[59] This meant that merchants from Alexandria had to pay taxes to export goods from their home city, but paid nothing to offload this same cargo in Rome.

The low rates set on *portorium* tax meant that the Roman government received relatively small revenues from internal commerce. Supposing the stocks of privately owned grain shipped from Alexandria to Rome matched the scale of the government grain dole (29,000 tons), this quantity of grain would be worth perhaps 8 million sesterces in Egypt, but would generate 200,000 sesterces for the government from the single low-rate export tax imposed at Alexandria.

The grain dole ensured the provision of a basic, stable diet for the male citizens of Rome and their closest dependants. But it also enabled people to afford other, non-essential items that could be purchased with their surplus income, including eastern products available in new food flavourings, perfumes and remedies. In Rome many people began to spend their surplus wealth on eastern spices, incense, ivory, gems and pearls. Tacitus describes how 'the consumption of edible luxuries reached substantial new levels in the century between the close of the Actium War and the struggle which established Servius Galba as emperor' (31 BC–AD 69).[60] Other eastern commodities imported during this era created fashions for popular new forms of jewellery, ornaments and clothing. Pliny confirms that 'pearls came into common use in Rome after Alexandria came under our power' (30 BC).[61] Throughout this era, the most fashionable, desirable and expensive items available to Roman consumers were the eastern goods delivered to Rome through the Red Sea trade.

The Commercial Significance of Rome
By the first century AD, Rome was a vital component in the Mediterranean economy. In the ancient world the long-distance transport of goods by sea was generally faster and more convenient than land haulage. Diocletian's *Price Edict* suggests that shipment by sea was twenty-seven times cheaper than land transport and these figures are confirmed by the recorded haulage costs in eighteenth century Europe.[62] The Roman Empire was structured around the Mediterranean Sea and Rome lay at the hub of a major maritime thoroughfare that could easily facilitate the mass movement of commodities between widely spaced regions.

The city of Rome possessed the advantage of being close to the geographical centre of the Mediterranean Sea. It was therefore ideally placed to control the sea-lanes and attract cargoes from all regions enclosed by this seascape. From Italy, the Romans could exploit the passage of goods between three continents, Europe, Africa and the Asian Near East. As Pliny comments, 'all benefits come to Italy from her situation – for the land juts out in the direction that is most advantageous to us, midway between the East and the West'.[63]

Rome performed an important function in the Mediterranean because in ancient times market information could only travel as fast as the movement of people, or commodities. It was therefore important to have a centrally placed city that could function as a nucleus for the regular exchange of goods. Over and above the normal transactions of local exchange, in any given year there would be seasonal food surpluses in many countries that bordered on the Mediterranean, while in other territories there would be shortages caused by unpredictable crop failures.[64] In both circumstances Rome acted as a central marketplace where those with excess could be certain to sell their goods at a competitive price and those with shortages knew that they could acquire immediate provisions at an appropriate market cost. As there were no customs taxes imposed at the Italian ports, merchants favoured places like Rome for their transitional deals. Aristides calls Rome 'the common trading centre of all mankind' and declares that 'whatever is grown, or made amongst every people, it is always to be found here in Rome at all times and in great abundance'.[65]

Rome, with its large population of up to a million inhabitants, provided unique opportunities for visiting merchants. Over 200,000 people in the city were eligible for the grain dole that enabled them to spend their earnings on products other than their basic staple foods. Large numbers of wealthy people also resided in Rome in order to be at the political and economic centre of the Empire. Their elite spending enriched the city and provided further opportunities for merchants to sell expensive products to the wealthiest in society. Aristides describes Rome as the place 'where merchant vessels come carrying many products from all regions and in every season'.[66] Although these factors meant that prices in Rome were competitively high, this was a further incentive that attracted foreign imports. As the author of *Revelations* notes, Rome was 'that great city, wherein all who had ships in the sea were made rich by reason of her prices'.[67]

Modern scholars estimate that Rome might have required over 1,000 ship-loads of cargo a year to supply the city inhabitants with grain, wine and olive oil.[68] The scale of Mediterranean trade is suggested by Tacitus when reporting a disaster that occurred at the Roman ports of Puteoli and Ostia in AD 62. He explains that 'two hundred ships at harbour were wrecked by a violent storm. One hundred more which had sailed up the Tiber to Rome, were destroyed by an accidental fire.'[69] The 'storm' may have been a tsunami tidal-surge that occurred when the volcano Vesuvius caused an earthquake in central Italy on 5 February AD 62.[70] This quake caused damage to the Roman towns of Pompeii and Herculaneum and was the precursor of a full scale volcanic eruption on 24 August AD 79.

Eastern trade provided further momentum to the Roman economy because foreign goods added greater value to Mediterranean commerce. Even the cheapest of eastern goods represented a low-weight, high-value trade investment in unique merchandise that could not be produced in Roman territories. A grain or wine dealer might find that there was a local glut in these commodities at his trade destination, but if he carried a quantity of spice, he would be more certain of a profitable trip. A single sack of black pepper was worth more than fifty sacks of grain (over a ton) and it was not quick to spoil, nor expensive to store.[71] Consequently, by taxing eastern imports the Romans had discovered a way to make international commerce pay for their Empire with the added benefit that exotic goods became widely available in Rome and other Mediterranean cities.

In the Republican period Rome took tribute from subject nations and the resources of defeated people were paraded through the city in military triumphs. However, in the Imperial era it seemed as though Rome had triumphed over the entire world, since resources from every region reached the capital in large quantities. But these goods were arriving at the city as a consequence of commerce, rather than tribute. In his address to the city, Aristides proudly boasted that in Rome 'there is clothing from Babylon and ornaments from the barbarian world far beyond'. Aristides suggests that 'there are so many cargoes from India and Arabia Felix that you might imagine that their trees have now been left bare and their people would come here, just to get their own produce back'.[72] In *Revelations*, the author says of Rome, 'your businessmen are the most powerful in the entire earth and with your bewitchments you have deceived all the nations of the world'.[73] This is an astute comment about a regime that financed itself from taxes based on international commerce.

The author of *Revelations* foresaw the destruction of Rome by the natural disasters of disease, famine and fire. This calamity was to be witnessed by foreign kings and by a multitude of merchants who owed their livelihoods to the city's fortunes. *Revelations* uses vivid imagery to compare Rome with a millstone through which a great wealth of tribute and trade is gathered together and worn down by a single grinding mechanism. The author describes the destruction of the city when 'the merchants of the earth weep and mourn over her, for no man buys her merchandise anymore; merchandise of gold, silver, jewels, pearls and fine linen, purple, silk and scarlet, all kinds of scented wood, ivory, articles of costly wood, bronze, iron and marble, cinnamon, spice, incense, myrrh and frankincense'.[74] Over half of the commodities mentioned in this passage are imports from beyond the Empire's eastern frontiers.

The author of *Revelations* understood that foreign goods were crucial to the economic foundation of the Empire and the supremacy of Rome would end when its international connections were severed. *Revelations* visualises the city plunged into oblivion as 'every shipmaster and the whole company of ships and sailors and everyone who trades by sea, will stand afar off and cry out when they see the smoke of her burning – what city is like this great city?'[75] There was no city in the ancient world comparable to Rome in terms of the scale of its trade business and the range of its commercial resources. But during the Imperial period the Empire faced a dilemma that threatened its long-term existence. International trade was supported by the large-scale export of gold and silver bullion to Arabia, India and China. However, these were finite resources and the Roman regime could not sustain this amount of commerce indefinitely.

CHAPTER THREE

Incense: A Unique Product

In the ancient world many regions had unique natural products that were valuable commodities in distant markets. Traders, traffickers and consumers were all prepared to pay large sums to obtain these goods. Foremost among these unique products was the incense formed from fragrant, hardened resin of certain trees that grew in hot, arid climates. Most incense trees were subject to particular environmental conditions and could only be grown in certain regions. Incense was a renewable crop and since it was a sap, it was rarely diminished by 'poor' yields caused by seasonal fluctuations in annual weather patterns.

Incense became a necessity for religious observance in places far from its place of origin, so transport systems were created to deliver this valuable crop to consumer markets. The demand for incense was large-scale and the markets to be supplied covered the entire ancient world from Western Europe to the cities of Han China. Incense stocks were so valuable that even a moderate amount was usually purchased using silver or gold. In the first century AD, Pliny the Elder records that the best frankincense was valued in Roman markets at 10 silver denarii per pound, while a similar weight of the finest resin-oil myrrh (*stacte*) could sell for up of 50 denarii (200 sesterces).[1] To give context to this figure, 200 sesterces represents about fifty day's pay for a skilled labourer in the first century AD.[2]

Incense production therefore had an important impact on world resources and increased the prosperity of the regimes engaged in this trade. Nations that controlled the incense trade had a continuous source of revenue that offered them an important and dependable long-term advantage in world commerce. Myrrh and frankincense in particular were renewable crops that brought great wealth into territories near the Gulf of Aden. By contrast, civilisations like Rome and Parthia had no equivalent product that could meet the cost of their incense imports and therefore had to rely on finite bullion reserves to pay for their consumerism.

Origins and use of Incense
Arabia was a leading participant in the ancient economy because it produced and trafficked large amounts of valuable incense. In particular, Roman consumers sought frankincense and myrrh to be used as burnt offerings for their gods and as ingredients in various aromatic potions. By the first century BC the main kingdoms in southern Arabia were cultivating large groves of incense trees as cash-crops and were prepared to offer this valuable product to foreign merchants in return for gold and silver in the form of bullion and coins.[3] Due to the value of

these commodities southern Arabia became known as 'Arabia Felix' meaning 'Arabia the Blessed'.[4]

The lands that surround the Gulf of Aden had a unique environment that combined extreme heat with abundant seasonal moisture from the ocean monsoons. The most well-known incenses harvested in this region were the dried sap produced by shrub-like trees called *boswellia* (frankincense) and *commiphora* (myrrh). These products were unique to the area and expensive to acquire in foreign markets.

Frankincense and myrrh trees grow wild in Somalia and southern Arabia, but since ancient times they have been planted and cultivated as a crop. The *boswellia* (frankincense) is a relativity small tree that favours a dry woodland habitat and can reach almost 16 feet tall. It has sparse branches and a papery bark that produces a thick whitish sap when lacerated. *Commiphora* (myrrh) trees favour more arid conditions and thrive in shallow rocky soils where they can reach heights of up to nine feet tall. Myrrh trees have spiny branches with sparse leaves and their potent sap is a reddish colour. The gum resin is extracted from both trees by cutting into the trunk and allowing the fragrant sap to ooze from the injury. These tear-shaped droplets are allowed to harden over several weeks before the solidified resin is collected from the tree.

Resin extracted from frankincense and myrrh trees had great significance in ancient religions and was burnt as an offering to the gods in Greek, Persian and Roman cultures. The hazy atmosphere and rich perfume from incense contributed to the sacred aura of temples and holy-places. Incense separated these special places from the unpleasant pervasive stench of the filth-polluted ancient towns, reeking of food waste, animal excrement, sewage and human body odours.

Egyptian papyri texts depict servants carrying pots of incense to embalming ceremonies. The *Book of the Dead* describes rituals when incense was burned to invoke the gods and used to anoint the mouths of the deceased as incantations were recited over their bodies.[5] The Greek historian Herodotus describes Egyptian animal sacrifices to the goddess Isis. The intestinal cavity of a slaughtered ox would be filled with bread, honey, raisins, figs, frankincense and myrrh, then the carcass would be roasted and consumed in a ceremonial feast.[6]

In early Judaism the books of *Exodus* and *Leviticus* mention incense. Frankincense was burnt as an offering and myrrh and cinnamon used as an ingredient in a special libation oil used to anoint the holy chamber which held the Ark of the Covenant. *Exodus* records how the God of Abraham described the components of this libation oil and Moses was commanded to 'put it before the testimony in the tabernacle of the congregation, where I will meet with you: it shall be unto you most holy'. These instructions came with a warning that anyone who used the holy perfume for personal enjoyment was to be expelled from the community.[7]

When the Jews journeyed through the wilderness, an incense altar was placed in a compartment of the Tabernacle next to the curtain that screened the Most Holy. Aaron was instructed to burn incense before the altar in the morning and evening as he tended the lamps and to instigate this practice as a perpetual tradition.[8] The original Temple of Solomon, dated by tradition to the tenth century BC, was provisioned with an altar where sacred incense was burned before the curtain that separated the Holy of Holies.[9] The Talmud suggests that nineteen spices were added to the *ketoret* (the holy mixture) including eastern cinnamon and spikenard from India.[10] Passages in the first century *New Testament* include incense and gold among the precious gifts the eastern magi gave to the infant Jesus.[11]

The Persians burned large quantities of incense at the Temple of Baal in Babylon which housed a gold statue of the god seated on a throne. Many animals were slaughtered and over 33 tons of incense was burned in front of the temple at the annual festival of the god.[12] Among affluent Babylonians, incense was also used for ceremonies within the household. Herodotus was told that Persian and Arabian couples ritually cleansed and perfumed themselves with incense before intercourse.[13]

Incense also reached the steppe peoples who lived in Central Asia. Herodotus heard that Scythian chiefs were embalmed with frankincense and aniseed before being coated with wax to preserve their bodies for prolonged funeral rites. Scythian women also prepared a fragrant paste with ground-down cypress, cedar and frankincense bark. When applied overnight the treatment gave their bodies a sweet odour and made their skin 'clean and glossy'.[14]

By 600 BC, Greek society was familiar with incense and when the female poet Sappho imagines the wedding of the Trojan prince Hector to Andromache, she describes 'bowls and cups filled with mixed myrrh and cinnamon'.[15] Burning a small quantity of costly incense became a more attractive alternative to killing an animal and burning its entrails. In 500 BC, the Greek philosopher and mathematician Pythagoras recommended offering frankincense to temple altars instead of sacrificing animals. Diogenes Laertius records that, 'Pythagoras burnt frankincense instead of burning sacrificial offerings and all his sacrifices consisted of innate things.'[16]

The amber-coloured beads of frankincense were burnt slowly over hot coals to release a pungent white smoke with an astringent and heady aroma. By contrast, the glossy dark-coloured resin of myrrh produced a lingering bittersweet smoke. The smouldering incense was burnt slowly on hot coals held in ornamental dishes, or placed in an indent carved into holy altars. The resin was also placed in special intricate lantern-like incense burners to allow the light and smoke to issue from patterns in the surface of the vessels. Ovid describes how 'cornmeal and glittering grains of pure salt were once the means for men to placate the gods'. But that was a time 'before foreign ships brought liquid myrrh extracted from tree's bark, over the ocean waves'.[17]

In the Roman Imperial period, incense became an essential element in state occasions when the authorities sought to invoke divine approval. Augustus ordered that all Senators attending meetings in temple grounds were to begin proceedings with an offering of frankincense.[18] Over time its use spread from public to private settings with incense becoming commonplace in many domestic religious rites. Incense was burnt to ensure blessings at feasts, marriages and births and it was routinely offered to household gods, or used as part of the ritual required at funeral ceremonies. During worship, fragrant oil was poured as a libation and incense was burnt to conceal the smell of animal sacrifices. Romans combined these customs by anointing the heads of animals before they were ritually slaughtered.[19] It also became common practice to offer incense before and after long journeys, including sea-voyages.[20]

But the amounts used did not need to be large. Heliodorus tells how a character in an adventure story approached a popular shrine, but could only give a merge offering. This included 'some frankincense and a libation of water that caused those around to wonder at the simplicity of the sacrifice'.[21] When Cynthia, the lover of Propertius, left Rome for the countryside among 'the fields of poor farmers there were no games to corrupt her and no sanctuary temples to give her countless opportunities for sin'. Instead she would carry 'a little offering of incense to some crude shrine, where a goat will die in front of a rustic altar'.[22] Offerings of incense were also believed to ward off imminent bad fortune. One of Martial's friends had predictive dreams and alarmed the writer with dire warnings. Martial's advice to the man, after claiming to have sacrificed animals and burnt 'mounds of frankincense', was to 'either stay awake or dream for yourself'.[23]

Ovid believed incense deterred the gods from inflicting misfortune as 'often Jupiter, about to hurl his lightning, will draw back his hand when offered a gift of incense'.[24] He lists some of the many rituals that occurred in the Roman religious calendar. On the first of April women took over the public baths to perform a ceremony with special burnt offerings of incense in honour of the goddess Fortuna. Also in April, grains of salt and incense were offered in hearths to the mother goddess Ceres to encourage a good harvest.[25] In his treaties on agriculture Cato recommended sacrificing a sow to Ceres before harvest in a ritual involving incense and wine.[26] Ovid reports that on 22 February many relatives gathered together to celebrate their kinship connections and 'burn incense to the gods of the family'.[27] He also records that on 23 April prostitutes congregated near the temples of Venus to 'offer incense and pray for beauty and men's favour'. On 15 May, a day sacred to Mercury, 'all those who make a living trading their wares offer incense and beg for an increase in their profits'.[28] Ancient documents found at Dura-Europos indicate there were fifty days in the military calendar when incense had to be burned, or animals sacrificed, in special celebrations.[29]

Incense had an important role in Roman funeral practices and Persius describes death and internment within an ancestral tomb. He imagines how 'the dear deceased who is thickly-coated with perfumed balm, is placed on a tall bier with his rigid heels extending towards the door'.[30] Propertius describes funeral rites of wealthy men involving 'a line of perfumed dishes'.[31] Incense was also used in cremation ceremonies where it honoured the spirit of the deceased and disguised the stench of the burning corpse. Upper-class Romans venerated their ancestors and many leading families competed to burn as much incense as possible in costly funeral rites. Martial refers to the thief who would steal 'that lavender and myrrh reeking of funerals, half-burned frankincense and cinnamon snatched from the midst of pyres'.[32] The Jews also used incense in ancient burial practices and the *New Testament* records: 'Nicodemus came bringing a mixture of myrrh and aloes, about a hundred pounds weight. So they took the body of Jesus and bound it in linen wrappings with the incense, as is the burial custom of the Jews.'[33] Special incense lamp-burners were used in the Persian cult of Mithras at a time when this secretive religion was spreading through the Roman army. Similar lamp burners have been found at sites sacred to Celtic deities showing that this practice was transferred from eastern to western religions.[34] Conversely, in his study of German culture Tacitus remarks that they 'do not heap spices on their funeral pyres'.[35]

Pliny describes how perfume was considered an 'appropriate tribute to the dead' and scented substances were often placed in urns alongside the cremated remains.[36] For this reason Persius warns that, 'if you decrease your property, your heir will put your ashes into the urn without any fragrance'. He suggests that an ungrateful heir could purchase cheap cinnamon that had lost its smell, or bundles of cassia that had been bulked up with ordinary cherry bark.[37] In grief Propertius imagined he was visited by the charred ghost of his dead lover Cynthia. She demanded, 'why weren't my flames redolent of nard? Was it such an effort to scatter cheap hyacinth flowers, or honour my tomb with a broken jar?'[38] Propertius asked for his own funeral to be a simple affair, with his remains placed in an alabaster jar filled with cheap nard-like fragrances. He instructed, 'when the fire below turns me to ashes let the little jar receive my spirit and over my poor tomb place a laurel'.[39] The use of incense in funeral rites became so common that some Romans would even offer incense to mark the death of their household pets.[40]

The Romans offered garlands of flowers to temple statues and protective household deities. They also displayed wreaths at graves and family tombs to publically honour the dead. These wreaths included colourful and exotic flowers and Pliny reports that 'no garland is fashionable unless it is stitched together with genuine petals and now these flower petals are fetched from India and the lands beyond'. Women in the household oversaw the arrangement of these devotional displays and Pliny confirms that 'the most acclaimed garlands are made from nard leaves, or multi-coloured silks steeped in perfumes – for this is the latest form of extravagance devised by our women'.[41] Vespasian was said to be the first person to offer chaplets made from African cinnamon and gold filaments to the gods when he made special peace dedications to the Temples on the Capitol in Rome.[42]

Incense was also burned during personal celebrations and Tibullus sent a verse to his friend Cerinthius on his birthday to say 'burn incense around the altars because today it is your birthday and we shall declare this with perfumes from Arabia Felix'.[43] These customs spread to the less affluent sections of Roman society and Propertius refers to the 'cheap incense from a poor man's rites'.[44] Pliny describes how the Roman population celebrated the coronation of the Emperor Vespasian by making personal offerings to the gods. Many rural peoples offered milk, while the urban populations burnt incense to mark the event. Only the very poor who could not afford frankincense had to make do with offerings of salted-cakes.[45] Martial also describes how incense was offered to Jupiter in the hope that the god might extend and favour the rule of the Emperor Domitian.[46]

Even people with limited income would spend part of their small earnings on incense to invoke the power and protection of the gods. A shopping list found in the ruins of ancient Pompeii provides evidence for the products regularly bought by a small Roman household that included slaves. Over eight days the household spent 160 sesterces on bread, dates, cheese and a tiny amount of incense. The incense was the cheapest commodity they bought during this period and cost one-sixteenth of a denarius.[47] But with millions of similar households in the Empire, even small-scale consumption could produce trade on a large scale.

Pliny understood how countless thousands of small, but frequent, incense offerings could generate consumption on an enormous scale. When he writes about southern Arabia, he asks his reader to 'take into account the vast number of funerals that are celebrated throughout our world each year and the heaps of incense that are piled on pyres to honour the bodies of the dead. Also consider the vast quantities offered to the gods bit by bit in single grains'. The result was the large-scale export of bullion from the Roman Empire to pay for large quantities of disposable incense. Pliny comments, 'the excess of extravagance is displayed even in the paraphernalia of death. Arabia deserves the title *Felix* (Fortunate) because we burn with the dead those products originally understood to have been produced for the service of the gods.' Pliny thought that ostentatious funeral displays were taking priority over temple dedications and he writes, 'I would like to know how much incense really goes to the gods of the heavens and how much is expended on spirits in the underworld.'[48]

The Roman State imposed quarter-rate import taxes (the *tetarte*) on the frontiers and these taxes could be collected as a share of the incoming goods. This meant that Roman government received large stocks of foreign products and could burn astonishing amounts of incense in public spectacles including shows and games, ceremonial processions, victory celebrations and State funerals. Tacitus says that the body of Nero's wife Poppaea was 'not consumed by fire according to Roman practice, but following the custom of foreign princes it was filled with fragrant spices and embalmed in the sepulchre'.[49] Pliny reports, 'those who are most knowledgeable in this matter assert that Arabia does not produce in a whole year the quantity of perfumes that was burnt by the Emperor Nero at the funeral observances of his wife Poppaea'.[50] But the ordinary citizens could also create spectacular events and Pliny describes how a grief-stricken supporter of one of the factions in the Roman chariot races threw himself into the funeral pyre of a deceased sports champion. Supporters of the other team scorned the incident by claiming that this person had merely fainted into the pyre because of the vast amounts of intoxicating eastern scents being burnt at the funeral.[51]

Pliny mentions a freedman named Gaius Caecilius Isidorus who left 60 million sesterces in his will along with instructions that 1.1 million sesterces was to be spent on his funeral rites.[52] The Emperor Vespasian was criticised for a lack of public spending and during his funeral it was suggested that to save money he might prefer his corpse dumped in the Tiber River. But Suetonius reports that even the restrained funeral rites of this moderate emperor cost the State 10 million sesterces.[53]

The Romans eventually developed incense-based libation oils that produced the pungent smell of the product without the act of incineration. These sacred oils were poured on altars and other objects connected with religious rituals, including animals prepared for temple-sacrifice. Some family tombs were fitted with libation funnels so that offerings could be channelled straight into the burial chambers of deceased relatives.[54] Cremation jars were sometimes buried so that the funnel projected above the surface to allow relatives to pour perfumed oil into the ashes.[55]

As consumerism increased within the Empire, Roman society found other uses for incense. Unguent-makers blended incense into pungent perfumes and Greek doctors dissolved the resin in remedies used for a range of aliments including salves to soothe pain. Celsus advised that myrrh or frankincense gum should be used to agglutinate a wound and ensure that flesh closed over the injury.[56] Myrrh in particular had proven analgesic properties and was offered in wine to Jesus to ease the suffering of crucifixion.[57] A mixture of frankincense, mistletoe and wax was used to ease muscle pains including backache.[58] The Romans also added incense to drinks as tonics and flavours and it became fashionable to add frankincense and myrrh to Roman wine along with nard, cinnamon and ginger. Pliny writes, 'I find that aromatic wine is made from the same ingredients as perfumes, the best using myrrh'.[59]

Roman consumers confused the distinction between incense-based perfumes made for religious ritual with fragrances intended for personal indulgence. Libations were used to bless the portico of a homestead, or anoint an instrument that was crucial to the livelihood, or fortunes, of an individual. But the same ingredients that evoked an association with divine favour were also used in personal perfumes.

Soldiers ceremonially anointed their regimental battle-standards with special libations to invoke divine approval and protection in battle. Pliny complains that 'it is an amazing development that this practice is now prevalent in the army camps where the grimy spikes of Eagles and Standards are anointed on festive days'. Military pay records from Egypt show that soldiers had 12 drachmas deducted from their wages every year 'for the Standards'.[60] If this was typical of expected contributions, then 300,000 military personnel offered over 3.6 million sesterces of incense to the Standards every year.

Some soldiers extended this ritual by anointing their helmets with oils and this perfumed the hair beneath. Pliny describes this practice as an indulgent gratification as 'the act provides precedent for those who now wear unguents beneath their helmets'.[61] It was widely known that the unpretentious emperor Vespasian disapproved of this and Suetonius reports an incident when a young officer reeking of perfumed oils came to thank the Emperor for a commission he had been granted. Suetonius claims that Vespasian turned his head away in disgust and cancelled the promotion, commenting; 'I would have preferred if he stank of garlic'.[62]

Pliny reveals how the incense trade had developed by AD 70 when he lists three grades of frankincense that ranged in price from 3 to 10 denarii per pound. There were also several varieties of myrrh including cultivated and wild myrrh, a summer-crop variety and *stacte* (liquid-resin). Incense was imported from different regions and Pliny lists 'wild myrrh from the Troglodytes (Somalia) and Minaean myrrh which includes the Astramitic, Gebbanitic and Ausaritic varieties from the Kingdom of the Gebbanitae' (Qataban in southern Arabia). Each variety had its own characteristics, for example the Somali variety 'is dry and dusty in appearance, but has a stronger scent than other sorts'. Pliny reports that *stacte* ranged in price from 3 to 50 denarii a pound, the top cultivated myrrh was 11 denarii and the more heavily-scented variety was valued at 12 denarii. Somali myrrh was more expensive and the Erythraean and Troglodyte products sold for about 16 denarii per pound. Like most eastern goods, market prices paid for myrrh fluctuated and Pliny reports that 'prices vary with the supplies available to buyers'.[63]

Medicines

With the market for incense well established, merchants had the incentive to import similar products from further afield. Ancient India possessed high-altitude Himalayan climates and southern tropical-zones with abundant jungle vegetation. Aelian confirms that 'our authorities report that India is rich in plants and remarkably prolific in the medicinal substances that can save lives'.[64] Pliny also writes that 'remedies are casually offered, Arabia and India are considered to be the source of medicines and even a small sore is treated with substances imported from the Red Sea'.[65]

The distant east produced many unique products that became highly sought after in Roman society for their properties as medicines, flavourings and perfumes. Pliny describes how a special red bark called *macir* was imported from India and when this substance was boiled with honey, it produced an effective remedy for treating dysentery.[66] Indian *lyceum* cleared up acne, reduced sores and soothed throat infections.[67] Other potions were ingested to cure impotence, relive digestive ailments, or induce vomiting. Arabian aloe was a potent laxative that was given to people and cattle that had intestinal blockages.[68] Warm ointments composed of fragrant eastern ingredients were also used to soothe aching muscles and menstrual pains.[69] Papyri from Egypt describe how incense gum was used to treat persistent nosebleeds, while Indian resins were used in special pastes to alleviate toothache.[70] Eye complaints were common in the ancient world and salves were prepared using resins that soothed strained optic-muscles and helped to clear infection.[71] Skin ulcers were also treated with special pastes made from eastern resins and indigo-dyes that would dry-out open sores and promote healing.[72] Pliny believed that a healthy diet was the best way to avoid illness and argues that eastern imports should be 'bought to make perfumes, unguents and luxuries, or used for worship'. He himself vowed 'never to take remedies imported from India and Arabia, or from the world beyond'.[73]

Some medical remedies combined a variety of different eastern ingredients. Celsus composed a compendium of medical texts during the first century AD and he describes popular healing salves that contained carefully proportioned quantities of pepper, cinnamon, nard, cassia, myrrh, frankincense, aloes, antimony sulphate and opium extracts from the poppy plant.[74] The celebrated doctor Galen identified five types of cinnamon that he combined with other ingredients to produce special *thetics* to serve as preventatives and cure-alls in the early stages of illness. He was engaged in studies to determine the treatment benefits of Somali cinnamon when his medical storeroom in the government-run warehouse, the *Horrea Piperataria*, was destroyed by a devastating fire.[75]

Flavourings
Roman cooks competed to develop compelling new tastes by combining different quantities of nard, cinnamon, ginger and incense in their dishes. Foreign ingredients were added to many Roman foods; as Pliny comments, 'flavours are blended and different ingredients added to gratify taste. These additives come from different regions and climates. Some foods receive ingredients from India, others additives from Egypt, Crete, Cyrene and every other land.'[76]

Eastern imports were also used to flavour wines and enhance the taste of Mediterranean olive oil, which was ubiquitous in the Roman diet. Virgil complains that indulgent cinnamon flavours were spoiling the principle of plain and decent olive oil and Martial refers to more expensive flavourings when he writes about wines infused with nard.[77] Persius also describes 'olive oil polluted with perfumed spice' and expresses longing for a past era when cornmeal was a sufficient offering in temple rituals.[78]

Pliny describes how expensive malabathrum (a type of cinnamon) was added to lukewarm wines to release a strong perfumed aroma.[79] Many ingredients were added to the crushed grape product used to make grape-juice and sweet-wine including, 'nard, cardamom, cinnamon bark, saffron, dates and butterbur flowers'. Pliny reports that 'some winemakers add a half-pound mix of nard and cinnamon-leaf to a gallon and a half of *must* (grape product). This is called 'savoury wine' and peppered wines can be made by adding pepper and honey.'[80] The practice of mixing together flavours to enhance taste became so popular among wealthy Romans that Martial commented on a friend's wedding that 'the couple are like precious cinnamon united with nard'.[81]

Colourful giant clams were also imported from the Indian Ocean and shipped across half the known world to astonish guests at Italian dinner tables. These three-foot-long seabed dwelling creatures were protected by a thick fluted shell that opens to reveal a fleshy organism that feeds off algae and plankton drawn from tropical water currents. In Rome these exotic molluscs became centrepieces in expensive banquets and Pliny calls them *tridacna* (three-bites). This was 'because they are so large it takes at least three helpings to consume them'.[82] Confirmation of these imports comes from Pompeii where the remains of giant clams have been found amongst deposits of Mediterranean shellfish.[83]

A giant clam would be flavoured with expensive eastern spices to give guests a unique dining experience. Apicius recommended that shellfish should be served with a touch of pepper and dry mint, but the finest seafood dish would be further enhanced by the addition of bay leaves and Indian malabathrum.[84] The price of malabathrum leaf was about 60 denarii per pound, which was more than a Roman soldier would receive for two months' service.[85]

Juvenal identifies clam dishes as the height of expensive excess when he satirised the behaviour of Roman matrons who gorged themselves on exotic foods. He describes how, 'drunk and indecent', they would indulge themselves late into the night 'consuming giant shellfish and pouring foaming unguents into their Falernian wine'. Juvenal imagines the scene when surrounded by flasks of scented potions, 'the room spins dizzily around her and the table seems to dance in her double vision'.[86]

The flavourings available in Roman markets are confirmed by the Pozzino shipwreck which was found off north-west Italy. Underwater archaeologists recovered rectangular wooden caskets from the wreck that were fitted with sliding lids. Inside the caskets were numerous tin-lined cases and within each case there were three small cylinders sealed with tightly fitting wooden caps. When the archaeologists broke the seals they smelled powerful aromas of ancient spices including cinnamon, cumin and vanilla.[87]

Personal Fragrances

The perfume trade was a widespread and lucrative business throughout the Roman Empire. African barks, Arabian incense, and Indian spices were all crushed, boiled and blended with carrier oils to create unique and attractive scents. In particular sweet-smelling cinnamon bark was a prime ingredient in many Roman fragrances. But other ingredients were added including substances closely associated with sacred observances. This meant that many perfumes crossed the divide between personal indulgence and religious ritual.

Certain regions were famous for perfume manufacture and Pliny reports a common saying that 'the Campanians produce more scent than other people produce olive oil'.[88] The Italian perfume industry was founded on rose extracts, but enhanced by many eastern ingredients. The Roman trade in perfumes is evidenced from the remains of alabaster vases, lead flasks and small glass bottles known as *unguentaria*. These glass vials were sometimes buried with the deceased in Roman Egypt where the dead were often interred rather than cremated and some coffin portraits picture women holding small perfume vases.[89] In ancient society lead and glass were routinely recycled and alabaster vessels were reused and refilled many times. Consequently, these finds show the geographical scope, but not the scale, of ancient consumerism.

By the first century AD, the popular fashion in Roman society was for perfumes that smelled intensely sweet, so cinnamon products from East Africa or South East Asia provided one of the core ingredients in these concoctions. Pliny suggests that all perfumes could be enhanced by the addition of cinnamon and reports that consumers in his own time considered concentrated cinnamon perfumes to be a 'prime scent' and one of the most desirable of all fragrances. Thick cinnamon unguent was often enriched by the addition of myrrh, honey and soothing balsam harvested in Palestine.[90] The purest cinnamon perfumes could fetch high prices and they ranged in cost from 35 to 300 silver denarii per pound, depending on ingredients. Prices could also fluctuate according to eastern supplies and on one occasion the cost of cassia bark imported from East Africa increased 50 per cent after a serious forest fire occurred in Somalia.[91]

Dyes including red cinnabar were sometimes introduced into the perfume formula to give the concoctions a pleasing colour, but not too much colorant or the wearer would find their skin and clothing stained by the product.[92] Women liked to display their perfumes in glass-crystal jars and delicate quartz vials, but sunlight caused perfumes to deteriorate, so it was better to store them in opaque containers. Unguents were brewed and blended in work-areas at the back of the perfume shop and it was said that customers who lingered in a shop too long would carry away the scent of the place. Seneca uses this as a metaphor to explain how even the most remiss student can gain from the benign presence of a great philosopher.[93]

Arabian white marble was the most sought-after material for containers, until fashion began to favour alabaster decorated with honey-coloured swirls. Alabaster jars became the preferred containers for perfumed oils, though the use of cheaper lead flasks was also popular.[94] Horace wrote to Virgil inviting him to sample a new wine from Sulpicius' cellar, suggesting a jar of wine could be earned with the gift of one small alabaster jar of nard.[95] Pliny explains that the best alabaster came from Iran, but next in value was the Indian material which was considered superior to Syrian varieties.[96]

The Himalayan plant called nard was made into expensive libation oils that were used in religious festivals and to anoint the dead. But nard was also a perfume that could be applied as a personal indulgence. The *New Testament* describes how Jesus was anointed with nard oil in an act that was symbolically linked with Jewish funeral practices. While Jesus sat in conversation with his disciples, a woman approached him and poured a pound-weight of nard oil from an alabaster jar on to his head and feet. Kneeling and weeping in front of him she then proceeded to methodically dry his feet, using her hair to wipe away the excess.[97] The disciples complained that the perfume, valued at 300 denarii, should have been sold to provide alms for the poor. But Jesus explained the significance of the ritual was that, 'when she poured this perfume on my body, she did it to prepare me for burial'.[98]

The *Muziris Papyrus* records that a Roman ship called the *Hermapollon* returned from India with sixty boxes of nard from the Ganges.[99] Each box was valued at 1,125 denarii and Pliny reports that nard-leaf sold in Roman markets at a price between 40 and 75 denarii per pound.[100] This price range is consistent with the *New Testament* figure of 300 denarii because perfumers making natural unguents expect a 6 per cent yield from raw product and this essence is usually diluted by a 75 per cent mix of carrier oils. This meant that four pounds of nard leaf were required to make a single pound of pure-nard perfume.

Nard was one of the premier perfumes of the Roman world and its pure essence was often blended with other ingredients in an effort to reduce the cost of the finished product, or create a hybrid fragrance that enhanced other scents. Juvenal writes about the fashionable Roman matron who 'wears spikenard for her lovers. It is for them she buys all the scents the slender Indians bring to us.'[101] Pliny reports that there were nine different species of plants resembling Indian nard that could be used to adulterate the pure product without spoiling the overall fragrance. A skilled perfume blender would use these substances to make his high-grade perfumes more competitively affordable and increase the profits he could make from each new batch. Other eastern ingredients would change the properties of the blend and Pliny was informed that nard perfumes 'can be rendered more pungent by the addition of costus and amomum which have an extremely powerful scent'. If the nard was to be used as a carrier for a healing ointment, or ingested as a remedy, then further ingredients would be added. Pliny reports that 'nard perfumes can also be made thicker and sweeter by the inclusion of myrrh, or made into a medicine by adding saffron'.[102]

Pliny was critical of all expensive perfumes, arguing that 'they are the most superfluous of all forms of luxury, because at least pearls and jewels pass to the wearer's heir and clothes last for some time, but unguents quickly lose their scent and diminish by the hour'. He explains that 'the greatest appeal of perfume for a woman is that she can pass by and attract the attention of men by her scent. For this purpose substances are bought that cost more than 400 denarii per pound.' Furthermore, he argued, 'all that money is paid for a pleasure enjoyed by somebody else, because after a while the person wearing a scent does not smell it themselves.'[103]

Money entered in business accounts as spending on incense and perfume was a good way to hide bribes and theft, since there was no lasting product to show from the transaction. Pliny the Younger describes how a civic official from North Africa bribed a Roman governor with 200,000 sesterces. He took the money from the civic treasury and entered 10,000 sesterces in the account books under the heading 'perfumes' since he expected that this figure would not arouse suspicion because the city regularly spent large sums on libations and incense.[104]

Since ancient scent was transitory, Seneca describes how many men began applying these scents several times a day to ensure a continued effect. He explains that 'nowadays it is not enough to use perfume, unless you put on a fresh application two or three times a day to keep it from evaporating fully from the body'. Seneca declares that a perfumed person from only a generation earlier would 'stink like a goat' compared with men of his day, who were drenched in cinnamon and other eastern scents.[105] Juvenal also ridiculed two men called Montanus and Crispinus who could 'out-stink two funerals' with the sweet smell of their personal perfumes.[106]

Athenaeus claims that Tarsus in Asia Minor produced the best nard perfume using the 'spikenard' root of the plant. He also reported that nearby Pergamon 'produced the most delicious unguent extracted from frankincense that was the invention of a certain perfumer in the city'. The perfume-blender at Pergamon only briefly enjoyed his fame before other fashions diminished his business. Athenaeus confirms, 'no one before him made this frankincense perfume and nowadays it is no longer made'.[107] Many retail workshops only held prominence for a short period before their production secrets were copied, or fashion-driven consumers shifted their attention to another innovative business.

In the late first century AD, the leading perfume-makers in Rome were Cosmus and Nicanor who each ran a business that manufactured and sold the best perfumes to the wealthiest and most fashion-conscious clients. When Martial expressed hopes for his new book, he imagined it being handled by so many wealthy readers that its very pages would be 'greased with the rich unguents of Cosmus'.[108]

Seneca describes how feasts were multi-sensual experiences with music played for the guests and the 'scent of various perfumes offered so that even the nostrils are not idle'.[109] Juvenal confirms that 'while we drink we call for garlands and perfumes'.[110] At the feast of Trimalchio the attending slaves sung as they washed and manicured the hands of the dinner guests so that the task resembled a stage performance.[111] A mural found in the House of the Heralds in Pompeii depicts servants providing guests with towels, garlands and a box of ointments.

It became practice for Roman hosts to offer scent to dinner guests during banquets and Martial complained about a patron named Zoilus who although 'drenched in essences from the stores of Cosmus' was 'not ashamed to divide amongst us, in a little gilded shell, the type of unguents used by only the poorest women'.[112] Martial mentions another host who offered excellent unguents to his dinner guests, but served only meagre foods. He complained that being 'perfumed and starved at the same time was the experience of a corpse'.[113]

An unguent-maker named Marcellus sold perfumed hair oils and when Martial complained about a wealthy ex-slave who was seen at the theatre wearing expensive sardonix rings, he added that the man smelt as though he was wearing 'all the essences from Marcellus's shop'.[114] Ovid also warned Roman ladies to avoid womanisers and 'do not be tricked by men with their hair gleaming with nard oil' because, 'what they tell to flatter you, they have already told a thousand girls'.[115] Pliny had heard that Nero used fragrant oils to deodorise his feet and he asks, 'how could a perfume be perceptible, productive, or pleasurable, when applied to that part of the body?' He adds that 'I have also heard of a person giving orders for his private bathroom to be fragranced with unguents'.[116] Theophrastus describes how long-lasting powders were added to clothing and bedding to scent the body.[117] Pliny mentions 'sprinkling powders' and says that cinnamon was placed among clothes to fragrance fabrics.[118]

Some Romans added fragrant substances to their drinks so that their breath would smell sweet. Pliny observed, 'nowadays some people actually put fragrances in their drinks and they accept the bitter flavour so that their bodies might enjoy lavish scents both inside and out'.[119] Cosmus endorsed this fashion by selling expensive crystal cups engraved with his name and Martial writes about taking 'a gem-cup bearing the name Cosmus to drink the luxury of perfumed wines'.[120] When Martial was given a small allotment in the suburbs by a friend, he remarked that he could find more foliage in the dregs of one of Cosmus's perfumed vases, or a package of pepper, than could be seen in that garden.[121]

Cosmus sold mouthwashes that he claimed would conceal the fetid aftertaste of a hangover and these potions were dyed attractive colours. Martial remarked that a female acquaintance no longer smelt of yesterday's wine because she had swilled a perfume by Cosmus, but added that it had stained her teeth. The potion was not swallowed, so it did not prevent 'foul emanations' escaping from the depths of her stomach.[122] Martial described a man named Coracinus who was 'always redolent of lavender and cinnamon and he exhaled the odour of Nicerotius's leaden vases'. Coracinus was said to 'smile with contempt at those who were unscented'.[123]

Roman poets confirm the association between courtship, sensual pleasure and perfume. Pliny describes how some Romans placed small leaves of malabathrum under their tongue to make their breath sweeter.[124] Propertius pictures his lover Cynthia with breath the sweet odour of Arabian perfumes.[125] Martial also compares the kisses of his favourite to the sweet contents found in 'the alabaster jars of Cosmus and the offerings made at the altars of the gods'.[126] The kisses of a lover named Diadumenus were said to be potent like frankincense or 'chaplets draped on locks of hair dripping with nard'.[127] Yet Martial complains about a woman named Gellia who wore so much fragrance that whenever she came near, it was as though Cosmus had moved his shop and spilled his perfumes.[128]

Phials of scent were popular gifts during courtship and Martial often rewarded his lovers with perfumes. He confides that 'beautiful Phyllis has delighted me in every way during a whole night of pleasure and in the morning I was thinking what present to give her – a pound of perfume from Cosmus or Niceros, or perhaps ten new gold coins of Domitian?'[129] In another epigram Martial expressed the view that 'the man who asks girls to give him favours for nothing is foolish and impudent', but in his opinion a young woman named Aegle asked for too much in exchange for kisses. Aegle had demanded 'either a pound of Cosmian unguent, or eight newly minted gold coins'.[130] These prices suggest that the most affordable unguents blended by Cosmus sold at perhaps 200 to 250 denarii per pound (nearly 1,000 sesterces).

Fragrant eastern substances were common ingredients in the popular beauty creams and special lotions that Roman women used to improve their attractiveness. Ovid offers a recipe for a 'beauty cream' that women could apply to their faces.[131] He writes, 'though incense pleases the gods and soothes angry spirits, there is no need to burn it all on the altars, with this cream on your face for a short time you'll have a beautiful complexion'.[132] Lucian also describes the 'numerous concoctions of scented powers, used by women to brighten up their unattractive complexions'. He imagines how rich Roman women might appear without their make-up, saying 'to see them rise in the morning, they must look like apes' until 'a throng of maids fix their ill-favoured faces with an assortment of treatments'.[133] Some medicinal ingredients were used to revitalise skin and Juvenal says that beauty-conscious ladies were treating their faces like open sores that needed creams and pastes to clear-up an ugly discharge.[134]

Affluent Roman women also followed various fashions for increasingly lavish hairdos that involved bee-hive coiffures and braided weaves. In many portraits wealthy women are depicted with curls and waves fashioned into the hair and this effect was achieved by setting the hair with perfumed oils, then styling it with heated metal tongs. Juvenal describes that 'important business of beautification; when numerous tiers and storeys of hair are heaped, one upon another on her head'. He also describes the finished effect when a seemingly tall matron with a heroic stature turned around to be revealed as a small lady supporting a high stack of coiffed hair.[135] Lucian stresses the time and effort involved in these elaborate hairdos that involved curls to be arranged and fixed with 'the perfumes of Arabia'.[136] Martial offers the gift of a gold hairpin with the verse, 'insert a pin to hold up your twisted hair so that your moistened locks may not damage your bright silks'.[137] When the Emperor Nero recited poetry praising the beautiful auburn hair of his consort Poppaea, Roman women began dyeing their hair this colour and perfumers developed a new fragrance, called 'Poppaean Unguent', said to be based on her personal preferences. Juvenal describes the fashionable woman who 'reeks of rich Poppaean unguents which stick to the lips of her unfortunate husband'.[138] Writing in the second century, Dio Chrysostom complained that some men were spending almost as much time as women by dyeing and perfuming their hair for the sake of vanity.[139]

Given the time-consuming effort required in hair-styling, many Roman women opted for elaborate wigs that could be quickly fitted to enhance existing hairdos. Braided extensions would be carefully woven into natural hair to provide extra length and bulk when fashion dictated a more elaborate style. The best quality hair available to Roman fashion-suppliers came from India where hair was collected in temple warehouses and sold to foreign merchants. In an ancient custom that has survived into modern times, Hindu women donated their hair to their gods as an offering of piety and to receive divine favour. A list of eastern goods subject to customs tax at Alexandria includes bales of this 'Indian hair' that would have been destined for use in the latest Roman fashions.[140]

Balsam

The study of balsam demonstrates the desirability of incense as a commodity worth the effort and expense of distant trade. The healing ointment referred to as 'balm' in the *Old Testament* is believed to be a unique form of myrrh known as *balsam* and ancient records suggest that the Jewish kingdom of Judea had a monopoly on this valuable substance.[141] Balsam was highly sought after for its medical properties and raised enormous revenues for whatever regime controlled its production.

The balsam tree is described by ancient authorities as a short evergreen scrub-like bush which produced a valuable sap-resin with a strong perfumed aroma. Its value and ritual significance was equivalent to the most expensive Arabian aromatics, yet balsam is a puzzle for modern botanists who find it difficult to connect ancient descriptions of the plant with any currently known species.

It seems that the balsam shrub, like frankincense and myrrh, was originally native to the desert fringes of southern Arabia. However, by the fifth century BC the crop was thriving in Judea, while the original Arabian sources had declined or vanished. The Judean variety of balsam was safeguarded for more than a millennium before it was wiped-out in the political turmoil of late antiquity.

It is not known when the balsam tree was first successfully grown in Judea, but the ancient sources are certain that the plant could only be cultivated in the Jordan Valley, close to the Dead Sea in the intense arid heat of the local climate. The Jordan Valley lies more than 900 feet below sea-level and is the lowest dryland depression on the earth's surface. In this unique environment balsam thrived in specially managed artificial groves, while attempts to cultivate the shrub in other Mediterranean territories met with failure. The Jordan Valley therefore preserved a valuable monopoly over balsam production. Archaeology confirms that an important site in the Jordan Valley called Engedi became a flourishing oasis closely connected with balsam cultivation.[142]

An early mention of the value of balsam occurs in *Genesis* in an account of how Joseph, the favourite son of Jacob, was sold into slavery by his brothers. Joseph and his brothers encountered a trade caravan from nearby Gilead that was passing through their territory on a route south into Egypt. The text describes how the caravan was formed from Ishmaelite and Midianite merchants who had loaded their camels with 'spices, balm and myrrh'. These merchants were willing to convey slaves to their destination markets and so Joseph was sold to the merchants for 20 silver shekels.[143] Later, when Jacob needed foreign grain for his household, he told his sons to travel to Egypt taking with them the 'best fruits in the land' to secure trading deals. He instructed them to give a gift to the Egyptian viceroy in charge of grain distribution and this diplomatic offering was to include 'a little balm, a little honey, spices, myrrh, nuts, and almonds'.[144]

Ancient texts connect the tenth century King Solomon with the first cultivation of balsam in Judea. Josephus believed that King Solomon was gifted shrubs of balsam by the Queen of Sheba (Sabaea), who ruled lands in distant southern Arabia.[145] In the *Song of Solomon* the bride mentions 'spice beds' to evoke the sweet desolation of her longing and this could be a reference to the balsam cultivated in royal gardens.[146] Talmudic tradition suggests that in seventh century BC King Josiah arranged that balsam should anoint the heads of Jewish royalty in place of myrrh.[147]

In the following centuries, balsam became a major source of prestige and wealth for the rulers of ancient Judea. In the book of *Jeremiah*, balsam from Engedi is mentioned three times in connection with healing and the soothing of grief.[148] Balsam perfumes also appear in the prophecies of Ezekiel when he refers to the great commercial wealth of Tyre on the Phoenician coast. Ezekiel reveals that merchants from the kingdoms of Judea and Israel offered wheat, honey, olive oil and balm for the wares available in the city.[149]

Through a careful system of water management, the ancient rulers of Judea transformed the rocky desert lands around Jericho into a series of verdant gardens. An abundant spring rose at Jericho and this water source was channelled across an area eight miles long and over two miles across.[150] On this ground the kings of Judea created a wide, oasis-like plantation of palms and rare fruit trees that thrived in the extreme dry heat of the Jordan Valley. Strabo describes how the fertile plain of the valley was like a vast amphitheatre surrounded by imposing arid mountains. Numerous small streams flowed through the valley and many dwellings were constructed within the confines of the oasis, including a royal palace.

Profits from Balsam
Biblical accounts emphasise the soothing properties of perfumed balsam and these claims are supported by ancient Greek authorities. The balsam produced in the Jordan Valley was an attractive alternative to the myrrh oil received from southern Arabia and some Roman writers regarded balsam perfumes to be superior to all other aromatics, possibly because of its soothing medicinal effects.[151] These properties ensured that balsam could be sold at high prices throughout the Greek and Roman Mediterranean.

The Greeks gained accurate knowledge about balsam cultivation in the 330s BC when Alexander the Great conquered the Near East. In this period there were two main balsam groves, one located at Engedi and the larger plantation situated in the royal grounds near Jericho, just north of the Dead Sea. The Jericho grove covered an area of about twelve acres in the midst of an artificial oasis full of palms and fruit-bearing trees. According to Theophrastus the two groves yielded 42 pints of resinous perfume per harvest and this precious substance was worth twice its weight in silver.[152]

Josephus calls the Jordan Valley 'the most productive part of Judea' and describes gardens thickly set with fruit-bearing palms that could not be grown successfully in any of the surrounding regions. Honey was also produced in these garden parks and it was reported that the air was so mild that people who resided in the valley could wear their linen garments in winter, even if the rest of Judea lay under a fall of snow. Josephus concludes his description of these oasis gardens with the comment, 'it is no exaggeration to call this place divine'.[153] Strabo uses the word *paradeisos* for the royal groves at Jericho, evoking the Persian word *pardessa* meaning a luxurious walled garden.[154] This phrase passed into later traditions as 'paradise', the word selected to describe the Garden of Eden.[155]

Strabo reports that the precious balsam groves lay deep within the oasis gardens at Jericho.[156] The plants resembled a bushy shrub, or stunted tree, with a strong aromatic essence. Attendants made incisions into the bark so that glutinous milk-white sap would bleed from the tree. Pliny explains that bladed metal would taint the resin, so attendants worked with specially fashioned tools made from pieces of glass, sharpened stone, ceramic blades, or animal bone. This ensured that the tree was not excessively harmed and Pliny describes how great expertise was required in making the correct cuts to maximise the seepage of resin without killing the plant, or harming future yields.[157]

Pliny explains how the balsam sap flowed like a tear-drop from the incisions and was collected with tufts of wool, then drained into small horn containers. The resin had the consistency of olive oil and was decanted into large earthenware vessels for storage and fermentation. The finished product was a congealed red substance with a highly potent fragrance. Balsam trees had to be carefully pruned to control their growth and the offcuts were gathered and diced into fragrant wood fragments known as *xylobalsam*. This woodchip was sold to perfume manufacturers who could crush any residual sap from the leftovers.[158]

Greek and Roman writers describe how important the balsam crop was as a source of revenue for local rulers. In the 160s BC, Judea managed to cede from the Seleucid realm and re-establish its position as a small independent kingdom. A century later, Roman armies under the command of Pompey annexed Syria and made Judea a client kingdom of Rome. While on his march to Jerusalem, Pompey established his camp near Jericho and he had a brief opportunity to investigate the balsam gardens.[159]

When the Roman general Mark Antony took command in the eastern Mediterranean he seized the groves at Jericho from the Judean Kingdom and granted them to the Ptolemaic Queen Cleopatra. The Judean King Herod was forced to rent his properties back at the enormous cost of 200 talents.[160] When Cleopatra arranged meetings with Herod she insisted these took place at the Jericho Palace and the gardens that had formerly belonged to the Judean Kingdom. In these luxurious surroundings, Herod was forced to disguise his contempt and it was said that he had to be persuaded not to have Cleopatra murdered.[161]

The value of the balsam crop is suggested by the rent that Cleopatra imposed on the gardens at Jericho. In Egypt, vineyard and orchard land was subject to tax rates of one-sixth and if the same charges were applied to the Jericho oasis, then the site was producing income worth over 1,200 talents every year. This figure is equivalent to about 7 million sesterces in Roman currency at a time when the total revenues of Judea were less than 22 million sesterces.[162]

Herod supported Octavian in his war against Antony and Cleopatra by sending funds to aid the Roman troops as they progressed toward Egypt. After his victory in 30 BC, Octavian rewarded Herod by placing the Jericho groves back under the authority of the Judean Kingdom. These harvests were an important addition to the revenues Herod received from his subject territories.

Roman Balsam

Balsam from Judea was the only major incense crop produced in the regions subject to Rome and whoever owned jurisdiction over the Jericho and Engadi groves had a monopoly on the production of this valuable commodity. During the Imperial period, uses for the product diversified as balsam was transformed into potent perfumes for ritual and personal use. Demand for balsam increased as markets expanded and Roman consumers sought further aromatic ingredients to use for medicines, as offerings for religious worship and as personal fragrances.

Pliny describes the significance of balsam as a perfume, but its medical properties were also well known to Roman society. Balsam remedies soothed pain and aided the treatment of eye conditions, so when Tacitus writes about the resin, he describes it primarily as a 'sap that is utilised by physicians'.[163] Balsam also appears in medical remedies promoted by Galen who recommends a particular variety of medical balsam that was grown at Engedi.[164] Strabo describes balsam as a cure for headaches and an effective treatment for early-stage cataracts and other conditions that diminished eyesight. The Greek doctor Dioscorides confirms that 'warming balsam juice has the most strength and it can clean away the things that darken the pupils'.[165] This medical demand greatly increased the cost of balsam, particularly as Judea remained the only producer of this rare substance.[166]

The balsam gardens at Jericho came under imperial control when Augustus made Judea a Roman province in AD 6.[167] Aware of the opportunities for profit, the revenues from the royal holdings were maximised by imperial agents. The Romans were familiar with hilly Italian landscapes and had generations of experience in the water management systems required for vineyard cultivation on terraces. Balsam could not be grown beyond its unique Dead Sea environment, but the Romans realised that the area under management could be increased by the introduction of methods learnt from Italian agriculture.

One of the Roman innovations was to cut terraces into the slopes that led down to the Jericho valley and add irrigation works to the new surfaces. Cuttings were taken from the balsam trees and the shoots planted on the terraces to grow through a supporting grid of wooden frames. Commenting on these developments Pliny informs his readers that 'at present balsam crops are more like a vine than a myrtle bush' and 'with the shoots tied to trellises, the crop can cover hillsides like a vineyard'.[168]

Under Roman management, continual pruning and cropping was undertaken to maximise the amount of productive balsam under cultivation. The Romans also increased the frequency of resin collections and incisions were made three times every summer to gather the perfumed sap. The redundant shoots and branches cut from the crop were sold to unguent-makers who developed new techniques to extract expensive perfumes from the crushed extracts. Pliny describes three types of cuttings, as thin twigs, small bushy branches and taller shoots with smooth bark.

The 'wood-balsam' made from these cuttings shared many qualities with traditional resin-prepared balsam and imperial agents also sold bark fragments 'at a considerable price, for its use in medicines'. There was even a market for the seeds which were sold as a spice that Pliny describes as having 'a sharp taste that is hot in the mouth'. These new products increased the variety of balsam available on the Roman market and substantially raised the revenues generated by the incense groves.[169]

Under careful Roman management, the balsam estates at Jericho reached new levels of productivity. Pliny reported, 'balsam is now cultivated by the treasury authorities and although the height of these shrubs does not advance beyond three feet, the production of the perfume has never been more plentiful'. Pliny also indicates knowledge of the scale of the revenue generated by the balsam gardens when he reports that a single tree was able to produce more than six pints of sap. The larger of the two balsam gardens covered more than twelve acres and the smaller grove may have been about four acres in extent.[170] This would represent at least 3,440 trees and with each plant producing six pints of sap every summer, the Roman authorities would have been receiving over 20,000 pints of balsam every year.[171] Pliny reports that balsam sold at about 1,200 sesterces per pint and this suggests that total resin production might have been worth over 26 million sesterces per annum.

To place this figure in context, the Jewish prince Herod Agrippa was granted rule over Judea and Samaria in AD 41. From these extensive territories, which encompassed most of ancient Palestine, the king received revenues of about 48 million sesterces per annum. Whoever had control of the balsam gardens could receive more than half this figure, just from the careful management of this precious incense crop. Income from balsam worth 26 million sesterces provided enough revenue to pay double the entire annual wages of the Roman Legion posted in Palestine.

In addition to the 26 million sesterces raised from the two main gardens was profit from the cuttings and sap taken from the vine-like balsam growing on newly trellised slopes. Pliny reports, 'there is such a market for these twigs, that in the five years since the Judean re-conquest, these loppings and shoots have raised 800,000 sesterces' (AD 70–75). Pliny gives the price of wood-balsam as 24 sesterces a pound and this suggests that over 16 tons (33,000 pounds) of waste cuttings were sold every year.[172]

The Roman government sold its balsam produce at special State run auctions. According to Pliny, unguent-makers who turned the pure balsam oil into more dilute perfumes could make a three-fold profit. A pint of pure balsam bought for 1,200 sesterces could make 4,000 sesterces when resold with the addition of further enhancing ingredients.[173] Martial confirms the popularity of this perfume when he writes: 'balsam delights me, for it is the perfume for men. Let matrons use the essences of Cosmus'.[174]

Such was their significance, the balsam groves at Jericho were attacked during the great Jewish uprising against Rome which began in AD 66. For the Roman treasury the plants were more valuable than entire cities and every effort was made to preserve this irreplaceable resource. The defence of the site was crucial for the continued prosperity of the region and the Romans took special measures to guard the gardens from the violence. Pliny reports, 'at the expense of their own lives, the Jews vented their wrath upon this plant. But the Romans protected the groves and there were pitched battles fought in defence of a shrub'.[175]

As the revolt continued and the fighting intensified around Jerusalem, a fanatical group of Jewish zealots known as the Sicarii took possession of Masada, a formidable cliff-top fortress. This stronghold occupied a high-plateau overlooking the southern shores of the Dead Sea and from this position the Sicarii prepared to make their final stand against the approaching Roman Legions. While their enemies delayed, the rebels sent out raiding parties to strip the surrounding land of food and supplies needed for the defence of their stronghold.

One group of Sicarii conducted a devastating night raid on the Jewish town of Engedi and its nearby balsam grove. Josephus reports, 'those who might have offered resistance were scattered before they could arm themselves and more than seven hundred women and children who could not escape, were butchered'. Then 'the Sicarii striped the houses bare, seized the flourishing crops, and brought their loot to Masada'.[176] Pliny confirms, 'once the town of Engedi was second only to Jerusalem in the fertility of its land and its groves of palm-trees, but now like Jerusalem it is a heap of ashes'.[177] With this act, the royal gardens at Jericho probably became the last refuge of the precious balsam crop.

The Jericho groves were preserved during the conflict so the local authorities were able to restore the allotments at Engedi. This was a major success for the Roman regime and balsam was prominent in the victory triumph celebrated in Rome at the completion of the Jewish War. Pliny describes 'the balsam tree exhibited at the Roman Capital by the Emperors Vespasian and Titus. It is a remarkable fact that ever since the time of Pompey the Great, shrubs have appeared as captives in our triumphal processions.' Vespasian could claim that he had preserved Judea for Rome and saved this valuable product from threatened extinction. With the war concluded, Pliny proudly boasts, 'the balsam-tree is now a subject of Rome and it pays tribute to us along with the race to which it belongs'.[178]

Solinus suggests that shortly after the Jewish War was concluded in AD 73, the Roman authorities increased the amount of land near Jericho given over to balsam cultivation.[179] Archaeologists investigating the area have unearthed ancient installations associated with the processing of unguents. They have found the remains of workshops with soaking pools, holding vats and heavy cylindrical stones used to pound the essence from offcut branches.[180] Latin papyri fragments found at Masada document Roman military operations to transport balsam-wood trimmings.[181]

During the second century AD, Roman authorities allowed members of the Jewish nobility to harvest their own balsam shrubs in small allotments. The *Babylonian Talmud* makes a distinction between 'the balsam of the Caesars' and balsam from the 'House of Rabbi Judah the Prince'.[182] Talmudic tradition suggests that Rabbi Judah visited Rome as an advocate of his people and developed a friendship with a prominent Roman named 'Antoninus' who could be Antoninus Pius.[183] Antoninus became Emperor in AD 138 and this would explain how a Jewish prince came to be favoured with permission to cultivate a special allotment of precious balsam.

The Romans also introduced balsam production at a military installation on the southeast coast of the Dead Sea. In the fourth century AD a Christian scholar named Eusebius composed a catalogue of biblical sites including a place called Zoara. He reports, 'a garrison of Roman soldiers is stationed at Zoara and there is a balsam and date-palm grove in the fertile land near this place'.[184] Writing in the fifth century AD, Jerome also referred to the 'balsam vines of Zoara and Engedi'.[185] Archaeologists excavating at Engedi have uncovered the ruins of a synagogue with an ancient inscription that condemns anyone who would betray the 'secret of the town'. This could be a reference to balsam production and the specialist cultivation skills preserved by this community.[186]

Balsam became extinct during the sixth century AD when serious revolts in Palestine were followed by Persian and Islamic invasions. But although no living samples of the balsam plant exist, archaeologists have recovered evidence of balsam resins in ancient containers. An empty jar was found at Masada bearing the scratched-on words 'balsam juice' in Aramaic letters, while at caves near Qumran an intact jug was found wrapped in palm fibres and crammed between some rocks. The ancient jug, dated to the time of King Herod, contained a dark viscous liquid that could not be identified with any currently known plant substance.[187] Archaeologists investigating the ancient terraces at Jericho and Engedi are currently screening the arid soil for the desecrated remains of balsam cultivation. Perhaps ancient balsam will soon be identified by botanists and with the assistance of science, revived from its long extinction. If so, then modern society will be able to experience an archaic essence acclaimed for its soothing medical benefits and associations with ancient religious worship. Incense was a unique, valuable and regionally specific product, but balsam was the rarest and most precious of all.

CHAPTER FOUR

The Intermediaries: Petra and the Nabataeans

Incense was a unique crop that could only be produced in particular areas and commanded high prices at distant market destinations. Consequently, the trafficking of incense generated wealth for those who conveyed the substance from the producer to the consumer. Among the intermediaries in this trade, a desert people known as the Nabataeans achieved a prime place in the trafficking of incense from southern Arabia to Roman markets. Their prosperity serves as an example of the riches to be made through the distant trade of valuable commodities.

The early Nabataeans were a nomadic people who occupied a territory on the northern desert fringes of Arabia. They led their camel herds across lands that had few natural resources to attract the attention of powerful foreign regimes. The Greek historian Diodorus reports the words of a Nabataean spokesman who claimed: 'we live in the desert, in a land that has neither water, nor grain, nor wine, nor anything else that is needed by you. But we are not willing to be slaves and so we have taken refuge in a land that lacks all the things that are valued amongst other peoples. We have chosen to live in the desert like harmless wild animals.'[1]

In the fourth century BC the Nabataeans moved their herds of camels and sheep between the seasonal grazing grounds of their homelands in northwest Arabia. Although their territory was poor, the Nabataeans had access to important land-routes and abundant livestock that could be used to transport commodities. Their travels led across large tracts of desert and brought them into contact with neighbouring peoples including fellow nomads from inner Arabia who traded incense. The Nabataeans realised that if they brought this product to eastern Mediterranean markets, foreign merchants would be willing to pay silver bullion for packages of this rare and costly substance. By using their indigenous camel herds as pack-animals, the Nabataeans transformed their small nation into a wealthy and successful kingdom.

The Origins of the Nabataeans
In the fourth century BC the growing wealth of the Nabataean nation began to attract the attention of foreign regimes, particularly the ancient Greeks. The Nabataeans had a central gathering site in Jordan called 'the Rock', which was to become the city of Petra. The Rock was a natural stronghold where men left their families and flocks in safety while they travelled north to the frontiers of Judea

to trade incense with Mediterranean merchants from Gaza. But their wealth attracted outside interest and in 312 BC the one-eyed Macedonian general Antigonus decided to attack the Rock while the menfolk were absent.

The operation was led by a Greek officer named Athenaeus who was given command of 4,000 lightly-armed infantry and 600 cavalry. After leaving their base in Judea, it took Athenaeus three days and nights to cross almost 100 miles of desert to reach the Rock. The Antigonid army attacked at night, plundering the settlement and seizing the women and children to be sold as slaves. The affluence of the early Nabataeans is demonstrated by reports that Athenaeus secured a large stockpile of incense and 500 talents of silver (almost 12 million sesterces) from the camp.[2]

As dawn broke, Athenaeus regrouped his forces and ordered an immediate retreat back to Judea. But his army had been observed as it marched into the desert and its movements reported to the main assembly of Nabataean men. Guessing the destination and intent of the Antigonid forces, the men immediately rallied and raced back to the Rock to defend their families. The first camel-riders reached Petra only hours after Athenaeus had left the site and learning about the attack from the wounded survivors, they began an immediate pursuit.

Athenaeus assumed it would take several days for the nomads to mobilise their fighting forces, so that same night he rested his army in a lightly defended desert camp. While his troops slept, some of the prisoners escaped into the desert and were picked up by trackers moving ahead of the pursuing Nabataean force. Under the cover of darkness a horde of 8,000 camel-mounted fighters galloped into the Macedonian camp to slaughter the aggressors and free the captive families. The Nabataeans fought with javelins, killing the Greeks where they lay, or lancing those who clambered awake to defend themselves from the sudden assault. Barely fifty wounded Greek cavalrymen escaped from the slaughter and fled into the desert.[3]

The Nabataeans sent spokesmen to the Macedonian General Antigonus, explaining that they wanted to avoid a war and had been provoked into attacking the Antigonid force. Antigonus publically accepted their explanation and placed blame on Athenaeus as a 'rogue' general who had acted without orders. Greek strategists reported that the Arabs 'possessed the wilderness as their inaccessible refuge' and a pursuing army would be divided and exhausted by any attempt to hunt down the individual tribes. The best tactic to defeat the Nabataeans was to surround and attack their seasonal assembly sites. So when peace had been restored, Antigonus placed his son Demetrius in charge of a larger force and gave him orders to attack the Nabataeans at their main gathering. Demetrius commanded 4,000 foot-soldiers and 4,000 cavalry, which he believed was a sufficient force to match the fighting strength of the entire Nabataean nation.

The Greek foot-soldiers led by Demetrius were lightly armed and selected from infantry units capable of fast-paced marching. The army was well-provisioned with food rations, so the troops did not need to forage, or light campfires that would betray their position in the desert. Demetrius marched his army straight to the Rock hoping to ambush and slaughter the gathered

Nabataeans before they could scatter into the surrounding desert. But the Nabataeans had not trusted the assurances given by General Antigonus and had posted watchmen on the hills to report the movements of any hostile forces entering their territory. When the lookouts sighted the Antigonid army, they lit a series of pre-arranged signal fires to convey a rapid warning across the wilderness.[4]

For three days the Antigonid army advanced quickly through arid tracks of land that had neither rivers, nor roads to permit easy passage. When they reached the Rock they found the Nabataeans fully prepared for battle. The Arabs had gathered together their flocks and herds and sent them out to the furthest pasturelands. They had brought their remaining material wealth to the Rock and posted their most able fighters around this naturally defensive stronghold. The Greeks attacked the Rock though a narrow pass, but the Nabataeans controlled the slopes and repelled each assault.

By the second day of the attack Demetrius was forced to concede peace terms with the Nabataeans. In spite of his preparations, his army had limited supplies and by this stage it was apparent that the Rock was extremely well-defended by determined fighters. The Antigonid army carried no siege machinery and their casualties were probably higher than expected. But as a condition of his withdrawal, Demetrius insisted that the Nabataeans provide him with political hostages from their leading families and offer him precious gifts to be displayed as tribute. Demetrius then abandoned the campaign claiming that Nabataean territory was not a viable acquisition for his father's domains. He justified this by arguing that the territories lacked grain, wine and other economic crops that were essential for Greek civilization.[5] Demetrius then led his army north to the shores of the Dead Sea to investigate the properties of this giant salt lake where asphalt deposits erupt from the depths. Bitumen was an important resource in the ancient world because it could be melted down to waterproof the outer hulls of sea-going vessels.

When Demetrius returned from the campaign, his father Antigonus rebuked him for not taking more aggressive action against the Nabataeans. However, when he learned that his son had located important bitumen deposits, he 'praised him for scrutinizing the lake and finding a further source of revenue for the kingdom'. Demetrius sent military forces to the Dead Sea shores to develop collecting and processing camps for the asphalt deposits that periodically emerged from the saline waters. But the surrounding Arab tribes objected to this intrusion and gathered a force of several thousand fighters to challenge the Antigonid presence in their territory. The Arabs approached the Antigonid boats on reed-rafts and killed almost all the Greek personnel in an overwhelming hail of arrow-fire.[6]

Antigonus had once again provoked local hostility towards his regime. Then, in 312 BC, his army was routed and pushed back into Syria by the rival Macedonian general Ptolemy I Soter. Ptolemy chose not to attack the Nabataeans and the prosperous incense trade that crossed their desert territory was permitted to continue without any further interruption. By the first century BC, the Greeks regarded Nabataea as 'a country with a large population and well supplied with pasturage'.[7]

Early Nabataean Trade

In the pre-Roman period Nabataea was the main connection point for inland caravans and cargo offloaded from Red Sea vessels. The Sabaeans in southern Arabia controlled the main groves that produced the valuable frankincense and myrrh, but other Arab nations were involved in bringing these incense stocks to Mediterranean markets. Diodorus reports that: 'by custom the Nabataeans bring down to the Mediterranean Sea their frankincense and myrrh along with the most valuable kinds of spices. They procure these goods from those who convey them from southern Arabia.' The intermediaries in this trade were Gerrhaeans from the Persian Gulf and a people called the Minaeans who occupied lands flanking the Red Sea. Diodorus explains that 'the Gerrhaeans and Minaeans convey frankincense and other aromatic wares from southern Arabia to Nabataea and Palestine'.[8]

Some of this ancient incense traffic was probably conducted through a network of inland caravan courses that connected various regional oasis stations in inner Arabia. This was not a straightforward route and most incense seems to have passed through a series of intermediate suppliers. Strabo describes how 'the Arabs who live close to one another receive in continuous succession loads of aromatics coming from the Sabaeans'. Through a sequence of regional deals, 'they convey this product to their neighbours as far away as Syria and Mesopotamia'.[9]

Strabo used similar sources to Diodorus in his account of the Nabataeans, including a work by the Greek author named Artemidorus who was writing around 100 BC. Artemidorus emphasised the importance of seaborne trade to the Nabataeans and describes how merchants from different Arab nations sent ships to the northern coasts of the Red Sea. Strabo explains that 'near the island of Phocae there is a promontory linked to the Rock of the Nabataeans and Palestine. The Minaeans, Gerrhaeans and all the neighbouring peoples convey their aromatics loads to this location.'[10]

By the first century BC, most incense was shipped aboard Arab dhows that visited ports in southern Arabia and carried cargo to harbours in the northern quarter of the Red Sea. On these journeys Arab vessels also visited settlements on the east coast of Africa and Strabo explains that 'the Sabaeans engage partly in agriculture and partly in the traffic of aromatics produced in their homeland and Africa. To acquire African aromatics they sail across the sea in leather boats.'[11]

The Minaeans also shipped incense through Ptolemaic Egypt and established trade agreements with Mediterranean sea-captains in Alexandria. Using these contacts, the Minaeans sent their cargoes to Greek cities across the eastern Mediterranean. The second century coffin of a Minaean frankincense merchant named Zayd'il has been found at the Egyptian city of Memphis and dedications from the sanctuary of Artemis on the Greek island of Delos record that Minaean merchants were operating on the island during the second century BC.[12]

Confirmation comes from southern Arabia where early Minaic inscriptions mention expeditions to Egypt.[13] The Minaeans brought their profits back to Arabia to buy further incense stocks from the Sabaeans and the result was an outflow of wealth towards southern Arabia. Strabo explains that 'from their trafficking of incense the Sabaeans and the Gerrhaeans have become richest of all the Arabians. They have a vast store of both gold and silver articles including couches, tripods, bowls, and drinking-vessels.' Palace-like residences in the Sabaean cities were said to have rich interiors, 'decorated with ivory, gold and silver, and fitted with precious stones'.[14]

Rome Invades the Sabaean Kingdom
By the first century BC, the Nabataean nation had developed into a settled kingdom with Petra as their prosperous capital city. It was during this period that the Nabataean Kingdom was incorporated into the Roman Empire and its ruler accepted as a client king. When the Emperor Augustus came to power he decided to preserve this arrangement, as the Nabataeans would support his ambition for further Arabian conquests.

Soon after Egypt was secured, Augustus decided that the Sabaean Kingdom should be conquered and southern Arabia added to the Roman domains. He was motivated by Greek reports that suggested the Sabaeans occupied 'a very fertile country' and were 'a very large nation' rich in incense and under-exploited gold reserves. When Pliny promises to 'catalogue the riches of Arabia and the reasons that it receives the name Fortunate (*Felix*)' he cites incense production in particular.[15] Large quantities of myrrh and frankincense were produced in Sabaean territory and Strabo believed that the Sabaeans also grew cinnamon, since their traders were important dealers in this Somali product.[16] Pliny confirms 'some authorities report that the Sabaeans import highly regarded myrrh from the islands (Socotra) and the Troglodyte Country (Somalia)'.[17] Strabo reports that the southern Arabians 'excavate gold nuggets that do not need to be processed' and there was a river in the southwest corner of Arabia 'that brings down gold-dust, but the inhabitants do not know how to work it'.[18] If the Romans seized this territory they could bring advanced mining methods and technologies into the region.

The conquest of Arabia Felix (the Yemen and Dhofar) would have given the Roman Empire ownership of one of the main incense producing regions of the ancient world and possession of a seaboard that faced the Indian Ocean. Strabo explains why the Roman governor of Egypt, Aelius Gallus, was selected to lead the conquest of Arabia. The Romans understood that Egypt could dominate the Red Sea coast of East Africa, known as the 'Troglodyte Country'. Augustus 'saw that the country which below Egypt approaches Arabia and the gulf which separates the Arabians from the Troglodytes, is extremely narrow'.[19] The Red Sea could therefore be made into a 'Roman Gulf' if both coastlines were made subject to the Empire.

At first Augustus thought that the best opportunity for success was to launch a fleet from Egypt and attack the coast of southern Arabia with a naval assault. He

therefore had 80 triremes and 130 troop transport ships built in Egypt for a
seaborne conquest of the Arabian Peninsula. Strabo reports that 'Gallus was sent
by Augustus to explore the tribes and the places of Arabia and Ethiopia'.
However, the ships that Aelius Gallus sent into the gulf reported back, saying that
sailing conditions and the positions of ports made the seaborne conquest too
difficult a prospect. A land campaign was therefore recommended and Augustus
was 'encouraged by the promise of assistance from the Nabataeans, since they
were friendly and promised to co-operate with him in every way'. Significant conquests were planned, 'for Augustus expected either to deal with wealthy friends,
or to master rich enemies'.[20]

As part of his main campaign force, Aelius Gallus was given command of
10,000 Roman troops. He also received the support of 500 Jewish soldiers sent by
the Judean King Herod and 1,000 Nabataean troops under the command of a
vizier named Syllaeus.[21] The Romans were confident of complete victory and
back in Rome the poet Horace wrote a verse entitled *Off to the Wars*. He writes,
'are you gazing with envy at Arabian riches and preparing for a bitter war against
the unbeaten kings of Sabae'.[22]

In early 25 BC Gallus led his army south to capture a network of oasis towns on
the main desert trails into central Arabia. The dune deserts of inner Arabia can
reach surface temperatures of up to seventy degrees and the Roman army made
slow progress towards Arabia Felix. It took Aelius Gallus eighty days to capture
a network of oasis stations that led across the sand-filled inner desert to the
Sabaean Kingdom. When the Romans seized the city of Negrana (Nejran) the
Sabaeans gathered nearly 10,000 fighters to protect their homeland. But their
army was inexperienced and poorly equipped, defending themselves with a dis-
ordered mixture of bows, spears, swords, slings and double-edged axes. The
disciplined Roman ranks drove the Sabaeans into full retreat and Gallus captured
several further towns on his march towards the royal capital Ma'rib, known to the
Romans as Sabae (Marsiaba).[23]

Ma'rib was a populous walled city, a dense cluster of multi-storey mud-brick
buildings positioned within a broad oasis valley. The city was equipped with
wealthy royal palaces and splendid temples.[24] Ma'rib was at the edge of the
coastal mountains and its oasis fields were watered by a giant dam built into the
hills to collect run-off from the seasonal monsoon mists. This dam redirected
streams of water through a sophisticated irrigation system that sustained a
panorama of fertile fields around the city.[25]

The Romans learned from captives that they were only a few days march away
from the first frankincense districts of the Sabaean realm. But by this stage the
Roman army was suffering from a scurvy-induced paralysis in their limbs, probably caused by the lack of vitamin C in the campaign diet of the soldiers. As the
Romans were unable to diagnose the true cause of their sickness, they assumed
that the water in southern Arabian was detrimental to non-indigenous peoples.
Fearing that some unknown element was killing his troops, Aelius Gallus ordered
an immediate Roman withdrawal from the region. The thousand-mile retreat
back to Nabataea took sixty days and during this period the Romans suffered

heavy losses due the debilitating effects of the disease. Any Roman garrisons remaining in Arabia Felix either succumbed to the sickness, or were expelled by native uprisings.

Strabo blamed the Nabataean viceroy for the losses, suggesting that if Syllaeus had led the Romans directly to Sabaea the region might have been conquered before the sickness took hold. He explains that 'Gallus discovered that the Sabaeans are unwarlike and if Syllaeus had not betrayed him, he would have subdued the whole of Arabia Felix'.[26] Campaign doctors concluded that the illness was a 'native ailment' of southern Arabia and 'this paralysis of the legs and mouth was the result of the local water'.[27] Aelius Gallus informed Augustus that southern Arabia could not be occupied by Mediterranean troops and the incense groves of Arabia Felix would never be added to the Empire.

But the conflict probably had a positive outcome for the Nabataeans who increased their position as intermediaries in the incense trade. Writing several years after the war, Strabo argues that Syllaeus must have used the Romans 'to investigate Arabia and destroy certain cities and tribes, so that he could master the country'.[28] The conflict had other consequences as the Roman assault destabilised the Sabaean Kingdom and as the realm fragmented, neighbouring Arab regimes seized the territory. The Himyarites subdued the Sabaean homelands in Yemen and the Hadramawt claimed the frankincense plantations on the seaboard of Dhofar. The rulers of these new kingdoms understood the threat posed by the Roman Empire and sent regular envoys to the imperial court in the hope of discouraging any future invasion. These envoys gave lavish gifts to the rulers of Rome and assured them that the new kings of Arabia Felix were committed to being the permanent 'friends of the Emperors'.[29] Arabia therefore remained permanently beyond Roman rule and in a secure position to slowly drain the Empire of its bullion wealth through the long-term processes of trade.

Nabataean Commerce in the Roman Era

During the Imperial period, Petra operated as a major hub for Arab caravan traffic heading for the Mediterranean coast. Ancient Petra was built at the site of the Rock, recessed into the cliffs of Mount Hor where an ancient dried-up river had cut a deep gorge through the desert on its route to the Aqaba Gulf on the northeast coast of the Red Sea (the Wadi Araba). Strabo calls Petra the metropolis (capital city) of the Nabataeans and describes its position, 'situated on a smooth and level site fortified all around by high rock-faces'. He reports that beyond the city and its irrigated grounds, 'most of the surrounding territory is desolate'.[30]

The Nabataeans constructed dams and water conduits around Petra to gather rainfall from periodical flash floods and direct the supplies into central cisterns. They created an artificial oasis around their city with enough stored water resources to overcome the desert droughts and sustain a prosperous settled population. Strabo reports that the outer parts of the site were precipitous and sheer, but the interior had abundant springs which were used for domestic purposes and for watering public gardens'.[31] Monumental buildings in the centre of Petra were carved directly into the pale surface of the salmon-coloured sandstone ravines. These buildings were influenced by Greek architecture and the city had a Roman-style amphitheatre constructed within its confines. Family tombs that were cut into surrounding cliff-faces were frequently carved to resemble classical buildings, complete with orders of decorative columns.[32]

The Roman merchants who conducted deals in Petra gave Arab traders gold and silver in return for the incoming incense stocks. They also offered the Nabataeans supplies of iron, brass, *storax* perfumes, purple cloth and crocus flowers that could be crushed to produce a yellow dye. According to Strabo the Nabataeans had an interest in classical art, including paintings, sculptures and expensive embossed silverware that could be exchanged for costly incense.[33] Pliny confirms that 'in Arabia there is a surprising demand for foreign scents which are imported from abroad'.[34]

During the Imperial era, most merchants from Petra ended their caravan journeys at the Mediterranean ports of Gaza in Palestine or Rhinocorura in Egyptian territory. Gaza was under the authority of Judea and the city was positioned midway between Jerusalem and Alexandria. The port was therefore well placed to supply important regional markets in both Judea and Egypt.[35]

The Nabataeans had two major ports on the Red Sea coast. These were Aila on the Aqaba Gulf and Leuke Kome ('White Village') which was several hundred miles further south. Many Nabataeans were full-time merchants who launched their vessels on to the Red Sea to reach markets in southern Arabia and visit trade-stations on the east coast of Africa. They sailed in shallow-draft dhows fitted with lateen sails for increased manoeuvrability. These ships could carry up to 30 tons of cargo and operate in difficult, or variable, wind conditions.[36] Procopius describes the unique construction of these vessels which had their hulls fastened with cord so that they could withstand a reef-strike without fracturing. He explains that 'these vessels are not smeared with pitch and the planks are not fastened together by iron nails. Instead they are bound together with a type of cording.'[37]

Strabo suggests that it took Arab ships about ten weeks to complete a voyage from southern Arabia to the Nabataean port of Aila, 'a city on the upper reaches of the Red Sea, near Gaza'. He explains that 'frankincense, myrrh and other aromatics are exchanged between merchants who arrive at Aila in seventy days.'[38] There were strong prevailing northerly winds in the upper part of the Red Sea and Strabo reports that 'this sea is hard to navigate, especially for those who sail to its innermost recesses (Suez and Aqaba).'[39] Consequently many returning ships chose to offload their cargo at the Nabataean town of Leuke Kome (modern al-Wajh).[40] Caravans then carried these cargoes about 300 miles north to Petra for immediate sale, or transport to further Roman markets.

Roman sources suggest that Leuke Kome became the main trade port for the Nabataean Kingdom and most eastern goods reaching Petra arrived via this route. In 26 BC, it was Leuke Kome that received the Roman fleet for the invasion of Arabia Felix when over a hundred transport ships from Egypt arrived under the command of Aelius Gallus. During this conflict the Nabataeans were able to accommodate 10,000 Roman troops in the town for several months.[41]

A Roman trade guide called the *Periplus of the Erythraean Sea* describes how the harbour at Leuke Kome was usually filled with numerous small ships importing freight from Arabia Felix. The author confirms that 'from the harbour there is a path inland to Petra which is ruled by the Nabataean King Malichus' and 'this harbour functions as a trade port for small craft that arrive loaded with freight from Arabia'.[42] Strabo was an associate of Aelius Gallus and heard first-hand reports about the scale of the trade conducted through Leuke Kome. He describes how 'aromatic cargoes are conveyed from Leuke Kome to Petra and from there they are sent to Rhinocorura near Egypt'. He also reports that 'from Leuke Kome traders travel safely and easily on the route to and from Petra, and they move in such numbers of men and camels that they resemble an army'.[43]

Although Nabataea was a Roman client kingdom, the Empire did not permit the region to have full autonomy over its frontier taxes. The Romans established a customs station at Leuke Kome to tax all incoming cargoes at the standard quarter-rate. This intervention was to increase imperial revenues and ensure that traders importing goods through Nabataea had to pay the same tax rates as merchants bringing cargo through Egypt. The *Periplus* explains that, 'as a safe-guard, a customs officer has been dispatched to the port to deal with an import duty of one-fourth on the incoming merchandise'.[44] Without this measure, many traders importing through Egypt would have shifted their business to Nabataea to avoid paying the high Roman taxes.

The *Periplus* records the presence of a fort at Leuke Kome that was either garrisoned by Roman troops, or a cohort of Nabataean allies. The author refers to 'a centurion with a detachment of soldiers', who was posted at the port to protect the customs post and ensure imperial order.[45] These measures were suc-cessful and Nabataean merchants submitted to paying Roman customs taxes at whatever Red Sea port they chose to offload their cargo. During the Imperial period, some Nabataeans transferred their import businesses to the Egyptian port of Myos Hormos on the opposite coast of the Red Sea. Nabataean pottery has been found at the harbour and these Nabataeans would have joined caravans through the Eastern Desert, possibly using their own camel-teams. This is con-firmed by Nabataean graffiti found carved on to rock-faces near ancient caravan stations on the road from Myos Hormos to Coptos.[46]

Pliny suggests that every year the Roman Empire exported more than 50 million sesterces of bullion wealth to Arabia to pay for incoming incense.[47] A large share of this wealth was procured by the Nabataean Kingdom which imposed tolls on caravans crossing their territory. However, when the Nabataean King Rabbel II Soter died in AD 106, the Romans decided to annex his kingdom. In AD 107, Nabataea was made an imperial province known as *Arabia Petraea* and its overseas possessions became the property of the Emperor Trajan.[48] This brought substantial new revenues into the imperial finances and led to increased Roman involvement along the Arabian coasts of the Red Sea.

CHAPTER FIVE

Beyond Egypt: The Nile Route and the African Kingdom of Meroe

The wealth of Egypt was crucial for sustaining Roman prosperity and the lands beyond its borders were of great importance to the ancient economy. The Sahara Desert covered North Africa with a belt of barren land almost 3,000 miles wide stretching from the Red Sea to the Atlantic Ocean. It extended nearly a thousand miles from north to south with an expanse larger than the entire landmass of the Roman Empire. The desert contained vast dune fields, stone plateaus, gravel plains, salt flats and arid valleys swept by severe sand-storms. In the ancient past, Berber caravans with knowledge of wells and oasis stations were able to cross this landscape, but the extreme conditions of the area confined the Roman Empire to the Mediterranean seaboard fringe of North Africa.

The land of Egypt was the exception and offered the Romans an important route into inner Africa. The Nile River flowed from sources deep within the continent northwards into the Mediterranean Sea, creating a strip of fertile terrain in an otherwise barren land. The White Nile begins in Tanzania nearly 4,000 miles from the Mediterranean coast of Egypt and the soil-rich Blue Nile emerges in Ethiopia to join with the White Nile in the Sudan. From there the river flows through desert landscapes towards the ancient city of Syene (Aswan) which stood on the frontiers of Egypt. Beyond Syene, the Nile flood waters fertilised broad field systems with the rich soil deposits it carried into Egypt. Pliny describes how 'for a certain part of the year the volume of the Nile greatly increases and it flows over the whole of Egypt, inundating the land with a fertilising flood'.[1] Most ancient Egyptian towns and cities were therefore positioned near the flood plain of the Nile Valley to exploit this resource in a landscape that would otherwise have been a bare wilderness.

From very ancient times, the river was a conduit that allowed extraordinary goods to be brought into Egypt. It was almost 600 miles from Syene to the coast and the Nile formed a major route for travel and communication as it flowed north into a broad delta that discharged into the Mediterranean Sea. Most of the Egyptian Nile was safe for riverine travel, except for seasonal surges in the volume of water coming downriver from distant sources in Sub-Saharan Africa. African goods entering Egypt passed Syene and the neighbouring temple-site of Elephantine which was located on an island in the Nile. Elephantine Island could have received its name from the import of ivory, or because the large boulders found on its shores resemble the hunched-shape of crouching elephants.

Between Syene and the confluence of the White and Blue Nile in Sudan there were Six Cataracts that impeded upstream travel. Some of these cataracts contained multiple rapids that stretched for miles, or resembled waterfalls when the river cascaded down a steep descent. Boats on the Egyptian Nile did not sail beyond the frontier city of Syene because of a dangerous series of rapids called the First Cataract. This First Cataract had shallow waters with protruding rocks that would puncture hulls, and turbulent fast-flowing currents that could overturn fragile river-craft. Ancient travellers therefore disembarked near Syene and followed the banks of the Nile to bypass these rapids. On the far side they boarded other vessels to sail south to the Second Cataract. It was just over 200 miles between the First and Second Cataract and the journey was also made by using pack-animals that followed caravan trails flanking the river. South of the Second Cataract it was advisable to travel entirely by land, rather than continue the journey by boarding further river-craft. Beyond the Second Cataract fixed trails followed the curving route of the Nile, occasionally branching off to connect with distant oasis sites in the surrounding desert landscape.

Nubia

The lands below Egypt were known as Nubia and in the time of the Pharaohs were ruled by an African people that the Egyptians called the Kush. Kushite civilisation was clustered around the upper part of the Sudan, but their influence extended north through a largely arid landscape where the Nile flowed through narrow gorges hemmed in by steep cliffs. The early Egyptians described Nubia as desolate by contrast with their own fertile valley. But Nubia produced gold and controlled the traffic of Sub-Saharan products into Egypt, including elephant ivory, dark-skinned African slaves, ebony wood, valuable leopard pelts and incense from Somalia.

During the New Kingdom period the Egyptian Pharaohs conquered Nubia as far as the Fourth Cataract (1552–1070 BC). This conquest extended their kingdom south by nearly 400 miles and incorporated the large looping bend of the Nile River between the Third and Fourth Cataracts. A place called Napata became the new frontier for this merged kingdom and over successive generations the Egyptians imposed many of their own state structures and customs on Nubian society. The Kushite ruling class adopted aspects of Egyptian-style culture and when Egypt began to decline in the eighth century BC, they led African armies north to assume control over the northern kingdom. The Kings of Kush established a succession of African Pharaohs that ruled both kingdoms for almost a century (751–656 BC). The reign of this Twenty-fifth Dynasty ended when a Near Eastern people called the Assyrians invaded Egypt and defeated the Kushites. The Egyptians restored a native Pharaoh to power in the reclaimed kingdom and the Kings of Kush retreated back into the Sudan. Most of these events are recorded in hieroglyphs, but the early Greeks also heard and preserved stories from ancient Egypt.

The Kingdom of Meroe

The Egyptian Pharaoh Psammetichus II attacked the Kingdom of Kush in 592 BC and sacked the capital city Napata.[2] After this defeat the political centre of the African Kingdom was transferred south to a site called Meroe which lay between the Fifth and Sixth Cataracts of the Nile. Meroe became the site of sophisticated temple buildings and royal burials which followed the Egyptian practice of encasing the dead in wooden, or stone, sarcophagi. The sarcophagi were deposited in steeply angled stone-pyramids and more than 200 of these Egyptian-influenced tombs have been found near the site of the ancient city. The rulers of Meroe used Egyptian hieroglyphics for their royal decrees and Diodorus reports that their priest-class resembled their counterparts in Egypt.[3]

Greek and Roman writers referred to the African population of Sudan as 'Aethiopians' and called their Meroitic Kingdom 'Aethiopia'. These Nilotic Africans were one of the tallest population groups in the ancient world and they are described as having exceptionally slender bodies with very dark skin and an athletic physique. Since the time of the Pharaohs, Nubians served in the Egyptian army as specialist archers and Herodotus reports that Nubian soldiers carried extraordinary palm-wood bows that were up to six feet long. They carried spears and dense clubs carved from knotted wood for close quarter combat. These Nubian soldiers often wore clothing fashioned from the skins of predatory animals such as leopards and lions. They also wore red and white war-paint and Herodotus describes their distinctive appearance on the battlefield, where 'they painted their bodies, half with gypsum and half with vermilion'.[4] Diodourus adds that 'when their arrows are exhausted they finish the fight with wooden clubs. They also arm their women, setting an age limit for female service and most of them observe the custom of wearing a bronze ring in their lip'.[5]

When the Persian King Cambyses II conquered Egypt in 525 BC he investigated prospects for an invasion of Meroe and sent spies and envoys south to establish contact. Deciding conquest was achievable, he led a large army south into Nubia, but his Persians were not equipped for a long-distance desert campaign. By the time they had covered one-fifth of the distance to Meroe (nine days march or 180 miles) the main army had exhausted its supplies and had resorted to eating their pack animals. When there were no more pack animals to consume, the Persian soldiers foraged for whatever grass and herbs seemed edible. But when the course of the Nile led them through bare sand dunes, there was talk of cannibalism in the army. Cambyses was so alarmed by these reports that he ordered an immediate retreat back to Egypt and by the time his army reached Thebes, 'he had lost vast numbers of soldiers'.[6]

The Persians had reached their operational limits in Egypt, but it seems that Cambyses was nevertheless able to achieve a degree of authority and influence in northern Nubia. The Persian King Darius I (522–486 BC) received tribute from the Nubians, which was possibly sanctioned by the Kings of Meroe. Every two years Darius was presented with 2 quarts (more than 60 pounds) of unrefined gold, 200 ebony-wood logs and twenty elephant tusks.[7] Nubian soldiers were also levied into the Persian army and when King Xerxes invaded Greece in 480 BC a large contingent of African troops were seen amongst his forces.[8]

After the Macedonian conquest of Egypt, King Ptolemy II Philadelphus (285–246 BC) established direct relations with the royal court at Meroe and sent Greek representatives to the African kingdom. Diodorus mentions a King of Meroe named Ergamenes who learnt Greek and 'was instructed in Greek philosophy'. Ergamenes was probably King Arqamani who is attested in ancient inscriptions and had a tomb built near Meroe.[9] During this period, several Greek authorities visited Meroe and produced studies about the Kingdom that unfortunately have not survived.[10] During this period Ptolemy Philadelphus took possession of lands below the First Cataract including the Dodekaschoinos which covered a 70 mile stretch of river between Elephantine and a Nubian settlement called Takompso. Ptolemaic forces also claimed a territory called the Triakontaschoinos, which extended south from the Wadi Allaqi to the Second Cataract.

In the Ptolemaic era, the Temple of Khnum on Elephantine Island wanted to obtain rights to collect customs taxes on goods passing their stretch of the Nile. To support their case they asserted that in ancient times the Pharaohs had granted them a one-tenth tax on all African imports entering Egypt. The story was retold on temple-*stelae* and expressed a hope that the Ptolemies might reinstate these rights. The Khnum Temple wanted income 'of one tenth of the gold, ivory, ebony, carob-wood, ochre, carnelian, *seheret*, *tiu*, *nefu*, all woods and everything that the Nubians beyond the frontier bring into Egypt'.[11] The list indicates the prosperity of Nile trade which must have been a lucrative source of revenue for the Ptolemaic regime.

The Roman Conquest of Egypt

With the defeat of Mark Antony and the death of Queen Cleopatra in 30 BC, the Roman general Octavian took possession of Egypt. Octavian had himself proclaimed as Emperor and Egypt was established as a Roman province. Octavian (Augustus) appointed a military colleague named Gaius Cornelius Gallus as the first governor of the new territory. Cornelius Gallus was a general of equestrian rank, but he also had a reputation as a poet and literary prodigy. His admirers in Rome included Virgil and Ovid who expressed the view that Gallus could expect 'literary fame that would extend as far as his military commands and endure longer'.[12]

When Gallus gained office in Egypt, he led a Roman army south to supress a revolt in the Thebaid district.[13] After regaining order in Syene, Cornelius Gallus crossed the First Cataract to establish Roman authority in northern Nubia and lay claim to the nearby temple-site of Philae. He brought a local Nubian ruler under Roman control and in return for paying homage to the Empire, this dynast was given the title of *Tyrannus* (Tyrant) of the Triacontaschoenus. Cornelius Gallus also received representatives from the King of Meroe, whom he acknowledged as a political associate of the Roman Empire.

To celebrate his exploits Cornelius Gallus had a trilingual *stelea* erected in Philae in 29 BC. The inscription had a message recorded in Latin, Greek and

Egyptian hieroglyphics. In the Greek text, Cornelius Gallus was awarded the title of *proxenia* (political-associate) by ambassadors sent from Meroe.[14] This arrangement suggests mutual obligations, with Gallus hosting representatives from Meroe and acting in their interest in affairs which involved the Empire.

The Latin inscription on the *stelae* offers a different interpretation of these political events. In the Latin text, Gallus claims that he had extended Roman authority further than the Ptolemaic rule by placing the King of Meroe under imperial protection. The Latin text explains that Cornelius Gallus 'received ambassadors from the King of the Ethiopians and accepted that king into protection (*tutelam*)'. This was often the first stage for bringing an independent State under Roman dominance as a vassal kingdom. The Latin text also describes the Nubian dynast in different terms. In the Greek inscription he is simply a ruler (*Tyrannus*) installed in the Triacontaschoenus, but the Latin version presents him as an agent of the Empire. The text announces that Gallus 'appointed a local governor for the district of Ethiopia known as Triacontaschoenus'.[15]

Gallus remained in office for just over two years, during which time he celebrated his exploits in grandiose acts that began to attract concern, then criticism in Rome. Dio describes how Cornelius Gallus 'set up images of himself practically everywhere in Egypt and inscribed a list of his achievements even upon the very pyramids'. By Roman standards these displays were judged to be insolent and when Cornelius Gallus was accused of making disrespectful remarks about the Emperor, he was removed from office. Augustus formerly renounced their friendship and Cornelius Gallus was threatened by numerous law suits. He committed suicide rather than endure the forfeit of his family estates and lose what remained of his reputation.[16] The death of Cornelius Gallus left the first political settlement between Rome and Meroe poorly defined and open to challenge.

War between Meroe and Rome

Augustus had three complete Legions, approximately 15,000 troops, posted in Egypt to secure the province. When Aelius Gallus was appointed as the next governor, many of these troops were redeployed to invade Arabia (26 BC). This offered the rulers of Meroe an opportunity to challenge Roman power and launch a large-scale military raid on southern Egypt (25 BC). Strabo explains that 'the Aethiopians were emboldened because part of the Roman force in Egypt had been taken away by Aelius Gallus to wage war against the Arabians'.[17]

Meroe gave no warnings before the attack on Roman Egypt. In late summer 25 BC a Meroitic army of 30,000 warriors sacked the island site of Philae and arrived at the First Cataract. An inscription from the Nubian site of Pselchis (Dakka) suggests that this army was commanded by a Meroitic King named Teriteqas.[18] It seems that Teriteqas had taken notice of Nubian complaints about Egyptian intrusions into their domains and decided to bring northern Nubia back under the authority of Meroe.

There was a small Roman garrison of three cohorts (about 1,500 troops) stationed at Elephantine Island to maintain order in Syene, but they were not prepared for a full-scale invasion. Strabo reports that the Meroitic army sacked Syene, stormed Elephantine Island and removed all symbols of Roman administration from both sites. They 'enslaved the inhabitants and tore down the statues of Caesar Augustus'. The Meroitic army then retreated south with thousands of Egyptian captives.[19]

When this news reached Alexandria, the acting governor Petronius set out immediately for the Egyptian frontier with a force of 10,000 Roman infantry and 800 cavalry. By then the Meroitic army had withdrawn with their captives and trophies to Pselchis sixty miles south of the First Cataract. Strabo calls Pselchis an 'Aethiopian city' and reports that when Petronius reached the site, 'he sent ambassadors to demand what had been taken and ask the reasons why they had begun a war'. But King Teriteqas had died suddenly due to sickness or injury, so there was nobody in supreme command of the Meroitic army.[20]

The acting leader sent spokesmen to Petronius claiming that the attack on the Roman frontier was in retaliation for abuses carried out by the Egyptian Nomarchs (district administrators) who had exceeded their usual authority. Perhaps the Nomarchs were claiming tax rights over autonomous Nubian communities allied to Meroe, or imposing increased taxes on the African traders who brought goods across the frontier. They might even have been granted this authority by Cornelius Gallus as part of his overstated claims to have established political control over northern Nubia.

Petronius explained that if the Egyptian Nomarchs had exceeded their authority, then they would be answerable to the Emperor for any transgressions. The leaders of the Meroitic force occupying Pselchis asked for three days to deliberate, perhaps hoping that the royal family in Meroe would send instructions. But when this period elapsed without response, the Romans resumed the initiative and Petronius assembled his forces to attack the African city of Pselchis.

The warriors of Meroe came forward to do battle, each carrying a large oblong shield made of raw ox-hide and armed with an array of axes, pikes and swords. But they were 'poorly marshalled and badly armed' compared with the well-drilled legionary ranks. Strabo records that the Romans quickly drove the enemy horde from the battlefield and parts of the Meroitic army fled in disarray into the city, or retreated into the surrounding desert. Some of the African soldiers escaped the battlefield by wading out into the Nile at a fording point where the current was weak and there were few crocodiles. They hoped to make a stand at a defensive position on a small island, but the Romans secured rafts and boats to capture the island and take them prisoner.[21]

With the city of Pselchis secured, Petronius sent large numbers of war captives back to Alexandria.[22] He also captured several African generals who he questioned about the leadership situation in Meroe. They told Petronius that the ruling family of Meroe had a royal residence in the African city of Napata in the northern part of their kingdom near the Forth Cataract. The captured generals told Petronius that a Queen named Candace had assumed power in their kingdom as 'the ruler of the Aethiopians'. Inscriptions from the kingdom suggest that 'Candace' (*kdke*) was a royal title, rather than a personal name and possibly signified 'Queen-Mother' as it appears alongside the Meroitic word 'Ruler' (*Qore*).[23] In this period a Queen-Mother named Amanirenas is attested as being in power, so she is likely to be the 'Candace' of Roman accounts. Strabo describes her as 'a masculine sort of woman who was blind in one eye'. Her 'masculine character' could refer to her physical height, or her commanding presence as a leader of men in both politics and war. Queen Candace acted as regent for a young prince named Akinidad who held court in the city of Napata, so this rendered it a prime target for Roman retaliation.[24] Petronius therefore led his army south to claim the former Triakontaschoinos and launch a direct assault on the frontiers of Meroe.

South of Pselchis the sands of the Sahara encroached into the Nile valley and Strabo reports that the Roman troops struggled 'across sand dunes'. Almost mid-way between the First and the Second Cataract they reached a fortified Nubian town called Premnis (Qasr Ibrim) positioned on a cliff-top site overlooking the Nile. The Romans took this town in their first assault and then continued their march south towards Napata. Along the Nile from the Second to the Forth Cataract, Petronius captured a succession of Nubian towns and drove out any occupying Meroitic forces. Pliny lists the captured towns as 'Pselcis, Primi, Bocchis, Cambyses' Market, Attenia and Stadissis'.[25]

As the Romans approached Napata, Candace sent ambassadors calling for an end to hostilities and 'offering to give back the captives and the statues taken from Syene'. But with his objective in sight, Petronius dismissed the opportunity to negotiate and immediately attacked the city. After the battle Petronius was informed that Akinidad, son of Queen Candace Amanirenas, had fled the city, probably to the main royal residence at Meroe. The Romans burned the city and rounded up its inhabitants for transport back to Egypt as slaves.[26]

Napata was a major city in the northern part of the Meroitic Kingdom, but if they followed the looping course of the Nile, the Roman army were still more than 330 miles from the main capital at Meroe.[27] The alternative was to leave the river and cut across almost 175 miles of open desert. The full heat of the African summer was approaching and Petronius had already marched more than 570 miles from Syene, a distance almost as long as the entire length of Egypt.[28] Based on earlier Greek reports, the Roman force could not be sure of the terrain, nor the true scale of the kingdom they were attacking.

Petronius was probably concerned not to exceed his imperial mandate and indulge in what could have been perceived as 'glory seeking' behaviour. The fear of 'campaign sickness' was probably another factor suggesting that a further advance was unwise. By this stage the Romans had demonstrated their military superiority and inflicted a loss on the Meroitic Kingdom that matched the attack on Egypt. The city of Napata had been destroyed in appropriate retribution for the sack of Syene by the Meroitic army. Roman victories at Pselchis and Premnis were sufficient retaliation for the damage to Philae and Elephantine. Strabo reports the decision by Petronius: 'when they had burned Napata to the ground and enslaved its inhabitants, he turned back with the booty. He had decided that the regions beyond would be difficult to traverse.'[29] Summer was imminent and Dio adds, 'Petronius was unable to advance farther on account of the sand and the heat. There was no advantage to be gained by remaining where he was with his entire force, so he withdrew, taking the greater part of the army with him.'[30]

On his return march Petronius established a Roman garrison of 400 men on the cliff-top at Premnis. This outpost was positioned on a 250 feet high headland that towered above the course of the Nile River. Premnis was enclosed by massive walls that dated back to the time of the Egyptian Pharaohs and the New Kingdom Period (1552–1072 BC). It was therefore an ideal location to control traffic between the First and Second Cataract and interrupt any future invasion from Meroe. Petronius strengthened the fortifications of the town and as a precaution placed two years' worth of provisions within the fortress stores. North of Premnis, the city of Pselchis and the complete area of Dodekaschoinos was secured under Roman rule.

The entire expedition was concluded in a matter of months, with eight weeks spent on the outbound and return marches from Syene to Napata. When Petronius returned to Alexandria he dispatched reports and war trophies to Augustus with the news that a hostile foreign enemy had been defeated and a new territory had been added to the Empire (the Triakontaschoinos). Many of the Meroitic prisoners had died from disease during the journey back to Egypt, but Petronius was still able to send a thousand captives to Rome for the attention of Augustus when he returned from Spain.[31] Peace seemed to have been secured.

However, two years after the war, Queen Candace Amanirenas led an army of several thousand Meroitic warriors north to the Second Cataract (22 BC). But, contrary to expectations, the Meroitic army did not immediately attack the fortress at Premnis. This delay gave Petronius time to arrive with a Roman army equipped with various war machines to reinforce the town garrison. When the Queen learned that a senior Roman commander had arrived in the area, she immediately sent ambassadors to establish political relations. She wanted to negotiate a permanent settlement with the Roman State and requested information about the imperial government. International negotiations were beyond the remit held by Petronius, so he told the Meroitic ambassadors to take their case to the Emperor.

It seems that the envoys from Meroe were confused by Roman terminology. The new imperial protocol recognised the Senate as a governing body, but promoted the Emperor as a first citizen (*princeps*) who held autocratic powers. Also, as head of the Roman army, Augustus was touring the Empire to resolve important political and military issues. Strabo explains that when the representatives from Meroe 'claimed that they did not know who the "Caesar" was, or where they could find him, Petronius responded by giving them escorts'.[32]

The envoys were taken under guard to the Greek island of Samos where Augustus was preparing for an expedition to Syria and was making plans for a permanent political settlement with the Parthian Empire which ruled ancient Persia (21–20 BC). Augustus treated the African envoys favourably and submitted to all the demands made by Queen Amanirenas, including that the Romans withdraw from Nubian territories claimed by Meroe. Strabo reports that, 'when the ambassadors had obtained everything in their appeal, Augustus went even further and remitted the tributes that he had imposed upon them'.[33]

The Greek geographer Strabo was in Alexandria at this time and he explains the imperial response when he describes the situation in Britain. It was considered to be expensive and dangerous to conquer and govern a new region. Foreign territories were 'suitable' conquests if they possessed rich revenues, or if they posed a threat to existing provinces. But in many cases Rome could obtain more revenue by taxing trade contacts with a free territory than they could gain by long-term conquest.[34] This was probably the case with Meroe and explains the decision by Augustus to surrender the Triakontaschoinos.

The Emperor probably received great prestige from receiving African ambassadors from distant Meroe. Their gratitude and respect was witnessed by foreign envoys visiting Augustus from many distant parts of the ancient world, including representatives from India. Augustus would have appeared conciliatory ahead of his crucial settlement with the Parthian Empire. It is also possible that a war with Nubia was not high on the imperial agenda after the Roman failure to conquer Arabia and the prospect of further conflict involving the Parthians.

The Romans retained the Dodekaschoinos because this part of northern Nubia gave the Empire access to the main gold mines in the Eastern Desert. The income from Nubian gold offset the high cost of garrisoning a region which produced relatively low revenues. Procopius describes how the Roman Emperor Diocletian finally abandoned the Dodekaschoinos in AD 298 when the gold mines had declined. It was said that Diocletian 'observed that the tribute from these places was very small, since the land is extremely narrow and surrounded by high rocky terrain. A large number of Roman soldiers had been stationed there from an early period and their maintenance was an excessive burden on the State.'[35] Augustus would also have considered these factors, but concluded that the income from the gold mines at that time justified the military occupation.

Around 20 BC, Roman troops left the Nubian town of Premnis and withdrew sixty miles north to the Dodekaschoinos. The Meroitic Kingdom then claimed supremacy over the greater Triakontaschoinos and became responsible for protecting this territory from the desert tribes who threatened the Nile route. It was a peaceful takeover, but the Meroitic forces symbolically toppled the statues of Emperor Augustus that had been placed in the occupied towns. The head of one of these bronze statues was taken to Meroe and in 1910 was found beneath the threshold of a royal temple to their god of victory. The head, which is now in the British Museum, belongs to a statue which for stylistic reasons possibly dates to the Roman occupation of Premnis (24–20 BC), rather than the attack on Syene (25 BC).[36]

Queen Amanirenas presented her settlement with Rome as a victory. Two large *stelea* found at the site of an ancient temple at Hamadab, just south of Meroe, provide a record of the war. Cursive Meroitic script is difficult to decipher, but the stone inscription was erected by Queen Amanirenas and Prince Akinidad. It refers to a conflict with *Arme* which is probably a Meroitic rendition of the word 'Rome'. *Arme* (Rome) appears in a formulaic triumphal inscription indicating that the kingdom of Meroe had overcome this foreign enemy.[37] Further evidence of the war came from excavations at this site in the early twentieth century. Explorers entering the ancient temple discovered wall paintings depicting foreign prisoners being made to kneel before a Meroitic deity. The ancient paintings have since been destroyed, but watercolour copies made by visiting scholars confirm details of the scene. The paintings depict captives with white skin and fair hair dressed in tunic-like clothes. These prisoners are shown chained alongside men with brown skin who are possibly Egyptians captured during the attack that began the war.[38] The paintings probably depict the opening stages of the conflict when prisoners and trophies from Egypt were brought to Meroe after the successful raid on Syene.

Further evidence of the conflict comes from the remains of the Roman garrison at Premnis (Qasr Ibrim). During the twentieth century the Aswan High Dam was built and the Nile valley between the First and Second Cataract was flooded to create modern Lake Nasser. For conservation purposes the ruins of the ancient temple buildings in the path of this vast reservoir were carefully rebuilt at new sites in the surrounding desert. The one exception was the cliff-top complex at Premnis which survives as an island surrounded by fortress walls lapped by the waters of a man-made lake. The hyper-arid conditions at the site have preserved unique ancient artefacts including remains from the Roman occupation (24–20 BC).

Archaeologists have found refuse heaps at Premnis containing coins, lamps, papyri documents and scraps of clothing. Thousands of stone *ballistae* found at the site indicate that Petronius delivered catapults to the Roman garrison so that they could fire heavy-weight missiles down upon the Nile route. However, the most extraordinary find in the debris was a fragment of papyrus scroll. This reclaimed document is one of the oldest surviving manuscripts written in Latin and virtually the only remains of the once celebrated verses written by the poet-general Cornelius Gallus.[39] Part of the surviving text refers to a scheme by Julius Caesar to conquer Persia and extend Roman territory to the very frontiers of India (44 BC). Cornelius Gallus writes, 'my fortunes will be blessed, Caesar, when you dominate Roman history. When you return, I will admire the temples of many gods enriched with your trophies.'[40]

But Caesar was assassinated three days before his scheduled departure to the east, while Cornelius Gallus suffered an ignominious death at his own hands. Perhaps the idea of far-off adventures in eastern territories had a special appeal to the unknown soldier who found himself stationed at Premnis with the words of Cornelius Gallus as his inspiration. The Latin verses celebrated conflict, but

Meroe's relationship with the Roman Empire was destined to be peaceful and profitable trade, not further wars.

Roman Trade with Meroe

Strabo describes the arid lands between Egypt and Meroe. Nubia was sparsely inhabited and consisted of 'a long, narrow, winding stretch of river-land, with a population that was not well equipped for warfare, or any other kind of life'.[41] Aethiopians from Meroe dominated most of Nubia, but other population groups inhabited the region and they still preserved some level of independence. The Nubae (Nubians) mostly occupied the west banks of the Nile and the sand-dune fringes of the Sahara. Lands to the east side of the river were subject to the Blemmyes who inhabited rocky and mountainous terrain on the frontiers of the Eastern Desert.[42]

The Roman Dodekaschoinos extended barely seventy miles south of Syene, but this territory gave the Empire control of at least ten Nubian settlements. It also secured Roman access to the main gold mines in the deserts of northern Nubia. At the southern limit of the Dodekaschoinos was the town of Hiera Sycaminos (modern Maharraqa) which became the outer frontier of this militarised Roman territory.

Travellers began their journey into Nubia from Syene where they docked their river craft and made a land crossing around the rapids that formed the First Cataract. The geographer Strabo was familiar with the southern Egyptian frontier and he travelled to the region with the Roman governor Aelius Gallus. The governor's party disembarked from their river craft at Syene and boarded wagons that took them across a level plain of hard earth.[43] But most people probably walked the four-mile distance by using an ancient footpath that followed the banks of the Nile. Ancient travellers were vulnerable to sudden attack from bandits and desert nomads on this stretch of their journey, so the footpath was flanked by a large defensive wall. This was probably first built during the Twelfth Dynasty of Egyptian Pharaohs in the Middle Kingdom Period (1991–1786 BC). The wall was improved by subsequent rulers and by the Roman era it consisted of two parallel mud-brick façades filled with granite rubble. With the addition of parapets, the wall was up to thirty feet high and nearly nine feet wide. From this fortified walkway Roman troops could watch the surrounding desert and supervise the travellers crossing back and forth between Egypt and Nubia.[44]

The defended footpath ended at the banks of the Nile opposite the island-site of Philae. On this stretch of the river the Roman army maintained a permanent fortified camp to guard the frontier. Roman troops possibly occupied a dozen outposts in the Dodekaschoinos by restoring a range of ancient fortresses established by the Pharaohs and the Ptolemais. These garrisons guarded important temple buildings on the banks of the Nile and monitored the movement of people approaching Egypt. Most Roman outposts were on the west bank of the Nile, suggesting that the main threat to these garrisons came from nomads from the Eastern Desert. Some of these settlements had small satellite posts on the east bank of the river that were probably connected by bridges. There was also a series of small Roman watchtowers on hilltops overlooking the river valley. Graffiti confirms that Roman sentries were stationed at these posts and would have signalled to the garrisons if trouble was sighted.[45]

Roman Nubia

The town of Hiera Sycaminos on the west bank of the Nile was probably the limit of the Roman occupation in Nubia. Its urban temples contained images of leading Egyptian gods, including Horus dressed in a toga and depicted in the classical Roman manner.[46] Nubians were recruited from the local population into the Roman army and left inscriptions in these temples. One of these Africans, named Paccius Maximus, reached the office of *decurion* (cavalry commander) and left several Greek dedications to the Nubian god Mandulis in the temple at Hiera Sycaminos.[47]

Traders from Meroe journeyed north through the Triakontaschoinos to Hiera Sycaminos by following the overland trails, but some carried lightweight river craft for use along navigable stretches of the Nile.[48] The designated trade site at Sycaminos was a short distance outside the town and the visitors from Meroe would set out their African goods and wait for the arrival of Egyptian and Roman merchants. These goods included linen fabrics, elephant tusks, gold nuggets and blocks of ebony wood that Roman craftsmen made into valuable furniture.[49] Meroitic traders were also able to offer incense from Somalia and exotic live animals from inner Africa, including leopard and lion cubs. These creatures were exported across the Empire to be exhibited in crowded Roman arenas. The profits made in this business are revealed in Diocletian's *Price Edict* which lists thousands of prices paid for ancient items. The edict values a live lion as the most expensive commodity available in Roman society and this could be purchased at a price greater than a worker could earn in sixteen years.[50]

At Sycaminos, traders from Meroe set out their goods then withdrew from the meeting place to allow the Roman merchants an opportunity to examine the products. The Romans laid out a number of exchange items in front of the goods they wished to acquire in the hope that their offers would be acceptable. If the trader was satisfied, then he took these wares and left his African goods in the possession of the Roman merchant. Philostratus explains, 'this is a market place where the Aethiopians bring all the products of their own country; and the Egyptians take these goods away, leaving in place their own wares considered to be of equal value'. All of this business was conducted on trust and although the exchanges were supervised, there were no guards present to watch over these valuable goods. Philostratus describes how the pagan philosopher Apollonius visited the trade market at Sycaminos just before the exchanges were due to take place. He saw gold, a quantity of linen and a live elephant tethered ready to receive trade offers. Other commodities offered for exchange included 'various roots, myrrh and spices with all these items lying around at the meeting place without anyone to guard them'.[51]

Pliny describes a range of valuable gems supplied by Meroitic traders including black obsidian, red garnets, a golden-yellow stone called *hammonis*, highly-reflective *heliotropes* and the best magnets 'which in our markets are worth their weight in silver'.[52] Shards of diamond reached Egypt via Meroe, but they were not as large as diamonds from India.[53] Heliodorus has a character meet an Ethiopian near the Egyptian frontier. The man could not speak Greek well, but said, 'I saw you buy those herbs and roots that grow in India and Ethiopia. If you are willing to purchase from me simply and without guile, I will show you what I have to sell.' He then produced a bag of large pearls and precious stones including emeralds, sapphires and purple gems.[54]

There was a Roman custom station on Elephantine Island to monitor imports and impose the quarter-rate tax due on trade goods crossing the border.[55] Pliny calls Elephantine 'the point of rendezvous for Ethiopian vessels which on reaching the cataracts are made collapsible for the purpose of portage'.[56] These craft sailed to the nearby city of Syene with cargoes that included ivory and incense from Meroe. Juvenal confirms the significance of this commerce when he describes fashionable Roman furniture made from solid ivory. He writes that this product was sent to Rome as 'tusks from the swift footed Ethiopians at the portal of Syene'.[57] From Syene, Egyptian river craft would bring the African cargoes north to Alexandria and the Mediterranean coast (a distance of about 600 miles).

Pliny identifies ivory as one of the most expensive organic materials produced by nature, so trade contacts with Meroe would have brought large revenues into the Roman State.[58] Details from Roman custom records indicate that ivory was about one-tenth the price of silver and a single tusk was worth perhaps 33 gold aurei.[59] Roman officials imposed a quarter-rate tax on all foreign imports crossing the frontiers (the *tetarte*) and if merchants could not afford to pay this rate, then officials would take a quarter-share of their goods as a substitute. This meant that large amounts of high-value African goods came under imperial control. These products were either auctioned in Alexandria, or shipped to Rome for sale to wealthy dealers, businessmen, craftsmen and other consumers in the imperial capital.

Enormous profits were made from the sale of state-owned foreign goods and the court poet Statius lists 'the glory of the Indian tusk' as one of the main revenue sources for the Roman treasury.[60] The Roman statesman Seneca held a trusted position in Roman government, but he was also involved in the ivory business. He is reported to have owned 500 identical ivory tables which may have been acquired from government stockpiles.[61] These objects were probably sold in public auctions to fellow collectors and dealers, or 'gifted' to political associates.

The quantity of African tusks managed by the Roman State was revealed during excavations at an ancient warehouse complex in Rome called the *Horrea Galbae*. Within the ruins was a store chamber filled with 675 cubic feet of ivory splinters from African elephant tusks. These fragments were probably offcuts stored for further use that had accumulated over many years. In terms of weight, the splinters are equivalent to about 2,500 complete tusks and verify a thriving business in this particular high-value product.[62]

There is evidence that royal agents from Meroe visited kingdoms in the Near East that were subject to Roman rule. During the first century AD, Philip the

Evangelist was travelling from Jerusalem to Gaza when he encountered a court official from Meroe who was on his way back to Egypt on his chariot. The peoples of Meroe were familiar with Judaism from contact with Jewish communities in southern Egypt including Syene.[63] The Meroitic official met by Philip was a eunuch in charge of the Royal Treasury, which by AD 33 was under another female ruler with the title Candace (Queen-Mother). Philip baptised the man into the Christian faith and he returned to his homeland in Africa to spread word of his new beliefs.[64] Christianity gathered many adherents in Meroe and in fourth century AD, Ethiopia and the Sudan were among the first regions to adopt Christianity as an official religion.

CHAPTER SIX

The Red Sea Route

India was central to the ancient world economy because its tropical climates produced spices that could not be grown successfully in the temperate Mediterranean or Western Europe. By the first century AD India had an estimated population of 60 million people and even the Romans were daunted by the size of their civilisation.[1] Pliny the Elder, a Roman commander who served on the advisory council of the Emperor Vespasian, reported, 'they say that India forms one-third of the whole earth and that its populations are innumerable – this is certainly possible'.[2]

Eastern contacts began in ancient times when the Egyptian Pharaohs launched ships into the Red Sea to make contact with a mysterious incense producing land named 'Punt'. These voyages were important because the Egyptians used incense in many religious rituals, including mummification of the dead. Most of their incense came from Somalia and was brought to the Nile River by African intermediaries, but when this traffic was interrupted by hostilities, the Pharaohs were forced to open the sea-lanes and send their own ships directly to Somalia.

In the temple-tomb of the Pharaoh Queen Hatshepsut there is important evidence for early Egyptian trade missions to Punt (1473–1458 BC). Pictorial carvings and hieroglyphs reveal how the Queen established a base on the Red Sea coast of Egypt. From there she sent five Egyptian galleys to explore a sea route to the edge of Somalia. The ships returned loaded with frankincense intended for the use of the Queen and the priests who managed her royal temples.[3]

During the sixth century BC, Egypt was conquered by the Persian King Cambyses II (530–522 BC) and incorporated into his vast Empire. Cambyses was succeeded by Darius the Great who conquered the Hindu-Kush and led Persian armies into northern India in 520 BC. The gold dust found in these mountains provided Darius with large amounts of bullion that greatly enriched his regime. The Greek historian Herodotus records that India thereby provided the Persians with a third of the tribute they received from their entire Empire.[4]

When the Persians reached the Indus River they saw Indian crocodiles that were similar to the large reptiles found in the Nile River. Darius wondered if the two crocodile species could have originated from some common place of origin, in which case there would be a water source connecting both rivers. To discover the truth, he ordered ships to be built on the Indus River to explore the ocean beyond where this water course emptied into the sea.

Darius appointed a Greek captain named Scylax to command vessels involved in this voyage. The crew included Greek and Phoenician sailors with a detachment of Persian troops to guard against possible threats. The Greeks were skilled seafarers, but they were better used to the enclosed Mediterranean Sea. For a Greek like Scylax, reports of dangerous reptiles and world-spanning oceans might have resembled a voyage from Homer's *Odyssey* and images of unfamiliar Hindu gods and the sight of ten-foot elephants would have reinforced these fears.[5]

The Persian forces explored the course of the Indus River through nearly 2,000 miles of uncharted territory. On reaching the Indus Delta they established a naval station called Pattala near the coast and prepared for a westward sea voyage. But Scylax and his colleagues were unfamiliar with the monsoon winds that blow seasonally back and forth across the Indian Ocean, so it took them several months to negotiate the southern coast of Iran. From there they eventually discovered a route around Arabia and reached Egypt almost thirty months after leaving India. Scylax wrote a report of his voyage including details about the Indian civilisations he encountered while exploring the Indus River. This work was later studied by Aristotle who was to become the Greek tutor of Alexander the Great.[6]

Alexander in India

Alexander, the Greek king of Macedonia, conquered the Persian Empire between 334 and 326 BC. He led an invading Greek army through the Hindu-Kush to the upper reaches of the Indus River and there he formed an alliance with an Indian king named Talixes.[7] With Alexander's help, Talixes defeated a rival raja named Porus, but during this conflict the Macedonian soldiers were exposed to the terrifying combat capability of Indian battle-elephants.[8]

War-elephants had a fearful presence on the ancient battlefield. These five-ton animals possessed enormous strength and with their tough hides they could be extremely difficult to kill. The actions of the elephant were directed by a 'mahout' who perched astride the animal's neck and directed the charge into enemy ranks. The enraged animal would disrupt enemy formations ahead of the main infantry engagement by goring and trampling the opposition troops. The loud trumpeting and unusual odour of these war-elephants would also cause horses in the enemy cavalry to panic and bolt.[9]

Alexander tried to march his armies beyond the Hyphasis River (the Beas), but his Macedonian troops were awed by the scale of the eastern kingdoms of India and they mutinied against him.[10] Alexander therefore turned his attention to the Indus and decided to replicate the voyage of Scylax and reach the world ocean. He had a fleet constructed on the upper stretches of the Indus and, dividing his army into several battle-groups, set out to chart the course of the river.[11] On reaching the ocean, Alexander appointed a Greek general named Nearchus as admiral of the fleet and placed 20,000 Hellenic troops under his command. Alexander then ordered this Greek fleet to explore the route from the Indus back to the Persian Gulf.[12]

Alexander marched his remaining land forces back to Babylonia through the deserts of southern Iran. Thousands died on the journey, but Alexander seemed undaunted by the experience. When he reached Babylon he made fresh plans for the conquest of Arabia and prepared a Greek battle-fleet in the Persian Gulf. However, Alexander suddenly died in 324 BC from unknown causes before this invasion could be launched.[13]

Alexander's Successors

Alexander's Empire was divided between his generals who declared themselves 'kings' and established powerful dynasties within their own realms. The Ptolemais seized possession of Egypt and the Seleucids gained power in Syria and Iran. Both regimes believed they needed to obtain formidable war-elephants to reinforce their armies, but only the Seleucids had direct access to India.

During this period Greek engineers began improving the combat effectiveness of elephants with extra armour and the addition of fighting platforms. The armour included crests that shielded the mahout from missile fire and leg-bands to prevent axe-armed troops from 'hamstringing' the elephant to cripple it. Engineers also strapped wooden turrets to the backs of the animals and these were able to accommodate up to three soldiers equipped with bows, javelins, or pikes.[14]

For the sake of prestige and to improve their military prowess the Ptolemais were determined to acquire battle-elephants. There were small forest elephants in the Atlas Mountains of northwest Africa, but the city of Carthage controlled access to their habitat and would not permit the animals to reach Hellenic kingdoms. Therefore, in 280 BC, Ptolemy II Philadelphus ordered the construction of shipyards and harbours on the Red Sea coast of Egypt in order to send ships to find the location of distant elephant herds.[15] A Greek port called Arsinoe was founded at the head of the Red Sea (modern Suez) and two further harbour towns named Myos Hormos and Berenice were established further down the coast.[16]

Greek ships were built at Arsinoe and launched from Berenice to explore along the east coast of Africa. These missions involved weeks spent at sea with crews that included Egyptian sailors and Greek mercenary troops given orders to establish hunting stations on the coast of Ethiopia and Somalia. When captured, the elephants were brought back to Egypt on giant transport ships called *elephantegoi*.[17] The African shore of the Red Sea was a bleak and sparsely inhabited place and voyages to some of the furthest hunting stations could take up to a month. On the return journey the live elephants proved to be a difficult and dangerous cargo in the confines of a ship.

Most returning vessels docked at Berenice on the southern frontiers of Egypt where the elephants were loaded into giant corrals surrounded by deep ditches.[18] From there, transport arrangements were made for a desert crossing to take the animals to the Nile River. It took two weeks to travel overland from Berenice to the Nile by following the course of ancient dried-up river-beds that wound their way through the mountainous Eastern Desert. The Ptolemais constructed wells and military stations along these routes, but the journey remained difficult and travellers had to carry large quantities of water to maintain their live cargoes.[19] The caravans bringing the elephants generally travelled at night, spending the heat of the day in natural rock shelters.

The animal handlers and their guards have left graffiti on the walls of these desert shelters, scratching their names, or making drawings of the elephants they were leading through the desert landscape.[20] For example, a man with the Greek name Sophon carved his name into the walls of the Pan grotto on the desert road from Berenice to Edfu. Sophon asked the Greek god Pan for a safe journey and described himself as an *Indos* (an Indian, or a mahout). The discovery of elephant drawings in the temple suggest that Sophon was managing these creatures using skills learnt from Indian animal trainers.[21] When the elephants reached their eventual destination on the Nile River they were taken aboard barges and transported north to begin their battle-training. The Ptolemais received large amounts of valuable ivory from these African hunting operations, which encouraged the regime to pursue these ventures, even when it became clear that the elephants from East Africa were smaller and weaker than their powerful Indian counterparts.[22]

By 200 BC the Seleucids had lost influence in India and could no longer acquire war-elephants from eastern sources. As the threat of Seleucid battle superiority subsided, the Ptolemaic regime abandoned its elephant hunting operations in East Africa. However, the infrastructure they had built for these operations remained in place and was used by Mediterranean merchants to make a profit from Red Sea commerce. An Egyptian papyrus from the second century BC confirms this development. It records how five people, including a businessman from Veii in central Italy and Massilia (Marseilles) in southern France, borrowed funds for a Greek trading venture to the 'Incense Land' (Somalia). The deal was managed through a banker named Gnaeus who was probably Italian or Roman.[23]

The Ptolemais gained valuable revenue from the customs taxes they collected on Red Sea imports. It was therefore in their interests to facilitate the trade and protect the Greek merchants who operated within the gulf. Diodorus reports that 'when the Ptolemaic kings in Alexandria opened the Red Sea to their merchants, the Arabs attacked those who were shipwrecked and fitted out pirate vessels to prey upon the voyagers'. These attacks came from the Arab kingdom of Nabataea on the far coast of the Red Sea. The Ptolemais took reprisals by sending *quadrireme* war-galleys to sink the Nabataean ships and destroy their ports. During this conflict, the Nabataean raiders 'were caught on the high seas by the *quadriremes* and punished just as they deserved'.[24] Strabo elaborates 'the Nabataeans had been peaceful, but then they launched small ships to plunder the vessels of sailors from Egypt. They paid the penalty when a fleet went over and sacked their country'.[25] After this engagement the Ptolemais maintained a small patrol fleet of warships in the Red Sea to guard Greek shipping from further Arab attacks.

The Sea Route to India

In 118 BC, a Ptolemaic patrol ship found the remains of a strange foreign vessel adrift in the Red Sea. They rescued a single emaciated survivor from the wreckage, a man who was an Indian sailor. He was taken to the court of Ptolemy VIII

Euergetes II, known as 'Physcon', to recover from his ordeal and while he was there he learnt to speak Greek. The mariner explained that he had been blown off course on a trade sailing from India and offered to pilot any Greek ship that would return him to his homeland. Physcon was enthusiastic about the prospect of direct contact with the rich kingdoms of ancient India and appointed a Greek navigator named Eudoxus of Cyzicus to command the expedition.

The Indian mariner revealed to Eudoxus how the seasonal monsoon winds could be used to make fast voyages across the Indian Ocean. Eudoxus reached the Indus kingdoms in a matter of weeks and exchanged royal gifts with the ruling rajas on behalf of the Ptolemaic regime. He also conducted trade deals in the Indian ports and acquired stocks of precious stones and valuable spices.[26] His voyage demonstrated to Greek merchants how they too could profit from direct trade with India.

The Greek discovery of fast sailing routes across the Indian Ocean began an important new era in the development of the ancient economy. It took more than ten weeks for Greek ships to sail to India, but the voyage was costly and dangerous. There was also the further expense of customs taxes, set at one-quarter rate in Egypt and one-fifth in India.[27] These conditions encouraged Greek and Indian merchants to meet at places midway between their home ports and exchange goods at sites where harbour dues were lower, or non-existent.

One of these early meeting places was Socotra Island near the Horn of Africa. When Agatharchides writes about these contacts, he reports 'it is possible to see merchant vessels at these islands and many come from the place where Alexander established an anchorage on the Indus River'.[28] Most of these intermediate operations were soon moved to the city-port of Eudaimon Arabia (Aden) on the Yemen coast. The *Periplus of the Erythaean Sea* describes this early era when 'vessels from India did not go to Egypt and ships from Egypt came only this far. Our ships did not dare to sail to the places beyond Eudaimon Arabia and for this reason the city used to receive cargoes from both Egypt and India'.[29]

By the mid-first century BC most Greek ships ended their voyages at Eudaimon Arabia where they met with eastern merchants to take on board cargoes of Indian goods. In this era few ships would risk piracy and storm damage to complete the full voyage from Egypt to India. According to Strabo, 'in these early times, not even 20 vessels would dare to sail beyond the gulf, or venture out-side the straits. Under the Ptolemaic kings only a few vessels would sail to India to carry back Indian merchandise.'[30] This was nonetheless an important achieve-ment and for the first time a direct commercial link between India and the Mediterranean world was developing.

The Roman Takeover

When Mark Antony was defeated at the Battle of Actium in 31 BC, Queen Cleopatra prepared an escape to India with the treasure of the Ptolemais. Accom-panied by Caesarion, her son by Julius Caesar, she had enough troops to guarantee the continuance of her royal court in some faraway eastern city. She made preparations to launch her galleys into the Red Sea by dragging them across the Suez Isthmus, but the Nabataeans had old scores to settle with the Ptolemais. Her soldiers were ambushed by forces sent by the Nabataean King Malichus who had allied himself with Octavian, and Cleopatra's ships were burned before they could be launched, thereby ending her prospects of escape to the Orient.[31]

With the fleet burnt, there was still one final hope for the Ptolemaic dynasty. Cleopatra's son Caesarion was almost an adult and he was both the prime successor to the Ptolemaic throne and the blood-line heir to Julius Caesar.[32] This made him a serious threat to Octavian who was the grand-nephew of Caesar and only his 'son' by posthumous adoption. Cleopatra planned to send Caesarion to safety overseas in lands that were far from Roman authority and beyond the political reach of Octavian. She arranged for him to sail to India accompanied by a staff of royal advisors carrying a large consignment from the Ptolemaic treasury.[33] Perhaps the Queen hoped that the prince could reach adulthood in India and one day return to avenge her by leading a military rebellion against Octavian.

When Antony committed suicide, Cleopatra and her maidservants chose to die from the bite of a venomous snake rather than endure the humiliation planned by Octavian. Meanwhile, her son Caesarion waited at the port of Berenice for the seasonal trade winds. But before the youth could embark on his voyage, an advisor convinced him to return to Alexandria. Octavian had him seized and executed on the grounds that 'too many Caesars are not a good thing'.[34]

With the defeat of Cleopatra, Octavian had overthrown the last of the Hellenic dynasties that gained power after the death of Alexander the Great (323 BC). With all opposition removed, the entire Mediterranean was brought under a single Roman regime ending centuries of conflict and decades of repeated civil war. As supreme commander of the Roman Empire Octavian had assumed power over an estimated 45 million people.[35]

With the Mediterranean domains pacified, the new Emperor was in a position to seek peace terms with the formidable Parthian Empire which ruled in ancient Iran. But first he had to secure Egypt and maximise its revenue contributions to the imperial State. During the final years of the Ptolemaic era, the Egyptian economy had been exhausted by extortionate taxes and its infrastructure damaged by State neglect.[36] By using the Roman army as a workforce, Augustus began programmes to repair the transport and irrigation canals and re-secure the caravan routes through the Eastern Desert. The next military target was to be the conquest of Arabia, so Aelius Gallus the Roman governor of Egypt was ordered to restore shipyards at the northern Red Sea port of Arsinoe. Gallus set about building 80 triremes and 130 troop-transports, a fleet capable of conquering the Arabian Peninsula.[37] The existence of these shipyards at the Red Sea ports provided opportunities for business investors by allowing Roman merchants to build dozens of new ships and undertake further voyages to India.

As part of a preliminary attack on southern Arabia, Roman ships were sent to destroy the Sabaean city-port of Eudaimon Arabia (Aden).[38] This raid had immediate consequences for international trade as Greek and Indian ships arriving at the port discovered the city ransacked and its merchandise removed.

They had no choice but to sail onward and meet their trade contacts at more distant ports.

The Greek geographer Strabo, an associate of Aelius Gallus, accompanied the governor on an official tour along the Nile River. The group travelled past the Nile city of Coptos, which was the main commercial centre for Greek and Roman traders crossing the Eastern Desert. At Coptos, Strabo heard a report that over a hundred Roman ships were sailing direct from Egypt to India every year. He reports: 'when Gallus was the prefect of Egypt, I accompanied him along the Nile River as far as Syene and the frontiers of Aethiopia. On this trip I learned that as many as 120 vessels were sailing from Myos Hormos to India.'[39] This was more than six times the number that had made the journey during the Ptolemaic era.

Coptos and the Egyptian Desert Route
Under Roman rule the Nile city of Coptos was the main clearing house for eastern imports and Strabo describes how goods from Arabia, India and Africa were 'transported to Coptos, the emporium which receives these cargoes'.[40] Pliny confirms that Coptos was 'the market for Indian and Arabian merchandise' and consequently the city became an important base for commercial businesses and transport companies involved in international trade.[41] Roman officials and customs agents had their headquarters in the city and they managed the personnel and taxed the goods involved in distant trade ventures.

It took about twelve days to sail from Alexandria to Coptos using river craft to transport cargo a distance of nearly 400 miles.[42] From Coptos merchants and other travellers joined overland caravans bound for the two main Red Sea ports of Berenice and Myos Hormos. It took nearly seven days to reach Myos Hormos, which was about 110 miles away.[43] The journey to Berenice was longer, taking twelve days to travel the 230 mile route to this more southerly port.[44] The cost of camel hire meant that most merchants therefore preferred to dock their ships at Myos Hormos and send their outbound cargo to the closer seaport.

Myos Hormos may have been closer to Coptos, but the port had disadvantages, in particular the strong northerly winds in the upper part of the Red Sea. These winds made voyages to the port slow and difficult, especially for heavily laden ships. Many Roman merchants returning from India therefore offloaded their cargo at Berenice, knowing that they could get their goods to Coptos faster by travelling overland with the camel caravans, rather than sailing against the wind to Myos Hormos.[45]

The main caravan routes that crossed the Eastern Desert of Egypt were simple trackways marked by rubble cairns. Travellers had to keep a constant watch for the mountain bandits, but the danger was reduced when the Roman administration built new fortified stations in the desert called *phrouroi* and some of these outposts were large enough to accommodate several hundred soldiers.[46] The Romans also improved security by placing watchtowers on the hills overlooking the caravan trails. If the sentries sighted people likely to be hostile, then a chain of signals was conveyed along the watch towers to alert the nearest Roman military outposts. The garrisons sent mounted troops to the scene to intercept the bandits, or assist the armed caravan guards. Roman patrols also accompanied some of the larger and more important caravans on their entire journey across the Eastern Desert.

The Romans had other reasons to enhance and protect the caravan routes that crossed the Eastern Desert. There were valuable stone-quarries on the road to Myos Hormos, including Mons Porphyrites which produced purple-speckled porphyry and Mons Claudianus where blocks of golden-coloured granite were cut from the hillsides.[47] Work at these sites was undertaken by imperial agents who took charge of slave work-teams including convicts and political prisoners. The Roman State maintained a large labour force at the site and used special vehicles to move stone objects through the desert. Supplies for the workers, craftspeople and guards were brought in by camel through the desert routes. Stone from the quarries was taken nearly a hundred miles overland to the Nile to be transported down to Alexandria and shipped to destinations across the Roman Empire.

The decorative stone was used to adorn monumental buildings including temples, basilicas, palaces, imperial villas and public baths. For example, the columns in the portico of the Pantheon in Rome, quarried at Mons Claudianus, are thirty-nine feet tall, more than four feet in diameter and weigh at least 60 tons. Larger commissions were undertaken and one of the giant pillars at Mons Claudianus was discarded when it fractured and broke. This monolithic column, destined for an unknown building, is over fifty feet long and weighs more than 200 tons.[48] There were also state-owned emerald and gold mines in the Eastern Desert that could be reached by using the Coptos route to Berenice.[49]

Not only did the desert outposts need regular supplies, but there were also hundreds of people living and working at the main Red Sea ports. These individuals needed food and other basic materials and it has been estimated that the population of Berenice required at least 500 camel loads per month.[50] Many transport operations conducted across the Eastern Desert were managed by small firms who owned several dozen camels. Camel teams from dozens of different firms would have joined together for support and safety when crossing the desert and some caravans would have included over a thousand camels.[51] These transport operations would have continued throughout the year.[52]

A collection of business receipts from Coptos, known as the *Nicanor Archive*, reveals how a family-run firm was hired to deliver cargo and supplies to the main Red Sea ports (AD 6–62). The largest operation undertaken by the Nicanor Company involved thirty-six camels and was a State contract to deliver grain to a Roman fort in the Eastern Desert.[53] The firm had contracts with at least twenty businesses that needed goods moved across the Eastern Desert to ports on the Red Sea coast of Egypt. The archive names about twenty-five businessmen and thirty commercial agents. These businesses involved people from across the Roman Empire including Greeks, Egyptians, Jews and Italians.

One wealthy Greek-Egyptian businessman named Parthenios son of Paminis hired the Nicanor Company and had his name recorded on a temple inscription at Coptos when he made expensive offerings to the deities Isis and Cronos.[54] A further Greek inscription from Coptos records when a businessman named

Hermeros son of Athenion dedicated funds to the goddesses Isis and Hera. Hermeros records that he was resident at the Arabian port of Eudaimon Arabia (Aden) during a period when the site had been restored as a trade centre.[55] Other Roman subjects travelled even further away on long-term business and part of a papyrus poll-tax register carries details of a Greek-Egyptian from Arsinoe who was overseas in India.[56]

The *Nicanor Archive* contains the names of at least seven Roman citizens who were involved in eastern businesses and many more are mentioned in custom receipts found at Berenice.[57] Amongst these citizens were wealthy Italian businessmen from Campania who shipped wine across the Indian Ocean. The remains of plaster amphorae plugs found at Coptos record the names of wine dealers who had labelled delivery batches being sent for export.[58] Batches marked with the emblem 'G. *Norbanus Ptolem.*' belonged to Gaius Norbanus who hired the Nicanor Company to deliver goods to Myos Hormos and employed a female business-agent named Isidora.[59] Some of the Roman citizens involved in these eastern ventures were managing very large operations and the Berenice receipts mention a businessman named Varus who owned, or managed, several cargo ships. One of the receipts reads: 'Herak to Drakon, son of Peisipmous Koud – let pass Peteasmephis son of Horos with six *koilopomata* for loading on to the (ships) of Varus'.[60]

Desert graffiti provides further evidence for the Romans involved in this international business. A Roman citizen with the Greek name Eros carved Latin graffiti on to a rock shelter on the road from Coptos to Berenice. Eros writes: 'Gaius Numidius Eros was here in the 28th year of Caesar's reign on the way back from India in the month of Phamenoth' (February or March in 2 BC). Further graffiti in the shelter indicates that this trip must have been part of a long-running business interest. A slave working for Eros named Thaliarchus left his name in this same desert shelter in 11 BC and when Eros revisited the site sometime after 2 BC he left another undated inscription on the wall.[61] While working for his master Calpurnius Moschas, a slave named Laudanes left graffiti at a further rock shelter on the road to Berenice.[62] The Calpurnii were an important business family in the eastern Mediterranean who were honoured in an inscription erected by Alexandria merchants and Syrian businessmen.[63]

Distinguished Roman women were also involved in business ventures across the Indian Ocean. This is evidenced by an inscription from the Egyptian temple at Medamoud in which two Roman businesswomen named Isidora and Olympias 'set up a dedication to the greatest goddess Leto'. They describe themselves as 'distinguished matrons, Red Sea ship owners and merchants' and mention their agent Apolinarios who was 'the captain of the fleet of Olympias and Isidora'.[64] Both women have the *gens* (title-name) Aelia indicating that they were possibly granted citizenship by the Roman Emperor Hadrian.[65]

To facilitate this desert traffic the Roman State built new fortified watering stations known as *hydreumata*. Roman military engineers constructed cisterns in these stations to store rainwater and dug deep wells to tap underground water reserves. Strabo explains the benefits of these facilities when he writes: 'in pre-vious times the camel merchants travelled by night using the stars as their guide, just as sailors do. They also carried water with them when they travelled. But now the Romans have built *hydreumata* by digging to great depths and constructed cisterns for normally scarce rainwater.'[66]

Some Roman *hydreumata* provided facilities that could accommodate hundreds of travellers during the oppressive day-time temperatures. Pliny reports that in his era, 'the greater part of the journey is made at night because of the heat and the days are spent at these stations'. One of the main stations mentioned by Pliny was 'an old *hydreuma*, called Troglodyticum, where there is a fort able to accom-modate 2,000 people'.[67] When Pliny was writing about eastern trade there were eight Roman caravan stations on the road from Berenice to Coptos. In later decades further stations and halts were introduced to cope with increased traffic and a recent survey has identified the remains of a probable eighteen halts along the route.[68]

Travellers leaving Coptos bought a pass to verify their business in the desert and this token granted them entry into the military-managed *hydreumata*. A stone inscription referred to as the *Coptos Tariff* records the kinds of travellers who made this journey. The list includes guards, sailors, craftsmen, shipbuilders' servants, helmsmen and ships' lookouts.[69] An *ostraca* found at Myos Hormos records the name of a helmsman named Satornilus Tessararis who was possibly serving on a military ship.[70] Early Christian sources claim that the apostle Thomas travelled to India as a carpenter and the *Coptos Tariff* shows that he would have been following a tradition that was based on known practices at that time.[71]

Weapons
There is evidence of a private arms market at Coptos where travellers and their guards could buy armour and weaponry for their eastern ventures. In AD 34 the Roman governor Avilius Flaccus became concerned that a revolt might occur in southern Egypt. He therefore sent an officer named Bassus south to confiscate all privately held weapons in Coptos and the Eastern Desert. Onlookers at Alexandria were amazed at the quantity of weapons that were returned from this operation. Philo recalls, 'a great fleet of ships full of every type of weapon was seen sailing down the Nile and anchoring at the river harbours'.[72]

Flaccus had the weapons taken to the nearby military base at Nicopolis for sortation and assessment. Philo describes how 'numerous beasts of burden were loaded with these arms' and 'almost all the wagons belonging to the Roman camp were filled with these weapons'. Bassus decided to make a spectacle of the event and 'displayed the weapons in rows and arranged each of the many types in order'. The confiscated arms were then taken to the governor's palace where they were placed in long-term secure storage.[73]

When the Roman regime relaxed its enforcement measures, the dealers in Coptos re-stocked with weapons. A papyrus letter from the second century AD records how a Greek named Apollonius bought his military equipment there. Apollonius was from Alexandria, but he was concerned that there would be a

Jewish uprising in his home city and wanted to have his own arms and armour ready for the conflict. He therefore sent a subordinate named Hermias down to Coptos to collect weapons that had been discreetly acquired by a business colleague who undertook commissions. Apollonius ordered and received 'a breastplate made of excellent yellow copper that is fine-meshed and very light so it will not burden the wearer'. This armour was bought for a bargain price of 360 Egyptian drachmas (360 sesterces or three months' pay for a labourer). Apollonius also received an 'Italian-style sword bought for only 80 drachmas, but worth far more'. He had asked for a suitable military-style belt-dagger, but nothing that matched his exact requirements could be purchased at the right price.[74]

The Ports of Berenice and Myos Hormos
Berenice had good landing sites for offloading cargo, but during the Augustan era its harbour had fallen into serious disrepair and was probably unusable. Strabo describes the area around Berenice as having a 'coast roughened by reefs and submarine rocks, while most of the time it is subject to tempestuous winds'. Nevertheless, 'Berenice has convenient landing places ... and at present Indian and Arabian merchandise, as well as African goods, are brought to the port via the Red Sea'.[75]

Myos Hormos was the favoured base for outbound voyages and Strabo describes how the port had a long winding entrance to its large harbour.[76] During the Augustan era, it is probable that a squadron of Roman galleys was kept on permanent standby at the port as Strabo mentions the existence of a naval station in the town, built to accommodate Roman sailors.[77] In 25 BC, when Gallus brought his army back from Arabia with more than 100 military transport ships, he was able to land the entire fleet at Myos Hormos.[78] Strabo also reports that the 120 Roman merchant ships involved in voyages to India sailed annually from this same port.[79]

Myos Hormos (Quseir al-Qadim) was primarily a business town and its streets were full of buildings that were temporary lodgings, or housed workshops connected with the seafaring industry. The remains of lead sheets near the ancient shoreline suggest that the harbour had workshops involved in ship repair.[80] Archaeologists have excavated an artificial foreshore at the port made from thousands of empty pottery amphorae set together in upright positions and packed with quarry sand. The harbour was prone to silting and large earth mounds on the ancient shore may be the remains of dredged heaps created from debris cleared from the seabed. There is also a large enclosure at the outskirts of the town that probably served as a *caravanserai* that would have accommodated thousands of camels.[81]

Berenice was about 180 miles south of Myos Hormos, which represents up to five days sailing if wind conditions were unfavourable. It was a larger town and during the Imperial period Berenice served as an important administrative headquarters for the Roman authorities.[82] The harbour facilities at Berenice were restored early in the reign of the Emperor Tiberius (AD 14–37) to enable merchant ships to have long-term docking facilities at the port.[83] The *Nicanor Archive* reveals that by AD 26 firms based in Coptos were making regular outbound deliveries across the desert to Berenice. An increase in ancient graffiti dating to this period confirms that more caravan traffic had begun to use this route.[84]

Ships involved in voyages to India spent at least four months at the Red Sea ports and this meant that outbound cargo was assembled from multiple deliveries. A team of two men can control up to twelve camels tied in tandem and most cargoes were broken down into manageable batches for close supervision, or easy delivery. Roman ships docked at Berenice took on board food and provisions including beets, onions and medicines known as *pharmakoi*.[85] But perhaps the most interesting consignment mentioned in the surviving custom receipts is jars of quince-flavoured honey that was rich in ascorbic acid.[86] It seems that Roman merchants had discovered a successful way to prevent outbreaks of scurvy on their long voyages across the eastern ocean. One delivery of *pharmakoi* by the Nicanor firm consisted of nearly 300 litres of medicine which was either an export commodity or sizable medical rations for passangers and crew.[87]

By the middle of the first century AD, Berenice and Myos Hormos probably had equal importance in eastern commerce. The *Nicanor Archive* mentions deliveries to the ports a similar number of times and some businesses had agents working in both towns. In one instance a Greek-Egyptian businessman named Paminis sent a son to each port.[88]

The dry desert conditions at Berenice have preserved remarkable organic remains, including stray finds from incoming cargoes and foreign food provisions. The site has produced peppercorns, fragments of coconut, mung beans from Southeast Asia and the seeds of the Amla fruit from the lower Himalayas.[89] The discovery of beads from the islands of Sri Lanka and East Java indicate the scope of the trade contacts conducted from this place.[90]

Further evidence for shipping activities at Berenice comes from custom passes recovered from a rubbish pit at the ancient port (AD 40–70). Merchants who paid their custom tax for outgoing goods at Coptos were given a pottery token as verification for the officials at Berenice. Possession of this token permitted the merchants to load the listed goods on board ships docked at the port.[91]

Customs officials at Berenice specialised in supervising different categories of goods such as olive oil or wine. Many of the surviving passes refer to Greek and Roman wines received from across the Empire. Although the largest consignment included forty-eight amphorae, most passes record much smaller batches.[92] The Berenice custom receipts also refer to *marsippia* which were money bags consisting of carefully weighed packages of coin. Some of the receipts mention hundreds of these coin pouches which were checked by a customs agent named Sarapion.

Receipts for Bullion Exports

Although the custom receipts found at Berenice document coin exports, they do not record where this bullion was being sent. The *marsippia* (pouches) were probably small bags filled with carefully weighed and packaged coin-batches.[93] Epiphanius suggests that each *marsippium* held 125 denarii and 'double bags' contained 250 coins.[94] A cargo of 320 coin bags (40,000 denarii) would therefore have contained enough silver to buy more than 5 tons of frankincense or black pepper.[95]

The *marsippia* recorded in the Berenice *ostraca* are for batches of silver denarii exported sometime before AD 70. Five of the custom receipts refer to coin consignments ranging from 194 to 320 *marsippia* (24,250 to 40,000 denarii). The currency value of these coin consignments would have been between 97,000 and 160,000 sesterces. This figure is consistent with other evidence. A receipt from the *Nicanor Archive* records that 3 talents-weight of silver bullion was sent to Myos Hormos in AD 62.[96] This quantity of silver bullion was equivalent to about 25,000 denarii and would have been worth over 100,000 sesterces. Perhaps this money was destined for southern Arabia, as the *Periplus of the Erythraean Sea* reports that a 'considerable amount of money' was sent to Muza in the Saba-Himyarite Kingdom, and the Hadramawt port of Qana received 'large amounts of coin'.[97] Pliny describes how a freedman of Annius Ploclamus was carrying a large consignment of silver denarii aboard his vessel on a sailing around Arabia.[98]

Another three customs receipts from Berenice record coin consignments consisting of between 73 and 120 coin pouches (9,125 to 15,000 denarii). This represents about 36,500 to 60,000 sesterces worth of silver bullion. Perhaps these silver consignments were bound for southern Arabia, or maybe they were destined for India ports. The *Periplus* records that in the Gujurat port of Barygaza, 'Roman money, gold and silver commands an exchange at some profit against the local currency'.[99] Many of these coin pouches could therefore have been destined for money dealers in the main cities of northern India.

The final four receipts from Berenice record smaller coin consignments. Two of the batches consisted of 56 and 68 pouches, which probably represented between 7,000 and 8,500 denarii (about 30,000 sesterces). A further receipt referred to 21 pouches (2,625 denarii worth 10,500 sesterces) and the smallest delivery consisted of only five *marsippia* (625 denarii worth 2,500 sesterces). Maybe these smaller deliveries of silver were for Roman ships bound for the main trade ports of East Africa. The *Periplus* advises Roman merchants visiting the Aksumite port of Adulis to bring 'a little Roman money (*denarion*) for the resident foreigners'. The Somali trade centres also took Roman coin with Malao, Mosyllon, the Spice Port and Opone accepting 'Roman money, in limited quantity, both gold and silver'.[100]

A final possibility is that some of these smaller silver batches were bound for the Tamil cities of southern India. Many of the Roman coin hoards found in southern and eastern India consist of silver denarii. The two largest examples are the inland Akenpalle and Budinatham hoards which consisted of 1,531 and 1,398 Roman denarii.[101] This is close to the smallest coin consignments mentioned in the Berenice receipts. The Berenice receipts therefore confirm that

eastern commerce was removing gold and silver wealth from the imperial
economy.

The Nile Canal

Herodotus describes an ancient canal that connected the Nile River to the Suez
Gulf. This aqua-passage was originally devised by the Pharaoh Necho II (610–
595 BC), but the Persians and the Ptolemais took credit for completing the
project and upgrading the canal. The original canal was thirty feet wide which
was large enough to allow two *trireme* war-galleys to travel abreast from the Nile
inland towards the Suez Gulf.[102]

Herodotus claims that the Red Sea canal was completed by the Persian King
Darius (522–486 BC), but the waterway silted-up and Ptolemy Philadephus
(283–246 BC) had to recut large sections of the passage. The enlarged canal was
100 feet wide and 30 feet deep, but Pliny claims that the improvement work
was halted before the expanded channel reached the coast.[103] In Roman times the
Nile canal entered the Red Sea near the port of Arsinoe, but the passage was
heavily silted. This explains why Aelius Gallus had his military fleet built on the
shores of the Red Sea, rather than transported from the Mediterranean through
the canal. Despite the existence of the canal, throughout most of the first century
AD it was easier for businessmen to have their return cargoes transported
through the Eastern Desert and Coptos.

Conditions changed when the Nile–Suez canal was restored during the reign
of the Emperor Trajan (AD 98–117).[104] The repaired route allowed passengers
to sail directly from Alexandria to the main Red Sea harbours where they could
board ocean-going vessels heading for India. Transport by barge canal was about
one-sixth cheaper than overland haulage and many travellers used this route to
bypass the hardships of the desert.[105]

The best time for travel along the Nile–Suez canal was between September and
January when the waters of the Nile were swollen with rainfall from sources in
inner Africa. The canal began at the Egyptian city of Babylon (just south of
modern Cairo), a prime centre for the production of grain, wines and textiles.
These products were popular Roman exports to foreign countries and the canal
probably encouraged the shipment of bulk staple goods from the Empire.[106]

One incident in the second century AD indicates how much the Red Sea canal
simplified Roman trade ventures to India. Lucian describes how a student in
Alexandria took time away from his studies to visit India without informing his
personal slaves, or his parents in Galatia (Asia Minor). The young man took a
ship along the Nile to the port of Arsinoe at the head of the Suez Gulf where he
was persuaded to take a sea-passage to India. Lucian explains, 'he cruised up the
Nile as far as Clysma (Arsinoe) and as a vessel was just putting out to sea, he was
induced to join others in a voyage to India'. When he failed to return from the
Nile sailing, his servants in Alexandria concluded 'that the young man either had
lost his life during his cruise upon the Nile, or had been captured by brigands,
who were numerous at the time'. A famous medium named Alexander the
Paphlagonian convinced the bereaved family that their son had been murdered by

his servants, who were condemned on this testimony and torn apart by wild beasts in the Roman arena. A few months later the young man returned, 'telling of his travels' and proving the medium to be a fraud.[107] Lucian says that Alexander escaped justice, but in spite of his own predictions that he would live to be a hundred and fifty and die from a lightning strike, he contracted gangrene soon afterwards. Despite the best medical attention he died a slow and miserable death.[108]

CHAPTER SEVEN

The Scale and Significance of Indian Ocean Trade

During the Imperial period the Roman Empire received enormous revenues generated by taxing international commerce. Each year, hundreds of Roman ships undertook voyages across the Indian Ocean to distant kingdoms in Africa, Arabia and India. Trade with India alone delivered more than a billion sesterces worth of eastern goods into Egypt for distribution and sale throughout Roman territory. Due to high-rate customs taxes, this commerce provided the Roman State with nearly a third of the funds it needed to finance its Empire. These revenues contributed to the cost of the professional army that secured Roman dominance and ensured the long-term peace and prosperity of the Empire – the *Pax Romana*.

Eastern goods transformed Roman culture by offering new food flavourings, perfumes, medical remedies, jewellery styles and clothing fashions. As Pliny the Elder observed, 'people used to gather all their ingredients from home and there was no demand for Indian pepper and these other luxuries that we now import from overseas'.[1] Describing the era before Roman domination, the Greek orator Dio Chrysostom spoke of 'the Indian Ocean, whose name was rarely heard in past times'.[2] But Roman control over Egypt changed this situation, fundamentally altering Mediterranean commerce and transforming its prospects within the ancient world economy. As eastern trade boomed, Alexandria became the prime market for international commerce and Strabo describes the city as 'the greatest emporium in the inhabited world'.[3]

Most Roman imports from the distant east concerned food products and other perishable consumables that are not well attested in archaeological remains. The extent of the problem is indicated by a Roman legal text describing goods subject to import tax at Alexandria. The passage reads:

Types of goods liable to tax: cinnamon; long pepper; white pepper; pentasphaerum leaf; barbary leaf; costum; costamomum; nard; stachys; Tyrian cassia; cassia-wood; myrrh; amomum; ginger; malabrathum; Indian spice; galbanum; asafoetida juice; aloe; lycium; Perian gum; Arabian onyx; cardamom; cinnamonwood; cotton goods; Babylonian hides; Persian hides; ivory; Indian iron; linen; all sorts of gem; pearl, sardonyx, ceraunium, hyacinth stone, emerald, diamond, sapphire, turquoise, beryl, tortoise stone; Indian or Assyrian drugs; raw silk, silk or half-silk clothing; embroidered fine linen; silk thread; Indian eunuchs; lions; lionesses; pards; leopards; panthers; purple dye; also African wool; dye; Indian hair.[4]

Unfortunately, few of these goods would have left any archaeological trace among a Roman population that probably numbered more than 45 million people.[5]

Many senior Romans viewed the development of international trade with pride as Pliny explains: 'mutual communication has been established throughout the known world by the majesty of the Roman Empire. No-one can deny that life has been advanced by the interchange of commodities in this partnership of peace. As a consequence, things that had previously been unobtainable are now in common use.'[6] Seneca also comments, 'we have made contact with the whole earth and can claim the entire world as our country.'[7]

But international commerce threatened the long term stability of the Roman system. Most of the products that the Empire received from the distant east were perishable consumables that could not be produced in the Roman Empire due to the unique environmental conditions in their countries of origin. The Romans had no comparable product that could meet the cost of acquiring these goods from distant markets. So, in order to sustain international trade, the Romans had to export bullion to pay for their spices, incense and pearls. As Pliny explains, 'both pepper and ginger grow wild in their respective countries, yet here we buy them by weight, using so much gold and silver'.[8]

Pliny indicates the scale of the problem when he considered the most valuable goods in Roman society. This list is dominated by eastern imports. He states:

The most valuable products known to us are these: at sea, pearl; in the earth's surface, rock-crystal; under the earth, diamonds, emeralds, gemstones and fluorspar. The most costly natural resources are scarlet kermes dyes and silphium, then spikenard and silks, citrus wood from trees, cinnamon, cassia and amomum. From saps: amber, balsam, myrrh and frankincense, and from roots: costus. As for land animals, the most costly product is the elephant's tusk, and at sea it is turtleshell. The most costly animal furs are the coloured pelts from Serica (China) and then Arabian *ladanum*.

Pliny concludes, 'our gold is scarcely tenth in this list of valuables, while silver, which we use to procure gold, is only twentieth'.[9]

The Muziris Papyrus
The best evidence for eastern cargo quantities comes from a Greek document discovered in Egypt, known as the *Muziris Papyrus*, which dates to the second century AD. This legal document contains cargo details from a ship called the *Hermapollon* that were checked by Roman customs officials and by agents of a money-lender. This money-lender needed to be certain that a borrower had proper security for a loan by using the ship's cargo. Some of the cargo manifesto recorded on the papyrus is incomplete, but the sections that do survive show that the *Hermapollon* was carrying over 220 tons of Indian merchandise.[10]

The *Muziris Papyrus* reveals how eastern imports were managed by merchants and taxed by the Roman government.[11] The *Hermapollon* had just returned from the Tamil trade port of Muziris in southern India and its cargo was valued by Roman customs agents at the Egyptian port of Berenice, or Myos Hormos. But the merchant owner needed immediate cash, perhaps to pay expensive caravan and river transport costs, toll-dues or storage expenses. He therefore arranged a loan from a wealthy businessman, promising to repay the money with the profits he made when he sold his eastern cargo at Alexandria. The Indian cargo removed from the *Hermapollon* was valued at 1,154 talents after payment of import tax. This is equivalent to nearly 7 million sesterces in imperial money.[12]

The *Muziris Papyrus* is a formulaic legal template written in careless hand-writing as though the scribe had copied out the same basic text numerous times. Details of the agreement were then filled in by a different writer.[13] This suggests that the document was a standard contract that could be used by financers and merchants to facilitate recurring agreements. The agreement included a cargo manifesto recording the value and quantity of bulk goods removed from the hold of the trade ship *Hermapollon*. The list includes pepper, malabathrum (cinnamon), nard and ivory, but not pearls, gems or silk. The merchant must have retained these small lightweight, but expensive items, perhaps expecting to pay off the loan with the profits he made by selling these goods in Alexandria.

The *Muziris Papyrus* records how the agents of the financer met the merchant at one of the Red Sea ports. They verified details about the cargo, including the quality and cost cited by customs agents who monitored offloading operations. The merchant then signed over legal ownership of these goods to the financer in return for an immediate cash loan. The merchant was then responsible for the safe transfer of these commodities to Alexandria and for their subsequent market sale. The financer would relinquish his claim over the goods once he had been repaid the full loan amount, plus an agreed interest payment. The merchant would then legally own the remaining commodities which he could sell on the free market for the highest possible profit.

The first section of the contract describes how cargo was taken by caravan from the Red Sea ports across the Eastern Desert to the Nile city of Coptos. The loan stipulates, 'under this agreement, I will give the goods to your other adminis-trators, or managers, and to your camel-driver and pay the extra charges for the journey to Coptos. I will convey the goods through the desert under guard and protection to the State tax-assessing warehouses at Coptos.'[14]

In the first century AD, businessmen like Alexander the *alabarch* bid for the right to collect customs tax on behalf of the Empire and they hired state-warehouses to manage incoming stock. Roman government probably took direct charge of taxing eastern imports during the reign of Vespasian, or his sons Titus and Domitian, as this is when large-scale facilities appear in Rome for managing eastern products.

The cargo manifesto records that the *Hermapollon* was carrying at least 220 tons of cargo that would have required over a thousand camels to transport across the desert.[15] The resultant caravan would have needed at least 160 camel drivers accompanied by armed guards.[16] Each camel driver could expect to be paid about 16 Egyptian drachma per day (4 sesterces), but other expenses were involved including the hire and daily supply-costs for each animal. The *Coptos Tariff* lists tolls to be paid on personnel and animals crossing the Eastern Desert.

The rates were 1 drachma per man, 5 drachma per guard and 1 obol per camel (1 drachma for a team of six camels).[17] These caravan expenses explain why many merchants who had their wealth invested in eastern cargo had to arrange short-term loans to transfer their goods to Alexandria. It was in their interests to have their cargo reach the city ahead of competitors and thereby guarantee profitable sales in the Mediterranean markets. Roman merchants leaving India in December could expect to have their cargoes reach Alexandria by early March when the Mediterranean sea-lanes became safe for summer voyages.[18]

Goods were declared to and assessed by State agents at the government warehouses at Coptos. Then they were bonded ready for river transport via the Nile to Alexandria. The loan agreement outlines responsibilities for the goods during this operation, 'I will place the goods under your authority and seal, or the authority of one of your present administrators, until they are loaded at the river. I will load them at the required time on to a safe ship on the river, and I will convey them down to the warehouse for receiving the *tetarte* "quarter-tax" at Alexandria'.[19] The *tetarte* customs-tax was assessed at the Red Sea ports when the cargo was first offloaded in Roman territory, but it was not seized by government agents until the goods had reached Alexandria. This meant that the State did not have to pay the expense of transporting its tax-percentage of the cargo, which could be taken as a quarter-share of the incoming goods. Government agents could sell or auction their tax-share of eastern goods to private merchants in Alexandria. Alternatively, they could ship these commodities to state-owned warehouses in Rome for further distribution, or sale by imperial agents in the capital.

By using his cash profits from the sale of pearls and gemstones, the merchant could repay his loan with interest before the agreed date. The financer would then sign custody of the *Hermapollon*'s cargo back to the merchant. The *Muziris Papyrus* outlines consequences if the loan was not repaid by the agreed date. In this situation the financer could sell any eastern cargo that had been signed over to him as security. The merchant agreed, 'regarding the loan agreement on the Muziris venture: If I do not duly repay the aforesaid loan – then you and your administrators or managers have the option and complete authority to exact the amount owed without notification or summons. You may seize and control the aforementioned security. You will pay the *tetarte* and offer the other three-quarters cargo to wherever you wish. You may sell or use these goods as security, or transfer them to another person (if you so choose). You may therefore dispose of the goods in whatever manner you wish. You may sell them at the price that is current at the time and you may remove and reckon any expenses arising from the aforementioned loan.'[20] It was therefore important for the merchant to repay the loan before the due date or he would lose both his cargo and his profits.

If the merchant repaid his loan in time, then he regained control over his cargo and was free to sell the goods to fellow merchants, business people and distributors in Alexandria. The goods could be sold wholesale at public auction with the State taking a further tax cut from the sales price, or the merchant could sell direct to business associates in the city, or to merchants with ships waiting in port to supply other Mediterranean cities.

Many eastern goods were processed in Alexandria, with cottons and silks made into Roman-style clothing in large urban workshops.[21] Stocks of expensive incense would be sorted and made into perfumes for sale across the Roman Empire. Security arrangements at the processing sites were strict, as Pliny explains, 'at Alexandria where the incense is processed for sale the workshops can never be guarded with sufficient care. A seal is placed upon the workmen's aprons. A mask and a net with very close mesh is put upon their heads. These people are stripped naked before they are allowed to leave their work.'[22]

Processing costs and profits could triple the price of many aromatics and increase the cost of the best fabrics by up to tenfold. For example, a *sextarius* of pure balsam bought for 300 denarii could be sold for more than 1,000 denarii when processed into perfume.[23] Diocletian's *Price Edict* records that one pound of fine purple-dyed silk was valued at more than twelve times the cost of basic un-dyed, white silk.[24] These unique goods were sold to further merchants who had ships operating in Alexandria and sent cargoes to many wealthy overseas cities, including Rome. Strabo explains that 'Egypt has monopolies for Alexandria alone receives these goods and the city is the main source of supply to the Roman world'.[25]

Dio Chrysostom depicts Alexandria as having 'a monopoly on all Mediter-ranean shipping because of the beauty of your harbours, the magnitude of your fleet, your abundant marketing of products from every land and goods from the outer seas, both the Red Sea and the Indian Ocean'. He describes Alexandria managing the trade 'of practically the entire world. For Alexandria is situated at the cross-roads of the whole world and it connects the most remote nations as if it were a market serving a single city.'[26]

However, the complexity of the ancient economy meant that prices paid for eastern goods fluctuated according to supply and demand. Pliny provides prices for many eastern products, but explains, 'the prices I have cited alter nearly every year, according to shipping costs, the terms on which a particular merchant has bought the product, or if some dealer is dominating the market and escalating the selling price'. Therefore, 'I have stated the usual prices in Rome, to give an idea of a standard value of commodities.'[27] Most Mediterranean products also fluctu-ated in price, and Roman law codes acknowledge 'location and time cause a dif-ference in price, olive oil does not sell at the same price in Rome and Spain and it does not have the same value in continuous bad years (causing scarcity) compared to favourable ones (providing surplus)'.[28]

The Cargo of the *Hermapollon*

The *Muziris Papyrus* records that the *Hermapollon* carried sixty boxes of nard, one hundred pairs of elephant tusks and enough ivory fragments to form a further seventeen tusks.[29] The names of three other commodities were lost when the papyrus was damaged, but the *Periplus of the Erythraean Sea* indicates that these goods were probably pepper, malabathrum and turtle-shell. Roman merchants visiting Tamil India also received silk-cloth, 'good supplies' of pearls and 'all kinds' of precious stones, but these lightweight items were not included in the loan agreement because they were not a bulky cargo.[30]

The identity of the unnamed goods listed in the *Muziris Papyrus* can be deduced from surviving details given about their weight and value. Imported goods were taxed at one-quarter their value and their customs-value was set by the sale price in Rome.[31] The main cargo removed from the *Hermapollon* consisted of Indian spices as the *Periplus* reports, 'ships in these ports of trade (Muziris) carry full loads because of the volume and quantity of pepper and malabathrum'.[32] The *Muziris Papyrus* lists a commodity that must be pepper because it was priced at 771 talents and 4,632 drachmas (4,630,632 sesterces) and weighed 135 tons. This means that the product had a customs value of 16 sesterces per pound, which is the price Pliny gives for pepper.[33] A further commodity removed from the *Hermapollon* is probably malabathrum (cinnamon) because it was valued at 220 talents (1,320,000 sesterces) and weighed over 83 tons. This is consistent with relatively ordinary cinnamon which sold in Roman markets at about 8 sesterces a pound.[34] The final unknown commodity removed from the *Periplus* was valued at 25 talents and 108 drachmas (150,108 sesterces). This probably represents over 3 tons of turtle-shell.[35]

The *Hermapollon* sailed direct to the Tamil lands, so its cargo was mostly comprised of relatively cheap spices from southern India. Roman ships that visited ports in northern India probably had a more varied cargo as these regions offered large quantities of cotton cloth. Cotton could not be widely produced in the Roman Empire so there is limited ancient evidence for its market price. Diocletian's *Price Edict* suggests that wool and hemp cloth was valued at about 4 sesterces per pound.[36] Using this as a guide, imported Indian cotton probably fetched slightly higher prices because of its foreign origins.

The Volume of Trade
The trade situation is complex, but the cargo figures for the *Hermapollon* can be 'scaled-up' to suggest the quantity of goods from India entering the Roman Empire every year. Assuming a fleet of 120 merchant ships, Roman Egypt could be receiving: 16,000 tons of pepper and cotton, 10,000 tons of malabathrum and other spices, 7,000 boxes or 50 tons of nard, 360 tons of turtle-shell and 576 tons of ivory (over 14,000 tusks), per annum.[37] Trade on this scale is feasible because the Romans were dealing with countries and populations that were as large as their entire Empire.

Support for these ancient trade estimates comes from later developments in world history. In the late fifteenth century Portuguese explorers established a new sailing route to India that bypassed the Middle East by sailing around the African continent. During the early sixteenth century the Portuguese began exporting more than 70 tons of silver to India per annum (equivalent to 16 million denarii or 64 million sesterces).[38] In return Portuguese merchants received 1,000–2,000 tons of pepper and over 1,000 tons of other spices that they sold to further

European markets.[39] Modern estimates suggest that by the start of the seventeenth century Southeast Asia was exporting 4,000 tons of pepper per annum.[40]

The Value of Trade

The value of Indian imports entering the Roman Empire is a more significant issue. The six commodities removed from the *Hermapollon* were valued at over 9 million sesterces by Roman customs agents.[41] This was not the entire cargo since the ship was probably carrying parcels of lightweight pearls, gemstones and silk. A million sesterces would purchase 160 of the finest pearls, or perhaps 3,000 large gemstones.[42] So the total value of the *Hermapollon*'s cargo was probably more than 10 million sesterces. This is significant because the Roman Empire took a quarter of this figure as customs tax.

The *Hermapollon*'s cargo can be used to suggest the overall value of goods from India entering the Empire. Assuming there were 120 ships in the merchant fleet, then Egypt would be receiving: 556 million sesterces worth of pepper and cotton, 158 million sesterces worth of malabathrum and other spices, 32 million sesterces of nard, 60 million sesterces of ivory and 18 million sesterces of turtle-shell.[43] Customs agents imposed quarter-rate taxes on all these imports, so the Roman regime could receive enormous annual revenues from this commerce.

A fleet of 120 Roman ships, each carrying a cargo worth approximately 9 million sesterces, would have added over 1,000 million sesterces to Mediterranean commerce every year.[44] That is a billion sesterces of goods from India, just from this one aspect of eastern commerce. This trade figure is larger than the annual income that the Roman government needed to sustain its entire Empire.[45]

The whole merchant fleet could have been importing over 26,000 tons of eastern goods per annum.[46] This quantity of cargo is similar to the size of the grain-dole that Alexandria sent to Rome (29,000 tons). There were over 45 million people living in the Roman Empire, so 26,000 tons of Indian imports is not a large figure. This represents an average of just over 1 pound of product per Roman subject.

CHAPTER EIGHT

International Business

The Ships

The Roman ships that sailed the Indian Ocean were large vessels by Mediterranean standards. This is confirmed by part of a pier excavated at Berenice with wide intervals for Roman ships to dock. These docking spaces were able to accommodate vessels that were up to 120 feet long and therefore had a cargo capacity greater than 350 tons.[1] Some of the larger ships could have been double this size with over 500 tons of space made available for cargo, crew and provisions.[2]

These Greco-Roman ships were probably the largest vessels operating in the Indian Ocean. A Greek author named Philostratus describes the ships in a biography he wrote about a pagan philosopher named Apollonius of Tyana. It was said that Apollonius travelled to India in the first century AD using an overland route. But while he was in India he talked with eastern philosophers about the nature of god and the universe, explaining these ideas through the analogy of Red Sea freighters managed by Roman businessmen in Egypt. The universe was likened to a great ship guided by a hierarchy of gods. Philostatus explains, 'the Egyptians build these ships on a scale whereby one of their vessels is equivalent in size to several of those used by the other races'.[3]

Site surveys at Berenice indicate that docked ships were secured to large cedarwood bollards and goods offloaded on gangplanks, or with the aid of cargo-nets.[4] The remains of cargo-netting, brailing-rings, sail fragments and mooring ropes are common surface finds at both Berenice and Myos Hormos. Many Roman Red Sea freighters were built out of Lebanese cedarwood, probably at shipyards in the northern port of Arsinoe. Large-scale repairs were conducted at Myos Hormos and Berenice, including the fitting of new timbers and the break-up of old vessels. Cedarwood beams, sometimes up to ten feet long, were removed from decommissioned ships and used in the construction of the town buildings at Berenice.[5]

Evidence of ship repairs comes from the *Coptos Tariff* which lists the toll to be paid on ships' masts transported across the Eastern Desert.[6] Wagons were used for these heavy loads and the wagoneers were permitted to carry timbers for the repair of their own vehicles. However, sometimes the rules were flaunted for profit. A military order scratched on a pottery fragment was found at the Roman fort of Krokodilo (the Crocodile) on the desert road from Coptos to Myos Hormos. The order is from a senior Roman commander named Artorius Priscillus who warns his soldiers that some shipwrights were buying timbers directly from the wagoneers to avoid paying the required transport tolls. He informed all garrisons along the route that this practice had to be stopped.[7]

The hulls of Greco-Roman ships were constructed from planks fitted together using strong mortise-and-tenon joints to create a rigid self-supporting structure. Once the hull was complete, large internal beams were fitted to reinforce the interior of the vessel. A coat of waterproof pitch was added to the finished hull with lead sheeting fitted below the waterline to prevent tiny marine creatures from burrowing into the timbers. Some Roman ships had extra protruding beams of thick planking attached along the length of the ship to reinforce the hull and stabilise the vessel.

Greek construction techniques were known in northwest India because of Alexander's fleet-building activities in the Indus Delta (325 BC). However, because there were few natural harbours in India, Indian shipwrights favoured alternative designs. They built shallow-hulled vessels that could be easily dragged ashore during monsoon storms, or safely docked in a shallow estuary. Indian shipbuilders also used cord fastenings, rather than joints and nails, to bind together their hull planking.[8] This meant that their craft could withstand the impact of striking a reef without fracturing the joints between the nailed timbers.

A merchant handbook, the *Periplus of the Erythraean Sea*, describes how Indian vessels delivered ship-building materials to Persian ports, including copper for nails and teakwood timbers.[9] These Indian ships probably made similar supply voyages to the Roman Red Sea harbours. Teak is a heavy and highly durable hardwood that is easily worked and it will not split, shrink, or alter its shape when used for ship construction. The evidence suggests that Roman shipwrights involved in the Red Sea trade maintained their traditional building methods, but made use of eastern materials to create even stronger vessels. Tropical teak-wood was imported from the distant East and Indian cotton was used to make a superior sailcloth. Nine-foot long teak beams marked with dowel holes and ship-nails have been identified in building ruins at Berenice and fragments of Indian cotton sails fitted with Roman-style brailing rings have also been found at the port.[10]

Standard Greek and Roman ships were deep-hulled freighters that used a large centrally-placed sail to run before the wind. The Roman ships engaged in eastern trade had higher bulwarks than usual, in order to withstand the monsoon winds and fierce waves of the Indian Ocean. These rampart-like barriers also made it harder for pirates and other hostiles to attack and board the ship. Philostratus confirms these design features when he writes, 'they rib the sides of the ship with bolts to hold the vessel together and they raise its bulwarks and its mast to a great height'. Philostratus also reports that Roman freighters bound for India were fitted with 'several compartments on the timber beams which run across the vessel'.[11] These were probably extra cabins fitted on deck for the crew to take shelter from the monsoon weather which could hit the vessel with Force Ten winds. Achilles Tatius confirms that some Mediterranean vessels had extra deck cabins for passengers.[12]

Each freighter probably towed at least one small ship-to-shore vessel for use in the eastern ports. A crewman would be stationed permanently aboard each of these small-craft and Petronius describes how 'one sailor is on watch, lying in the boat, night and day. You couldn't get rid of that watchman except by cutting his throat or throwing him overboard by force.'[13] This shore-boat could be hoisted aboard the ship if the main vessel was caught in a storm.[14]

Roman vessels designed for Indian ventures had a larger mast and mainsail to maximise wind-power on the ocean voyage.[15] They also had a smaller sail called an *aremon* positioned at their prow. Pliny describes how 'nowadays we are not satisfied until sails are larger than ships and single trees are scarcely big enough for the yardarms that carry the sails. Extra sails are added above the yards and others are spread at the bows and sterns'.[16] Alexandrian ships were known for their high topsails and Seneca explains, 'nothing sends a ship along so well as its upper canvas; that is where the most speed is obtained'.[17] A picture scratched on a pottery fragment found at Berenice shows a Red Sea freighter with these topsails fitted to the upper levels of the mainmast.

The mast-head on large ships was strengthened by decorative brass fittings since iron had a corrosive effect on wood.[18] Pendants were flown from the main-mast and the end-beams to indicate the prevailing wind conditions high above the decking.[19] The picture of a Roman two-masted freighter called the *Europa* was scratched on to a plaster wall at Pompeii. The illustration depicts a large ship in full sail with a prominent name-plaque fitted on the prow. Two giant rudders at the stern steer the vessel through the water and it tows a smaller support vessel that was probably designed for ship-to-shore operations.[20] The heads of about half a dozen crewmembers are visible on-deck, manning the rigging or con-ducting other ship's business. High above their heads a lookout signals from a platform on the top mast.[21]

Some Roman ships had vivid red sails, while others had colourful images from classical mythology painted on their canvas. The Torlonia Relief shows a Roman sail painted with a double image of Romulus and Remus being suckled by a she-wolf.[22] Lucian describes a freighter called the *Isis* with a figure of the goddess on the prow and further decorations which included, 'paintings of Isis and a scarlet topsail'.[23] Roman military ships used on scouting missions had their sails and rigging dyed venetian blue as camouflage on the open sea.[24] Pliny suggests that many ships displayed colourful bunting, but only the Emperor's vessel was per-mitted to have a sail dyed imperial purple.[25]

The deckhouse of the ship was near the stern and usually included the cook-house and captain's quarters. The roof of the block formed an elevated deck where the helmsman stood enabling him see over the bow of the boat as he operated the tillers to steer the ship. The tiller-bars were long levers attached to two giant rudders positioned on either side of the stern. By pushing or pulling two steering-levers the helmsman could pivot the rudders and control the direction of the vessel and its drag-speed through the water.[26] This equipment required more skill than strength and Lucian describes seeing the helmsman of a giant grain-freighter who was 'a tiny little old man who just now brought the ship to safety, pivoting those huge rudders with only a fragile steering bar'.[27] Lucian explains how the largest ships 'scudding and wave-skimming' might be slowed to a halt when the crew would 'throw out two-tongued anchorage and iron-stoppers and ship-fetters to block her foaming course'.[28]

The sterndeck did not cover the entire width of the vessel so that on each side a narrow gangway allowed access to an overhanging gallery. Ships carried bright lanterns on the stern to signal other vessels and prevent collisions.[29] Most of the Red Sea ships followed the Mediterranean custom of having large goose-head ornaments carved on their sternposts. Lucian describes an Alexandrian grain freighter which displayed 'a grand stern with a gradual curve and gilded beak'.[30] These figureheads were sacred to the Egyptian goddess Isis who was believed to offer special protection to sailors. Ancient Tamil poetry describes seeing these large carvings at night-time, when the Roman ships moored on the Indian coast were lit up by bright oil-lamps fitted on their gooseneck sterns. The *Perumpanar-ruppatai* describes a gem that 'shone as though it were a lamp seen on the swan timbers of a *Yavana* (Roman) ship. It sparkled like the distant star that heralds the dawn.'[31]

Some ships had a stone altar on the rear deck where the captain could offer incense and libations to the gods.[32] The Torlonia Relief shows a ship coming into harbour at Ostia with the captain and his wife burning incense in gratitude for a safe voyage. Other ships carried statues of guardian deities that were thought to offer special protection to the vessel and the Torlonia Relief depicts a statue of Victory holding a laurel wreath.[33] The vessels owned or operated by wealthy businessmen often displayed statues that were gilded or made from expensive materials. A delicately carved ivory hand from an ancient wooden statue was found on the Pozzino shipwreck, but Seneca warned that good construction mattered more than colourful decoration and a ship was not seaworthy and safe just because 'its guardian deity is carved of ivory'.[34]

Roman ships could be decorated with bright colors and a mosaic depicts the stern of a Mediterranean vessel that had its black-tar hull painted with blue and yellow lines and lateral red stripes. A giant eye and the image of a pale-blue sea-monster are depicted on the hull and the gooseneck sternpost is embellished with horizontal bands of brown and white stripes while banners fly from horizontal bars.[35] Ovid sailed on a ship called the *Minerva* that had a golden-yellow bust of the goddess painted on the bows and Apuleius imagined a ship with its 'gleaming goose-head stern covered in gilded foil'.[36]

Grain cargoes could be stored aboard ship in sacks or the loose grain poured into a common hold. Roman law indicates that some vessels had separate compartments, so that shippers could hire cargo areas divided 'by planks or partitions'. This meant that if the cargo was damaged those who had incurred losses could be easily identified.[37] Cargo ships often contained multiple decks accessed by ladders, including lower levels fitted for the confinement of captives or slaves. The Jewish book of *Maccabees* describes 'prisoners tied to the crossbeams of the ship', but 'their eyes were in complete darkness because of the thick deck just above'.[38] Large ships also had stalls for horses and other animals including compartments for fodder fitted on either side of the vessel.[39]

Fresh water could be stored in large wooden compartments within the ship's hold. These were lined with waterproof canvas and sealed with pitch.[40] In emergencies the sails or hide coverings used for awnings could collect rainfall or condensed dew.[41] Large vessels would also be fitted with saltwater compartments for live fish and Athenaeus describes a Mediterranean super-freighter where 'next to the cistern there was a large water-tight well made with beams of wood and lead. This compartment was kept full of water and filled with great numbers of fish.'[42]

Ships were equipped with lead weights to measure sea-depth and buoyant cork floats to mark the position of anchors.[43] These cork floats were thrown to those who fell overboard, but rescue was difficult in turbulent weather or if the ship was in full sail. Lucian describes a Mediterranean sailing when a frail young man named Damon 'was seasick on the rough sea and was leaning over the side of the vessel when an unusually violent lurch of the ship in his direction, combined with the rush of water across the deck, hurled him headlong into the sea'. His friend Euthydicus 'heard his cries and flung himself into the waves. He succeeded in overtaking the exhausted Damon and supported him as the crew and passengers threw cork floats and a gangplank into the sea.' In the moonlight those on deck saw Euthydicus swimming for a considerable distance, but the men disappeared from sight among 'the surging billows, the roar of crashing waters, the hissing foam, the darkness, and their prospects seemed hopeless'. Remarkably both men survived. They eventually drifted ashore on the Greek coast clinging to the gangplank.[44]

Roman ships entering the Indian Ocean must have adapted their vessels to resist pirate attack. Athenaeus suggests that a well-equiped lookout post on a large transport vessel might be manned by 'four young fully-armed men and two archers'.[45] Wooden palisades with iron fittings could be raised when the ship was in hostile waters and stones were stored on deck for guards and crew to hurl down upon their attackers.[46] Baskets of stones were also hauled up to the mainmast for the riggers to cast stones from a higher vantage point. Some Roman ships sailing the Indian Ocean had small bolt-throwing catapults fitted on buttressed deck-platforms.[47] These machines could be fitted with special grapples called 'ravens' to grip the enemy vessel and winch it into an exposed position.[48] The wide yardarms of the main sail could carry large torpedo-shaped lead weights called 'dolphins'. If a hostile ship drew alongside in an attempt to board the vessel, these weights were dropped upon the enemy to smash their deck timbers.[49]

The names of some of the Roman ships that operated in the Indian Ocean have been preserved in the surviving sources including the *Hermapollon* which sailed to Muziris in southern India.[50] Hermes was the Greek god of merchants and a messenger deity who crossed boundaries at great speed and Apollo was the Greek solar god who travelled through the heavens along the path of the sun. The *Hermapollon* therefore invoked the protection of these two powerful deities.

A pottery shard from Berenice records the name of another Red Sea ship called the *Gymnasiarchis*.[51] A Gymnasiarch was a rich benefactor who provided Greek gymnasiums with oil and wine. These institutions were fundamental to Greek culture and the Gymnasiarch was a highly respected individual. Perhaps the owner of this particular ship was a benefactor to his home-city, or funded a gymnasium with profits he made from international commerce. Perhaps the name of the ship refers to its outgoing cargo of oil and wine, delivered for the benefit of foreign cities.

Evidence from Egyptian papyri reveal the names chosen for the military ships that protected the Roman trade vessels. A man called Gaius Valerius Gemellus enlisted in the Roman navy, thereby annulling a marriage agreement he had with a woman named Demetria. The papyrus records that Gemellus joined part of the Alexandrian fleet and served on a warship called the *Draco* (*Dragon*).[52] Roman inscriptions reveal the names of other military ships operating in the Egyptian fleet including the *Fides* (*Faithful*), *Lupa* (*She-Wolf*), *Taurus* (*Bull*), *Neptunus*, *Mercurius* and *Sol* (*Neptune, Mercury* and *The Sun*).[53]

The Red Sea coastline drops steeply into deep waters and the thin sand that covers the seabed does not generally protect or preserve ancient remains. Coral growth in these warm waters also tends to destroy or obscure any wreckage that remains on the seabed. Despite these difficulties, the remnants of a Roman shipwreck have been identified on the coast near ancient Myos Hormos (Quseir al-Quadim). Little now remains of the ship apart from the scattered fragments of pottery amphorae that either held provisions, or were part of the outbound cargo.[54]

Another Roman wreck has been identified at a site just north of Berenice called Fury Shoals. The cargo consisted of over forty Roman amphorae including wine containers that were probably taken on board as crew provisions. There was also a scattering of volcanic ballast-stones around the vessel that must have been loaded aboard the ship in southern Arabia and in their midst was an Arabian storage jar.[55] The ship was probably heading back to Myos Hormos with a cargo of incense when it struck a reef on the treacherous Fury Shoals.

Another Roman shipwreck has been located at the Abu Fendera Reef, near Zabargad Island, about fifty miles south of Berenice. This Roman ship was carrying more than forty amphorae, including wine jars and olive oil containers from France and Spain. An underwater survey recovered two bronze bowls and the head of a Roman javelin that had been manufactured from a rust-resistant copper-alloy. Finds of copper-alloy nails and lead sheeting on the seabed confirm evidence for Roman shipbuilding techniques. The vessel was also equipped with at least five exceptionally large lead anchors including one that was almost ten feet long.[56]

The Ship's Crew

Roman ships sailing to India were commanded by a captain known as a *naukleros*. This man had responsibility for the crew and passengers, including the merchants and their agents. The captain also commanded the mercenary teams who maintained on-board security. Some *naukleroi* had control over a small fleet and commanded subordinate captains. The name of one of these captains is known from an inscription found at a small shrine on the road to Berenice. A man named Severus, son of Moschion, left a message on a wall of the shelter and described himself as a *naukleros*.[57] Apolinarios also took this title when he managed the ships owned by the wealthy businesswomen Olympias and Isidora.[58]

Some ships also had an officer who took special charge and responsibility for the cargo. When Apollonius compared Indian wisdom to a cargo of eastern goods, a student named Nilus requested, 'then let me share your goods – for I would gladly embark with you in your ship as a supercargo and a clerk to check your merchandise'.[59]

Each Roman ship was crewed by a staff of subordinate officers, a team of pilots, specialist lookouts and dozens of sailors. When Eudoxus explored the Indian Ocean he included physicians amongst his crew.[60] Philostratus describes how Roman managers 'set several pilots aboard the ship and made them subordinate to the oldest and wisest man. They also post several officers on the prow and set skilled sailors to man the rigging.'[61] Most freighters would have carried a team of carpenters and sail-makers to undertake any repairs needed during the voyage.[62]

Some passengers could have a religious motive for travel to the distant east. Philostratus describes a philosophy student whose 'father was captain of one the ships which the Egyptians send to India and from his dealings with the Indians of the seaboard, he brought home stories of the wise men of that region'.[63] Lucian also mentions a student of Cynic philosophy named Demetrius who was wrongly accused of temple-theft and imprisoned in Egypt along with his friend Antiphilus. The two men were freed with compensation, but Demetrius 'went off to India to visit the Brahmins, leaving his 2,000 drachmas with Antiphilus'.[64] Plutarch describes a Spartan traveller named Cleombrotus who 'had made many expeditions from Egypt to the land of the Troglodytes and sailed beyond the Red Sea. His journeys were not for business for he had sufficient wealth, but he was fond of seeing things and acquiring knowledge.'[65] Cleombrotus claimed to have met an eastern holyman, a vegetarian 'demigod' who smelt of perfumes, lived on a diet of herbs and spoke in a melodic voice.[66]

Arabian pirates operated along the east coast of the Red Sea and there were further pirate bases around the entrance to the Persian Gulf. Roman freighters therefore carried teams of mercenary archers on board to repel possible attacks. Philostratus explains that 'in the crew there is a detachment of armed men. They are needed to protect the ship from the savages of the Red Sea who are living on the eastern coast. These savages always lie in wait to attack and plunder ships on the high seas.'[67] Pliny confirms this situation with his statement, 'the voyage to India is made every year with companies of archers on board, because these seas are greatly infested by pirates'.[68]

Papyri letters reveal the type of equipment that could be carried by Roman marines and mercenary guards. A marine serving in the Alexandrian fleet decided to acquire his equipment privately rather than from the State military outlets. He wrote to his family asking for 'a cloak with belted tunic and trousers' and 'low-cut leather boots and a pair of felt stockings'. The recruit also asked his father to obtain 'a battle sword' and 'an axe, grapnel and two of the best quality spears'. He had to send for a replacement axe when his equipment was appropriated by a junior officer.[69]

The crew would have to work together to perform their particular tasks and Statius describes setting sail when the sailors 'brace the mast's rigging ropes, raise the topsail high to the upper mainmast and spread the canvas to the winds', while other crewmembers 'plumb the shallows, secure the boat that's destined to trail astern, some dive into the depths to loose and raise the fluked anchor'.[70] Philostratus describes further activity aboard a large three-masted ship as it set out to sea. He explains that, 'some of the crew row tugboats, others wind up and secure the anchors, others spread the sails out into the wind and others keep outlook at bow and stern. He added, 'if they can work in harmony, each according to his naval task, then the ship will reach the best of all safe harbours and they will make fair sailing in good weather. They will be as safe as if the god Poseidon watched over them.'[71]

Some Roman businessmen ran their own trade operations through a network of subordinate agents. Others leased out cargo space on board their ships to fellow merchants, or business associates. This meant that a single vessel could be carrying a dozen or more merchants, all expecting to make a profit in some distant market. These commercial travellers would have consulted shipping guides, such as the *Periplus of the Erythrean Sea*, in order to plan their business deals according to the ship's schedule.

Successful Roman Merchants

Most Roman merchants involved in Indian Ocean voyages probably began and finished their commercial operations in Alexandria, passing their goods on to business associates and traders who conveyed these commodities to Rome and other Mediterranean cities. But some leading Italian businessmen had connected interests that extended all the way from Rome to India. The Anni, like many prominent Italian associations, were a network of people formed from an extended family and its freedmen. They had business interests and operatives at the Italian port of Puteoli, tax-collection rights in the Red Sea and associates involved in voyages across the Indian Ocean.[72]

The Anni business-family that produced Annius Ploclamus began as grain merchants during the Republican period. In 70 BC, Cicero listed Roman merchants who could testify against a corrupt governor named Verres for his criminal actions in Sicily. One of these grain merchants was Marcus Annius, 'a most illustrious man who stood up and testified that a Roman citizen had been executed while a pirate captain had been spared'.[73]

An Italian merchant family with the name Peticii had similar commercial interests that demonstrate how international business could develop in ancient times. The Peticii were from Apulia in southern Italy and during the Republican era they established a profitable business exporting Italian wine and importing Egyptian grain to sustain the growing city of Rome. The Peticii are first mentioned during the Roman civil wars of 48 BC when Pompey was defeated at the battle of Pharsalus by Julius Caesar. Pompey fled to the coast with a few followers where he was picked up by an Italian merchant ship that had just left port in Greece. The master of the ship was a businessman named Peticius who was heading to Egypt to collect a grain cargo.[74]

Peticius and his sons also imported grain from North Africa in exchange for batches of Italian wine. A fragment of amphora found at Carthage was painted with the label C. Peticius and the name Peticius Marsus was carved on to a large pottery vat (a *dolium*) recovered from a shipwreck off the Italian coast. The Carthage find dates to about 20 BC and reveals the development of the family business across the Mediterranean shipping lanes. When Egypt became a Roman province, the Peticii expanded their wine export business to include Red Sea trade. Graffiti found on the desert road from Coptos to Berenice records the presence of a C. Peticius who was possibly a son of the merchant who shipped wine to North Africa. This younger C. Peticius carved his name in Greek and Latin on the walls of a desert shrine sacred to Pan, the Hellenic god who presided over the wilderness. Pan was part of the entourage of the Greek god Dionysus who was said to have led his followers to India and given eastern cultures a taste for wine.[75] It was therefore fitting that C. Peticius left a message at the shrine of Pan, asking for protection in the wilderness for a business that dispatched wine to India.[76]

Further evidence reveals how Red Sea trade became an important aspect of the Peticii family business. A funeral monument from the family home in southern Italy was decorated with stone panels including a relief sculpture that depicts a heavily laden camel loaded with three wine amphorae. This is a scene from the Eastern Desert and the camel is shown being led by a small figure wearing a short work-tunic. In the foreground are five men dressed in togas standing next to a Roman matron. This is perhaps a depiction of C. Peticius and his wife accompanied by their four sons who would inherit and expand the family business far beyond the Roman frontiers.[77] Generations later a further wealthy member of the family had the name 'M. Attius Peticius Marsus' inlaid in silver on a bronze statuette depicting Hercules.[78]

Some Near Eastern merchants operated Mediterranean business networks based on kinship connections. The Nabataeans had Mediterranean shippers who received incense from colleagues based at Gaza and Alexandria. Aramaic inscriptions from Puteoli reveal the presence of a Nabataean temple and trade-station at this important Italian harbour.[79] A Greek grave *stele* found nearby commemorates 'Tholomiaos son of Thaimallos, from Petra, died age 33' who was also known by the Roman name 'Maximus'.[80]

The Profits of Trade

Modern historians have deduced that there was a large increase in Mediterranean trade during the Roman era, indicated by the greater number of shipwrecks dated to this period (200 BC–AD 200).[81] Eastern trade would have contributed to this growth in Roman commerce by adding value and volume to the cargoes carried along the traditional Mediterranean sailing routes. International commerce is therefore an important factor to consider when studying the internal trade-traffic of the Roman Mediterranean.

A 200 ton cargo of black pepper was valued in Roman markets at over 6 million sesterces or 1,000 Greek talents.[82] This sum could have paid the annual wages of 6,000 legionaries (more than the manpower of an entire legion) and pepper was one of the cheapest imports from India. The profits from international trade therefore gave Roman businessmen vast sums of disposable wealth to spend on their community. In the mid-fourth century BC the tribute contributions collected by the Athenian Empire came to about 460 Greek talents per annum (equivalent to about 11 million sesterces).[83] In the Roman Imperial era, the wealthiest businessmen could match this income with the profits of their international dealings.

The ancient economy thrived through the efforts of international merchants who created unprecedented levels of interconnection, prosperity and economic development. The Roman businessmen who became successful from eastern trade ventures found that they could fund extraordinary lifestyles. Some retired to palace-like villas near the shores of the peaceful Mediterranean, established plantation-like estates and employed hundreds of agricultural workers. Others lived in city mansions and redirected their wealth into civic building programmes for the benefit of their fellow citizens. Inscriptions from Roman towns and cities reveal the costs involved in commissioning major public buildings. A medium-sized temple cost up to 70,000 sesterces to build, a theatre could be constructed for 600,000 sesterces and a small paved forum with porticoes could be established with funds worth around 200,000 sesterces.[84] A trade fortune worth 6 million sesterces could therefore fund the building programme of an entire town.

Throughout the Mediterranean, civic munificence reached significant new levels under Roman rule. This development was partly due to commercial wealth being redirected back into the community by business benefactors who valued the reputation that came from acts of public generosity. Petronius lampoons the lavish lifestyles of successful Roman businessmen when he describes the actions and attitudes of a fictional freedman named Trimalchio. Trimalchio declares, 'in one voyage I gained a good ten million sesterces. I immediately bought back all my old master's estates. I built a house, invested in slaves and in haulage. Whatever I touched grew like a honeycomb.'[85]

Trimalchio explains how his commercial exploits had prospered. 'When I was receiving more money than the entire revenue of my native country, I retired from business and began advancing loans to freedmen.' This suggests a genuine situation, as the richest Roman businessmen earned more than the tribute of entire provinces. Trimalchio describes investing in business ventures worth up to 30 million sesterces and sending ships to Rome loaded with cargoes worth 6 million sesterces.[86] This could have been a regular practice for Roman merchants involved in trade ventures to India, including the merchant named Varus who operated several ships from Berenice and the businesswomen Olympia and Isidora who had a small commercial fleet at the Red Sea ports.[87] Juvenal describes merchants such as these when he writes about traders 'who run the risk for the sake of 1,000 talents (6 million sesterces) or a hundred mansions. Look at our ports and observe how our seas are crowded with big ships.'[88]

Philostratus describes a businessman named Proclus who made a fortune in Alexandrian commerce, 'but wanted to enjoy the peace and quiet of Athens'. He therefore, 'moved to Athens, bringing with him a large sum of money, many slaves and a range of splendid and ornate household furnishings'. He arrived to find that a friend in the city was in financial difficulty and was being forced to sell his home. Proclus repurchased the property at a cost of 10,000 Greek drachma (40,000 sesterces), then bought four city mansions in the area for his own use. Two of these residences were in Athens itself, one was at the port city of Piraeus, and the other was at nearby Eleusis. Proclus conducted his business activities from his new headquarters in Greece and he regularly received eastern imports forwarded by his commercial contacts in Alexandria. Philostratus explains that 'Proclus used to receive regular supplies of incense, ivory, myrrh, papyrus, books, and other merchandise directly from Egypt. He would sell these goods to those who traded in such things.'[89] With the profits, Proclus decided to establish his own academy of philosophy at Athens with a suite of monumental buildings.

The most successful merchants might have five or more large vessels in service at any one time. Although fictional, Trimalchio claims to have started his business by having five ships built to transport wine and Lucian dreamed of owning 'five ships, larger and finer than the *Isis*', with each vessel consisting of 'that unsinkable Three-Mast type'.[90] Egyptian papyri provide additional information about Alexandrian businessmen, including a ship-owner who had eight vessels with an aggregate capacity of 1,300 tons. A further businessman registered three ships able to carry a total of 500 tons (average 165 tons per ship).[91]

Philostratus suggests that some Roman merchants formed groups of four investors to fund Mediterranean voyages.[92] A papyrus from Theadelphia in Egypt records how a Roman banker loaned money to four Greek shippers from Ascalon in Palestine to finance a Mediterranean trade run.[93] If four or five business partners each contributed 200,000 sesterces gained through loans, or the profits of Mediterranean commerce, they could finance a trade venture to India worth a million sesterces.[94] This was possible since a 200-ton grain cargo bought in Alexandria for 50,000 sesterces could be sold in Rome for 100,000 sesterces, providing market conditions were favourable and the transport costs were low.[95] The accumulated profits of several voyages could therefore be used to finance eastern ventures. Modern historians estimate that it would have cost between 170,000–300,000 sesterces to build a 300 ton merchant ship, so new vessels could easily be built from the profits of grain trade.[96]

The profits from international trade were enormous, but the risks were equally great. During the height of the Pax Romana, distant commerce offered prime opportunities for high-risk excitement and riches. As Juvenal explains, 'a merchant will load his ship up to the gunwale with goods with only a plank between him and the deep. He will endure hardship and danger for a few pieces of silver.' Juvenal pictures the scene when 'the clouds and thunder threaten and the merchant who is shipping grain or pepper cries out, "We will go! See that black sky? Those dark clouds are nothing but summer lightning."' But if the merchant misjudged conditions, his ship could be smashed apart by storms. As Juvenal reminds his readers, 'this very night the poor wretch may be cast adrift among broken timbers and engulfed by waves. But he will still clutch his purse with his left hand, or even grip it in his teeth.'[97]

These were the risks involved on voyages to build-up a commercial business, but for many Romans who sought prosperity and adventure, the rewards offset the danger. As Juvenal explains, 'if you are too lazy to endure the weary labours of the military camp, if the sound of the horn and war trumpet withers your soul, buy something that you can sell at half as much again . . . and you should make no distinction between animal hides and unguents because the smell of profit is good whatever it comes from'.[98]

Rich businessmen offered loans to merchants who lacked the funds they needed to conduct their own ventures. In the Republican era, the Roman elite became involved in complex business enterprises involving overseas commerce. Plutarch describes how Cato the Elder 'required his borrowers to form a large company and when there were fifty partners and as many ships, he took one share in the company. His business interests were represented by his freedman Quintio, who accompanied his clients in all their voyages. In this way only a small part of his funds were at risk and large profits were guaranteed.'[99] These deals channelled money from landed estates into commercial enterprises and since the loans were repaid with interest, both the lender and borrower profited from a successful venture.

Foreign Merchants in Roman Egypt

Trade from the Red Sea was not confined to Roman subjects and pottery shards scratched with Himyaritic and Sabaean writing have been found at Myos Hormos. These fragments indicate the presence of south Arabian merchants in Roman territory.[100] The homeland of the Minaeans was a landlocked region in southwest Arabia, but graffiti from their merchants has been found on the road leading from Myos Hormos to Coptos.[101]

Indian merchants travelled to Roman Egypt aboard their own ships and businessmen from the subcontinent were regular visitors to Alexandria. Indian pottery has been found at Myos Hormos including fragments of fine tableware and ordinary cooking pots. A few of these pieces are marked with Prakrit letters, which was a common form of the Indian language Sanskrit. Others were labelled with Tamil-Brahmin script, the preferred writing system in southern India.[102] Some of the pottery is scratched with Tamil names, including 'Catan' and 'Kanan', who were probably senior merchants.[103] Fragments of Roman amphorae are also marked with Tamil names, possibly to indicate ownership of the delivery batches being forwarded to India.[104] One piece of pottery recorded the names of three individuals called Halaka, Vinhudata and Nakada along with a list of possible stores including oil, meat and wine.[105]

The Greek orator Dio Chrysostom mentions how Indian people could be seen at large gatherings at Alexandria, including the crowd that came to hear his speeches. He describes how 'Ethiopians and Arabians from distant regions and Bactrians, Scythians, Persians and a few Indians all help to make up the audience in your theatre and sit beside you on each occasion'.[106] These exotic travellers caught the imagination of Roman subjects and Xenophon of Ephesus wrote a popular fiction set in Egypt which included an Indian character named Psammis. Psammis is a Greek name, but in the story he is an Indian merchant-prince, 'an Indian ruler, come to see the city and do business'. Psammis purchases the heroine Anthia, who has been wrongfully sold as a slave in Alexandria. He then takes her on a caravan journey back through the Eastern Desert with 'a host of camels, asses, and packhorses carrying a great deal of gold, silver and clothing'. But fate intervenes and the caravan is attacked by bandits who kill Psammis and capture Anthia before she can be sent to India.[107]

Some Indian businessmen visiting Alexandria travelled onward to Rome. This is evidenced by Martial who complained about a Roman woman named Caelia who gave her affections to exotic foreigners. Martial depicts Caelia associating with Egyptians from Alexandria and a 'dark-skinned Indian from the Eastern Ocean'.[108]

Slaves

In Roman society the ownership of rare and exotic eastern slaves signalled wealth and status. Roman women sought Indian slaves as personal attendants to escort them through public places, or as maidservants to attend to their fashion interests. The Roman poet Tibullus describes a matron who was often seen in public with 'dark Indians, scorched by the sun'.[109]

Many slaves imported from the distant east were bought by Roman households to be trained for prominent domestic duties. Eastern males were selected to serve guests at banquets where their presence indicated the host's wealth and cultural sophistication. Horace mentions a slave from the Indus region named Hydaspes who served expensive wines to the favoured guests of his wealthy master and Petronius describes how 'long-haired Ethiopians' waited on visitors attending a grand feast.[110]

Juvenal speaks about receiving his cup from the 'bony black hands of a Moor, so dark that you might walk straight into him at night'. Meanwhile, the host Virro and his favoured guests were served 'by the choice youth of Asia, bought for a sum greater than the entire fortune of the warlike Tullus or Ancus when they were kings of Rome'. Virro was personally served by one particular Asian youth who Juvenal describes as 'that Getulian Ganymede, who cost so many thousand sesterces'.[111]

When the philosopher Favourinus died he bequeathed his personal library and his Indian servant to his friend Herodes. Philostratus describes how this Indian had served wine to the two men during their philosophical debates and would sometimes join in their discussions, speaking with a curious mix of Greek and Indian words.[112] Juvenal mentions that wealthy Roman women paid Indian astrologers to reveal their fortunes since they were 'skilled in the stars and celestial spheres'.[113] Eastern slaves were also employed in the Roman arena to add further spectacle to the games. They are described by Petronius as the 'dark skinned' servants with 'long hair' who watered the sand in the amphitheatre to disperse blood trails, or lay the dust that might obscure combat.[114]

The rarest and most expensive servants imported from eastern kingdoms would have been eunuchs. Eunuchs were employed at feasts to personally serve their masters with the best wines. Martial describes how a eunuch watched for his master 'to signal him with snapping fingers and pour him wine'.[115] The *Alexandrian Tariff* records that Indian eunuchs were subject to Roman import taxes which confirms that they were being sold to private buyers.[116] The prices paid for eunuchs were extraordinarily high and could reach more than 100,000 sesterces for a single person.[117] This Roman fashion for exotic attendants attracted criticism from the Emperor Tiberius who addressed the Senate with the words, 'Where should I begin my prohibitions and attempt to revert to older standards? Shall I begin with the vast mansions, or these cosmopolitan hordes of servants?'[118]

But some of the poorer classes in Roman society also owned slaves from distant regions. Virgil describes a simple Roman farmer who owned a female servant named Scybale. She rose in the morning and kindled the fire as the farmer prepared a basic meal for them both before going out to work on the land. Virgil describes Scybale with 'every part of her figure proclaiming her native land as Africa; her dark skin, her full lips and her curly hair'.[119]

Roman servants were sometimes given names relating to their place of origin and this included slaves imported from the distant east. Names including 'Indos' and 'Indicos' appear in the classical records, but coincidently these were similar to a personal name used by Celtic peoples.[120] There is a further complication because some Roman parents possibly named their child 'India' to evoke the image of something precious and exotic. This is evidenced by a papyrus letter written by a Roman lady called 'Indica'.[121] An urban inscription from the Empire records the name C. Sornatius Indus, but the man was freeborn and his parents had Greek names.[122] Women called 'Inde' are also attested in a few inscriptions from the city of Rome, but their origins remain obscure.[123]

New DNA evidence also confirms that people with Far Eastern ancestry were living in the Roman Empire. Archaeologists excavated an imperial estate at Vignari in southern Italy which included a cemetery containing the bodies of slave-workers. One of the remains belonged to a man who possessed Far Eastern ancestry inherited from his mother. Perhaps this man was descended from some eastern concubine and being born a slave, he was drafted into the workforce at Vignari to assist with textile production at the site. When he died he was buried with the other slaves in a simple grave on a bleak hillside in southern Italy. His sole possession was placed next to his body, a plain wooden food-bowl to take with him into the afterlife.[124]

Cargoes of Sand

One of the most unusual imports from the east to reach Rome was sand. The Emperor Augustus believed that one of the greatest public legacies of his reign was to provide the city of Rome with permanent civic buildings constructed in marble and designed with grand architectural features. Suetonius explains that before the Imperial era, 'Rome had not been adorned as the dignity of the Empire demanded' and that Augustus made great efforts to 'beautify the city so that he could justly boast that he had found it constructed of brick and left it built in marble'.[125] During the height of the Roman Empire there was a fashion for marble as a building material to adorn temples, civic buildings, palaces and private mansions. This transformation of Rome from brick buildings to marble edifices was made possible by imports of abrasive sand from the east that enabled the mass quarrying of monumental masonry blocks.

In ancient times, blocks of marble were extracted from the hillside by using a long iron blade suspended in a rectangular wooden frame. The sides of a quarry were almost perpendicular and the workers would cut blocks and slabs by making downward vertical strokes with the saw-blade. The blade was pushed back and forth, but the real incision was made by abrasive sand that was washed into the deepening groove around the saw. By using this technique an iron blade could eventually cut through even the hardest marble, providing the sand chosen for the task was sufficiently abrasive. Pliny confirms that 'marble cutting might seem to be done with iron, but it is actually achieved with sand. The saw merely presses the sand into a very thinly-traced line and the rapid back and forth friction cuts the stone.'[126]

The technique created thin slabs of marble that were used to pave plazas and clad the façade of Roman buildings constructed primarily from brick, or ancient concrete. For circular pillars, a thin wire or blade could be held under tension to cut curved surfaces with a bow shaped rig. In the early part of the twentieth century American quarry workers used similar sand-cutting techniques to hew stone blocks. Even with modern refinements to the process they could only achieve an average cutting speed of one or two inches per hour. They also found that the amount of sharp sand required to cut a single, square block of marble was approximately the same size as the block itself.[127]

Sand-cutting techniques allowed Roman masons to mass produce blocks and slabs of marble for the ambitious construction schemes devised by the early emperors. Pliny reveals that the best sand for these marble-cutting operations came from the east and in particular 'the Ethiopian variety of this sand is the most highly esteemed'. The minute particles of this abrasive mix flowed easily through the water that lubricated the cutting blade, without snagging, or creating jagged scores into the sliced stone. As Pliny explains, 'the sand from Ethiopia is finer and therefore cuts without leaving any roughness'.[128]

Many raw blocks of newly-cut marble would have been transported in a relatively rough state as surface damage could be expected during haulage. On the building site the block would be polished using a wet-paste made by fine-particle sand in a process that created a smooth luminous surface for the finished marble. Indian sand was coarser and this meant that labourers who worked with this material could achieve a faster finish with less effort. The marble floors of public buildings in Rome and the gleaming surfaces of monumental edifices required continual maintenance and slaves would polish the stonework with Indian sand. Pliny reports that 'the Indian sand will not give the hewn stone such a smooth surface, but it is strongly recommended by the people who polish marble and it is also needed to clean marble surfaces as they deteriorate'. Consequently, 'the Indian variety is almost as highly praised as Ethiopian sand'. Enormous quantities of abrasive sand were utilised in Roman building projects and Pliny reminds his reader that this material was coming from an overseas territory that only a few generations earlier Romans would never have conceived of visiting, even for something as attractive and valuable as a pearl.[129] Now men were crossing storm laden oceans and facing shipwreck, piracy and great perils, for the sake of a cargo of sand.

The Periplus of the Erythraean Sea
A Roman merchant guidebook called the *Periplus of the Erythraean Sea* contains a list of the main products available from eastern ports. The *Periplus* is a short practical handbook that contains sixty-six concise paragraphs written in a popular form of Greek known as *koine*. It describes Roman trade ventures across the Indian Ocean, including contacts with ports and markets on the East coast of Africa, exchanges with the regimes of southern Arabia and commerce with the kingdoms of ancient India.

The unnamed author was probably a Greek merchant from Roman Egypt who was based at Coptos or Alexandria.[130] This man had first-hand experience in sea voyages to India and seems to have written his trade report in about AD 50. The author of the *Periplus* was probably writing to inform fellow merchants and investors interested in the possibilities of international trade. The report became part of a collection of merchant documents assembled by Roman government around AD 52.

The unnamed author describes three connected trade courses that led from Egypt across, or around, the Indian Ocean. One route led down the east coast of Africa from Ethiopia to Somalia and from the Horn of Africa to a distant trade post in Tanzania. Another course led around Arabia to connect with ports on the southern seaboard of the Arabian Peninsula in Yemen and Dhofar. A final course took Roman ships across the Indian Ocean using the seasonal monsoon winds to reach city-ports on the west coast of India.

The *Periplus* describes important markets and ports along these three main trade routes listing what foreign goods were available at different trade centres and what Roman commodities could be offered in return. This information would have been useful to less experienced merchants and also to speculators who lent money to the traders and businessmen who specialised in particular goods. The author of the *Periplus* describes the monsoon sailing from direct experience and uses phrases such as 'we set a course' and 'we put on extra speed'.[131] He had visited ports in northwest India and his account of the region contains several first-hand observations concerning tides and sailing hazards. The *Periplus* also offers key information about which particular regime, or ruler, held power in certain regions and who had authority over the leading ports. This was important because ancient regimes controlled a large share of many local products either from tax, tribute, or state-owned resources.

During the time of the *Periplus* most Roman ships regularly sailed no further than the Tamil ports on the southwest coast of India. But the author gives his reader a brief account of the east coast of India as far as the Ganges. His information probably came from accounts offered by the few Roman captains who had explored this route. Indian merchants may have been another of his sources, but they offered Roman traders only limited information about their voyages around the Bay of Bengal.

The Date of the *Periplus*

The date of the *Periplus* can be determined by the political and geographical information offered by its author. The *Periplus* mentions the Nabataean King Malichus II who was in power from AD 40 to AD 70.[132] The author also describes how the Saka Kingdom in western India was ruled by a warlord named 'Manbanos', who must be King Nahapana because of the phonic similarity and the match of dates. Indian coins and inscriptions confirm that Nahapana held power in northwest India during the mid-first century AD.[133]

The *Periplus* describes how the Sakas seized territories on the Konkan seaboard from the Satavahana realm. Inscriptions from an Indian holy site called Nasik confirm that the Sakas held the territory for several years, during which time they offered royal gifts to Hindu shrines that were commemorated in dedicatory inscriptions. These inscriptions offer dates based on a royal calendar that counted from about AD 10. This was the year when the last Indo-Scythian kings lost power in the Indus region and the Saka regime in Gujarat became an independent realm. Saka inscriptions at Nasik dated from 'year 41' to 'year 46' were probably set up between AD 51 and AD 56. The *Periplus* must date to this short period before the Satavahanas reclaimed their former territories, which included Nasik.

There is also the issue of Sri Lanka which is described in the *Periplus* as a vast unexplored island beyond the scope of regular Roman trade voyages. Roman merchants speculated that Sri Lanka and Madagascar might be part of the same enormous island. The *Periplus* reports that in Sri Lanka 'only the northern regions are civilised' and the island 'extends almost to the part of Azania (East Africa) that lies opposite'.[134] This viewpoint must pre-date the reception of a Sri Lankan embassy in Rome by the Emperor Claudius (AD 41–54).

The *Periplus* was probably amongst a collection of trade reports assembled by the governor of Egypt when Sinhalese ambassadors arrived in his province (AD 52). The reports were copied and sent to Rome with the ambassadors so that central government could appraise the possible significance of Sri Lanka and the scope of eastern trade. Some of these reports entered imperial archives and were later read by Pliny the Elder who cites Indian Ocean sailing times dated to this period. Pliny reports that Roman ships left for India on 'the sixth day of the Egyptian month Mechir, just before January the thirteenth in our calendar'.[135]

The two calendars were misaligned, so these dates only coincided in the four years between AD 48 and AD 52.[136] The surviving *Periplus* was probably archived in Alexandria where it was transferred into Byzantine State records in late antiquity. The *Periplus* is the only document of its kind to survive and it therefore offers modern scholars a unique insight into the scope and significance of international maritime commerce in ancient times.

CHAPTER NINE

East Africa and the Aksumite Kingdom

In ancient times territories on both sides of the Aden Gulf produced and traded large quantities of incense and fragrant woods. Since the time of the Pharaoh Queen Hatshepsut, the Egyptians had used the Red Sea to bypass Nubia and deal directly with Somalia (1473–1458 BC). This was the route chosen by the Ptolemais when they established new Red Sea ports to stage elephant hunting expeditions down the east coast of Africa (283–217 BC). From the Augustan era onwards Rome dominated Red Sea trade and most East African products entered the Empire through these sea-lanes. Strabo confirms that 'at the present time most aromatics are transported via the Nile to Alexandria'.[1] Beyond Ethiopia, the Romans called Somalia and the Horn of Africa the 'Far-Side' since in their terms this coast faced Arabia.

With sea transport nearly thirty times less expensive than land haulage, the Red Sea route was the most advantageous course for Roman merchants to make direct contact with markets in Sub-Saharan Africa.[2] Furthermore, Roman ships making voyages to East Africa did not need to be large vessels in order to make a sub-stantial profit from this commerce. A cargo-hold filled with just 30 tons of frank-incense could be worth more than a million sesterces in Roman markets.[3] There were probably more than a hundred ships involved in this commerce since Strabo mentions large fleets bound for Somalia and India in the same sentence. He confirms that 'at this present time large fleets are sent as far as India and the extremities of Africa, from which the most valuable cargoes are brought to Egypt'.[4]

Roman ships entering the Indian Ocean attempted only one sailing per year when the seasonal monsoon winds favoured relatively safe, fast travel. Wind conditions permitted Roman ships to make voyages down the African coast anytime from January to September, but most vessels sailing to Somalia sailed in September, nearly two months after their colleagues had left for India.[5] This schedule meant they could dominate loading activities at the Egyptian Red Sea ports during the month of August. It also allowed a prompt return when the incoming northeast monsoon reached east Africa in November.

Below Egypt, the African shoreline of the Red Sea was largely desolate. The seaboard was fronted by a thirty-mile wide stretch of coast that was generally unsuitable for agriculture. The native peoples occupying this region tended to be coastal fishermen, or inland hunter-gatherer nomads subject to local chiefs. The *Periplus* describes how the *Ichthyophagoi* (Fish-eaters) occupied the coastline, 'living in scattered groups in primitive huts built in limited areas'. Inland regions were 'inhabited by *Barbaroi* (Barbarians) and beyond them, *Agriophagoi* (Wild-animal-eaters) and *Moschophagoi* (Foliage-eaters) who are organised in chief-doms'. Roman sailors called this part of Africa 'the Country of the Barbaroi' or the 'Troglodytes'.[6] Somewhere inland was the metropolis of Meroe, but this Nilotic kingdom had no trade presence on the Red Sea coast.

Roman ships sailing 450 miles down the Barbaroi coast reached the first African trade-station at Ptolemais Theron (Ptolemais of the Hunts).[7] This out-post was founded as a hunting-station by the Hellenic King Ptolemy II Phila-delphus (283–246 BC) who sent expeditions of Greek mercenaries into the region to capture live elephants. A Greek general named Eumedes established Ptolemais Theron as a defensive outpost and enclosed a rare stretch of arable land suit-able for farming. At first the Greek intrusion was opposed by the local African population, but Eumedes was able to win their support. Strabo describes how, 'unannounced, Eumedes built a ditch and wall across the peninsula. Then, by his courteous treatment of those who tried to hinder his work, he persuaded them to be his friends instead of his foes'.[8] When the Greek hunters had decimated the nearby elephant herds, they moved their base-camps to more distant coasts. Sometime after this Theron fell back under the control of the local population.

The history of Theron was known to the author of the *Periplus* who reports that, 'in the days of the Ptolemies, the royal huntsmen made their way inland from this site'. However, by the Roman period there were no elephant herds nearby and ivory could only occasionally be found at the settlement. The *Periplus* describes Theron as 'a small port of trade' and explains that 'the place has no harbour and only offers refuge to small craft'. The main product on offer was turtle-shell obtained by offshore fishing, and a limited amount of small light-coloured tortoise shields gathered from local land hunts.[9] Few Roman ships stopped at Theron and the *Periplus* does not recommend any cargo suitable for trade ashore. Pliny estimated that Ptolemy Theron was on the same latitude as Meroe, but the two sites were not connected by any significant trade routes.[10]

The Aksumite Kingdom of Ethiopia

By the time of the *Periplus*, Ptolemais Theron was under the authority of an African King named Zoskales who ruled an inland kingdom called Aksum (AD 50).[11] The main trade port of the Aksumite Kingdom was a Red Sea settle-ment called Adulis which was about 340 miles, or five days' sail, south of Theron.[12] Pliny calls this region 'Anzania' and uses accounts from the Augustan era in his description of its resources. He reports that large quantities of turtle were fished near islands in the Azanian Sea and most of this shell was brought to Adulis for international trade.[13] Back in the Roman Empire, the shell was cut into panels and polished to decorate expensive furniture with lustrously patterned veneers.

There were legends that Adulis was founded by runaway slaves from Egypt and the settlement was therefore known as Freeman's Town. In reality, its origins were obscure and it is possible that the site began as a Ptolemaic hunting station similar to Ptolemais Theron.[14] Like Theron, Adulis was situated on a small area of arable land that could support a permanent community with locally grown produce. Pliny describes early Adulis as 'a very large trading centre of the Troglodytes and the Ethiopians that is five days' sail from Ptolemais Theron'. In the Augustan era, African people brought 'a large quantity of ivory, rhinoceros horn, hippopotamus hides, tortoiseshell, apes and slaves to the site'.[15]

When Pliny describes Adulis he makes no mention of the inland Ethiopian kingdom of Aksum that by AD 50 had seized control of Adulis and designated the settlement as its primary port. The *Periplus* describes Adulis as a 'legally limited port of trade' (*emporion nominon*) positioned on a deep bay that extended due south (Zula Gulf in modern Eritrea). Before the Aksumite takeover, Roman ships could moor at a small landmass on the outer part of the bay called Didoros Island. The custom was to name islands and landmarks after the Greek captains who discovered important features of the coastline. When Strabo describes east Africa he lists a range of headlands, harbours and elephant hunting grounds that were named after the commanders of early Ptolemaic expeditions.[16] Didoros Island was connected to the coast by a tidal causeway which limited access and offered some defence for Roman shore-camps. But the site was vulnerable to attack from local raiders and the Aksumite regime could not provide sufficient protection for visitors. The *Periplus* describes how 'the Barbaroi dwelling nearby used to over-run the island' and seize cargo headed for Adulis. In response, visiting Roman traders moved their operations about twenty miles offshore and occupied a new island called Oreine (Hilly) which was opposite Zula Bay and could only be reached by boat. The *Periplus* explains, 'at the present time incoming vessels moor at Oreine because of raids from the mainland'.[17]

Adulis received traffic from both sides of the Red Sea and was visited by Arab ships from Yemen.[18] Procopius reports that local ships took five days to cross the gulf between Africa and Arabia on voyages involving sailings that continued throughout the night.[19] In the time of the *Periplus*, Adulis was considered 'a fair-sized village' and its residents included Roman subjects who remained at the site all year for trade purposes.[20]

During the first century AD, one of the main products shipped from Adulis was turtle-shell, 'brought to the trade port by the Ichthyophagoi' who hunted turtles around the sandy-shores of nearby islands. The *Periplus* also describes a beach about ninety miles south of Adulis where obsidian could be collected from black volcanic rocks deep beneath the sand. The resource was 'a natural creation of that place alone' and although the area was claimed by the Aksumite Kingdom, it was not fully exploited for this valuable, glass-like material.[21] Pliny reveals that the Romans used obsidian to make cult statues and dark mirrors that reflected 'shadows rather than clear images'.[22] A flake of obsidian could also be used to test precious stones since it would scratch a white mark on glass copies.[23]

The Aksumites controlled the ivory trade and sent the product to Adulis via an Ethiopian city called Koloe. The *Periplus* describes Koloe as 'the first trading station for ivory' and reports that the city was three days inland from Adulis. Roman merchants making this journey had the option to travel further inland to the Ethiopian capital Aksum situated five days from Koloe and a total of eight days from the coast.

The *Periplus* calls Aksum a metropolis which confirms its position as the capital of the Aksumite Kingdom. The city stood in the fertile highlands of northern Ethiopia in a region grazed by herds of forest elephants and white rhino. The *Periplus* explains that 'into Aksum is brought all the ivory from beyond the Nile and the Kyeneion for transport down to Adulis'. The Kyeneion could be the Tekeze River which flowed through deep canyons to join with the Blue Nile. It was reported that 'the mass of elephants and rhinos slaughtered inhabit the upland regions, though on rare occasions they are also seen along the shore near Adulis'.[24]

Evidence for the rise of the Aksumite Kingdom comes from the discovery of fragments of first century Roman glassware near the site of their ancient capital, along with contemporary coins minted by Arab regimes in Yemen. The Ethiopian King Zoskales had his royal court at Aksum and from there he controlled the traffic in ivory and horn. These products probably entered the Aksumite treasury as taxes from subject communities, tribute from vassal peoples and income from royal hunts.[25]

Turtle-shell and Ivory

The prime exports from the Aksumite Kingdom were ivory, tortoise and turtle-shell. This trade was highly lucrative since the Romans had a great desire for expensive craft items made from exotic eastern materials. In the Republican period senior magistrates conducted State business while seated on special ivory decorated chairs known as *curule* seats.[26] But by the first century AD, many members of the Roman elite had developed an obsession with lavish ornaments and fitted out their mansions with expensive ivory and turtle-shell furnishings.

Martial writes about a wealthy acquaintance named Amoenus who bought a large property for 100,000 sesterces. Amoenus decorated the household with so much fashionable furniture and costly decoration that he demanded 200,000 sesterces as the sale price. Martial suggests that Amoenus was 'trying to cheat the purchaser by art and cunning, for his real house is hidden amid rich furniture and gorgeous decoration'.[27] Plutarch confirms that a finely decorated house was a platform to impress influential people and functioned 'like a theatre and stage prepared for visitors'.[28]

Ovid describes an earthly mansion visited by the gods imagining its inner rooms richly decorated with ivory and tortoiseshell.[29] Virgil describes a traditional rural villa that lacked these current fashions as a building without 'doorposts inlaid with beautiful tortoiseshell, no attire of gold brocade, no connoisseur's bronzes. No foreign dyes to stain the white fleeces and no exotic spices like cinnamon to spoil the olive oil'.[30] Horace denounced 'vain riches' explaining that there was 'no ivory or gilded panelling gleaming in my house'.[31] Propertius expressed similar sentiments when he explained that his reputation depended on poetry, since his house contained no 'ivory ceilings with gilded beams'.[32]

The expense of this consumer fashion is revealed by Martial who challenged a wealthy Roman collector named Quintus. When Quintus boasted about the vast fortune he had spent in acquiring a few pieces of exquisite furniture, Martial retorted, 'so your fairly small collection cost you a million sesterces? Well Quintus, you might think that this proves your cleverness, but you are wrong. Only a small intellect could spend this amount of money on that furniture.'[33]

The town houses and country villas of wealthy Romans were stocked with fashionable ornamental furniture made from ebony and other exotic woods, embellished with bright turtle-shell veneers and ivory inlays. These materials were used to make dining couches, centrepiece tables and more private furniture, including beds. There was also a fashion for veneering objects with iridescent nacre, the light reflective surface of certain sea-shells known as 'mother of pearl'. A business client or political associate invited into a household furnished with these ornaments would immediately recognise that he was dealing with an important, wealthy man.

Pliny explains that 'the practice of cutting tortoise-shell into plates and using it to decorate bedsteads and cabinets' was introduced by a man named Carvilius Pollio in the first century BC.[34] Juvenal describes this era as a period 'when no one seriously considered what species of turtle swimming in the ocean-wave might make a fine and notable headrest for the elite'.[35]

But the fashion took hold and when Varro offered a metaphor to illustrate how foreign words were entering the Latin language, he explained 'we prefer to have some couches inlaid with ivory and others with tortoiseshell and in a similar manner we adorn our speech'.[36]

Ancient texts suggest that ivory was valued at 9 denarii per pound and turtle-shell at perhaps 6 denarii per pound.[37] The *Hermapollon* was carrying a cargo of Indian ivory valued for customs tax at almost half a million sesterces.[38] When Seneca demands 'bring before me the trophies of luxury', first on the list is 'the shell of the tortoise, an unpleasant and slothful brute, bought for immense sums and ornamented with the most elaborate care'. Seneca also mentions that 'the contrast of colours is enhanced by the use of dyes resembling the natural tints'.[39] Pliny suggests that turtle-shell could be dyed with expensive Tyrian purple pigments or stained to resemble the most expensive woods and create 'a more costly citrus and counterfeit maple'.[40] In wealthy homes these shell veneers decorated everything from inlaid panel doors to the surface of musical instruments. Further evidence comes from Juvenal who suggests that the sons of the Roman nobility were exhibited in cradles adorned with delicate tortoiseshell.[41] Tortoiseshell was frequently displayed alongside ivory and Martial writes about Libyan table-tops balanced on Indian tusks. He describes a character named Mamurra 'walking long and anxiously through the bazaars where golden Rome proudly displays its riches'. There he 'uncovers various tables, square ones and round; next he asks to see some rich ivory ornaments, those displayed on the upper shelves. Then, four times he measures a dinner couch for six guests, adorned with tortoiseshell.'[42]

Shell-inlaid couches were displayed as centrepieces at Roman feasts attended by clients and specially invited guests. Martial composed the following verse, 'accept this semi-circular couch decorated with crescents of tortoise-shell – it will accommodate eight people so let your friends take a seat'.[43] In another gift-verse, Martial plays upon Roman consumer confusion about the origin of the shells used to create their specially veneered furniture. He writes about a dinner table, 'if you think that I am adorned with female tortoiseshell from the land, you are mistaken; I am embellished with shell from the male sea-turtle'.[44]

Distinctive twisting shapes in the wood-grain of ebony furniture added value to the object when the finished piece was polished to a smooth finish by Roman craftsmen. Seneca confirms the value of the most expensive imports when he writes, 'I see tables and pieces of wood valued at the price of a senator's estate (1 million sesterces) and these are all the more precious when the surface is twisted with the outline of tree knots.'[45] Part of the appeal of these exotic woods was their fragrant sap and Pliny reports that ebony wood-shavings produced a pleasing smell when burnt. By his era, the Romans were importing small thickets of ebony branches to be burned as a form of incense.[46]

Juvenal suggests that a mansion crowded with valuable furniture would be a burden to the owner because of the risk of fire-damage and theft. He claims that a wealthy man named Licinus had troops of slaves with fire-buckets stationed around his property at night in case a house-fire might destroy his precious collection of ornamental objects, which included valuable ivory furniture and turtle-shell plaques.[47] According to Juvenal, 'nowadays a rich man takes no pleasure in his dinner, his turbot and his venison have no taste, his unguents and his roses no sweetness, unless the broad slabs of his dinner-table rest upon solid ivory'.[48]

The Jewish philosopher Philo was critical of Roman competition to purchase and display the most expensive furniture. He reports, 'now even the poles of our ladders are ornamented with ivory feet and craftsmen inlay our beds with costly mother-of-pearl and variegated tortoise-shell – all at a great expense of labour, money and time'.[49] Clement of Alexandria likewise criticised 'ebony furniture, tripods fashioned of ivory, couches inlaid with ivory on silver feet, and folding-doors variegated with turtle-shell and studded with gold'. He argues, 'a simple loaf can surely be served on something other than an ivory footed table' and 'a simple box bed can offer the same rest as an ivory couch'.[50] But ivory received the endorsement of the Emperors and when Statius describes the imperial palace he depicts rows of the most expensive tables fitted with ivory legs.[51] Apuleius also imagines the house of a Roman noblewoman containing ivory tables as an indication of her status and wealth.[52]

Ivory furniture was a treasured item and when Propertius requested a humble funeral he instructed his friends, 'do not lay out a bed or couch with ivory posts for me'.[53] Archaeology has confirmed that some wealthy Romans were laid out on their ivory funerary couches for cremation. The charred remains of human bone and ivory fragments were interred in the same receptacle for burial.[54]

Ivory was used in religious rituals and Propertius describes an animal sacrifice at the Temple of Apollo accompanied by the music of an ivory flute.[55] Virgil also imagines an animal sacrifice on a rural Etruscan altar accompanied by the playing of an ivory pipe.[56] The interior of temples was sometimes decorated with ivory and when Petronius wanted to emphasise the modesty of a rural shrine he wrote that the place, 'had no Indian ivory and was without the gleam of gold'.[57] By tradition only a few statues of the gods were carved from expensive ivory. Lucian has Zeus and Hermes viewing all the cult statues venerated by mankind. Hermes comments, 'you see the Greek contingent, they have grace, beauty and artistic workmanship in marble or bronze, but only the most costly are ivory and there is just the occasional gleam of gold'.[58] Vertumnus, the Italian god of seasons had simple religious rites and Propertius has him saying 'I enjoy no ivory temple: it's enough that I oversee the Roman Forum.'[59]

The fashion for items manufactured in ivory extended to smaller everyday artefacts including writing implements (*styluses*), combs and hairpins which are often recovered during excavations of Roman remains.[60] Delicate ivory ornaments carved by Roman craftsmen were popular gifts exchanged between friends and associates during the midwinter Saturnalia festival. Martial composed verses to accompany gifts of costly ivory everyday objects including back scratchers.[61] For the gift of ivory writing tablets he recommends, 'if dull-coloured waxen-tablets strain your sight, let the black letters be depicted on snow-white ivory'.[62] For ivory dice, Martial comments, 'when these dice come up lucky you will surely say they were a great present'.[63] For costly ivory cash-boxes he uses the words, 'it is not right to fill these coffers with any coin other than gold' and to accompany the gift of an ivory medicine-chest he says, 'fill this with the appliances of the healing art'.[64] Ovid also describes medicines stored in an ivory casket and explains that 'ivory from India is carved and cut to suit the luxury of our times'.[65] Propertius mentions an ivory plectrum in one of his poems and complains about shopping trips into the centre of Rome where his lover would demand expensive items 'wanting to hold a cold crystal ball in her hand and longing for ivory dice or whatever glitters on the Sacred Way'.[66] But ivory had more pragmatic uses and Martial describes a woman who had teeth re-created in the material.[67]

When Juvenal wanted to stress his 'humble status' he explained that 'I am destitute of ivory, my dice and abacus beads are not made of it and even my knife-handles are made of bone'.[68] By the time Pliny was writing, demand for ivory was so great that craftsmen began to split and whiten imports of dense elephant bone to make it resemble tusk.[69]

Pliny reports that some Roman soldiers paid for their swords to be enhanced with ivory hilts and silver chains.[70] Brightly polished turtle-shell was also used to veneer small objects including combs, brushes and brooches. Rhino-horn was carved and polished to make cups and Juvenal describes a wealthy Roman man who carried a prized oil-flask made from this exotic material into the public baths.[71] Martial recommended the gift of a rhino-horn oil-flask with the phrase, 'accept this horn like the one recently seen in the Ausonian arena of the Emperor, when the rhino threw a bull'.[72] Girls from wealthy families had delicately carved dolls made from white ivory. These figurines were clothed in miniature dresses and are sometimes found buried in ancient graves, placed alongside a deceased child.[73]

The use of ivory for personal adornment extended to the distinctive black shoes worn by the patrician class as a mark of status. This footwear bore a crescent-shaped clasp that Juvenal says was often carved from ivory.[74] Some

Romans also wore ivory bands around their arms and Petronius describes the freeman Trimalchio, 'afraid that all of his finery would not be displayed, he bared his right arm which was adorned with a golden arm-band and an ivory circlet clasped with a plate of shining metal'.[75]

Exports to Ethiopia

Roman traders offered commonplace and inexpensive goods to the merchants at Adulis who dealt in ivory and turtle-shell. These included large quantities of Egyptian fabric including linens, double-fringed items, scarves from Arsinoe and coloured cloaks made from printed cloth. Roman merchants also traded in vividly-coloured glass stones and glass-globes with multi-coloured millefiori decorations made in Diospolis. These gem-like items were probably used in local jewellery and attached as ornamental fittings to other objects. Many of the goods offloaded at Adulis would have been delivered, or passed on to, consumers in the Ethiopian cities of Koloe, or Aksum.

There was a market for low-value Roman metals in Ethiopia and Aksumite traders accepted brass and copper pans and drinking vessels from the Empire. The African craftsmen cut apart these metal objects to make decorative armlets and anklets for local women to wear. Sheets of copper and brass were also cut into regular pieces to serve as token coinage in the kingdom. There was a market for Roman woodworking tools in the Aksumite Kingdom including axes, adzes (a wood-cutting tool with a right-angled blade) and knives. Local iron supplies were insufficient, or of poor quality, so Roman traders provided local dealers with iron to manufacture better weapons for hunting and warfare. The *Periplus* explains that Roman iron was used 'in spears for use on elephants and other wild animals and for war'.[76]

There were foreign traders residing long-term in the Aksumite Kingdom including Roman subjects who sourced and stockpiled African goods for export to the Empire. The *Periplus* therefore advised visiting traders to bring 'a little Roman money for the resident foreigners'. These dealers were also prepared to accept a limited quantity of Italian wine and olive oil as an alternative to cash, since these essential Mediterranean goods were not produced in Ethiopia.[77]

Royal agents probably controlled the bulk of ivory stocks available in the Aksumite Kingdom and the *Periplus* records that most of the valuable goods sent into the region were destined for the king. The Aksumite King Zoskales was on good terms with the Romans who visited his royal court, but he was notorious as a hard bargainer when it came to making deals with foreign merchants. The *Periplus* reports that 'Zoskales is astute about his possessions and in his dealings with us he is always holding out for more. But in all other respects he is a fine person and he is well versed in Greek reading and writing.'[78]

Roman dealers offered Zoskales valuable gold and silver tableware from the Empire that had been 'fashioned in the local manner'. In the Aksumite court communal drinking and feasting from expensive tableware was an important social feature. The Ethiopian highlands experienced cold winters, so the Aksumite King also accepted batches of heavy Roman cloaks, 'with no adornment and modest in price'.[79] These garments were probably issued to Aksumite soldiers and royal retainers in the African capital.

Roman merchants also offered King Zoskales valuable goods from India in order to acquire precious Aksumite stocks of African ivory. This included 'Indian iron and steel' produced using eastern techniques unknown to Roman metal-workers. The king also accepted a variety of Indian cotton fabrics, waistbands and a limited amount of pre-made cotton clothing.[80] A final commodity on the trade list is Indian lac-dye which the Aksumite king possibly used to equip his royal soldiers, or court officials, with scarlet-coloured uniforms.

The Somali Far-Side Markets
The Roman ships that continued their voyage down the east coast of Africa prepared to leave the Red Sea and make contact with markets in Somalia. The northern seaboard of Somalia was mostly flat and barren, and beyond the coastal plain there were arid mountains and a large inland plateau. All manner of exotic aromatic trees grew wild in this highland zone, including some ancient species of cinnamon that are now thought to be extinct due to the effects of deforestation (slash-and-burn land clearing) and the overgrazing of livestock.

The Romans called these trade-stations in northern Somalia 'the Markets Across' or the 'Far-Side ports' because they faced the seaboard of southern Arabia. There were no cities or indigenous kingdoms in this part of Africa and the native peoples lived in small self-governing communities. The *Periplus* explains that 'the area is not ruled by a king, but each port of trade is administered by its own chief (*tyrannida*)'.[81] Most settlements were inland, but there were a series of six markets on the coast that received goods for international trade. Each of these Far-Side markets had its own distinct character with some considered unruly or quarrelsome and others peaceful, depending on local conditions and the attitude of the native people. Roman traders generally referred to these African populations as *Barbaroi* (Barbarians).

When the Greek philosopher Apollonius argued with religious instructors from Meroe who challenged his ideas, he compared his accumulated wisdom to a ship loaded with foreign freight making landfall on the African coast. He asked, 'I would offer my goods to those who asked, but if someone came down the beach and began to criticise my cargo and abuse me, saying I come from a country that produces nothing worth having, or my cargo was shoddy, and if he should persuade others to think that way, then I would not cast anchor and secure the cables, but hoist the sails and put out to sea, trusting that the winds would carry me to a people less obtuse and inhospitable.'[82]

From the Red Sea to Cape Guardafui, the coast of northern Somalia was over 500 miles long and the distance between markets was divided into sailing-runs (*dromoi*) between landmarks. The Roman captains who undertook these voyages left Egypt in July at the same time as their colleagues sailed for India. This gave them extra time to reach the outer Horn of Africa before the onset of the north-east monsoon in November. Some of the larger Roman ships specialised in certain trade exchanges and sailed directly to particular Far-Side markets to acquire specific incense products, but other vessels sailed along the coast and took advantage of whatever opportunities were available at the various African markets. The *Periplus* explains that 'some ships sail principally to certain Far-Side trade ports, but some follow the coast and take on whatever cargoes come their way'.[83] Roman ships engaged in these Far-Side voyages would keep near the shore and moor at some sheltered place as night approached.[84]

Somalia produced large quantities of high-value products that were prized throughout the Roman Empire. Pliny records that in Rome a single pound of Somali myrrh was priced at 16 silver denarii, more than a labourer earned in two weeks.[85] African cassia could sell for up to 50 denarii a pound and Somali cinnamon fetched even greater prices in the Roman market for use as a potent perfume ingredient.[86] As none of these products could be grown successfully in the Roman Empire, most of these supplies were imported directly from Somalia.

The true appearance of Somali cinnamon trees remained a mystery to most Romans, but Pliny saw a living cinnamon-root on display at the Temple of Apollo Palatinus in the centre of Rome. This temple was built by the Emperor Augustus to honor his patron god Apollo and exhibit extraordinary natural wonders. The Emperor's wife Livia Drusilla gifted the stunted cutting to the temple and it was displayed in a golden bowl to be admired by worshippers entering the sacred precinct. Pliny describes the plant as a heavy root that somehow remained alive, but could not continue its growth in the temperate Italian climate. Every year small drops of fragrant resin wept from the living root and hardened into grains of sweet-smelling perfume. This strange living sample continued to attract interest until the temple and its cinnamon-shrine were accidently destroyed by fire sometime before AD 77.[87]

The first Far-Side market reached by Roman ships sailing south of the Aksumite Kingdom was Avalites. Avalites stood near the entrance to the Red Sea where the gulf narrowed at the straits of Bab-el-Mandeb. The *Periplus* describes Avalites as a small port of trade with a population that could be 'unruly'. Rafts from Somalia and other small crafts piloted by African and Arabian merchants came to this settlement. African traders sailed from Avalites to Arab ports on the opposite side of the Red Sea and the *Periplus* refers to 'transport to Ocelis and Muza which is carried out by the Barbaroi on rafts'. There was no king in the region and Roman merchants offered mostly low-value goods including colourful glass baubles that resembled precious stones and Egyptian olives from Diospolis which were shipped in an unripe condition so that they would not spoil before they reached their destination. There was also a market for used Roman clothing that was cleaned before export, Egyptian grain and a small amount of tin. In return the African traders at Avalites were able to provide a little ivory, local turtle-shell and a minimal amount of myrrh that was recommended because of its high quality.[88]

Ships leaving Avalites sailed through the straits of Bab-el-Mandeb and continued their voyage along the north coast of ancient Somalia to the Horn of Africa. The five Somali ports on this coast were indigenous settlements near large bays where cargo could be easily taken ashore and large ships could shelter in relative safety. The *Periplus* explains that the ports 'lie in a row and offer anchorages, roadsteads and suitable mooring when the occasion demands'.[89] Pliny describes how raft-like African craft sailed across the Gulf of Aden from Somalia to southern Arabia. These African traders carried Somali cinnamon which they exchanged for cloth, buckles, bracelets, necklaces, glass stones and copperwares.[90]

The first Somali port reached on the Horn was Malao (modern Berbera) which was about ninety miles east of Avalites. Malao was considered to be a better trade-market because it was positioned on a good natural harbour and its occupants were generally peaceable. The *Periplus* describes how 'the harbour at Malao is an open roadstead sheltered by a promontory extending from the east'. Malao offered supplies of myrrh, local incense, a harsh variety of cassia and several un-identified fragrant woods known to the Romans as *duaka*, *kankamon* and *makeir*. At Malao Roman merchants had to compete against Arab traders and the *Periplus* reports that incense and woods from Malao 'are exported to Arabia'. On rare occasions the market was also able to supply African slaves, perhaps as a con-sequence of local conflicts.[91]

Romans visiting Malao offered the same goods that were sent to Avalites including used clothing, coloured glass-stones, tin, grain and olives. There was a market for used Roman tunics and Egyptian cloaks from Arsinoe that were specially cleaned and re-dyed before export from the Empire. Roman merchants also offered the traders at Malao iron for tools and weapons, and a limited quantity of copper pans and drinking vessels. Coin was exchanged for valuable incense stocks and the *Periplus* advised bringing 'Roman money, in limited quantity, both gold and silver'.[92]

From Malao, Roman ships sailed two days further east to reach a market called Mundu (modern Heis). The *Periplus* reports that at Mundu vessels could 'harbour safely at an island that lies very near the shore'. Mundu was in the same region as Malao, so it offered similar goods with the addition of an incense called *mokrotu*. There was a market at Mundu for all the same Roman clothing, food, glassware, iron and money that was also shipped to Malao. Shards of Roman pottery and glassware have been found in the area, confirming the existence of these distant trade contacts.[93] However, the dealers living at Mundu had a reputation for being 'hard-bargainers'.[94]

The Somali trade port of Mosyllon was two or three sea-runs east of Mundu, but it accessed different inland regions with other unique natural products. Mosyllon offered large quantities of African cassia (cinnamon) and some Roman captains specialised in this trade by sending large vessels directly to the port. The *Periplus* explains that 'bigger ships are sent to Mosyllon because a great quantity of cassia is exported from this area'.[95]

Mosyllon was near a promontory on a beach with a poor harbour, but this did not discourage business at the site. In addition to cassia, the market offered other aromatics including a type of *mokrotu* incense that was considered poorer than the Mundu variety. Mosyllon also exported a little low-quality turtle-shell and on rare occasions some ivory and Somali frankincense. To acquire these goods,

Roman merchants offered the usual cargoes of clothing, coloured glass-stones, food and money. But the cassia stocks required further high-value exchanges and Roman merchants offered Mosyllon traders silverware and precious stones.[96]

Roman ships sailing east of Mosyllon were leaving the regions that produced myrrh and entering territories where the frankincense trees grew wild. Two days sail from Mosyllon, Roman pilots sighted thickets of mangroves on the coast and passed a promontory called Cape Elephas where a large river flowed into the sea. The *Periplus* reports that 'this place produces the most Far-Side incense and the product is high-quality'.[97] So much incense and fragrant wood grew in this part of Somalia that the region was known to the Romans as the 'Spice Promontory'.[98]

The Spice Promontory formed the outer tip of the Horn of Africa and included Cape Guardafui. The *Periplus* describes how Roman ships approaching the Cape sighted a steep promontory and reached an important regional market called the Spice Port (*Aromaton Emporion*). The harbour at the Spice Port was open to the sea and was dangerously exposed to any storms coming in from the north. The *Periplus* warned captains, 'when the sea becomes turbid and changes colour, this is a sign that a storm is coming and all ships take shelter at a site called Tabai at the big promontory'. But the value of the products on offer at the Spice Port made the risk worthwhile. Spice Port dealers offered large quantities of frankincense along with cassia, *gizeir*, *asyphe*, *aroma*, *magla* and *moto*.[99]

Cape Guardafui was at the eastern edge of the Horn of Africa and many Roman ships reaching the Spice Port then sailed out across the ocean to India.[100] However, ships that specialised in African trade continued sailing around the cape to reach a further Somali market called Opone (modern Hafun). Opone was less than fifty miles from Cape Guardafui, but by this stage Roman ships had sailed around the Horn and were heading south along the main seaboard of the African continent. African traders at Opone offered the Romans cassia, *aroma* and *moto*. Foreign ships from India and Arabia visited Opone to acquire African slaves, but the Romans were the main participants in this trade. The *Periplus* describes how Opone offered 'better-quality slaves, which mostly go to Egypt'. Opone also exported 'large quantities of turtle-shell that is better quality than other types'.[101]

It probably took Roman ships about forty days to sail from Egypt to the edge of the Horn of Africa. At this point Roman merchants reaching Opone were almost 1,500 miles from the southern frontiers of their Empire. During the time of the *Periplus*, this was the limit for most Roman voyages along the east coast of Africa and, after visiting Opone, Roman ships would return to Egypt on the winter monsoon winds. These merchants would have spent more than three months overseas in search of their costly aromatic cargoes.

Roman ships returning from India in November could also visit the Somali markets on their voyages back to Egypt. They could trade some of their Indian cargo for Somali incense and offer African merchants rice, ghee, sesame oil, cotton cloth, waistbands, cane sugar or gems.[102] The *Periplus* reports that, 'it is common to ship goods to the Far-Side from the inner regions of Ariake and Barygaza' (northwest India).[103] In this business, Roman ships would have competed with the Indian craft that also sailed to Somalia in November with the northeast monsoon.

East Africa

During the time of the *Periplus*, Roman ships on African voyages did not generally sail beyond the Horn. Distant trade connections continued down the east coast of the continent, but these routes were managed by Arab merchants who sailed in small dhow-like vessels with lateen sails. Some of these Arab trade runs extended hundreds of miles down the east coast of Africa to markets and trade outposts in Kenya and Tanzania. One of the main products shipped through this route were the large tusks of Bush Elephants hunted on the African Savannah. These supplies became more important as hunting operations in North Africa brought Forest Elephants closer to extinction. Pliny reports that by AD 77, 'only India can supply an ample supply of tusks, as luxury has reduced all other stocks'.[104]

Early Roman merchants knew from Arab traders about a route down the eastern seaboard of Africa. Ships sailing south passed a series of steep cliffs on the African coast known as the 'Small and Great Cliffs of Azania'. It took six days to sail past these heights with ships averaging about fifty miles during daylight hours and mooring offshore at night. The following coast, known as the 'Small and Great Beaches', was also desolate and devoid of towns. It took a further six days to sail along this long featureless stretch of the African coast.[105]

Past the beaches, the route was divided into a long series of runs between various river-mouths and natural harbours. Each of these courses could be completed in about a day's sailing beginning with the Sarapion Run and then the Nikon Run. The *Periplus* explains that each part of the sequence 'is separated by daily stops and there are seven runs to the Pyralaoi Islands and the place called the Canal'. The Pyralaoi Islands are the Lamu Archipelago which is separated from the mainland by a narrow stretch of water.[106] The islands are a thousand miles from Opone, which corresponds to a voyage of about twenty days.

Ships reaching the Pyralaoi Islands sailed south for two days on a course divided between four separate night and day runs. This took them down the Kenyan coast to a large island named Menuthias that must have been either Pemba or Zanzibar.[107] The *Periplus* describes Menuthias as a low-lying island with rivers and woodland that offered habitat to a wide variety of birds. There were also large monitor lizards on the island, which the Romans described as 'crocodiles that are not harmful to people'. Mountain tortoises were found inland and turtle was hunted on the coast by local people operating from dugout canoes and small craft that had timber hulls fastened with flexible wooden-cord ('sewn-boats'). The islanders were skilled at fishing and the *Periplus* reports 'they have their own way of capturing turtles with baskets, which they lower into the sea instead of nets'.[108]

Two runs, or about 100 miles, beyond Menuthias was a trade-station called Rhapta. Rhapta was on the Tanzanian coast and the *Periplus* calls the outpost 'the very last port of trade on the coast of Azania' (East Africa).[109] Local African ships brought turtle and tortoiseshell to the port and this accounted for the name of the settlement, 'Rhapta' meaning 'Sewn'. The *Periplus* describes how the indigenous people in this part of Africa were 'very big-bodied men who are tillers of the soil and each place has its own chief'.[110]

Rhapta was more than 1,400 miles, or 24 day's sail, from Opone on the Horn of Africa. But despite this distance the settlement was managed by Arab traders and was considered the possession of a Saba-Himyarite King who held power in Yemen. Rhapta carried on regular trade with a port in southwest Arabia called Muza which was near the entrance to the Red Sea. The *Periplus* reports that 'they send merchant craft from Muza to Rhapta staffed mostly with Arab skippers and agents. Through continual transactions and intermarriage these Arabs have become familiar with the area and the local language.' By AD 50 a consortium of merchants from Muza were running Rhapta as a business and had purchased the royal charter to collect taxes at the port.[111]

The *Periplus* reports that Rhapta traded 'great quantities of ivory and turtle-shell'. Bush elephant tusk is relatively dense and difficult to carve, so the ivory stocks at Rhapta are described as 'large volume, but inferior to the product from Adulis'. By contrast the turtle-shell was high-quality and considered the 'best product after the Indian variety'. Dealers at Rhapa also received rhinoceros horn and a small quantity of nautilus shell.[112] This shell was sought after by Roman craftsmen as a veneer that displayed beautiful geometric shapes with a pearl-like lustre.

Arab merchants offered traders at Rhapta weapons and tools from Muza including spears, axes, knives and small awls (a pointed tool for boring holes in wood or leather). They also traded 'numerous types of glass stones' which were probably replica gems produced in the Roman Empire and passed on to Arab dealers. Merchants from Muza shipped large quantities of grain and wine to Rhapta which they freely offered to visiting traders and gifted to African communities near the port. The *Periplus* explains that this cargo was 'not for trade and is given to ensure the goodwill of the Barbaroi'.[113]

Claudius Ptolemy explains how Roman merchants gained knowledge of the route to Rhapta in the period after the *Periplus* was written (AD 50–150). He describes how a Greek captain named Diogenes was blown off course on an ocean voyage back from India. Diogenes made landfall below the Horn of Africa and was unable to sail north because of the strong oncoming winter winds. He therefore took the opportunity to sail south to explore the east coast of Africa and made contact with Rhapta. Ptolemy explains, 'Diogenes was one of those people who sail to India and he was returning for the second time when he was driven back from the Aromatic Lands by the wind. He therefore sailed south.'[114]

This route was charted by another Roman captain named Theophilos who took twenty days to sail from the Horn of Africa to Rhapta. By this period there were two new settlements on the east coast of Somalia known as Apocopa and Essina. There was also a new trade port beyond the Small and Great Beaches called Sarapionis. Ptolemy describes Sarapionis as an emporium and a 'station' meaning that it was probably established by one of the regimes in southern

Arabia. Beyond Sarapionis was a 'market-place' called Tonice which was on the Nikon Run. Ptolemy calls the Far-Side ports 'market-places', so perhaps Tonice had a similar function. It was probably an indigenous settlement subject to a local chief who approved a gathering place for exchanges with foreign merchants. By the second century AD, Rhapta had become a regional capital and is described by Ptolemy as the 'metropolis of Barbaria'.[115]

A papyrus letter dated to 5 June AD 97 reveals the concerns of a merchant who had just returned from a long-distance voyage down the east coast of Africa. The merchant was in charge of several ships that returned late in the season as the Red Sea trade winds were shifting against incoming vessels.[116] The merchant informed his master that 'the winds are against us and the boats stalled from entering the harbour at Berenice for five hours'. He retained some of the out-bound cargo of multi-coloured cloaks and 'aboard the boat there are still varieties of "parrot" fabric left over by the *berbers*'. The long voyage and late sailing gave him little time to restock before the next expedition and to his dismay the new cargo was not waiting in its designated place. He writes, 'you did not prepare the blankets. But with the help of the gods, I shall go forth quickly. Be well.'[117]

Roman vessels making the voyage to Rhapta took at least sixty days to reach a location that was nearly 3,000 miles from the Empire.[118] This was the limit of Roman ventures along the east coast of Africa and the seaboard beyond Rhapta was unknown territory. Roman captains speculated that the African continent ended somewhere beyond Rhapta and believed it was possible to sail from the Indian Ocean into the Atlantic Sea. The *Periplus* explains that 'beyond Rhapta lies an unexplored ocean that bends to the west and extends along southern Africa, beyond Ethiopia and Libya, to join with the western sea'.[119] But Roman captains had no incentive to explore this route and the Red Sea offered them a fast and easy route back to the Empire.

CHAPTER TEN

Southern Arabia and the
Saba-Himyarites

Most of inner Arabia consisted of desert and included the sand-filled expanse of
the Empty Quarter (known today as Rub' al-Khali). By contrast the seaboard of
southern Arabia was swept by misty monsoon clouds and its well-watered highland territories sustained seasonally fertile forests. The ancient Sabaean Kings
who ruled this region oversaw the construction of dams and irrigation works
that redirected highland streams into bountiful field systems at the base of the
mountains. The steep woodlands in the Yemen and Dhofar produced abundant
quantities of honey and beeswax.[1] There were ancient reports of gold mines in
the region and Southern Arabia possessed one of the few climates where frankincense and myrrh trees could thrive and produce large quantities of highly
valuable resin.[2]

Roman authorities received reports regarding the incense production in
southern Arabia from visiting envoys and allies in foreign governments.[3] This
information included details about the size of the incense harvests and the
amount of land under cultivation. Pliny reports that frankincense trees covered an
area of about 1.3 million hectares in the coastal highlands of Dhofar. Every year
these territories were capable of producing at least 1,000 tons of frankincense for
the Sabaean Kingdom. Based on supply ratios, this total suggests that the amount
of myrrh produced in the neighbouring territory of Yemen must have been at
least 200 tons per annum. Taken together, the combined output represents over
50 million sesterces of incense gathered per harvest.[4] To give this figure a context, 50 million sesterces is more than the tribute that Rome received from Gaul.[5]

Roman sources reveal the long-term dilemma this trade created for the
Empire. Incense was essential in many popular religious practices that were conducted throughout the Roman world. But incense was so expensive that it was
generally purchased from Arab suppliers by using gold and silver in the form of
bullion or imperial coin. The Romans had no high-value commodity that could
meet this cost and the result was a steady drain of precious metal from the
Mediterranean economy. As Strabo explained the Arabians were wealthy because
they sold aromatics and valuable gemstones for gold and silver. But they never
expended the wealth they received from this trade with outsiders.[6] Pliny describes
gemstones trafficked through Arabia including sardonyx and glittering red
quartz, blood-red *haematitis*, translucent coloured crystals, diamonds and distinctive types of honey-coloured and mottled yellow gems.[7] Arabia produced black

onyx with white bands and Pliny describes Petra as a centre for the trade in purple amethysts.[8]

To the Greeks and Romans it seemed as though the gods had blessed southern Arabia with extraordinary good fortune. The Empty Quarter isolated southern Arabia from outside attack and their fertile forests produced a sustainable product that had unique international value. For this reason, many Greeks and Romans called the region Arabia Felix.[9] When Pliny wrote about eastern trade he identified Arabia Felix as one of the main regions responsible for draining more than 100 million sesterces from the Empire per annum.[10] If the Roman regime was not able to rectify this trade imbalance, then its financial system was in danger of irreparable decline.

Sabaean Trade

The Sabaeans were a leading power in southern Arabia as early as the tenth century BC. In the *Old Testament*, the *Book of Kings* records that the Jewish King David was visited by the Queen of the Sabaeans, known to them as Sheba. The Queen had heard about the rise of the Jewish Kingdom and came to Jerusalem 'with a very great caravan – with camels carrying incense, large quantities of gold, and precious stones'. The Queen was shown the Royal Palace and the Temple of the Lord, and David established formal relations between their realms. According to ancient tradition, David was said to have received diplomatic gifts that included nearly 4 tons of gold and large quantities of incense and precious stones.[11]

When the Queen returned to Sabaea, David ordered the construction of seagoing ships on the Gulf of Aqaba. He sent the ships into the Red Sea under the command of a royal agent called Hiram who was ordered to sail south to make contact with Sabaean settlements on the Yemen coast. Hiram entered the Gulf of Aden and brought back cargoes from Yemen and Somalia. He visited a port called Ophir, a settlement that received timber and scented woods from the Horn of Africa. The *Book of Kings* records that 'Hiram's ships brought gold from Ophir and great cargoes of almug-wood and precious stones'. The imported wood was used to refurbish the Temple of the Lord and adorn chambers in the Royal Palace. It was also carved into harps and lyres for the musicians who played for King David.[12]

By the sixth century BC, most of the incense reaching the Near East was trafficked through the Arab nations who occupied northern Arabia. One of these groups was the Gerrhaeans who controlled territories near the Persian Gulf. When the Persian Empire conquered the Near East it imposed tribute payments on the Gerrhaeans. Herodotus reports that King Darius (522–486 BC) received 1,000 talents (over 25 tons) of frankincense a year 'from the Arabians'.[13]

Nabataeans on the fringe of Judea supplied incense to the city of Gaza on the Mediterranean Coast. Over time Gaza became an important hub for the incense trade that supplied wealthy Greek civilisation with this sought-after product. Plutarch describes how, when Alexander the Great was a boy, he was seen making a sacrificial offering by using 'both hands to scoop up incense and throw it upon the altar-fire'. Alexander was cautioned by a tutor named Leonidas not to be so over-generous and wasteful when making such sacrifices.[14]

Alexander remembered this episode long after the event. During his conquest of the Persian Empire, Alexander besieged Gaza using large war-engines to breach its high outer-walls (332 BC). The Greeks looted a vast store of incense from the city which Alexander sent back to Macedonia to impress his royal court. Plutarch reports that Alexander sent Leonidas 500 talents (nearly 13 tons) of frankincense and 100 talents (over 2 tons) of myrrh, with the message, 'I have sent you myrrh and frankincense in abundance so that you can stop being so stingy before the gods'.[15] But Alexander and his Greek successors never managed to conquer Arabia and this meant that the peninsula retained its independent character and its control over the lucrative incense trade.

Red Sea Piracy
During the Roman era, the central seaboard of western Arabia was occupied by fiercely independent peoples who had a reputation for piracy. Strabo describes this coast as 'rugged and difficult for vessels to pass because high rocky mountains stretch along the shore and there is a lack of harbours and anchoring-places'. Furthermore, 'when the Etesian winds blow with rain, this coast is a danger to sailors because they are far beyond all help'.[16] The *Periplus* describes how Roman captains tried to avoid the coast by taking a course down the middle of the Red Sea and sailing as quickly possible past the main pirate bases. The author confirms that 'a course along the coast of Arabia is risky as the region lacks harbours and offers poor anchorage. It has many rocky stretches and the land cannot be entered because of cliffs. It has a fearsome nature.' Pirate dhows would attack any trade vessels venturing near their coasts and capture Roman crews who were unable to defend themselves. The *Periplus* warns 'these coastal people are vicious: they plunder any who stray from sailing a course down the middle of the gulf and they enslave anyone who they rescue from shipwreck'.[17]

The Saba-Himyarite Kingdom of southern Arabia waged a long-running conflict against these Red Sea pirates. In their operations the Saba-Himyarites probably received assistance from the Nabataean regime. The *Periplus* explains that 'the pirates are constantly being taken prisoner by the governors and kings of Arabia'.[18] Both kingdoms would have sent expeditions along the coast to capture the pirate ships and destroy any communities that supported their activities. But they could not eliminate the danger and Pliny suggests that there were occasions when some of the Arab raiders also threatened the African ports of the far coast of the Red Sea. One notorious group called the Ascitae operated from an island base near the Farasans and used rafts to stealthily approach ships moored near the African port of Adulis. Pliny describes how 'commerce is greatly exposed to the attentions of a piratical tribe of Arabians called the Ascitae who dwell upon the islands. They place two inflated skins of oxen beneath a raft of wood and they conduct their pirate raids with the aid of poisoned arrows.'[19]

Throughout the first century AD Roman merchants had to take their chances in the Red Sea shipping-lanes and hope that the nearby Arab kingdoms were prevailing in their war against piracy. The mercenary archers aboard Roman freighters could relax their guard when the ship's lookouts sighted Burnt Island (Jabal al-Tair). This landmark indicated that the ship had reached the security of the Saba-Himyarite Kingdom in Yemen. The *Periplus* explains that 'beyond Burnt Island, there is a succession of shores with peaceful inhabitants, camels and animals at pasture'.[20]

The Farasan Command

During the second century AD, the Romans secured the western seaboard of Arabia by establishing a naval base on the Farasan Islands. The Farasans were over 600 miles from the southernmost frontier of the Empire and the Roman military presence on these islands represents a significant interest in eastern maritime affairs. This island chain is about forty miles from the coast of southern Arabian and lies in a position to control important sea-lanes across the gulf.

The Farasans were less than sixty miles from Muza in the Saba-Himyarite Kingdom and about 120 miles from the African port of Adulis. The islands are part of a reef system that runs parallel to the Arabian coast, so Roman vessels could monitor traffic sailing through breaks in the coral bank between the two ports. From the Farasans, the Roman navy could also have watched over ships entering and leaving the Red Sea through the Eastern Pillars of Hercules (the straits of Bab-el-Mandeb) which controlled the passage into the Indian Ocean.

The Roman outpost on the Farasans is attested by two Latin inscriptions that were erected by garrison forces sent to the island from Legions based in Syria and Egypt. The first inscription dates to AD 120 and records that a *vexillation* (task-force) from the Legio VI Ferrata (the Sixth Ironclad Legion) was posted to the island.[21] Legio VI Ferrata was based in Syria, but assigned to Nabataea when the territory first became an imperial province in AD 107.

The troops sent to the Farasans were probably dispatched by the Emperor Trajan as part of Roman plans to annex Nabataea and extend Roman rule into the Indian Ocean. Trajan restored the ancient Suez canal, and Eutropius reports that 'he fitted out a fleet for the Erythraean Sea (Red Sea) so that he might use it to lay waste to the coasts of India'.[22] Trajan invaded the Parthian Empire in AD 114 and Rome was briefly able to occupy Mesopotamia (Iraq) and secure full access to the Persian Gulf. The Emperor probably hoped for further conquests in Iran with the assistance of a Roman fleet launched from the Red Sea or the Persian Gulf. The Farasan base and the monsoon trade routes would have provided a way for Roman reinforcements, supplies and equipment, to be sent east as far as the Indus River.[23] But the invasion never occurred as there was a series of violent uprisings in Mesopotamia and Trajan succumbed to a terminal illness in AD 117. His successor Hadrian withdrew Roman forces from Mesopotamia rather than continue the conflict.

By occupying the Farasans the Roman Empire engaged in a pattern of expansion that was occurring across the Arabian Sea. During the first century AD, the Saba-Himyarites claimed Rhapta, which was a Tanzanian trade post nearly 1,600 miles south of Arabia.[24] The Hadramawt King who ruled parts of Yemen and Dhofar also owned the African island of Socotra as a territory that could be leased out for its native resources.[25] In southern Mesopotamia, the King of Charax took possession of territories in the Persian Gulf, including the island of Bahrain which controlled lucrative pearl-fisheries.[26]

The Romans could have seized the Farasans as an unclaimed territory, or taken the islands as an already existing outpost. Pottery finds suggest a Nabataean presence on the islands that possibly predate the arrival of the second century Roman garrison.[27] Perhaps Trajan received the Farasans as a grant from the Saba-Himyarite Kings who presented themselves as 'friends of the Emperor' and sent regular envoys to Rome.[28] The island could have been given to Rome in the same manner that Rhapta, or the island of Socotra, was granted to merchant consortiums who maintained their own garrisons.[29] The Romans imposed a custom station at Leuke Kome when Nabataea was still a client-kingdom, so there was precedent for the Empire to impose its tax interests beyond the imperial boundaries.[30]

Once established, the Farasan base would have been maintained to supress piracy, or control valuble marine resources. Although the largest island on the Farasan chain is barely thirty miles long and four miles across, it would have been a useful staging post. The Nabataean Kingdom conducted military operations against pirates on the west coast of Arabia, so the Roman army probably assumed this role when the region became an imperial province. The legionaries based on the island would have been involved in clearing pirate settlements from the Arabian coast, or escorting groups of merchant ships on their seasonal sailings through the Red Sea.

The fleet and garrison posted on the Farasan Islands were possibly involved in managing the pearl fisheries positioned near Bab-el-Mandeb. In a list of income received by the Roman treasury the court poet Statius refers to wealth 'gathered by the divers who search the eastern seas'.[31] This could be a reference to state-managed pearl fisheries in the Red Sea and the Romans would have leased the collection rights to private businesses. Pliny reports that the Italian business-man Annius Plocamus 'gained a tax contract for the Red Sea from the Roman treasury'.[32] The rights might have included the pearl fisheries and Pliny writes that pearls from the Red Sea were 'specially praised' because they were smaller and brighter than other Indian Ocean varieties.[33]

The Farasan base could also have been involved in the collection of more distant resources and there is evidence that Nabataean merchants took control over markets in northern Somalia. Pliny describes 'a colony from the Naba-taeans' that was established in Somalia, 'at the edge of the cassia and cinnamon district' (between the ports of Malao and Mosyllon).[34] Perhaps Roman vessels based on the Farasans were responsible for protecting or taking tithes from this settlement. African cinnamon sold in Rome at the price of 10 silver denarii per pound, so this was a resource worth the investment of military personnel.[35]

The Farasans were hundreds of miles from the frontiers of the Roman Empire and the imperial garrison stationed on the island would have required regular provisions to be brought in by ship. It was easier to deliver these supplies through

Egypt since there were already Roman squadrons based in the ports of Berenice and Myos Hormos.[36] Sometime before AD 140 the Roman base on the Farasans was therefore placed under the authority of the governor of Egypt. The garrison from Legio VI Ferrata was replaced by a *vexillation* from the Legio II Traiana Fortis (the Second Valiant Trajanic Legion) and a supporting unit of auxiliaries.[37] Legio II Traiana Fortis was based near Alexandria and this confirms that the Farasan outpost was under the command structure of Roman Egypt.

The second Latin inscription found on the Farasans was discovered on the main island near the modern site of Gharrain. It was carved on a rectangular block of calcareous stone that probably adorned a medium sized Roman monument. The inscription reveals that the monument was erected by the Roman commander Castricius Aprinus in AD 143–144. Aprinus describes himself as 'Castricius Aprinus, son of Publius, Prefect of the Port of Farasan and of the Sea of Hercules' (Bab-el-Mandeb). He dedicates the monument 'on behalf of the *vexillation* of the Second Legion Traiana Fortis and its auxiliary troops'.[38] There is no mention of the ships under his authority, but Aprinus would have had command of several military transports and a squadron of war-galleys adapted for Red Sea service.

Pliny calls the east coast of Africa 'Anzania' and suggests that this region began mid-way down the Red Sea near the port of Adulis.[39] When the Chinese Empire received reports about the Roman presence in the Red Sea they heard the name 'Anzania' and rendered it 'Zesan'. Han records list Zesan as a territory subject to Rome alongside 'Lufen' (the Nabataean port of Leuke Kome). The *Weilue* explains that 'Da Qin (Rome) divides the various branch principalities of their territory into small countries that include the ruler of Zesan (Anzania) and the ruler of Lufen (Leuke Kome)'.[40]

This information was probably supplied by Roman merchants from Egypt who reached the Han court in AD 166.[41] It provides an important insight as to how Roman power was perceived in the Red Sea region. The *Weilue* also claims: 'the king of Zesan (Anzania) is subject to Da Qin (Rome). His seat of government is in the middle of the sea and to the north you reach Lufen (Leuke Kome)'.[42] This is probably a reference to the Farasan command and a situation where the Prefect of the Roman port claimed jurisdiction over the coastline of East Africa. Under protection from the Farasan command, Roman ships sailed through the Sea of Hercules to reach the Saba-Himyarite Kingdom.

The Saba-Himyarites

In the first century AD, the *Periplus* records that Roman merchants sailing to the Yemen usually left Egypt in September nearly two months after ships bound for India left the harbours. This schedule meant that merchants engaged in Arabian trade could prioritise loading operations in the summer months while many of their colleagues were overseas. If a ship could be loaded quickly, then it could leave early and this was advisable for sailings to the more distant Arab ports. The *Periplus* suggests 'the best time for sailing is around September, the month of Thoth, though there is nothing to prevent leaving even earlier'.[43]

The first stop for Roman ships sailing to Arabia Felix was a port called Muza, which was on the Yemen coast close to the Farasan Islands and the entrance to the Red Sea (near modern Mokha). The voyage from Berenice to Muza was less than 800 miles, but the *Periplus* estimated the distance to be over 1,300 miles. This represents difficult sailing conditions and the voyage probably involved nearly three weeks sailing.[44] Muza had a large sandy cove where cargo could be easily taken ashore and the surrounding seabed was free from concealed reefs and other underwater dangers. The *Periplus* explains that 'Muza has no harbour, but the site is a good roadstead and mooring location, because all around the bottom is sandy with positions for anchorage'.[45] Muza was usually crowded with Arabian craft involved in trade voyages to Somalia and northwest India. The *Periplus* describes how 'the whole place teems with Arab ship-owners, charterers and sailors. It is busy with commercial activity because they trade with the Far-Side (Somali) coast and with Barygaza, sending out their own ships to visit these places.'[46]

The Himyarite Kingdom ruled the myrrh-producing territories on the south-west corner of Arabia.[47] Their rise to power came after the Roman attack on Arabia Felix (25 BC) which left the Sabaean Kingdom vulnerable to regional rivals. The Himyarites seized the Sabaean homelands and made the population subject to a new Saba-Himyar regime. The Himyarites controlled the main sea-lanes that led from the Red Sea into the Gulf of Aden and grew rich from managing imports from across the Indian Ocean. They also generated substantial wealth from exporting myrrh produced in their subject territories. A single pound of this incense could be sold in Roman markets for 16 denarii.[48]

As there was little incense available offseason, Roman ships that sailed to India in late July rarely visited Muziris on their outbound voyages. Pliny explains that Muza 'is not called at on the voyage to India and is only used by merchants trading in frankincense and Arabian perfumes'.[49] Roman crews specialising in voyages to Arabia sailed later in the season and generally reached Muza in late September when the first of the summer incense crop was reaching the local markets.[50] Any Roman merchants planning to travel inland to the main cities of the Saba-Himyarite Kingdom were left ashore to be collected on the return voyage.

Dealers at Muza offered Roman traders large quantities of 'select-grade' myrrh and thick scented oils called *stacte*.[51] Pliny explains that most *stacte* was myrrh-sap that was collected before it could harden into resin. He describes *stacte* as 'a juice exuded before the tree is properly tapped and it is therefore the most highly valued of all myrrh'.[52] Some of the myrrh offered at the port was from an inland territory ruled by the Minaeans, so the Himyarite King must have permitted regional traders to sell their own product at Muza. Romans could also acquire Somali incense at Muza which was imported by Arab merchants who dealt in African products, including frankincense.[53]

Arab traders sailed back and forth between Muza and the African port of Adulis on the opposite coast of the Red Sea.[54] This meant that traders at Muza were able to offer 'all the merchandise from Adulis across the water', including ivory, rhino-horn and tortoiseshell. Roman merchants who were not scheduled to visit Adulis took advantage of this opportunity to acquire African goods at Muza, providing the exchange rates were reasonable.[55]

The Himyarites offered another interesting cargo for Roman merchants specialising in Arabian voyages. The pure-white marble that was quarried in southern Arabia had a fine crystalline texture and Roman merchants took aboard this heavy material as ballast to stabilise their ships. On their return to the Empire, this valuable marble was sold to stoneworkers and carved into elegant unguent jars that resembled radiant alabaster.[56] Pliny describes how Arabian marble had a brilliant white-lustre like ivory, but the material was brittle. When disintegrated by heat and ground-down it produced an abrasive calcined residue used to clean stained teeth and remove tartar.[57]

At Muza, Roman traders offered Arab merchants bales of cloth including expensive purple-dyed fabrics and clothing specially styled to suit Arabian fashions. These included sleeved tunics, chequered garments, cloaks, colourful striped waistbands and outfits decorated with gold thread. Traders at Muza also accepted Roman blankets that were dyed a single colour or had patterns that matched 'traditional local adornment'.[58]

Other Roman goods were more specialised, including yellow saffron dyes and a plant with medical properties called cyperus. Cyperus grew in Arabia Felix, but Arab demand for this substance was greater than local production could provide.[59] A moderate amount of Roman perfume could also be exchanged at Muza, either for local use, or as stock for Arab merchants to take to India. The *Periplus* also advised Roman merchants visiting Muza to bring a 'considerable amount of money' to the port in order to facilitate their deals.[60]

Romans ships offloaded only a limited quantity of grain and wine at Muza. These commodities were exchanged with local dealers, or offered to merchants from the Empire who resided long-term at the port. The *Periplus* explains that interest in these goods was limited because, 'the region produces moderate quantities of wheat and larger stocks of wine'.[61] Arabian wine was made from dates, or the fermented sap of palm-trees that were tapped to release their syrupy juices.[62] Many expatriate Romans probably preferred Mediterranean grown grape-wines to this sweeter alternative.

Caravan routes led inland from Muza to the main cities of the Saba-Himyarite Kingdom. Three days inland from Muza was a city called Saue which was under the authority of a Himyarite *tyrannos* (governor) named Cholaibos. The *Periplus* explains that Cholaibos administered the surrounding province called Mapharitis and kept a court residence at Saue.

A further nine days travel from Saue was the capital Saphar where the Himyarite King Charibael had his royal court. Saphar was the ancient city of Zafar which stood in the Yemen Mountains between the coast and the inner desert. The *Periplus* calls Saphar a metropolis and describes Charibael as 'the legitimate king (*basileus*) of the two nations, the Himyarite people and the adjacent Sabaeans'. 'Charibael' was probably the Greek rendition of the royal dynastic name 'Karibil'. Inscriptions from the region indicate that in AD 50, the ruler of this kingdom was Karibil Watar Yuhanim I, who combined dynastic titles from both the Sabaeans and the Himyarites.[63]

The Himyarite King Charibael had authority over distant sites in East Africa including the trading settlement at Rhapta in northern Tanzania. He leased this settlement to a merchant oligarchy from Muza who ran trade operations from the port and collected taxes on any incoming business. The *Periplus* explains: 'the region (Rhapta) is under the rule of the governor of Mapharitis, since by some ancient right it became subject to the Kingdom of Arabia when it was first established. The merchants of Muza hold it through a grant from the king and collect taxes from it.'[64]

The *Periplus* reports that the Himyarite King Charibael was, 'a friend of the Emperors, thanks to continuous embassies and gifts'.[65] When writing about eastern geography, Pliny refers to 'the ambassadors that have come from Arabia in my own lifetime'.[66] Possible confirmation of these contacts comes from a Roman gravestone found at the inland site of Baraqish in southwest Arabia. Written in both Latin and Greek, the gravestone commemorates a man named Publius Comelius who was an *eques* (knight). It could be that Comelius was a cavalryman who died during the Gallus campaign (25 BC), or perhaps he had been involved in a later diplomatic mission.[67]

The Himyarite Kings sent the Emperors gifts of the finest incense and the Greek physician Galen describes how the best grade of remedy materials could be found in the imperial palace storerooms.[68] Other gifts included natural wonders sent to impress the imperial court. Pliny records that the tallest person ever seen in Rome was 'a man named Gabbara brought from Arabia in the reign of Claudius'. Gabbara was said to be over nine feet tall and may have been a gift sent from an Arabian king.[69]

Some Roman merchants arriving at Muza brought their own pack-animals. They offloaded their trade-goods on to these animals and joined the caravans headed inland to Saue and Saphar. In these cities they could conduct business with state-officials working for the Governor Cholaibos, or King Charibael. Government agents supplied state-owned stocks of the finest myrrh grown in royal plots, or taken as a tithe from Himyarite harvests. It is also possible that the regime controlled marble quarries within their territory and supply orders were conducted through royal agents.[70]

Roman merchants offered expensive goods to the Himyarite authorities including horses and pack mules, gold objects and embossed silverware. They also provided the administration with valuable clothing and costly copper artefacts. Arab kingdoms issued their own silver currencies which were based on Hellenic models. The Himyarites therefore appreciated the value of silver denarii and probably received large quantities of these imperial coins as payment for their incense.[71] Pliny describes how a freedman of Annius Ploclamus had a consignment of silver denarii aboard his vessel when he sailed *circa Arabiam* (around Arabia).[72]

Roman merchants travelling inland to the main Himyarite cities would have probably conducted their best deals in early autumn when the bulk of the local myrrh crop became available for sale.[73] They aimed to be back at Muza by late October when Roman ships returning from more distant ports headed into the Red Sea to collect colleagues onshore and conduct any further business. Merchants taking passage aboard these ships could be back in Egypt by November, or they could await the return of the Roman ships from India who would pass the coast between December and late January.[74]

The *Periplus* describes a Himyarite village called Ocelis that was positioned about thirty miles south of Muza near the Straits of Bab-el-Mandeb where the Red Sea merged with the Gulf of Aden. The village was a shore-station that offered fresh water to Roman ships headed for India. The *Periplus* therefore describes Ocelis as 'not so much a port of trade as a harbour and a watering station, the first stopping place for those sailing on'.[75] Pliny verifies that 'those sailing to India find that Ocelis is a very convenient place for departure'.[76] When Claudius Ptolemy composed his geography in the second century AD Ocelis had become a market-town offering off-season supplies of myrrh for Roman ships heading for India.[77]

At Bab-el-Mandeb the African and Arabian coasts converged to form a narrow strait about twenty miles across. To Roman sailors this passage between tall headlands resembled the 'Pillars of Hercules' where ships sailed from the Mediterranean into the Atlantic Ocean between the Rock of Gibraltar and Jebel Musa in Morocco. Bab-el-Mandeb therefore formed a second Pillars of Hercules where Roman ships sailed from a land-bounded sea into a world-spanning ocean.

There was a small landmass midway across Bab-el-Mandeb Strait named Diodorus Island (modern Perim) which divided the passage into two narrow channels. Many Roman ships chose the Arabian channel, but they had to take care because 'a wind blows down from the surrounding mountains and there are strong currents alongside the island.'[78] Ships passing safely through this channel entered the Gulf of Aden.

Eudaimon Arabia

As the Roman ships sailed along the southern seaboard of Arabia, they passed by a deep inlet in the coast and the ancient ruins of Eudaimon Arabia (Aden). During the first century BC, Eudaimon was a thriving Sabaean metropolis where merchants from Egypt and India met to exchange their native goods and receive valuable stocks of Arabian incense. This was an era when only a few Greek ships sailed directly to India and vessels from India did not risk voyages onward to Egypt. Consequently, Eudaimon served as an intermediary market where foreign vessels could receive trade goods from more remote regions. During this period, Eudaimon became renowned as the main port of Arabia and early Greek sailors called the city 'Eudaimon Arabia' meaning 'Blessed' or 'Prosperous Arabia'.[79]

It seems that Eudaimon was attacked by Roman forces, probably during a pre-emptive seaborne operation ordered by Aelius Gallus in 26 BC. The *Periplus* explains that 'not long before our time, Caesar sacked the city' and Pliny confirms that 'Aelius Gallus, a member of the Equestrian Order, is the only person who has taken Roman forces into this country'.[80] After the Roman attack most merchants abandoned the Sabaean port and when the Himyarites laid claim to the territory they redirected all regional trade to Muza. By AD 50, Eudaimon was little more than a village clustered amongst the ruins of the once great city. The *Periplus* explains that the site still had 'suitable harbours and sources of water much sweeter than at Ocelis', but there was no trade business conducted at the port.[81]

In the time of the *Periplus*, Eudaimon and the surrounding coast was under the control of King Charibael and the powerful Saba-Himyarite Kingdom. However, one of the main routes leading inland from Eudaimon headed north towards the city of Timna, the capital of the landlocked Qataban Kingdom.[82] The Qataban produced myrrh in their homelands and during the mid-first century AD they became allies of the Himyarite nation. As a consequence, the Himyarites granted Eudaimon to the Qataban as an outlet for the sale of their incense stocks and the development of their maritime trade.[83] Roman evidence confirms the re-emergence of Eudaimon as an important regional trade centre during this period. A Greek temple inscription from Coptos records that a wealthy merchant from Eudaimon was visiting Egypt in AD 70.[84] By the time Claudius Ptolemy compiled his geography, Eudaimon was designated as a market centre (an emporium).[85]

The Qataban were known to the Romans as the Gebbanites and classical accounts describe the development of their maritime interests. After taking possession of Eudaimon, the Qataban King gained authority over Somali settlements on the far side of the gulf and began to import valuable African incense. Within decades the Qataban were managing the main groves involved in producing Somali cinnamon and shipping large volumes of the product back to Eudaimon. Consequently the Qataban King was able to fix the international price paid for this valuable product. Pliny explains that 'only the king of the Gebbanitae (Qataban) has the authority to control the sale of cinnamon and he opens the market by public proclamation'.[86]

The Qataban trade system functioned well, but disruptions were still possible. On one occasion Qataban operations in Somalia were severely damaged by a forest fire that was possibly started by local people opposed to the Arab incomers. Pliny reports 'it is said that infuriated barbarians started the fire; but it is not certain whether this action was provoked by injustice on the part of those in power, or was due to some accident'. After the fire, supply shortages affected sales in the Empire and the price of Somali cinnamon rose steeply in Roman markets. Pliny explains that 'prices rose by half their usual amounts after the forests had been burnt'.[87] This incident indicates how events occurring in distant regions could effect prices on Roman markets.

An ancient inscription from the Qataban capital Timna indicates how the regime would have controlled the prices paid for valuable products.[88] The *Mercantile Code of Qataban* dates to about 110 BC and is a market proclamation designed to centralise trade in recognised markets, facilitate the collection of taxes and regulate prices. The code specifies that 'the King of Qataban has authority over all transactions and goods within his territory'.[89] These powers allowed the king to set prices paid for cinnamon imports in Eudaimon and

Timna. The prices would be fixed so that royal agents could maximise the profits gained by selling state-owned stocks of the incoming aromatics. The Qataban also established a presence at the nearby Himyarite port of Ocelis on the Strait of Bab-el-Mandeb. There they sold stocks of cinnamon to Roman ships visiting the port on the way to India. Pliny calls Ocelis 'a harbour of the Gebbanitae' which suggests a strong Qataban presence at the port.[90] Ships sailing onward along the coast from Eudaimon would reach an ancient kingdom under the rule of the secretive Hadramawt regime.

CHAPTER ELEVEN

Arabia Felix and the
Hadramawt Kingdom

Roman ships sailing beyond Eudaimon Arabia (Aden) left Saba-Himyarite territory and entered the Hadramawt Kingdom which ruled east Yemen and Dhofar.
The Hadramawt were a well-defended regime who had risen to power after the
collapse of the Sabaean Kingdom in the late first century BC. During the Sabaean
decline the Hadramawt seized the seaboard of Dhofar and captured the main
frankincense groves on the highland coast. Under Hadramawt administration
these trees were managed as a state-run business and all produce belonged to the
king. By the first century AD the Hadramawt controlled a seaboard approximately
500 miles long which stretched from Yemen to Oman. The *Periplus* calls
Hadramawt territory, 'the Frankincense-Bearing land' or 'the Kingdom of
Eleazos'.[1] Eleazos is probably a Greek rendition of the dynastic name Il'azz which
is attested in Hadramawt royal inscriptions.[2]

The main Hadramawt port was 220 miles east of Eudaimon at a fortified
outpost called Qana. The coast between these trade centres was populated by
communities of local nomads and the inhabitants of small fishing villages.[3] As
Roman ships approached Qana they passed sandy shorelines where jagged black
volcanic rocks jutted into the sea. It was possible to sail from Berenice to Qana in
just over four weeks, provided the summer trade winds were blowing and the
merchants did not delay at any intermediate ports. Pliny confirms that from
Egypt, 'it takes about thirty days to reach the Arabian port of Cane (Qana) in the
frankincense-producing district'.[4]

Qana was just outside the frankincense-growing region and it functioned as the
main depot for gathering incense from the Hadramawt Kingdom. The harvests
were collected at outposts in the incense-producing highlands and from these
places all loads were sent west to Qana by land and sea. The *Periplus* explains that
'all the frankincense grown in the land is brought into Qana as if it were a single
warehouse'.[5] The land routes passed through mountain valleys where guard-
stations and checkpoints could monitor the caravans headed for Qana.[6] Other
stocks were shipped by sea, aboard 'boats and rafts of a local type made of leather
bags'.[7]

The port of Qana lay on a large sandy bay overlooked by a flat-topped volcanic
promontory that rose 450 feet above the beach.[8] As Qana was the reception
centre for Hadramawt incense, the promontory was a guarded installation
managed by royal agents. The regime had built stone storerooms into the cliff
face to contain the incoming frankincense. Excavations have revealed several

Roman merchant ship depicted on the Sidon Relief. (*Louvre, Paris*)

Roman ship graffiti from a wall at Pompeii: The *Europa* (first century AD).

Roman relief showing armoured marines on a bireme warship. (*Vatican Museum, Rome*)

Silver Egyptian tetradrachm issued by the Emperor Nero (AD 54–68).

...oman grave relief showing the Peticii business-family who exported wine to India.
...bruzzo Museum, Italy)

...utinger Map showing a Roman temple in Southern India.

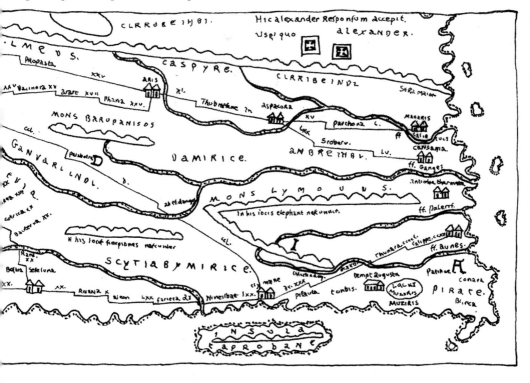

Relief depicting Prince Arikankharer of Meroe (AD 25). (*Worcester Art Museum, New York*)

Gold Coins of the Aksumite King Ousanas (AD 300).

Silver Saba-Hymarite coin displaying emblems from Greek drachmas and Roman denarii (Athenian owl and laureled head of Caesar).

Indian ship depicted in a painting from a temple-cave at Ajunta (western India).

Silver Coin of the Indo-Parthian King Gondophares (AD 20). Obverse: Bust of the King with Greek legend. Reverse: Winged Nike crowning the King. Legend: *King Gondophares the Saviour.*

Silver Coin showing the Saka King Nahapana (AD 50). Obverse: Bust of the King with Greek legend. Reverse: Arrow with Brahmi legend.

Silver Roman denarius found in India. Obverse: The Emperor Augustus. Reverse: His two grandsons, the Imperial Princes Gaius and Lucius Caesar.

A denarius of the Emperor Tiberius. Obverse: The Emperor. Reverse: Seated female figure, perhaps his mother Livia.

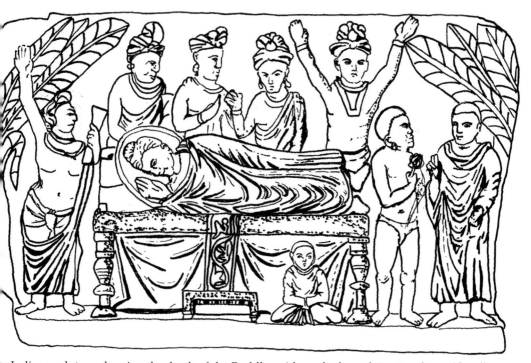

An Indian sculpture showing the death of the Buddha with a robed monk in attendance (Gandhara, Indus Region, second century AD).

Indian Ivory Statuette found at Pompeii (first century AD).

Relief Sculpture from the Stupa at Sanchi depicting an Indian City (first century AD).

Portrait Bust of a Buddhist Roman (second century AD). (*National Museum of Rome*)

large chambers, each with rows of internal pillars and a storage area of about 1,000 square feet.[9] More than eight of these chambers would have been needed to store the entire summer harvest of frankincense as it arrived at the installation and was stacked in wicker baskets.[10] Adjacent to these facilities was a trade-station inhabited by a cosmopolitan community of merchants from many parts of the Indian Ocean.

Trade at Qana
The high-promontory at Qana was heavily fortified and probably off-limits to most foreign merchants. Checkpoints guarded the steep stone staircases that wound upwards to the summit. These walkways were enclosed by walls to pre-vent rock-falls and were overlooked by square watch-towers.[11] There was a citadel at the summit of the cliff containing a temple structure that probably operated as a beacon for incoming ships. Large cisterns in the fort collected and stored rainwater for the Hadramawt garrison.[12]

Excavations reveal evidence of an attack on Qana sometime in antiquity when a fire destroyed the incense storerooms at the base of the promontory. Archae-ologists recovered the charred remains of large woven bags and palm baskets among the carbonised remains of destroyed frankincense stocks.[13] This was possibly a raid conducted by a rival Arab power whose troops had been unable to breach the inner walls of the summit fortress.

There was a caravan road from Qana that led north to the inland Hadramawt capital Sabota in the Wadi Hadramaut.[14] Some of the stock of frankincense col-lected at Qana would have been sent to Sabota to be burned in the royal temples, used by the court of King Eleazos, or distributed amongst his subjects. But most of the main harvest remained at Qana where it was sold to Arab dealers from neighbouring nations and various foreign merchants who visited the port.

Ships came to Qana from the Persian Gulf, the Parthian Empire, southern Iran, the Indus region and the Saka Kingdom in Gujarat. Merchants from all these territories sought frankincense to take back for sale in their home cities. They also used the opportunity to trade with other foreign merchants who visited the port and thereby obtained a range of cargoes from distant regions that were not on their usual sailing schedules. The *Periplus* explains that 'Qana carries on trade with the ports across the sea, including Barygaza, Scythia, Omana and its neighbour Persia'.[15]

Merchants from the Red Sea reached Qana in October and ships from Persia and India that had waited for the shift in trade winds arrived at the port in November.[16] The Hadramawt probably made their main stocks of incense avail-able for sale when the port was at its busiest as competition would ensure them the best deals. Foreign goods acquired from the exchange of state-owned incense stocks were sent by caravan to Sabota and sold to the Hadramawt people by agents of the king.

Archaeological evidence confirms the full extent of foreign activity at the ancient port. For example, only a quarter of the pottery fragments found at the ancient site belong to locally made containers. Archaeologists found shreds of elegant pink-clay tableware from Nabataea and rough pottery from Adulis in East Africa. They also recovered pieces of green-glazed pottery from the Parthian Empire and fragments of black and grey storage vessels from the Persian Gulf. These containers would have once held dates and palm wine produced in the fields of ancient Mesopotamia, while Indian involvement at Qana is demonstrated by finds of red polished tableware at the port.[17]

Roman merchants visiting Qana offered local traders and state-agents a large quantity of printed fabrics and Arab-style clothing either with or without adornment. They also traded goods that were valuable in Indian markets including copper, tin, red coral and storax perfumes. Other Roman goods sent to Qana were the same as those traded in Muza including purple cloth, patterned clothing with sleeves, garments interwoven with gold thread, striped waistbands, cloth bundles, blankets, saffron, cyperus, fragrant unguents and imperial money. Roman ships offloaded a limited amount of Egyptian wheat at Qana either for trade with the Hadramawt garrison, or to supply merchants from the Empire who were long-term residents at the port.[18]

Roman merchants arriving early in the season had to wait several weeks at Qana for eastern ships to arrive at the harbour and for the Hadramawt to release their incoming frankincense crops.[19] A significant portion of the Mediterranean pottery found at the site could therefore be from Roman crews who had gone ashore to await scheduled contacts and trade deals. More than half of the pottery fragments found at Qana belong to Roman amphorae that had been either taken ashore as supplies or offered to foreign merchants. These containers would have held popular wine vintages and were mostly manufactured in Italy, Egypt and the eastern Mediterranean. Some of the Roman shards found at Qana were from containers that once held garum fish sauce from Spain.[20]

About a fifth of the Roman pottery fragments found at Qana have black volcanic specks in their composition which indicates that they were manufactured in the Italian district of Campania near Vesuvius.[21] The eruption of Vesuvius in AD 79 had a detrimental impact on this trade because the volcanic ash cloud and pyroclastic blast damaged the wine-growing industry in the surrounding areas. After the disaster, Roman merchants probably increased their export of bullion to Qana, as the wine stocks available for trade exchange were suddenly reduced.

Fine quality Italian-made tableware (*terra sigillata*) from the Augustan era has also been found at ancient Qana. One of the shards bore the impression of a small stamp marked with a foot symbol and the name 'AGATE'. This symbol identifies the manufacturer as Agathemerus who owned workshops in eastern Sicily and was producing this style of tableware in the period between 15 BC and AD 15.[22] The fragments of Roman glassware that have been found during excavation at Qana were either used by visiting traders, or examples of yet another Roman export commodity.[23]

The *Periplus* mentions expensive Roman goods destined for the Hadramawt royal court including embossed silverware and 'large amounts of coin'. Roman merchants provided the Hadramawt King with prized horses, classical statues and expensive clothing.[24] Along with bullion, these costly items acquired the best stocks of state-owned frankincense being offered from the Qana ware-houses.[25] The *Periplus* does not record the journey time from Qana to Sabota, so it is possible that these deals were conducted mostly through royal agents stationed at the port. Local officials would then manage delivery of bullion profits and royal property directly to the ruling court at Sabota.

Roman ships visiting Qana took on board mainly frankincense grown in the highland plantations under Hadramawt authority. By AD 50, the Hadramawt also had control over the African island of Socotra and its frankincense crop was shipped across to Qana along with a sought-after plant substance called aloe.[26] Aloe was in high demand in the Roman Empire because its cooling juices soothed burns and helped treat abrasive skin irritations. It was also ingested as a laxative and given to grazing animals to treat intestinal blockages.[27] Roman merchants who ended their voyages at Qana also had the opportunity to trade with other foreign visitors to the port. The *Periplus* explains that 'further exports to Qana are through its connections with the other ports of trade' and from these deals Roman traders could acquire incoming African, Persian, or Indian goods.[28]

Some Roman ships visiting Muza had problems with ballast because they off-loaded heavy cargoes at the port and took on board only lightweight and compact stores of incense. This change in the weight and distribution of cargo in their holds made many vessels unstable. To alleviate this problem, Roman ships head-ing for India took on board Arabian wines.[29] Local containers used at Qana were large vessels with a porous surface that were suitable for storing foods, rather than liquids.[30] Palm wines exported from Qana were therefore shipped in goat-skin flasks, or decanted into Mediterranean amphorae that could provide important weight and stability for Roman ships headed further east.

During the era of the *Periplus*, most Roman ships specialising in Arabian trade ended their voyages at Qana. Ships heading straight back to Egypt therefore took on board volcanic rocks to act as ballast in their holds and these stones were dumped at Egyptian harbours before replacement Roman cargo was loaded in preparation for the next voyage. Stacks of volcanic rocks found at Berenice and Myos Hormos provide evidence for this ancient solution to the ballast problem.[31] At least a third of the ballast found at Myos Hormos comes from the shoreline near Eudaimon (Aden) and must represent trade in the Ptolemaic era, or Roman commerce conducted after the revival of this port. But almost all the ballast found at Berenice comes from Qana and represents trade conducted during the early Roman Imperial period.

Socotra Island

Socotra lay on the Horn of Africa, but the island held an important position in Arabian seaborne commerce. The island is eighty miles long and thirty miles wide and was closely associated with southern Arabia. Greek merchants from Egypt visited the island in the first century BC to meet foreign ships coming from India. Some of these early merchants settled on the north side of the island and the *Periplus* describes the population in this era as 'a mixture of Arabs and Indians and even some Greeks, who have sailed out there to trade'. The Romans called the island 'Dioscurides' and regarded it as part of Arabia.[32] Indian merchants were important in the early development of this island as a trade outpost and the name Dioscurides was a Greek adaptation of the Sanskrit *Dvipa Sukhadhara* meaning 'Island of Bliss'.

Socotra was about 250 miles south of a port called Syagros Fort in the Hadramawt Kingdom and nearly 150 miles west of Cape Guardafui in Somalia. Due to Hadramawt control over the main sea-lanes leading to the island, the author of the *Periplus* wrongly thought that Socotra was positioned closer to Syagros than to Africa. The *Periplus* describes Socotra as a large island filled with stretches of desolate terrain and damp regions watered by inland river systems. Its unusual wildlife included 'crocodiles, numerous vipers and large lizards that are eaten for their flesh, while their fat is melted down to produce oil'. The *Periplus* suggests that no farm products were available on the island and the few settlers who lived there had to import essential supplies of grain and wine.[33]

Socotra was subject to extreme heat and was in the right climatic zone to grow frankincense. Its native trees grew in strange hemispherical shapes that shaded the surrounding soil with a canopy of tightly-twisted branches and long stiff leaves. The sap from these trees (*dracaena cinnabari*) was a resin with a deep red pigment known in ancient times as 'dragon's blood'. Dragon's blood was highly sought-after in the ancient world because it could be applied to wounds as a coagulant or ingested to soothe internal ulcers. The product could also reduce fever and was effective at treating bouts of dysentery.[34] The *Periplus* calls the red sap 'Indian cinnabar' and knew that it was 'collected as an exudation from the trees'.[35] Most of the frankincense and aloe that was grown on Socotra was probably shipped to Syagros before being transferred to Qana where it was sold to Roman merchants.

One of the main exports from Socotra was the tortoiseshell that the Romans used for furniture veneers. Hawksbill turtles were hunted around the coast and land tortoises were commonplace on the island. These included leopard tortoises with large, brightly patterned shells. The *Periplus* reports that 'the island yields great quantities of tortoiseshell generally offered as large shields. Varieties include the standard kind, the land-type and the light-coloured product.' Usually Roman craftsmen were only interested in the shield (the dorsal shell) of the animal, but one of the tortoise types on Socotra had ventral plates that were thick enough to be carved into small objects. The *Periplus* informs traders: 'the oversize mountain variety of tortoise has an extremely thick shell and the parts that cover the belly are useful. They are tawny and will not take regular craft-cutting, but they can be used for small boxes, plaques, disks and similar items that are completely cut up'.[36]

In the Augustan era, Roman ships sometimes visited Socotra after finishing their business at Muza. Socotra was probably closed to most seaborne traffic during the peak of the summer southwest monsoon, but ships were able to reach the island in autumn. Roman ships would therefore approach Socotra on winter sailings back from India and could offer the settlers some of the Indian cargo in return for tortoiseshell. The *Periplus* explains that 'some of the shippers from

Muza and those sailing out of Limyrike and Barygaza trade if they chance to put in at the island'. They exchanged rice, grain, cotton cloth and female slaves for 'large cargoes of tortoiseshell'.[37] Fragments of ancient pottery have been found near Hajrya on the north part of the island and these finds include Arab pottery from Qana, black and grey wares from the Persian Gulf and a few fragments of Roman amphorae.[38]

The opportunity for direct trade ended when the Hadramawt seized possession of Socotra. After the takeover, the Hadramawt King leased the island to a consortium of Arab merchants who ran the territory as a business venture. The syndicate hired private guards to protect their investment and Roman ships were no longer permitted to land on the island. The *Periplus* explains that 'the island is subject to the king of the Frankincense-Bearing land' and 'at the present time the kings have leased out the island and it is under guard'.[39]

Ancient stonewall boundaries have been identified on the island and perhaps these were part of the plantation plots established by the consortium.[40] Myrrh trees could have been introduced during this era as the tree is now a recognisable feature of the modern island.[41] The consortium would have sold the products of Socotra in the main Arab ports, or perhaps taken their valuable cargoes to Roman markets in Egypt or Palestine. Confirmation comes from ancient documents and inscriptions found in a cave at Hoq on the northeast coast of Socotra. Some of the texts are on wooden tablets and the writings include Nabataean, Indian, Ethiopian and Palmyrene languages along with graffiti depicting eastern ships.[42]

Roman vessels trading with Qana were advised to leave Egypt a little before September to accommodate the longer sailing.[43] From Qana it was a voyage of at least thirty days back to Egypt and most Roman ships returned to the Empire in November at the earliest. By contrast, Roman captains involved in voyages to India left Qana in August and headed east along the seaboard of the Frankincense-Bearing Lands.

The Frankincense Coast
Beyond Qana there was a deep inlet called Sachalites Bay which was on the western edge of the Frankincense-Bearing Land. Beyond Sachalites Bay was the headland of Ras Fartak which was known to Roman sailors as 'Syagros', or 'Wild-Boar Promontory'. The *Periplus* describes Syagros as a 'mighty headland facing east' and it was from this projecting landmark that Roman ships sailed out to sea on their ocean crossings to India.[44]

This stretch of the Arabian Sea contained large humpbacked whales that sometimes approached too close to Roman ships and sprayed them with water from their blowholes. Strabo reports, 'those who now sail to India speak of the appearance and size of these creatures. They say that these whales can be scared away by shouts and trumpets and they do not often appear in large groups or attack ships.'[45] Philostratus confirms that 'the entire sea is full of sharks and groups of whales'. He claims that Apollonius travelled on an Indian vessel that carried bells at the bow and the stern to frighten away these sea creatures.[46]

Syagros was the furthest location in Arabia regularly visited by Roman merchants from Egypt. Writing a decade after the *Periplus* the Greek pharmacist Dioscorides mentions a distinctive variety of frankincense called 'Syagros' that was shipped from this place.[47] The Hadramawt had a fortress on the east side of Syagros Promontory that protected the harbour and acted as a temporary storehouse for the collection of frankincense destined for Qana. By AD 50 Syagros was probably the main port for Hadramawt ships bound for Socotra Island on the nearby Horn of Africa.

Pliny locates the main frankincense growing region about eight days travel from the Hadramawt capital Sabota. The territory was called 'Sariba' which the Greeks claimed meant 'Secret Mystery' in the native language.[48] When Herodotus described this region he imagined that 'winged serpents' guarded the incense groves.[49] These stories might have been based on distorted accounts of Arabian fat-tailed scorpions with large pronged pincers and arching tails able to deliver a powerful neurotoxin. But Pliny dismissed the accounts as 'stories invented for the purpose of enhancing the prices of these commodities'.[50] By the mid-first century AD the Hadramawt Kings of southern Arabia were collecting a second harvest on their incense crops. Pliny reports: 'in former times, when they had fewer opportunities for sale, the Arabs used to harvest their frankincense only once a year. But at present there is a much greater demand for the product, so they now gather a second, additional crop.'[51]

Few Romans had seen the coast of the frankincense-producing lands that lay east of Syagros. The incense trees grew in limestone highlands that were arid in the winter months and during summer were obscured by the heavy clouds of the oncoming monsoon. The *Periplus* explains that 'the land is mountainous with difficult terrain and an atmosphere that is misty and oppressive'. Roman merchants were correctly informed that the frankincense woodlands consisted of medium sized trees that produced resins, 'congealed from the bark'.[52]

Pliny describes the frankincense region as 'surrounded by impenetrable rocks and bordered by a seacoast with inaccessible cliffs'. Furthermore, these highlands had, 'hills rising to a great height with natural forests that spread down to the plain'. Foreign travellers were not permitted to venture into this region, so there are few details known about the incense crop. The clay-like soil was 'a milky white colour with a tinge of red' and the local springs were said to be heavily alkaline. Based on reports from the pre-Hadramawt period, the frankincense-growing region was estimated to be about a hundred miles across and fifty miles wide.[53]

Pliny describes how the frankincense crop was collected in the period before the Hadramawt conquered the region. In the first century BC the Sabaeans managed the wood-lands as a series of inherited family plots. These landholdings were cultivated by family members who had to maintain certain ritual purities during the harvesting period, such as avoiding contact with corpses. Pliny reports, 'it is said less than 3,000 families retain the right of producing frankincense as a hereditary property'.[54] The resultant crop was shared out between the families and sold to merchants from neighbouring regions.

When the Hadramawt controlled the region they confiscated the frankincense groves and used slave-workers to manage the harvests. Describing conditions in the mid-first century AD the *Periplus* explains that 'the frankincense is handled by royal slaves and convicts'. Roman crews were discouraged from visiting these shores by stories that the local climate was harmful and it was said that the slave-workers were severely mistreated by their Hadramawt masters. Some of these reports may have been deliberate disinformation spread by Hadramawt agents, but the tactic was successful. The *Periplus* reports: 'these districts are very unhealthy, harmful to those sailing by and absolutely fatal to those working there. The workers frequently die due to lack of nourishment'.[55]

According to the *Periplus*, the seaboard of the incense-producing region was over 120 miles long. East of Syagros Fort was a wide bay called Omana that covered nearly seventy miles of coastline. Beyond this bay the seaboard was dominated by 'high mountains, rocky and sheer, where men live in caves'.[56] Arab vessels sailing fifty miles along this coast reached another Hadramawt harbour-fortress called Moscha Limen (modern Khor Rori).

Moscha Harbour was a fortified collection point positioned at the eastern limit of the frankincense-producing region. The *Periplus* describes Moscha as 'a desig-nated harbour for loading *sachalite* frankincense' from nearby production sites. Hadramawt ships based at Moscha Harbour delivered these stocks to Qana, several hundred miles west of the port.[57] Together Syagros Fort and Moscha Harbour guarded the two opposite ends of the frankincense-producing highlands and ensured that only approved traffic was allowed to venture along this shore-line.

Moscha was established on a natural harbour in a sheltered lagoon that was reached through a narrow inlet. During the autumn season, Hadramawt camel teams worked in relays to bring the collected frankincense crops down from the highlands to the stronghold. A pound of the best grade frankincense could be sold in Roman markets for 10 denarii, so security was paramount at the facility.[58] The harbour-town was surrounded by thick stone walls and defensive towers that guarded a single reinforced entrance to the complex. The entrance-passage through the narrow main gates changed direction several times and passed through further buttressed doors. Travellers therefore had to zigzag through narrow passageways to gain admittance to the town.[59] Moscha was at the centre of a network of security features. Further walls and check-points on the main approaches to the town monitored caravan traffic approaching from the north.[60]

The fortified ruins of Moscha Harbour (Khor Rori) have been excavated and more information has been discovered about the ancient site. Archaeologists suggest that over 200 people lived and worked at Moscha. The town had paved streets, well-planned residential zones, warehouses, temples and a large open market-place where trade deals could be conducted. An inscription found near the town gates explains how Moscha was founded by a royal Hadramawt direc-tive. The population of Moscha were conscripts from an inland territory called Sumhuram in the homelands of the Hadramawt nation. Inscriptions from the site suggest that the colonists were selected for settlement at this eastern outpost and brought to the harbour as a subject labour force.[61] The entire facility seems to have been planned and built sometime in the last decades of the first century BC. This is consistent with the Hadramawt having conquered the region during the breakup of the Sabaean Kingdom and establishing a series of new ports (Qana, Syagros and Moscha) to manage the collection and sale of the incense harvests.

Ancient grains of desiccated frankincense have been found scattered across the excavation layers at Moscha Limen. The discovery of grinding stones and hand-mills suggests that there were farmsteads in the vicinity that provided some locally grown food for the settlers. However, the coast was not well suited to agriculture and the colonists were probably dependent on food supplies sent from the main Hadramawt homeland.[62]

Sometimes Roman ships heading for India suffered a delay and reached Syagros Promontory when the summer monsoon winds were already subsiding. On these occasions they could seek safe harbour at Moscha and remain there during the winter under the protection of the Hadramawt authorities. After the winter monsoon, these vessels could continue their voyages to India. It was a rare occurrence for Roman ships to miss the southwest monsoon, but Indian vessels were often caught out by the seasonal change because they sailed slightly later in the summer when the winds were already subsiding. Consequently, many Indian ships heading for Egypt carried extra supplies in case they were forced to harbour at Moscha Limen on the return sailing. The *Periplus* confirms that 'ships sailing from Limyrike or Barygaza may spend the winter at Moscha if the season is late'.[63] This explains why the image of a two-masted Indian trade vessel was found scratched into the plaster wall of a building in the town. The broken remains of Roman cookware have also been found at ancient Moscha confirming that merchants from the Empire spent time in the harbour.[64]

Many Indian ships were well stocked with food produce destined for sale in East Africa. The harbour service organised at Moscha therefore helped to alleviate supply difficulties in the town. The *Periplus* reports that 'by arrangement with the royal agents, visiting ships may take on board a cargo of *sachalite* frankincense in exchange for cotton cloth, grain and oil'. The Hadramawt made these exchanges at a time when favourable winds had returned and foreign ships could resume their voyages. The author of the *Periplus* had never visited Moscha, but he heard stories about the deals conducted at the site. It was said that 'the pier is unguarded because some power of the gods watches over this place and no one can load frankincense aboard a ship either in plain sight, or by stealth, unless royal permission is given. Even if a single grain is taken aboard without approval, then the ship cannot sail since it is against the will of the god.'[65] These stories confirm the authority that the Hadramawt had over all the frankincense produced in Arabia Felix.

In AD 50, Moscha Harbour was the furthest outpost of the Hadramawt Kingdom. There was a mountain range called Asichon (Ras Hasik) about 170 miles east of Moscha that Arab ships used as a landmark on voyages into the Persian Gulf.[66] The seven isles of Zenobios (Khuriya Muriya) were on this coast and their beaches provided nesting grounds for turtles to come ashore and lay their eggs.[67]

In modern times up to 10,000 turtles come ashore to bury their eggs on these coasts during spring nights when the moon is large and full.[68] The *Periplus* reports that the coast beyond Zenobios was 'inhabited by an indigenous people who are part of a different kingdom – that of Persia.'[69]

Claudius Ptolemy indicates that the Hadramawt took control of the coast near Asichon sometime after the *Periplus* was written. He records the existence of a naval base called Neogilla positioned east of Moscha Harbour.[70] From Neogilla a squadron of Hadramawt warships was probably involved in policing shipping, or controlling important offshore resources. By then the Hadramawt had probably seized the Zenobios Islands to control the collection of valuable turtle-shell.

CHAPTER TWELVE

The Indo-Parthians

Roman ships bound for India left the Red Sea ports in July when the seasonal northerly winds blew down the gulf. The first stage of the journey was a 700 mile sailing to the Arabian port called Ocelis. It took three weeks to reach Ocelis and Roman ships arriving at the town took on board fresh water and waited for the onset of the monsoon trade winds.[1]

During the first century BC, Greek ships tended to follow the coasts of Iran on their eastern voyages to India. The *Periplus* describes this era as a time when 'men formerly used to sail in smaller vessels, following the curves of the bays'. But when Greek pilots charted the shape of the Indian coast, they realised that shorter sea crossings were possible. Maritime folklore claimed that the first trans-ocean voyages were undertaken by 'a captain named Hippalos, who, by plotting the location of trade ports and the configuration of the sea, was the first to discover the route over open water'.[2] The *Periplus* claims the southwest monsoon was renamed in honour of this early navigator.

Pliny received further information on monsoon travel from a government report compiled sometime between AD 48 and AD 52.[3] This report called the southeast monsoon the 'Hippalos' and gave sailing times to ports in southern India. Pliny explains that in his own time most Roman ships took forty days to sail from Ocelis to southern India, but some of this journey time was spent visiting the trade ports in the Gulf of Aden.[4]

Roman ships would enter the Gulf of Aden in early August when the southwest monsoon was just beginning to blow across the Indian Ocean. Some ships followed the Arabian coast as far as Qana, while others sailed along the Horn of Africa to Cape Guardafui. From these locations Roman captains sailed out into the open ocean, trusting that the powerful monsoon winds would take their ships directly to the Indian coast. The monsoon blows at Near Gale Force Seven (40 miles-per-hour, heaped waves and moderate ocean spray) often rising to Whole Gale Force Ten (60 miles-per-hour winds, high waves with overhanging crests, white foaming sea, with pounding waves and airborne spray that reduces visibility). The *Periplus* explains that Roman ships heading for the Tamil lands 'set out with the wind on the quarter for most of the way, but those bound for Barygaza or Scythia hold course for only three days and take the rest of the run on their own direction. Thus they are carried away from the shore on to the high seas'.[5] Pliny explains that the southern voyage to the Tamil lands was considered 'the most advantageous way of sailing to India' and observed that 'the desire for gain brings India ever nearer'.[6]

When driven by gale-force winds, even the largest and most cumbersome Roman freighters were able to travel at speeds greater than six knots (nautical miles per hour). Roman ships heading for northern India crossed 1,000 miles of ocean in about seven days, while those sailing to the Tamil lands launched on a southern course and crossed more than 1,600 miles of open sea in just over ten days. The *Periplus* confirms 'those who sail with the Indian winds leave in July (*Epeiph*) and although this voyage is hard going, it is absolutely favourable and shorter'.[7]

Roman captains timed their voyages so that they reached India in early September when the monsoon winds were subsiding and the coastal trade-routes re-opened. Altogether, it took nearly seventy days to complete the entire voyage from Egypt to India. The Roman voyagers who disembarked at the Indian ports were almost 3,000 miles from the nearest frontiers of their Empire. They would spend at least two months in India, as the trade winds that returned them home did not begin to blow until early November.

The Indo-Scythian Kingdom
The seven outlets of the Indus River expelled a vast quantity of fresh water into the Indian Ocean. The *Periplus* called the Indus 'the mightiest of all the rivers along the Indian Ocean' and reports that Roman pilots could recognise signs of the river water while still far out to sea. The pilots knew they were on the correct course when the sea around their vessel became pale in colour and the ship's lookouts sighted '"eels emerging from the depths" to swim around the hull'. The first stop for Roman merchants was a port called Barbaricon which lay on the central mouth of the Indus River and served an inland capital called Minnagar that lay just upstream.[8]

During the first century AD, the Indus Region was ruled by Indo-Parthian warlords who controlled the main cities in the Sindh. The apocryphal *Acts of Thomas* describes how the apostle sailed to this region sometime before AD 40. Thomas was taken to an Indian city known as Andrapolis and was assigned work overseeing the construction of a regional palace for an Indo-Parthian King named Gondophares.[9] The *Acts* describe the encounter when the king questioned 'what craftsmanship do you know in wood and stone?' The apostle replied: 'in wood: ploughs, yokes, goads, pulleys, boats, oars and masts; and in stone: pillars, temples, and courthouses for kings. And the king said: Can you build me a palace? And Thomas answered: Yes, I can build it and furnish it too'.[10]

Evidence from ancient coins and inscriptions indicate that Gondophares was in power between AD 20 and AD 45, but his death caused serious instability in the region.[11] Consequently, when the *Periplus* describes the kingdom in AD 52 the territory was 'under the control of Parthians, who are constantly ousting each other from the throne'.[12]

Although Roman ships moored at Barbaricon, trade exchanges were conducted at the royal city of Minnagar. Minnagar was the district capital of southern Indo-Parthia and the *Periplus* reports that 'all cargoes are taken up the river to the king at the metropolis.'[13] This was a royal directive and made it easier for government agents to tax and control international trade. Indian policies towards foreign commerce are outlined in an ancient Sanskrit guide to statesmanship called the *Arthasastra*.[14] The *Arthasastra* contains a section offering advice to the Superintendent of Commerce who fixed market prices for state-owned goods sold in the capital.[15] Another royal official called the Superintendent of Tolls was responsible for taxing trade goods entering the main city.

Roman cargo offloaded at Barbaricon was assessed by a customs officer known as the *Antapala* (Officer in Charge of Boundaries). According to the *Arthasastra*, the *Antapala* examined the quality of the incoming cargo and stamped delivery batches with his distinctive seal. He also collected road and ferry tolls on merchants heading to the main city with their bonded goods. The *Antapala* kept customs records and maintained a network of 'spies in the guise of traders' who he could send 'to the king with information about the quantity and quality of incoming merchandise'. The king would forward this information to the Superintendent of Tolls so that agents in the main city knew exactly what goods foreign merchants were bringing into the capital. The *Arthasastra* recommends that the superintendent confronts merchants with this knowledge so that they understand 'that nothing can be kept secret and all information is known through the omniscient power of the king'.[16]

The *Arthasastra* advises Indian kings to impose different toll rates on the trade goods brought into their main cities and suggests that customs taxes on foreign goods arriving through seaborne commerce be set at one-fifth value. Taxes set up to one-tenth value were to be collected on 'fibrous garments, cotton cloths, silk, mail armour, sulphate of arsenic, red arsenic, vermilion, metals, colouring ingredients, sandalwood, pungents, ferments, clothing, wine, ivory, skins, raw materials for fibrous or cotton garments, carpets, curtains, insect products and wool'. Other items were subject to specially assessed higher tolls and this category included diamonds, precious stones, pearls and corals.[17]

The *Arthasastra* describes how the Superintendent of Tolls would have operated a customs station at the main gates of Minnagar, where a flag or banner signalled his presence. His toll booths would be manned by a team of four or five staff who stopped and questioned incoming merchants. They examined the state-seal on bonded merchandise to ensure that no goods had been removed on-route to the city. The *Arthasastra* instructs the agents to record 'who the merchants are, where they come from, how much merchandise they bring and where they received their first customs seal'.[18] The details taken at Minnagar could be compared with custom records from Barbaricon to ensure that no-one was evading taxes.

The *Arthasastra* suggests that goods without a seal mark should be subject to double-rate tax and merchants who used a counterfeit seal were to be charged eight times what they would usually pay. For Roman traders who transgressed, this meant their entire consignment of goods might be confiscated. Foreign merchants were also forbidden to sell weapons and armour to Indian subjects and if these goods were found, they were forfeited. The *Arthasastra* advises, 'whatever causes harm, or is useless to the country, shall be shut out; and whatever is of immense good, as well as seeds not easily available, shall be let in free of toll'.[19]

Once through the gate, incoming goods were placed under the banner of the toll-house and merchants were required to cry out the quantity and price of their goods three times. Merchants were forced to give a realistic market price because anyone watching the proceedings was permitted to buy the goods at the declared price. If the merchant cried out an unrealistically low price, then nearby competitors could immediately begin bidding for his stock. But if he cried out a high enough price, then this would deter bidders and he could keep his merchandise for sale in the city. If there were no challenges, then the supervising customs agents would collect tax at the stated value. If there was a bidding contest, then the percentage tax was due from the winning bidder.[20] Indian rulers sometimes made their own subjects exempt from import tax so that local merchants could thrive and this enabled them to expand their foreign business. The *Arthasastra* advises rulers that 'subject mariners and merchants who import foreign merchandise shall be favoured with remission of the trade-taxes, so that they may gain profit'.[21]

The Indian system responded to market prices, so visiting merchants needed good knowledge of local conditions in order to secure the best deals. This situation encouraged Roman merchants to settle in Indian cities where they could act as brokers, or stockpile sought-after produce. They could advise those arriving at Barbaricon about market conditions in Minnagar and suggest what goods were worth taking ashore.

Goods Sent to Minnagar
Indo-Scythia received ships from Egypt, India, Arabia and the Persian Gulf. The *Periplus* records that Roman merchants visiting Minnagar offloaded bulk clothing, multi-coloured textiles and printed cloth. Roman dealers also offered costly storax perfumes, glass vessels and expensive silverware for luxury dining. Mediterranean workshops had developed techniques for making crystal-clear glass that could be coloured in beautiful pale hues. Roman subjects had also devised the first glass-blowing methods that allowed large thin-walled vessels to be created with minimal effort and expense. Glass ornaments produced in India and China tended to be small and heavy with opaque impurities, so there was demand for Roman glass in the Indian markets.

High-value deals at Minnagar were also conducted with the use of Roman money, red coral and peridot gemstones known as *chrysolithon* (golden-stones). These yellow-green stones were mined on Zabargad Island which lies just south of ancient Berenice. Romans also brought incense to Minnagar which they collected from the Arab and African ports they visited on the outbound journey. Only a limited amount of wine was sent to Barbaricon, but there was great interest in Mediterranean red coral.[22]

In ancient times red coral grew in the western Mediterranean between the island of Sicily and the Balearic Sea. Most coral becomes brittle and discoloured when brought to the surface, but the Mediterranean variety was exceptional. It grew in branch-like growths that resembled skeletal bushes that were up to half the height of a person. Pliny describes how Roman divers cut coral branches from the seabed using sharp iron instruments and gathered them into net bags to be taken to the surface. When hauled ashore the branches hardened into a dense porcelain-like material that displayed vivid colours ranging from pink to deep red. The branches were cut and polished to produce valuable semi-precious stones to adorn special jewellery and ornaments.

Roman tradition claimed that red coral came from the blood of a female monster named Medusa who was slain by the Greek hero Perseus. Medusa was a Gorgon whose gaze could turn creatures into stone and fossilise living tissue. Andromeda, daughter of King Cepheus, was chained to a rock-face as a sacrifice and Perseus used the severed head of Medusa to rescue her. But drops of blood from the head fell into the sea, creating a living organism that hardened to stone when removed from its element. Ovid explains, 'the seaweed's porous tendrils absorb the monster's power and congeal. They take on a new stiffness in their stems and leaves. The sea nymphs test this wonder on more tendrils and seed them in the sea. Even now coral has retained this property so that stems, although placid under the water, turn to stone once exposed to the air.'[23]

In Roman society smooth red coral was used as a protective charm for people who were vulnerable. Concerned parents would provide their babies with amulets made from red coral and the substance was believed to have a supernatural influence over both water and fire because of its vivid warm colours and aquatic origin. Coral is rich in calcium carbonate and Greek doctors realised that powdered coral was a strong antacid that was useful for treating indigestion.[24]

Ancient India was well informed about the origins of Roman coral. The *Arthasastra* explains that red coral came from *Alakandaka* which is a Sanskrit rendition of the name Alexandria.[25] The study also mentions coral from Vaivarnaka which is described in a Sanskrit treaty on words and grammar as 'a sea near the island of the *Yavanas* (Romans)'.[26] This is probably the Mediterranean Sea around Sicily or Sardinia, both of which have coral producing coasts.[27] The *Arthasastra* describes coral from this region as having 'a ruby-like colour and a very hard structure that is free from the contamination of other substances'.[28]

Authorities in Rome were amazed at the value Indian society placed on Mediterranean coral. Pliny reports that 'coral berries are valued by Indian men as much as large Indian pearls are prized by Roman women. Indian soothsayers and seers believe coral to be a very powerful amulet for warding off dangers. So they enjoy it as a beautiful item and an object of religious power.'[29] Sanskrit texts confirm the value of red coral received from *Romaka* (the Roman Empire). They praise the vivid colour and supposed magical properties of this prized substance which was classified as *ratna* (jewels).[30] Hindu and Buddhist scripture tells how a primordial serpentine deity called Vasuki defeated the Lord of Demons and had his mutilated body dragged through the heavens. Drops of the demon's blood fell to the earth to form rubies and his entrails were cast into distant seas. A Hindu text called the *Garuda Puranam* explains that coral grew from these entrails, 'the best kind are red like the blood of a hare, orange like the Gunja berry, or pink like a Chinese rose'.[31]

The *Garuda Puranam* reports that red coral 'is empowered with the virtue of augmenting the riches and filling the granaries of its wearer'. Coral amulets were also said to be 'the best eliminator of poison and a safeguard against all dreaded evils'.[32] An early Indian study on gemstones called the *Ratnapariksa* explains that 'good coral is tender, smooth and shining and has a beautiful red colour. In this world it procures richness and gains; gives women marital bliss; destroys corruption and illness, and wards off perils such as poison'.[33] The *Arthasastra* recommended that valuable stores of red coral should be stockpiled in royal treasuries along with pearls, rubies, beryls and diamonds.[34]

Pliny explains that the Gauls used to ornament their swords, shields and helmets with coral fittings, but this 'was before the Indian love of this material became known'. He reports that 'nowadays, coral has become scarce because of the price it will fetch in eastern markets and it is very rarely seen in the countries where it grows'.[35]

Exports from Minnagar

Under Parthian rule, the Indo-Scythian Kingdom extended north into the Hindu-Kush and received trade goods from the Himalayas. The region also received merchandise from Bactria (ancient Afghanistan) delivered by caravans leaving the Central Asian silk routes. Roman traders visiting Minnagar could therefore find Indian, Afghan, Iranian, Scythian and Chinese goods on offer in the city.

An important part of the international commerce conducted at Minnagar involved spices, aromatics and plant-based drugs. Roman merchants received locally grown bdellium, nard and lyceum from the Himalayas and costus from Kashmir in Afghanistan. Silk route traffic reached the Indus, so Barbaricon offered silk and exotic animal furs, including mink and sable from the Asian steppe. Roman merchants also received locally produced indigo dyes, turquoise stones from Iran and blue lapis lazuli crystals mined in Afghanistan.[36]

During the time of the *Periplus* Afghanistan was under the rule of a powerful new regime called the Kushan. The Kushans were a population of steppe warriors who had come from a homeland on the western edge of the Chinese Empire. They conquered Afghanistan and established a kingdom in Bactria under a supreme ruler named Kujula Kadphises. The *Periplus* describes the Kushan as 'a very warlike people' and reports that these 'Bactrians are now ruled by a single king'.[37]

Excavations at a Kushan palace in Begram revealed the importance of ancient trade routes through Afghanistan. Subterranean storerooms at the site contained costly Indian, Iranian, Chinese and Roman art objects. These items date to about AD 100 and were probably associated with royal feasting and palace display. The Roman finds include plaster moulds with classical motifs, bronze statuettes, serving bowls, colourful glassware and brightly painted vases. The vases display images from Greek myth and scenes from the Empire including a Roman gladiator and a view of the Pharos lighthouse at Alexandria.[38] Wine was produced in Bactria and Kushan nobles would have enjoyed their vintages in crystal-clear

Roman glassware. Kushan warrior graves at Tillya Tepe also contained numerous items of gold jewellery fitted with turquoise and lapis lazuli. These objects display Greek and Scythian motifs reworked to suit Bactrian fashions.[39]

The Chinese referred to the Indus region as *Tianzhu* and they collected reports about its trade resources. The *Hou Hanshu* records that Tianzhu produced elephants, rhinoceroses, turtle-shell, gold, silver, copper, iron, lead and tin. When the Han authorities investigated India's trade contacts with Rome, they were informed: 'to the west, Tianzhu communicates with *Da Qin* (the Roman Empire). Precious things from Rome can be found there, as well as fine cotton cloths, excellent wool carpets, all sorts of perfumes, sugar-loaves, pepper, ginger, and black-salt'.[40]

When Claudius Ptolemy described India, Barygaza was no longer operating as an emporium for foreign trade. Instead, Roman merchants visited an Indus city called Bardaxima which was close to a naval site called 'Canthinaustathmus Station'. Canthinaustathmus was possibly the naval base of an Indus ruler who maintained warships on this coast.[41] Roman merchants visited several powerful kingdoms in ancient India who fought wars involving naval battles as well as large-scale land conflicts. In the time of the *Periplus*, Roman ships sailing south of the Indus region prepared to enter the territory of kingdoms at war.

CHAPTER THIRTEEN

The Saka and Satavahana Kingdoms

Roman ships leaving the Indus region sailed hundreds of miles south to a port in Gujurat called Barygaza. This was a treacherous sailing for the deep-hulled Roman vessels that might run aground on underwater hazards and be torn apart by powerful currents. The *Periplus* warns that east of the Indus was a bay called Eirinon where 'there is a succession of shallow eddies reaching out a long way from land. Here, vessels often run aground with the shore nowhere in sight'.[1]

Roman ships might also be drawn by ocean tides into the Gulf of Barake (Kutch). The *Periplus* warns that 'vessels blundering into the basin are destroyed, for the waves are very big and oppressive. The sea is choppy and turbid with eddies and violent whirlpools.'[2] The crews of Roman ships caught by these currents threw down restraining anchors, but the coast had sheer drops and sharp rocky outcrops that sometimes cut their anchor lines. These dangers have been confirmed by the discovery of Roman amphorae fragments and the remains of lead anchors on the seabed near the island of Bet Dwarka.[3] An indication that the ship was close to currents came when the pilots sighted 'sea-snakes, huge and black, emerging to meet the ship'. Most Roman ships would head out to sea and only re-join the coast when small golden-yellow eels were seen in the waters about their hull.[4] This was a sign that they had reached the Cambay Gulf which led to the city-port of Barygaza.

Barygaza was ruled by a dynasty of Saka kings who came from homelands on the Asian steppe. The Roman Emperor Augustus received envoys from these Sakas in 26 BC, when he was campaigning in Spain. Suetonius explains that these Indo-Scythian ambassadors 'were from nations previously known to us only through hearsay and they petitioned for the friendship of Augustus and the Roman people'.[5] This was a period when the Sakas still ruled most of the Indus region, but were being threatened by the Parthians. The Sakas were probably looking for a military alliance with Rome in the expectation that Augustus was planning to conquer Persia. This would explain why Orosius links the embassy to eastern conquests and claims that the ambassadors came to 'praise the Emperor with the glory of Alexander the Great'.[6]

This embassy was probably sent by Azes who was the last Saka king to rule in Indo-Scythia. The Sakas were influenced by Greek culture and Azes issued currency displaying images of the goddess Athena. He also used Greek titles on his coins and referred to himself as 'The Great King of Kings'.[7] King Azes was probably responsible for a second embassy that reached the Roman Empire in 22 BC. On this occasion the Saka ambassadors sailed to a port on the Persian Gulf and travelled overland to Roman Syria. In Antioch they were received by

Roman authorities and taken to the Greek island of Samos where Augustus was holding court and receiving African envoys from Meroe. Strabo reports that only three of the ambassadors survived the journey from India, 'the rest had died chiefly by consequence of their long trek'.[8]

The ambassadors carried a letter from Azes to the Emperor written in Greek on a vellum scroll. In it Azes explained that he held the allegiance of 600 minor sovereigns in northern India and 'was anxious for an alliance with Caesar Augustus'. His Indus possessions were about to be conquered by the Parthians and he proposed a military pact similar to the deal agreed between Alexander and the Indian King Porus. Strabo had an acquaintance named Nicolaus who saw the letter from Azes when the ambassadors were being taken to Antioch. He reported that Azes was 'ready to allow Augustus passage through his country, wherever he wished to proceed and co-operate with him in anything that was honourable'.[9] According to Dio a 'treaty of friendship' was agreed between the two rulers, but by this stage Augustus had begun to seek peace terms with the Parthians and these superseded his plans for any further eastern conquests.[10]

This diplomatic contact occurred in the first decade of Indo-Roman trade when the sight of Indian visitors was still a novelty for most subjects of the Empire. Nicolaus describes how the 'gifts brought to Caesar Augustus were presented by eight naked servants besprinkled with sweet-smelling odours and clad only in loin-cloths'.[11] Roman crowds marvelled at an armless Indian youth sent by Azes who was proclaimed a 'living Hermes' because he resembled the pillar-statues erected in Greek cities to honour the god of expeditions and commerce. Dio describes how the boy could 'use his feet as if they were hands and with them he could pull a bow, shoot missiles, and put a trumpet to his lips'. The traditional symbols of Hermes included the tortoise, the rooster and a staff called the *caduceus* which was decorated with two intertwined snakes. This is probably why Azes sent Augustus an exotic pheasant, a large tortoise, a brood of colourful Indian snakes and a giant python. The bird was probably a Himalayan Monal Pheasant which displays metallic-coloured plumage ranging from blue-greens to purple and copper-reds. It was probably symbolic of the mythological phoenix that was said to make its nest from cinnamon twigs.[12] Dio claims that the envoys also brought tigers, and 'this was the first time the Romans and probably the Greeks had seen these animals'.[13] Augustus displayed these exotic wonders to astonished crowds in Athens and Rome. Strabo reports 'I myself have seen this Hermes – the man born without arms'.[14]

The Saka ambassadors who visited Augustus were accompanied by a Buddhist or Jain missionary who came from the Gujurat city of Barygaza. This holy man was known in India as a *shramana* (a monk or religious instructor), but the Romans took this title to be his personal name and called him 'Zarmarus' and 'Zarmano-chegas' ('Teacher' or 'Master of Shramanas'). Zarmarus probably sought patronage from Augustus and may have requested permission to establish a Buddhist or Jain monastery in Rome, Antioch or Alexandria. His request was denied, but Zarmarus remained in the company of the Emperor when he travelled to Athens in 21 BC.

In Athens Augustus was accepted into a secretive and exclusive Greek cult called the Eleusinian Mysteries which promised its followers rewards in the afterlife. Augustus used his influence to have Zarmarus initiated into this cult so that he could witness some of the most ancient and enigmatic practices involved in Greek religion. Zarmarus decided to exhibit his Indian faith and asked to be burned alive in a funeral pyre. His request was granted by the Emperor and Dio indicates the bewilderment of the Greek crowds who gathered for this occasion. He writes, 'for some reason Zarmarus wanted to die' and concludes, 'maybe he wanted to make a display for the benefit of Augustus and the Athenians'.[15] Plutarch pointed out that the event resembled a ritual performed for Alexander the Great, when an Indian sage named Calanus renounced his position as advisor to the king and immolated himself on a funeral pyre in front of the assembled Macedonian army.[16]

Strabo describes the scene witnessed in Athens by the Emperor when Zarmarus 'anointed his naked body with fragrances and wearing only a loin-cloth, leaped upon the lighted pyre with a laugh'.[17] Augustus arranged that the cremated remains were placed in a tomb at Athens and the event commemorated with the text, 'Here lies Zarmanochegas, an Indian from Barygaza, who immolated himself in accordance with his ancestral customs'. When Plutarch wrote his *Life of Alexander*, he describes the self-immolation of Calanus and mentions how the memorial to Zaramos had become an attraction in Athens. He reports, 'the same ritual was performed by an Indian who came with Caesar to Athens and they still show you the Indian's Monument'.[18]

Augustus took great pride in elevating the Roman Empire to a position of world recognition. His memorial testimony is preserved in an inscription that records, 'to me were sent embassies of kings from India, who had never been seen in the camp of any Roman general'.[19] However, his interest did not go as far as military intervention and by 10 BC the Parthians had conquered most of the Indus Region (Indo-Scythia). The Saka Kingdom was reduced to Gujurat with Barygaza becoming the main port for the diminished regime. During the first century AD Gujurat was ruled by a Saka King named Nahapana known to Roman traders as 'Manbanos'.[20]

Trade at Barygaza

There were few natural harbours on the west coast of India and the coastline around Gujurat was fringed with marshes and wastelands. The main wealth of the Saka Kingdom lay inland where the regime ruled over rich and well-populated agricultural territories. The *Periplus* reports: 'the region is very fertile and produces grain, rice, sesame oil, ghee (clarified butter), cotton and ordinary quality Indian cloths. There are a great many herds of cattle in this place and the men are of very large stature with a dark skin-colour.'[21]

The Romans imported new crop types from this part of India and Pliny describes how a variety of millet was successfully transplanted to Italy where it thrived on marginal lands and produced a greater yield than traditional crops. He reports that 'within the last ten years a new type of millet has been introduced to

Italy from India – black in colour, with a large grain and reed-like stalk'. This plant was considered 'the most prolific of all kinds of corn, one grain produces three-sixteenths of a peck, but it should be sown in damp ground'.[22]

The Saka rulers of Gujarat called themselves the *Kshatrapas*, which was an ancient term adapted from the Persian word for governor (*satrap*). *Kshatrapas* was a royal title, but also it denoted the position of the Sakas as warlords who claimed authority over the local population. Barygaza (modern Bharuch) was almost thirty miles upstream along the Narmada River at the head of the Cambay Gulf (Khambhat).[23] The approach to the port was dangerous because there were strong currents, shoals and reefs in the gulf. There were also few natural land-marks from which ships could take their bearings to avoid these concealed hazards. The *Periplus* explains: 'it is difficult to moor in the gulf because of the current and because the rough and rocky seabed cuts the anchor cables. Even if you manage the gulf, the mouth of the river leading to Barygaza is hard to find because the land is low and nothing is clearly visible, even from nearby. And even if you find the river mouth, it is hard to negotiate because of the shoals in the stream.'[24]

To lessen these dangers the Saka King Nahapana arranged for local rowing boats to guide Roman freighters past the sandbanks and tow them upstream to large sheltered docking basins in the Narmada River. The *Periplus* reports that 'local sailors in the king's service come out with rowers and long ships, known as *trappaga* and *kotymba*, to meet vessels on the gulf and guide them up to Barygaza'.[25] The *Arthasastra* suggests that Roman captains probably paid for this service and the funds went to the royal treasury.[26] Incoming ships docked in the river next to Barygaza while the merchants went ashore to trade at the city-port.

Eastern Gemstones

One of the main commodities that attracted Roman merchants to northern India was the range of colourful gemstones produced at inland mines. Only a few of the ancient territories ruled by the Roman Empire produced precious stones and the variety of these gems was limited. By contrast, India and the distant east yielded a stunning range of gems with a bewildering variety of colours and attractive properties. Prized for their beauty and expense, eastern gemstones became an essential feature in widespread Roman fashions and Pliny identifies 'India as the most prolific provider' of these attractive and costly items.[27] The subject was so important that Pliny devoted the final book of his *Natural History* to the origin and character of gemstones.[28]

The ancient sources reveal how affluent Roman women wore colourful eastern gemstones in their rings, necklaces, earrings, hair-clasps and tiaras. In the first century AD, a single rare and costly jewel was considered enough to attract male attention and incite envy from other fashion-conscious women. Propertius describes how a typical unmarried lady at the theatre wore her hair clasped at the crown with an Indian jewel.[29] Writing in the second century AD, Lucian describes the full development of this fashion as women adorned their carefully braided beehive hair-styles with multiple gem-studded tiaras and 'star-like arrangements of Indian gems'.[30] Tertullian confirms that by this period many Roman matrons possessed an 'array of gems'.[31] Sometimes an imperial consort would appear at a public event in a glamorous outfit that encouraged a new fashion for similar-styled jewellery. When the prospective Emperor Titus was rumoured to be having a love affair with a Judean princess named Berenice, affluent Roman women tried to emulate her glamorous jewellery which included diamonds imported from 'beyond India'.[32]

Martial condemns the demands of young women for eastern gifts, which he calls 'their cunning plunder, levied from us for the sake of infatuation'. Addressing his mistress, he writes, 'sometimes a ring drops off your finger, or a precious stone is lost from your ear'. On other occasions, 'I hear that your silk dresses are getting threadbare, or a scent casket is brought to me, and shown to be empty'.[33] When this occurred the suitor was expected to lead his mistress on a shopping trip down to the commercial centre of Rome. Martial criticises a wealthy woman named Chloe who spent a fortune on her young lover. He received 'Indian sardonyxes, Scythian emeralds and a hundred newly coined gold pieces, for you never fail to give him whatever he asks for'.[34]

Clement of Alexandria criticised 'foolish women' who wear 'amethysts, *ceraunites*, jaspers, topaz and emeralds, fastened to chains and necklaces'. But many women followed these fashion trends: as Ovid explains, 'you like to scent your hair and change your hairstyle. You like to have your hands ablaze with gems and round your neck you like to wear great eastern jewels with stones so large that no ear could take a pair. That's not bad taste: you need to be attractive.'[35]

Roman men also wore rings decorated with expensive eastern gemstones in ostentatious displays of their wealth. Pliny describes how 'gems of exquisite brilliance are added to rings, so that people's fingers are loaded with wealthy revenues' and that 'having images engraved on these items by craftsmen adds to their value'.[36] The most delicate engravings were carved with the assistance of iron tools fitted with a tiny diamond-shard for a fine cutting edge.[37] Solinus explains that diamond shards were the only tools hard enough to engrave vivid blue eastern sapphires.[38]

When Pliny examined old statues of Roman nobles, he observed 'it was originally the custom to wear rings on only one finger, the one next to the little finger'. However, this practice changed as Roman men began to collect gemstone rings and sought every opportunity to display these as trophies on their hands. Pliny says that by his era 'only the middle finger tends to be without a ring, while all the others are burdened. Sometimes each finger-joint has another smaller ring of its own.'[39] For wealthy men, most rings held coloured Indian gemstones engraved with images of classical gods and heroes. Martial pays a compliment to a fellow poet named Stella Severus who 'wears sardonyxes, emeralds, diamonds and jaspers on his fingers' adding 'there are as many gems in his poetry'.[40]

Pliny explains that the value of particular gemstones was decided by popular fashion and 'the matter is settled by the decrees of our women'. But male fashion also had an impact on price and Pliny confirms 'an individual's caprice sets a value upon an individual stone and rivalry will ensue'. This occurred when 'the Emperor Claudius took to wearing a green gemstone or a sardonyx'.[41]

Crimson-coloured sardonyx gemstones were sent to the Roman Empire from cities in northwest India. Sardonyx received special attention in Roman fashion because it could be carved into large opaque stones displaying pink and cream-coloured bands. Martial describes how his mistress demands the finest perfumes and 'matching sardonyxes'.[42] Juvenal also writes about 'that sort of wife who is always handling musical instruments. See her with her thick sardonyx rings sparkling over the tortoise-shell veneers as she plays the chords.'[43]

Small ring-mounted stones could be cut into an intaglio, a negative reverse-image carved as a motif on to the surface of the gem. This device was popular in the signet-rings Romans used to validate documents by imprinting a small distinctive image into warm wax. Affluent Romans would pay high prices for their signet-rings because this emblem represented their personal authority and status. Juvenal describes court cases where written agreements were contested and the proof that a contract was genuine was demonstrated by the wax mark of signet-rings carved from 'the best sardonyx stones, kept in an ivory case'.[44] Pliny explains that sardonyx became a popular signet-stone, 'because the gemstone will not carry away the sealing wax'.[45]

Sardonyx gemstones were perceived as ostentatious and Martial refers to a wealthy former slave who sat on the front benches of the theatre with his hands 'glistening with sardonyxes' so that he could attract attention even at a distance. He criticised another man called Zoilus because the sardonyx in his ring was 'overwhelmed by an excessive weight of gold'.[46] Martial describes how a man named Mamurra perused the market stalls in the centre of Rome, but could not afford their costly contents. Mamurra 'counted emeralds set in chased gold, examined the largest pearl ear-pendants, looked on every counter for real sardonyxes and questioned the value of some large jaspers'.[47]

Some Romans began to hire expensive gemstone jewellery in order to convey the image of wealth and status when appearing in court or conducting financial business. Juvenal suggested that the lawyer Paulus 'has hired a sardonyx ring so that he will seem to be worth the higher fees he charges'.[48] He also comments, 'nobody today would employ Cicero as his lawyer unless a large ring worth 200 sesterces was blazing on his finger'.[49] Martial was critical of a man named Clearinus who was seen at many public events proudly displaying his expensive rings. But it was rumoured that he hired, rather than bought, his jewellery. He wore six rings on each of his hands and never took them off; even in the public baths when he appeared naked. It was rumoured that Clearinus even slept wearing his precious rings.[50]

A fashion also developed in Roman society for bronze and gold goblets to be decorated with gemstones. Philostratus describes dedications made to a temple altar that displayed 'two gold vases decorated with the rarest and most beautiful jewels that India can provide'.[51] But the practice spread to dinner parties and Pliny admitted that this trend could not be controlled by Roman sumptuary laws. He comments, 'we are unable to censure the use of drinking-cups adorned with precious stones and rings that sparkle with gems, since these articles are now in common use'.[52] Martial admired a costly goblet, writing 'see how the gold glistens when it is decorated with Scythian emeralds, but how many fingers have to do without jewels for the sake of that cup?'[53] Juvenal describes a patron named Virro who coveted 'fine and much admired jasper gemstones and like many others he has transferred his jewels from his fingers to his cups'. Hosts offered favoured guests the best goblets, while lesser clients would be placed in the outer circles of the dining group and served from cups fitted with less expensive gems. Juvenal found himself in the outer circles at these social gatherings and he describes a scene that must have been familiar to many Romans. Looking at the inner group of privileged guests, he admires the best tableware from a discreet distance: 'That cup in Virro's hands is richly studded with amber and beryl, but you aren't trusted with gold items. If you are, a servant is posted nearby to count the gems and keep an eye on your sharp finger-nails'.[54] Some guests must have felt an urge to unpick and pocket some of the costly gemstones and hope that the theft was not noticed until after their departure. Petronius describes how Trimalchio ordered games and entertainments for his dinner guests that included precious metal gaming pieces and gemstone dice.[55] The fashion spread throughout Roman society and Pliny mentions a popular yellow-brown Indian gemstone called a *xuthos*, which was 'a gem regarded as suitable only for the common people'.[56]

Trade at Barygaza

Barygaza was a major hub for Indian Ocean commerce and the *Periplus* records that the port received incoming ships from Arabia, east Africa and the Persian Gulf.[57] The port is referred to more times in the *Periplus* that any other trade centre, appearing twenty-eight times in nineteen of the sixty-six chapters.[58] The author of the *Periplus* knew about Barygaza from personal experience and he devotes a large part of his report to its maritime dangers. He also saw evidence of Greek campaigns in the region that had been staged by an Indo-Greek King named Menander I (*c*.155–130 BC). Roman traders wrongly attributed these remains to Alexander the Great and the *Periplus* reports 'in the area there are still preserved to this very day signs of Alexander's expedition, ancient shrines and the foundations of encampments and huge wells'.[59]

Barygaza served an inland city called Minnagara which was the capital (*metropolis*) of the Saka Kingdom in Gujurat. Minnagara in Gujurat shared its name with the Indus city of Minnagar in Indo-Parthia. This was because Indian civilisation called the Sakas the 'Min' and their capitals were therefore known as 'Minnagara' meaning 'City of the Min'.[60] When Minnagar on the Indus was captured by the Parthians, the new capital of Minnagara was created in Gujurat.[61] The *Periplus* describes how the new metropolis of Minnagara was a hub for regional exports and 'sent great quantities of cloth to Barygaza'.[62]

As for more valuable merchandise, the *Arthasastra* study on statesmanship explains how Indian governments could control the collection and sale of precious stones in their subject territory. Mines were taken under royal authority and prohibitions placed on private dealers bringing stocks of crystals into designated trade cities. These measures ensured that foreign merchants had to buy their precious stones mainly from government agents and the profit from this sale went into the royal treasury.[63]

This was probably the situation in the Saka Kingdom which had a second royal court at the city of Ujjain in central India. Valuable goods were collected at Ujjain including gemstones obtained at inland sites. The Sakas collected these items as royal tribute and sent them to Barygaza to be sold by state-agents to the visiting maritime traders. The *Periplus* explains that 'in the east is a city called Ozene (Ujjain) which was the former royal residence. From this place came things that contributed to the region's prosperity and supplied trade with us.'[64] Goods sent the 200 miles from Ujjain to Barygaza included onyx, agate, Indian cotton garments and a large amount of cloth. However, by AD 50 the Satavahana Kingdom of central India had declared war on the Sakas. During the fighting Saka forces were expelled from Ujjain and the Satavahanas took possession of the city. When the Sakas lost Ujjain, the state-run business ceased and Roman traders had to rely on merchant-managed trade networks to acquire inland goods, including gems.

Romans visiting Barygaza sought bright agate with stratified colours and dark onyx with light streaks. Roman jewellers cut these stones into disks, or carved portraits and classical images into the flat surface where the contrasting colours met. If the jeweller was making a cameo, he would cut into these horizontal bands to create a strong colour contrast between the raised relief and the background detail. Wealthy Romans emulated Julius Caesar by collecting and displaying precious stones. Caesar dedicated six cabinets of engraved gems to the Temple of Venus Genetrix in the Roman Forum to be viewed and admired by the Roman public.[65]

At Barygaza Roman ships took on board large stocks of cotton and spices. The spices included costus, bdellium, lyceum and Himalayan nard coming from northern India. Some of these products arrived via a land route 'through the adjacent part of Scythia' (the Indus Region leading to Central Asia).[66] Local products included valuable long pepper that the Romans reserved for medical remedies.[67] Further cargo space was filled with Chinese silk yarn and silk-cloth, ivory and precious stones, including onyx, agate and quartz.[68] Some Roman ships also took on board rice, ghee and female slaves, either at Barygaza or one of the other Indian ports.[69]

The ivory that the Romans received from Barygaza would have included whole tusks and locally worked artefacts. Ovid writes about 'India offering carved ivory to charm us' which could be a reference to foreign art objects.[70] An ivory statuette carved by an Indian craftsman was found in the remains of a moderately sized Roman townhouse in Pompeii buried by volcanic ash in the Vesuvius eruption of AD 79. The statuette depicts a semi-naked Indian female standing with her arms raised and two tiny acolytes by her side. A hole drilled down through the centre of the object suggests that it was once part of a larger piece, perhaps the handle of a mirror, or the leg of a small decorative table or stool. The figure is often interpreted as the Hindu goddess Lakshmi who is the embodiment of beauty and prosperity.[71] Perhaps the figure was brought back as a souvenir from India, or maybe some citizen of Pompeii purchased this object as an attractive piece of exotic art.

The *Periplus* concludes the list of business at Barygaza by mentioning that the city offered 'items brought here from other ports of trade'.[72] This would have included commodities from southern India, Arabia, East Africa and Persia. The *Periplus* reports that Indian vessels visiting Barygaza sent copper and tropical hardwoods to shipyards in the Persian Gulf.[73]

Roman Exports to Barygaza

Italian wine was one of the main Roman products exported to Barygaza, but merchants from the Empire also offered stocks of Laodicean wines from Asia Minor and Arabian wine acquired on their outbound voyage.[74] Tradition suggested that the Greek god Dionysus (Bacchus) travelled to India to give eastern peoples a taste for Mediterranean wines. A surviving Roman mosaic from North Africa shows the classical god of wine in a chariot drawn by four large tigers.[75] Lucian suggests that, 'owing to climate, when the Indians drink wine they quickly become drunk and behave twice as mad any Greek or Romans'.[76]

According to the *Periplus*, other Roman exports included raw glass, copper, tin and lead.[77] Confirmation of this trade comes from a Roman shipwreck found off the northern coast of Gujurat loaded with lead ingots and wine amphorae.[78] Other Roman exports included plain clothing, printed fabrics and multi-coloured waistbands. There was a market in Barygaza for red coral, peridot gemstones, storax, perfumes and fragrant yellow sweet clover. Indian dealers also accepted antimony sulphate (for alloys and eye-cosmetics) and a red mineral called realgar (arsenic sulphide) which was used to make vivid paints. Pliny reports that caustic realgar was also used on wounds to stop excess bleeding and employed as a treatment for asthma and other breathing conditions that involved excess mucus.[79]

The *Arthasastra* describes how Indian kingdoms would fix prices for certain goods being sold in the city markets.[80] The Saka probably followed this practice and offered generous rates to traders who made their purchases in the local currency. This encouraged Roman merchants to exchange imperial money for Indian coins before they did business in the city.[81] State authorised money-dealers offered good exchange rates on Roman coins and the *Periplus* reports that 'Roman money, gold and silver commands an exchange at some profit against the local currency'.[82]

The Sakas encouraged these coin exchanges because the Roman Empire was rich in precious metals. Roman denarii were minted on a pure silver standard (3.9 grams) and aurei were issued in solid gold (8 grams). By contrast most Indian kingdoms had no gold coinage and the highest value silver currency contained a large proportion of base-metal.

The Sakas used Roman aurei to make high-value monetary payments in India. A Prakrit inscription dated to AD 62 records how Usavadata, the son-in-law of King Nahaphana, gave gifts to a Hindu shrine at Nasik in the Western Deccan.

The gift was valued in debased silver coins (*karsapanas*), but the total was also given in gold issues that are probably aurei (*suvarnas*).[83] The dedication reads: 'a gift was given of 70,000 *karsapanas* with each 35 coins making a *suvarna*. The sum was therefore worth 2,000 *suvarnas*.'[84]

The details given in the inscription by Usavadata indicate that Indian society placed a premium value on silver. Based on the ratio of *karsapanas* to *suvarnas*, the Indians considered ten quantities of silver to be worth one quantity of gold. By contrast early Roman currency had a ratio where twelve quantities of silver were worth one quantity of gold.[85] A Roman merchant could therefore acquire 20 per cent more product by buying Indian goods with silver than if he used gold in bullion or coin.

The Sakas imposed favourable exchange rates to draw precious metal from the Roman economy and enrich the silver reserves of their own kingdom. They collected denarii stocks from local moneychangers and melted these coins down to produce a higher-grade Saka currency. During his reign, King Nahaphana began to mint new Saka coins with a superior silver content and modern metal analysis confirms that these issues were made from Roman denarii.[86] This meant that trade with India increased the drain of silver from the Roman economy.

Most Indian rulers permitted outdated foreign currency to circulate in their kingdom. This included old drachmas issued by the Indo-Greeks who briefly ruled this part of India during the second century BC. The *Periplus* reports 'there are to be found on the market in Barygaza even today, old drachmas engraved with the inscriptions, in Greek letters, of Apollodotus and Menander, rulers who came after Alexander'.[87] Roman coins are sometimes found in the remains of ancient Buddhist *stupas* (relic temples) in northern India. These coins tend to show heavy wear and they are deposited along with local currency as tokens given as votive offerings.[88]

Roman coins became a popular symbol of wealth in ancient India and Indian craftsmen copied imperial designs on to small ornamental disks made from brightly-polished base metals or ceramic red-clay. These '*bullae*' depict stylised images of the Roman Emperors and crude attempts to copy the semblance of Latin words. *Bullae* moulds were found near the ancient city of Ter (Tagara) and these objects would have been used to cast stylised metallic imitations of Roman coins. Many *bullae* were pierced or have a loop so that they could be worn as ornaments, while others were probably held in jewellery clasps.[89]

When the Sakas ruled Ujjain the Romans were able to do profitable business with the royal court. They offered high-value products to Saka royal agents in return for the precious stones the regime received as tax and tribute from Ujjain. According to the *Periplus* this included silverware, slave musicians, female concubines for the harem, fine wines, expensive clothing and choice unguents.[90] Sanskrit drama confirms that Indian kings received Roman slaves who served as royal attendants. When the Indian playwright Kalidasa describes a royal court he gives stage directions to a female character described as a '*Yavana* attendant', who 'enters with a hunting-bow in her hand'.[91] The *Acts of Thomas* also mentions how a flute-playing slave girl from Judea served in the court of King Gondophares. She recognised Thomas as someone from her home country, so she 'came to the place where the apostle was. She stood over near him and played for a long time: for this flute-girl was by race a Hebrew.'[92]

Part of a Greek comedy play called *Charition* has been preserved on a second century papyrus found in Egypt. In the story a hero travels to India aboard a Roman ship to rescue his sister Charition, who had been wrongfully sold to an eastern king. While being pursued by the king and his female archers, Charition escapes by hiding in the temple of an Indian goddess. A Greek character reassures her: 'Mistress Charition, I see the wind is rising so we can start crossing the Indian Ocean.' The heroes make their escape when the Indian characters become drunk on undiluted Mediterranean wine. Charition's brother explains, 'in places like this wine is not for sale, so when they get hold of it they drink it straight away'.[93]

Once the Sakas lost Ujjain, the opportunities to conduct high-value exchanges diminished. When the *Periplus* describes Roman business with the Saka court, it specifies that 'these items were sent to the king in previous times'.[94] However, overland trade continued during the period when the Saka and Satavahana kingdoms were at war with one another. The *Periplus* describes how Indian caravans made the journey from Barygaza south to the Satavahana capital Paithana in about twenty days.[95] Caravans at Paithana undertook a further ten-day journey east to reach a 'very large' inland city called Tagara (Ter). The *Periplus* reports that 'from these cities to Barygaza, wagons convey goods over very great stretches of land with no roads. They bring large quantities of onyx from Paithana and large quantities of ordinary quality cloth and all kinds of cotton garments from Tagara.'[96] Indian texts that record the teachings of the Buddha mention a figure of 500 carts (250 tons) as the typical trade business of a prosperous merchant.[97]

Hazards at Barygaza
The *Periplus* describes the hazardous conditions at Barygaza for 'those who are inexperienced, or entering this port for the first time'. In particular Roman ships were exposed to tidal danger while their merchants went ashore at the port. The *Periplus* explains that 'all along India there are many rivers with extreme ebb and flood tides that occur during the new and full moon. The tides can last for up to three days, diminishing between these intervals. But they are much more extreme near Barygaza than anywhere else.'[98]

During these lunar cycles the Narmada River was prone to tidal floods when seawater surged upstream along the course of the river. At first, people would perceive that the water level was dropping rapidly. As the sea suddenly withdrew, large Roman ships would be left immobile on the riverbed, or start to tilt over at a dangerous angle. When the alarm was sounded, work-crews would dive into the water with heavy beams to prop up the vessel in an attempt to keep the hull upright. The *Periplus* explains that 'suddenly the seabed becomes visible and certain coastal stretches that had ships sailing over them become dry land. Then there is an inrushing flood tide that sends a concentrated mass of seawater head-long upstream against the natural river flow for a good many *stades*.'[99]

The Roman crews had little time to prepare before the ocean flood arrived with a noise that sounded like the roar of an approaching battle army. This turned into a loud hiss as the water streamed over the sandbanks. The returning tidal surge could dislodge restraining anchors and swamp any unbalanced ships. Smaller vessels would capsize and larger ships could break free of their moorings and be propelled upstream to collide with sandbanks and other concealed underwater dangers. Roman lookouts had to remain vigilant, especially in the darkness of the night. The *Periplus* reports, 'if the flood arrives at night, when the tide is just beginning to come in and the sea is calm, people at the mouth of the river hear something like the rumble of an army heard from afar. After a short while the sea races over the shoals with a hiss.'[100]

When Claudius Ptolemy compiled his geography, Barygaza was no longer visited by Roman ships. The port was replaced by a new Saka emporium called Monoglossum that probably offered safer docking for visiting vessels.[101] The Sakas would have diverted their inland trade routes to connect with this newly designated commercial centre. These routes would have been prone to attack while the Sakas continued their conflict with the neighbouring Satavahanas. Roman merchants heading south would need to avoid rival armies as they ventured into contested territory.

The Satavahana Kingdom
Roman merchants who sailed south from Gujarat entered the Satavahana Kingdom. The heartland of the regime was in central India and the realm covered most of the Deccan Plateau including the eastern seaboard of the subcontinent. But the Satavahana also had a political presence on the Konkan Coast of western India.[102]

The Konkan Coast was flanked by the Western Ghats and inland communication was restricted to valleys that breached this mountain chain. The *Periplus* describes how journeys inland led travellers through a 'hinterland that contains many barren areas, great mountains and all kinds of wild animals'. There were said to be 'a great many populous nations between this region and the Ganges'.[103]

There were ten trade ports on the Konkan coast, but most of these centres dealt with regional exchanges. The only city-port on this coast was Kalliena on the Ulhas River, which served the Satavahana Kingdom as an *emporion enthesmon* (state-nominated trade centre). Goods from across the Satavahana Kingdom were directed to this trade outlet to engage with visiting merchants involved in Arabian Sea commerce.

Trade was important to the Satavahana regime and lead coins issued by King Vasisthiputra (AD 78–114) depict large, two-masted Indian ships. Sixth century paintings from the Buddhist caves at Ajanta in western India depict similar vessels with their unique rounded hulls and multiple masts.[104] The image of a twin-masted ship was also found during excavations at the fortified southern Arabian port of Moscha Harbour. The distinctive shape was scratched into plaster on an ancient wall.[105]

Roman merchants visiting the Satavahana city-port of Kalliena offered local traders Italian wine, lead ingots and antique bronze objects. Excavations of an ancient residential building near Kolhapur city uncovered a cache of more than ten classical bronzes, including mirrors, tableware and a statuette depicting the sea god Poseidon dating to the third century BC. These items were manufactured in Campania and were probably considered to be 'antique junk' in most Roman markets where consumers were seeking newer styles.[106]

In AD 50 the Saka King Nahaphana seized and occupied the Satavahana possessions on the west coast of India, including the rich city-port of Kalliena. The Satavahana opposed the conquest and by way of retaliation began to attack foreign shipping associated with the Sakas. This included Roman ships attempting to sail down the Konkan Coast.[107]

When Nahaphana conquered Kalliena he placed a Saka governor named Sandanes in charge of the city and gave him command of warships. It became unwise to land at Kalliena while the war continued and most of the international business that had been conducted at the port was redirected north to Barygaza in Gujarat. Roman ships that strayed into the conflict, or sought protection in Kalliena, were given a guard of Saka warships to take them safely back to Barygaza. The *Periplus* reports that Kalliena 'was a designated emporium where everything used to go, but since Sandanes has occupied it there is great hindrance; for Greek ships that by chance come into these places are brought under guard to Barygaza'.[108] Inscriptions from the region indicate that Kalliena remained under Saka rule for more than a decade.

During the AD 60s, the Satavahana were able to reclaim their former west coast territories including Kalliena.[109] The timing was fortunate because Kalliena was a major exporter of exotic animals and the Emperor Vespasian had only recently come to power in the Roman Empire (AD 69–79). Vespasian ordered the construction of an enormous new arena in Rome called the Flavian Amphitheatre, now known as the Colosseum. Many displays in this stadium involved exotic eastern animals in mock hunts and fights between closely matched beasts. The shows also involved public executions where the condemned person was torn apart by predators, or forced to combat other unusual animals, including rhinos. Dealers at Kalliena could provide Roman merchants with leopards, tigers, large snakes, hyenas and monkeys.[110]

Kalliena probably remained vulnerable to Saka raids, so the Satavahanas designated one of the more southerly ports as their main west coast trade centre. When Ptolemy wrote his geography, Kalliena was no longer marked as an emporium, but Semylla had already attained this status.[111] Roman ships docked at Semylla would have received cotton fabrics, spices and onyx coming from inland sources.[112] Roman merchants began to reside long-term in the Satavahana ports and established business communities in the nearby towns. Some of these men converted to Indian religions and were recorded as being generous benefactors to the local Buddhist monasteries.

The Buddhist Romans

The ancient Buddhist monasteries of the Western Deccan made use of cave systems in their religious practices. The monks established communities in the valleys and hired stoneworkers to carve their religious edifices into the hill-side rock-faces. Prakrit inscriptions from these ancient rock structures record how *Yavanas* (Romans) were active in the region.

Ancient Sanskrit and Tamil texts generally refer to the Greeks and Romans as *Yavanas*. The word *Yavana* is derived from the Old Persian term '*Yona*' which originally referred to Ionian Greeks. Indians called all Greeks *Yavanas* and due to the spread of classical civilisation this term became applied to subjects of the Roman Empire.

Yavanas are mentioned in inscriptions from the remains of the ancient monasteries at Nasik, Junnar and Karle. The inscriptions commemorate donations made by Roman subjects who adopted Indian beliefs and took indigenous names to integrate themselves into their new religion. An inscription from Nasik celebrates a *Yavana* known by the Indian name Indragnidatta who refers to himself as *Dharmatma* (Righteous). Indragnidatta described himself as a *Yavana*, claimed his father was 'Dharmadeva from the north', and recorded that he was originally from 'Dattamitra'. Indragnidatta donated funds for a new relic chamber to be built at the Nasik monastery that included stone cisterns.[113]

A further inscription from Nasik mentions a donor named Romanakas, which is probably a Prakrit rendering of the Latin term *Romanus* (Roman).[114] Inscriptions from the Buddhist monastery at Junnar record donations by three further *Yavanas* who paid for cisterns, a hall façade and a refectory.[115] Two of these donors named Cita and Irla record they came from 'Gata' which is most likely a Prakrit rendition of Coptos in Egypt.[116]

The Romans mentioned in the Karle inscriptions lived at a nearby community called Dhenukakata which is described by Indian donors as a *vaniya-gama* (a community of merchants). They adopted Indian names based on concepts such as Dharma (religious practice) and referred to themselves as Dhammadeva, Dhammarakhita, Yasavadhama, Culayakha and Sihadhaya.[117] Roman devotees provided the Karle monastery with funds to carve decorative pillars into the main relic hall and these columns were inscribed with their names.[118] The Karle inscriptions reveal that Romans were also operating at another unidentified Indian town called Umehanakata. One inscription reads 'this pillar is the gift of the departed *Yavana*, Cita from Umehanakata'.[119]

Unlike other donors the *Yavanas* rarely mention their profession, perhaps because it was widely understood that they were businessmen involved in foreign trade. One possible exception is a donor at Karle called Milinda who described himself as a physician resident at Dhenukakata.[120] Milinda is a Prakrit rendering of the Greek name Menander, so perhaps this was a Roman doctor practicing in India.[121] Milinda paid for a relatively plain pillar to record the names of his Indian wife and children.[122]

Other Romans residing in India may have been received into Brahmin communities where they adopted Hindu customs. Hindu and Roman civilisation shared a common interest in astrology and these beliefs depended on accurate astronomy which included star-charts. Roman navigators brought Greek treatises on astronomy to India where the texts were studied by Hindu scholars. A sixth century Hindu astronomer named Varahamihira wrote a book on astrology called the *Pancasiddhantika* when he was studying in Ujjain. In the introduction Varahamihira mentions the existence of five well-known *Siddhantas* (doctrines or studies) concerning the stars and the position of the earth in the cosmos.[123] Two of these studies originated in the Roman Empire, the *Romaka Siddhanta* (*The Roman Tradition*) and the *Paulisa Siddhanta* (*The Paulus Tradition*). There was a Roman astrologer named Paulus Alexandrinus active in Alexandria in the fourth century AD, but it is difficult to match his ideas to the *Pancasiddhantika*. Consequently, the *Paulisa Siddhanta* is probably a lost work compiled by a different author, also named Paulus.

Varahamihira respected Roman doctrines on astronomy, but regarded the Hindu studies to be more accurate. He explains that 'the Siddhanta made by Paulisa is correct, the Siddhanta proclaimed by Romaka (Rome) is almost as precise, but the *Savitra* is more accurate'.[124] Varahamihira also suggests that some Romans had been included in Hindu religious practices and exchanged knowledge with their Indian counterparts. He recognised that '*Yavanas* who have studied the science are respected as *Rishis* (Hindu Seers)'.[125]

Some of the early Roman converts to Buddhism continued to practice their eastern beliefs when they returned to the Empire. This could explain why several portrait busts from the Imperial period depict Roman men with the reflective composure of philosophers and hair fashioned in Indian styles. They are shown with long hair styled into a special cranial knot known as the *ushnisha* worn by Buddhist holy men to signify the attainment of an exceptional spiritual knowledge. In modern times one of these portrait heads has been fitted on to a torso depicting the chest and shoulders of a general in Roman armour.[126] But whatever the interpretation of this particular sculpture, its reference to two distinct cultures is striking.

CHAPTER FOURTEEN

The Tamil Kingdoms of Southern India

The southern tip of India was ruled by three rival kingdoms known as the Chera, the Pandya and the Chola. Most Roman ships visiting northern India sailed south to finish their voyages in these Tamil Kingdoms.[1] On reaching the Tamil ports the Roman traders offered the local merchants large quantities of gold and silver bullion. From first-hand experience as a merchant the author of the *Periplus* reports that 'the market here is mainly for a great amount of our money'.[2] His words have been verified by dozens of Roman coin-hoards found in southern India containing hundreds, and sometimes thousands, of imperial coins. This Roman money consists of gold aurei and silver denarii.

The Cheran controlled inland gem mines in the Coimbatore district and their subjects harvested crops of black pepper in the highlands. Their rivals the Pandians had access to larger pepper harvests and managed substantial pearl fisheries on the southern tip of India. By contrast the Chola controlled a coastline on the eastern seaboard of India and dominated trade with the Ganges, Burma and Malaysia.

Many Roman ships visited northern India and then sailed south along hundreds of miles of coastline to the Tamil Kingdoms.[3] The first Tamil trade-stations reached by these vessels were the village-ports of Naura and Tyndis. The voyage down western India took several weeks and Roman ships had to avoid the pirate bases that controlled stretches of the coastline south of Kalliena city. The *Periplus* lists a series of islands along this coast and warns that 'around these places there are pirates'.[4] Confirmation of this fact comes from a medieval copy of an ancient Roman map called the *Peutinger Table* which displays the words 'PIRATE' in bold red letters near that part of southern India.[5]

Sometimes Indian kings declared war on foreign vessels entering their territorial waters and in these instances Roman mercenaries were called upon to protect the freighter from eastern warships. The Satavahana were known to attack foreign craft during their war against the Saka Kingdom.[6] Tamil sources also record an incident when a second century Cheran King named Netunceral attacked and seized Roman ships. The *Patirruppattu* describes how the king 'captured the uncivilised *Yavanas* of harsh speech, poured oil on their heads, tied their hands to their backs and took their precious and beautiful vessels and diamonds'.[7] The Cheran army had attacked the Roman merchant fleet, rounded up imperial traders and either forced them into slavery or imposed a ransom for their release.

The Cheran Kingdom

Many Roman captains chose to avoid the northern coast of India by sailing directly to the Tamil lands from Africa, or Arabia. By the time of the *Periplus*, most Roman ships ignored the village-ports on the Konkan Coast and headed straight for the city of Muziris.[8] Pliny explains: 'the most advantageous way of sailing to India is to set out from Ocelis. Utilising that port it is a forty day voyage, with the Hippalus blowing, to Muziris the first trading centre in India.'[9] Roman lookouts watched for signs that they were approaching the Malabar Coast near Muziris. The *Periplus* reports that 'vessels coming from the open sea get an indication that they are approaching land from the short black eels that emerge to meet them; creatures with dragon-shaped heads and blood-red eyes'.[10] When these strange eels were sighted, the crew knew that they were in Tamil waters near *Limyrike* (the Malabar Coast).

The *Periplus* calls Cheran territory the 'Kingdom of Ceprobotos' and reports that its king ruled from an unnamed inland capital.[11] Muziris was the main port of the Cheran Kingdom and the city was situated several miles upstream on the Periyar River. Deep-hulled Roman vessels could not sail safely upriver due to treacherous shallows, so ships sheltered in the lagoon while their cargo was unloaded aboard smaller craft for transportation upstream.[12] Ancient Tamil literature describes these contacts and reveals how Romans used large quantities of gold to acquire incoming harvests of local black pepper and newly mined gemstones. The *Akananuru* refers to 'rich Muziris, where the large and well-crafted ships of the *Yavanas* (Romans) come with gold and depart carrying pepper'.[13]

Muziris was a hub for international commerce and its inhabitants became wealthy from their dealings with the Roman Empire and contact with Indian ships coming from Gujarat and the Konkan Coast (Ariake). The *Periplus* explains that 'Muziris owes its prosperity both to trade from Ariake and Greek shipping'.[14] Black pepper was one of the main exports from the Cheran Kingdom and the producers brought their harvests to warehouses in ancient Muziris. The *Purananuru* describes activity at the port when 'small boats take ashore the gifts of gold brought by the large ships. The port is crowded with the turmoil created when sacks of pepper are piled up high in the surrounding buildings. Here King Kuttuvan presents to the visitors the rare products of the mountains and the seas.'[15]

The remnants of ancient Muziris have been found near modern Pattanam and include the ruins of warehouse structures and wharves made from fired brick. Wooden artefacts found at the site include teakwood bollards and the remains of an eighteen-foot boat carved from a single timber. These robust vessels probably carried pepper cargoes down the Periyar River from inland collection sites. They could also have conveyed cargo back and forth between the port and the Roman ships moored offshore. Finds at Pattanam include thousands of ceramic shards from Roman amphorae and fragments of fine Mediterranean tableware (*terra sigillata*). Other finds include copper-alloy beads, lead Cheran coins, fragments of frankincense resin, shards of Roman glassware and peridot gemstones from Zabargad Island near the Red Sea port of Berenice.[16]

The Cheran kings were on good terms with the Romans and permitted merchants from the Empire to reside at Muziris. The *Peutinger Map* records the presence of a Roman temple in the Indian city with the label '*Templum Augusti*' (Augustan Temple).[17] Similar buildings existed in the Parthian Empire where wealthy Roman merchants established Augustan temples in the Persian cities connected with their commercial interests.[18] The imperial cult was strong in Alexandria and Philo describes the city's Augustan temple as a large building positioned opposite the harbour. He boasted that it was superior to other Imperial temples built in rival cities and was 'full of offerings, pictures, statues and decorations in silver and gold'. It was said to be 'a hope and beacon of safety to all who set sail or come into harbour at Alexandria'.[19] The Augustan temple at Muziris probably formed a similar function for Alexandrian merchants making the voyage to India.

Further evidence of a permanent Roman presence at Muziris comes from the *Periplus*. The local Tamil diet was mainly rice-based and the *Periplus* indicates that the incoming ships supplied the Roman community resident at Muziris with regular grain supplies. Ships were advised to bring 'sufficient grain for those involved with shipping, because the [local] merchants do not use it'.[20] There would have been thousands of Roman subjects living as temporary residents in the Tamil ports during the peak of the sailing season, including large numbers of armed mercenaries, artisans and craftsmen.[21]

There is evidence that Roman subjects brought Christianity to Tamil India. In the second century a Christian theologian named Pantaenus travelled to India hoping to establish a church movement. Pantaenus found that Christian communities were already worshipping in India using the *Gospel of Matthew*. These converts claimed that the apostle Bartholomew had brought Christianity to their kingdom and had given them a gospel written in Hebrew. The Christian scholar Eusebius explains: 'when Pantaenus visited the Indians he found that among them there were people who already knew about Christ through the *Gospel of Matthew*. Tradition suggests that the apostle named Bartholomew preached to these Indians and that he had left them the writings of Matthew in Hebrew, letters which they still preserved.'[22] This is significant because the earliest surviving gospels from the Roman Empire are written in Greek.

The existence of a Hebrew gospel in India suggests that eastern society probably had contact with a very early branch of the Judeo-Christian tradition. This is plausible since Roman sources confirm that leading Jews managed prominent businesses involved in eastern commerce. For instance, the Jewish businessman Tiberius Julius Alexander was responsible for collecting the quarter-rate import tax in Roman Egypt. He is mentioned in the *New Testament*, and receipts from the *Nicanor Archive* confirm that he established his son in a business that hired personnel and exported goods across the Indian Ocean.[23] Converts to Christianity from these Jewish businesses could have introduced the religion to different parts of India. In the medieval period there was a Jewish community living in southern India who claimed to be the descendants of fugitives from Roman persecutions conducted after the destruction of the Temple in Jerusalem (AD 70).[24]

Tamil literature refers to the inland capital of the Cheran Kingdom as Karuvur (modern Karur on an upper branch of the Kaveri River). Karuvur was known to the Romans as Karoura and this is the name used by Claudius Ptolemy when he lists the city as a royal centre.[25] To reach Karuvur, merchants visiting Muziris had to travel inland through a mountain pass in the Western Ghats called the Palghat Gap. Most Roman coin hoards found in southern India have been recovered in this region near gem mines in the Coimbatore district.[26]

The *Periplus* records that Tamil merchants at Muziris exported 'all kinds of transparent gems; diamonds (from the Ganges) and sapphires (from Sri Lanka)'.[27] Beryls were expensive to obtain in the Tamil kingdoms because they were also valued in Indian society as jewellery pieces. Ancient Hindu texts explain how costly gems were believed to bestow different attributes of fortune and good health on the wearer. The *Garuda Puranam* explains 'the most outstanding jewels are the diamond, pearl, ruby, emerald, topaz, blue-sapphire, crystal and red coral'.[28] The status and value of these jewels explains why the Romans had to use gold and silver bullion to pay for beryl in the Tamil ports.

The beryl mines were probably under state management, which meant that the Cheran regime received large profits from this commerce.[29] Beryls were popular in the Roman Empire and were used to adorn fashionable jewellery. Pliny reports that 'India is the sole producer of beryls which display the best qualities of the most valuable gems, including the subtle-fires of the ruby, the flashing-purple of the amethyst and the sea-green tint of the emerald'. The most valuable beryls displayed aquamarine colours, but Pliny also mentions golden-yellow *chrysoberyls* and vivid-blue *hyacinthizonte*.[30] For many Romans these Indian gems became an indispensable mark of their status.

Beryl rings were cherished items and many of these stones were unique and distinctive because of their hues and colour shifts. Martial writes of a little maltase dog named Issa, who was the much-loved pet of his friend Publius. He explained that 'Issa is more precious to Publius than Indian gems'.[31] Unique beryls were sometimes left on the deceased rather than passing into the possession of family members as heirlooms. Propertius was haunted by the image of his dead lover Cynthia with 'her garment charred and the fire consuming the beryl ring from her finger'.[32]

Pliny's information on Roman voyages to southern India is based on a report collected between AD 48 and AD 52.[33] But Pliny updated these details with more current information about the condition of the Cheran Kingdom between AD 52 and AD 77. In this period pirates had expanded their operations and began to attack Roman ships moored near Muziris. This meant that many Roman captains preferred to trade with the nearby Pandian Kingdom which offered better loading facilities for visiting vessels and a greater range of trade goods. Pliny explains: 'Muziris is not rich in merchandise and it is not a desirable port because of nearby pirates who occupy a location named Nitrias. Moreover, the anchorage for the ships is far from land and cargo has to be fetched and brought by boats. As I publish this, Caelobothras is its ruler.'[34] Pliny names the current Cheran king as

'Caelobothras', but this is probably a Roman rendition of the dynastic title Keralaputras ('Sons of Kerala').

Muziris remained an important trade centre during the second century when Claudius Ptolemy calls the city an *emporium*. The second century *Muziris Papyrus* found in Roman Egypt confirms this evidence and lists trade goods brought back from the Tamil port. The document records that a Roman merchant secured a loan using a cargo from Muziris which included pepper, Gangetic nard, malabathrum, ivory and turtle-shell.[35]

The Pandian Kingdom
The main Pandian port was called Nelcynda and lay about sixty miles south of Muziris.[36] It was an export centre for large amounts of black pepper harvested in the Pandian highlands and valuable pearls farmed in the Mannar Gulf. In the *Periplus*, pearls appear second on the list of goods exported from the Tamil lands.[37] The Pandian pearl fisheries were renowned throughout the ancient world and Roman writers told stories of how an 'Indian Hercules' established the Pandian Kingdom for his only daughter Pandaea.[38] Arrian explains that 'Heracles collected all the jewels from the sea and brought them to this part of India to adorn his daughter'. He also tells his readers that 'these are the same pearls that merchants purchase today in India at great expense and bring back to us to be sold at a high price to the foremost Romans'.[39]

The pearl fisheries in the Mannar Gulf were worked by a slave force of condemned criminals. The *Periplus* explains that 'diving for pearls is conducted here by convicts and this area is under the control of King Pandian'.[40] Royal agents sold the pearls to Roman merchants visiting Nelcynda and the proceeds enriched the Pandian treasury.[41] The *Periplus* records that the area produced 'good supplies of fine-quality pearls' and other Roman sources confirm the high-value of these items. Pliny reports that 'pearls have the highest price of all valuable objects and they are sent to us mainly from the Indian Ocean'.[42]

The Pandian fisheries produced thousands of pearls every year which represented millions in foreign currency. But pearls were also highly valued in India so the Pandian Kingdom derived enormous revenues from its fisheries. An ancient Hindu text called the *Garuda Puranam* suggests that half a *tola* (5.8 grams) of the finest pearls could be worth 1,305 silver-based coins. Beneath this grade there were more than ten further categories of lower-quality pearls that were nonetheless valued at substantial coin totals.[43] The ancient Indian guide to statecraft, the *Arthasastra*, recommended that rulers stocked their treasuries with bullion, jewels and strings of pearls (*indracchanda*). The longest *indracchanda* were threaded with 1,008 pearls and there were five further categories of pearl-strings used in treasury accounts with the smallest containing only ten pearls.[44]

Early Pandian Kings were keen to foster contacts with the Roman Empire and they 'sought friendship' with the Emperors.[45] Augustus received a Pandian embassy in 20 BC which was sent to display Tamil wealth to the Roman court and encourage trade contacts. They presented the Emperor with pearls (possibly strung as *indracchanda*), precious stones and a giant Indian elephant. Suetonius records that Augustus subsequently offered 50 million sesterces worth of pearls and gemstones to one of the most important religious buildings in Rome, the Temple of Jupiter Optimus on the Capitoline Hill.[46] Perhaps this was the Pandian gift which Augustus dedicated to the leading god of the Roman pantheon. As a comparison, a figure of 50 million sesterces is more than the revenues that Rome received annually from Gaul or Judea, and was enough to pay the annual cost of four Roman legions.[47]

In verses addressed to the Emperor, Horace mentions an extraordinary white elephant displayed in Rome during this period. He claimed that public readings by poets could not compete with the sight of this animal which amazed and excited the crowds.[48] Perhaps this was a gift from an Indian King as rare white elephants are sacred in Buddhist and Hindu faiths where they symbolise auspicious achievements, earthly power, justice, peace and prosperity.[49]

The Romans were astonished to learn that the Tamil ambassadors had completed their entire journey by land. It had taken them four years to cross India and Iran, but during their journey they received the assistance of many intervening regimes who also hoped to profit from the growth of world commerce. Florus describes the Pandian ambassadors as 'Indians who live immediately beneath the sun' (the Tropics). He writes that 'they regarded their four-year journey as the greatest tribute they could render. Their dark completion proved that they came from beneath another sky'.[50] Their trade initiative fuelled the fashion for imported pearls and encouraged Roman ships to sail as far as the Pandian Kingdom.

Pearls in Roman Fashions

Pliny explains how Roman society valued pearls for their radiance, size, roundness, smoothness and weight. The greatest praise was awarded to pearls that had the faint translucence of alum crystals and pearls elongated into tear-shapes were considered to be particularly charming. Pearls needed to be handled with care for they could be worn away by continual use and their colour and lustre damaged by contact with oils or other perfumes. However, if well looked after, expensive pearls became heirlooms and were passed down through several generations. Pliny explains that 'this article is an almost everlasting piece of property, for it passes to its owner's heir, or can be offered for public sale as if it were a landed estate'.[51] Teachings in the *New Testament* use pearls as a metaphor for a prize investment and in the *Gospel of Matthew* the Kingdom of Heaven is considered 'like a merchant who seeks fine pearls: when he had found one pearl of great price, he went and sold all that he had to buy it'.[52]

In the *Satyricon*, Petronius describes how a freedman merchant named Trimalchio lost his main cargo investments when his leading ships were wrecked by a severe Mediterranean storm. Trimalchio explains that his wife Fortunata 'showed her devotion and sold her jewellery and dresses to give me 10,000 gold pieces' to reinvest in further enterprises. This was a million sesterces, 'all that I needed to see my fortune rise again'.[53]

By the mid-first century AD, even moderately wealthy women could display one or two pearls amongst their finest jewellery and Pliny reports that 'nowadays even poor people covet pearls'.[54] The Romans recognised a difference in the appearance of pearls, with those found in the Red Sea having a bright lustre, while Tamil pearls were larger and had the sparkle of mica.[55] Pearls were an ideal gift for a wealthy suitor to offer a potential lover, as Propertius reveals when he praises the marvellous effect of his own poetry. He explains, 'I could not dissuade her from leaving by offering gold and Indian pearls, so I won her over with flattering song and now Cynthia is mine'.[56]

Pliny explains that some women wore 'little bags of pearls suspended by gold chains around their necks'. These were worn at all times and usually remained hidden, 'so that even in their sleep women may retain the consciousness of possessing gems'.[57] Martial writes about a woman named Gellia who swore oaths 'not by any of our gods and goddesses, but by her pearls. She caresses these objects, covers them with kisses, calls them her brothers and sisters; loves them more ardently than her two children'. She lived in fear of thieves and claimed that she could not endure their loss or live even an hour without her pearls.[58]

Wealthy Romans placed valuable pearl beads on their calendars to mark special days. Martial, rejoicing at the return of a friend from an overseas voyage, commented, 'my dear Flaccus is restored to me from the coast of Sicily; let a milk-white gem mark this day'.[59] He also advised celebrating a wedding anniversary with the lines, 'the deities have given fifteen full years of married bliss to you and Sulpicia; these happy nights and hours should all be marked with precious pearls from the Indian shore'.[60] After the death of a very young slave girl, Martial commended her spirit to his deceased parents by writing that 'no one could prefer the pearls of the Indian Ocean, or the newly polished ivory of the Indian elephant, to this girl'.[61]

There was a fashion for pearl earrings in the Empire and portraits painted on coffin lids from Egypt show how Roman women wore pearls fixed to trident-shaped earrings by threads of golden wire, or hanging from multiple necklaces that ranged from tight chokers to long, dangling loops.[62] Excavations at Berenice uncovered an earring made from five small pearls held together by twisted gold wire.[63] Fashion dictated that pearls should be displayed next to emeralds to complement the colours of each gem and many of the most affluent Roman women would have appeared in public wearing pinkish-purple dresses and displaying multiple precious stones strung or fitted on to numerous items of jewellery.[64] Horace described how Roman matrons exhibited rows of pearls and emeralds until they were 'ornamented with snowy-white and green precious stones'.[65] This fashion spread across the Empire and stone funeral monuments from Palmyra show that rich Syrian women also wore pearls and gemstones as part of their elaborate costumes. These sculptures also show the Roman fashion for tiaras and headbands studded with multiple pearls and precious stones.

Lucian describes how affluent Roman women were often seen with 'eastern sea-pearls worth many talents dangling heavily from their ears'.[66] An Egyptian talent was about 6,000 sesterces and more money than a Roman labourer could expect to earn in four years of work. As the fashion spread, some wealthy women tried to outdo their peers by wearing multiple pearl necklaces and earrings designed to display several gems in a single fitting. Pliny describes how 'our ladies glory in arranging pearls on their fingers and using two or three for a single earring'. This fashion created a new jewellery-style called the 'castanet pendant' that was popular amongst Roman matrons. Pearls hung on gold fittings so that the precious stones rattled and clicked together, making a pleasing sound. Pliny reports that 'it is now a common saying that a pearl is as good as a *lictor* (public herald) for announcing the presence of a lady when she is about'.[67] Over time, the swaying pearls would have been chipped and scratched by clattering together, but this was further proof to onlookers that the woman was someone of wealth and status who could wear out and replace even the most expensive jewellery.

When Pliny was a young man in Rome, he saw a senior member of the Roman nobility named Lollia Paulina dressed in a unique outfit layered with precious stones. Lollia was briefly married to the Emperor Caligula in AD 38 and Pliny recalls, 'I saw Lollia Paulina, not at some solemn ceremonial celebration, but at an ordinary betrothal banquet. She was covered with emeralds and pearls alternatively interlaced and shining all over her head, hair, ears, neck and fingers'. The total price paid for this jewellery was more than 40 million sesterces and Lollia was ready at a moment's notice to show her receipts as documentary proof of the purchase. Pliny compared the honour and wealth won by past generals to the 'spoils displayed by Lollia Paulina, a tiny gem-clad woman reclining beside the Emperor'.[68]

Seneca denounced this fashion, writing: 'I see pearls, not single ones designed for each ear, but clusters of them on earlobes that have been trained to carry these loads. The earrings are joined together in pairs and above each pair still others are fastened. Feminine folly tries to overwhelm men with two or three fortunes hung from each ear.'[69] The weight of heavy pearl jewellery sometimes caused disfigurement and Juvenal describes wealthy women who encircled their necks with green emeralds and fastened huge pearl pendants to their elongated earlobes.[70] Ovid observes that Roman men were persuaded by jewellery and dress so that appearance mattered more than traditional female virtues. Many women from wealthy families were 'concealed by gems and gold' so that 'the actual woman is only a minor part of this display'.[71]

Wealthy fathers were expected to buy jewellery for their daughters as wedding gifts. Pliny the Younger was deeply upset when he heard that the teenage daughter of his friend Fundanus had died shortly before her intended wedding. He writes 'no words can express my grief when I heard Fundanus giving the order that the money he had intended for clothing, pearls and jewels was to be spent on her funeral incense, ointment and spices'.[72]

Roman husbands provided their wives with expensive jewellery to display the wealth of the household and family estates. But Martial describes a Roman patron who indulged the costly fashions of his mistress at the expense of his friends and clients. He says of this man, 'your mistress shines resplendent with pearls from the Indian Ocean and while you are immersed in pleasure with her, your client is abandoned to his creditor and dragged away to prison'.[73] Seneca published a homily addressed to his mother praising how she had maintained the traditional values of an earlier era and 'unlike so many, never succumbed to immodesty, the worst evil of our age, nor been charmed by jewels and pearls'.[74] He also has the lead character in his tragedy, *Phaedra*, renounce the new fashions with the words, 'no necklace at my throat, no snowy-pearls, no gift of the Indian Ocean weigh down my ears. Let my hair hang loose unscented by Assyrian nard.'[75] Petronius declares through a character in his satire, 'excess luxury ruins the State and why are Indian pearls so precious when your wife, decorated in these sea-sought gems, lifts her legs in adultery?'[76] Horace also compares the respectable Roman matron with a prostitute, asking 'does the matron with her pearls and emeralds have a softer thigh, or more delicate limbs?'[77]

The wealthy elite could afford even more extravagant displays and began having pearls sewn into items of clothing including the laces of their sandals. This was the ultimate statement of wealth as the precious stones were scuffed and covered in filth from the streets. But someone seen wearing these sandals at a public event probably travelled to the venue in a private sedan chair, carried in a curtained booth through the jostling crowds. The Emperor Nero wore slippers studded with pearls and had his sceptres and travelling couches all adorned with these precious decorations.[78] The practice attracted criticism and Pliny comments, 'now people are not content with wearing pearls and they must have them fixed to their shoes'.[79] These fashions had added resonance for early Christians who recalled the Sermon on the Mount when Jesus preached 'give not that which is holy unto the dogs, for you would not cast your pearls before swine, lest they trample them under their feet, then turn and attack you'.[80]

Ostentatious and competitive displays of wealth involving jewellery often caused discord in early church communities. In the AD 60s, the apostle Paul wrote to Timothy in Asia Minor advising him that the women in his congregations should be encouraged to dress modestly and avoid expensive fashions. In particular, Paul objected to braided hair, gold jewellery, costly clothing and pearls.[81] These ideas were repeated by the Christian theologian, Clement of Alexandria, who writes that 'the highly prized pearl has invaded female surroundings to an extravagant extent'. He advises, 'do not let the ears be pierced, contrary to nature, in order to attach ear-rings, for there is no better ornament for the ears than to hear true instruction'.[82] The fashion for pearls was a major feature of eastern commerce and when Pliny mentions bullion exports from the Empire he includes the condemnation, 'this is what our women and luxuries cost us'.[83]

Nelcynda

The Pandian city-port of Nelcynda lay inland about thirteen miles upstream on the Pambiyar River. It had important advantages over Muziris, and Tamil literature describes the port as a large urban centre surrounded by a wide defensive moat. The *Maturaikkanci* refers to 'the city of Nel with resplendent buildings which is full of noise from the deep moat that leads to the southern sea'. It was 'here that the big ships descend bearing splendid prosperity and excellent gold to increase riches. Here the war-drum resounds, the sails unfurl and the high banner flies. They reach shore with the strong wind, breaking the tall waves of the fearsome great sea in the ocean that joins the sky.'[84]

Roman sources confirm that the Pambiyar was deep enough to allow large freighters to sail up the river to dock in the sheltered waters next to the city. Large ships offloaded their cargo at Nelcynda then sailed downstream to a shore-station called Bacare. There were sandbanks in the Pambiyar River and it was dangerous for Roman ships to cross these hazards when burdened with a full cargo. It was therefore better to transport goods downriver on smaller craft and then load heavy spice cargoes aboard at Bacare. The *Periplus* explains that: 'the river has sandbanks and channels, so vessels drop downriver from Nelkynda to the settlement at Bacare. They anchor at the very mouth of the river to take on board their cargoes.'[85] This setup suggests that the Romans received most of their heavy spices from the Pandian Kingdom, since their ships were still relatively buoyant after visiting Muziris. It also confirms that there was a weight imbalance in the cargo exchanges at Nelcynda, probably because lightweight but high-value bullion was paying for large volumes of heavier spice.

When Pliny writes about Roman trade with the Tamil lands he explains that the loading difficulties at Muziris made Nelcynda 'a more serviceable port'. He also describes how 'pepper is brought to Becare by boats made of single logs called *Cottonara*'.[86] The eighteen-foot vessel found at Pattanam (ancient Muziris) is probably an example of one of these barge-like craft that served the Tamil ports. Tamil producers brought their pepper crops downriver in these vessels and some of the native suppliers may have dealt directly with the Roman ships, offering sacks of black pepper in exchange for leather pouches filled with gold coin.

Pliny knew about ancient Madurai which was the inland royal centre of the Pandian Kingdom. He also refers to a king named Pandion who was probably the Tamil ruler who sent the embassy to Augustus in 20 BC. Pliny informed his readers that 'Pandion ruled this region from a city called Modura (Madurai) which is far inland from the market at Nelcynda'.[87] The actual name of this Tamil king is not recorded in the classical texts since *'Pandian'* is a dynastic epithet similar to the Roman title *'Caesar'*.

When the Pandian Kings went to war with their Cheran rivals, the nearby port of Muziris was a prime target for their attacks. Tamil literature describes how a Pandian army besieged Muziris to destroy its trade dominance. The Pandian King is depicted issuing orders from his royal chariot, while his war-elephants trample Cheran troops underfoot. The *Akananuru* describes the 'great suffering of the mortally-wounded warriors slain by the war-elephants when Celiyan came on his flag-bearing chariot pulled by horses with plumed manes to besiege the port of Muziris'.[88] When the Pandian army finally broke into the city, the king rode a giant battle-elephant through the streets to display the priceless treasures seized from Cheran temples. The *Akananuru* describes the scene as 'Celiyan came on his great war-elephant with the seized sacred images after besieging rich

Muziris, where the large and well-crafted ships of the Romans come with gold'.[89] Perhaps the Pandian King also captured the Roman Temple dedicated to Augustus and had its sacred artefacts rehoused in Nelcynda.

Roman Troops in Tamil Service
Claudius Ptolemy confirms that the Pandian ruled their kingdom from an inland city called Madurai on the Vaigai River.[90] Ancient Tamil literature describes Madurai as a large urban centre with palaces, temples and celebrated literary academies. The city was surrounded by towers and tall ramparts and was encircled by a deep moat.[91] Since their business interests concerned the ports, only a few Roman merchants went inland to cities such as Madurai. As Dio Chrysostom comments, 'those who go to India travel there in pursuit of trade and they mingle mostly with the people of the coast'.[92] But Roman ships also carried mercenaries and artisans amongst their crew and people from these professions were prepared to travel inland to find employment with Tamil rulers.

Roman carpenters were active in the Tamil cities and their skills were highly sought after by the Pandian Kings. It seems these artisans were employed to carve wooden statues and craft decorations on royal buildings. The *Manimekalai* refers to a *Yavana*-built pavilion and the *Perungadai* describes how 'the bowl of a lamp was held in the hands of the beautiful crafted statue made by the *Yavanas*'.[93] These statues possibly depicted Tamil Kings, or Indian deities rendered in Greek and Roman art styles. Early statues of the Buddha found in northern India display certain influences received from Greek and Roman sculpture. During this period images of the Buddha appear displaying a Greek-style halo and dressed in a *himation*, or light robe similar to a toga.[94]

The Roman mercenaries in service with the Pandians were employed as high profile guards and posted at the city gates of Madurai. These men were probably military veterans and were noted for their assertive posture that intimidated onlookers. Tamil literature describes these Romans as 'excellent guards with murderous swords' who carefully scrutinised passers-by with their 'stern' gaze. The *Silappatikaram* describes how people entering Madurai would take care not to, 'alarm the suspicions of the *Yavanas*'.[95]

Tamil accounts describe how Roman troops also guarded the command tent of the Pandian King when he went on campaign. The *Mullaippattu* recalls how 'the inner-tent has double walls of canvas held firmly by iron chains and protected by powerful *Yavana* guards'.[96] These Roman troops would have formed up as an elite bodyguard around the king on the field of battle. They appear in the Tamil sources wearing clothing that was loose-fitting and belted at the waist in the style of imperial military tunics. The *Mullaippattu* describes 'the powerful *Yavana* guards, whose stern looks strike terror into every beholder, wear long and loose clothes that are fastened at the waist by means of belts'.[97] The Tamil poets use the word '*mattikai*' for the whips that the *Yavanas* carried on their belts and this word seems to be borrowed directly from ancient Greek.[98]

The Roman army used a long-range torsion-powered bolt-thrower called the 'Scorpion' which launched harpoon-like metal javelins. Some Roman merchant ships could have had large bolt-throwers and other military machines fitted on their decks to repel attackers. It seems that Roman mercenaries used this same technology in the service of Indian kings, and ancient Tamil literature mentions strange 'war-engines' constructed using *Yavana* engineering. These machines were built into the fortified gateways of Indian cities to destroy attackers with their lethal blades and unfamiliar missiles.

The *Sivakasindamani* lists 'machines invented by the *Yavanas* and made with the help of their intelligence'. The list includes the 'hundred-killer' and the 'mechanical bow'. Other strange weapons could be versions of the Archimedes Claw which used a crane-like apparatus to grapple and overturn enemy ships (the 'mechanical owl and beam that crushes heads'). There may also be a reference to petroleum-based incendiary weapons in the description of 'human statues and figures of swans that spit out red flames'.[99]

Black Pepper

The *Periplus* puts black pepper top of the list of exports from the Tamil kingdoms. The *Periplus* explains, 'pepper is mostly grown in only one region known as Kottanarike, which is connected to both trade ports (Muziris and Nelcynda).[100] The Roman demand for this product was so great that Indian merchants began calling the spice *Yavanapriya* (*Yavanas*' Passion).[101] Pliny was amazed by the popularity of black pepper in the Roman Empire. He comments, 'we admire some substances because of their sweetness or appearance, but the berry of the pepper-plant is desirable only because of its pungency and for this reason we import it all the way from India'.[102] Most Roman ships left the Tamil ports with all their remaining space entirely filled with black pepper and an eastern cinnamon called malabathrum. The *Periplus* explains that 'ships in these trade ports carry full loads because of the volume and quantity of pepper and malabathrum'.[103]

The black pepper plant is a climbing vine that attaches itself to other trees and produces dense clusters of small bead-like fruit on dangling spikes. It is indigenous to the hillsides of southern India where it thrives in the high altitude and hot, moist, tropical climate.[104] The early pepper crop was picked in autumn before the fruit had an opportunity to fully ripen and lose its pungency. After several weeks drying in the sun, the peppercorns were packed into sacks and brought down to the main trade ports. Roman ships visiting northern India would time their arrival in the Tamil ports to receive these incoming pepper harvests (November). Merchants who sailed directly to southern India could take on board pepper that had been processed late in the previous season (November–March).[105]

Numerous black peppercorns have been found scattered across the ruins of ancient Berenice where Red Sea ships offloaded their eastern cargoes in Egypt. During four seasons of excavation at Berenice, archaeologists found almost 1,600 peppercorns in the ancient remains of streets, buildings and rubbish deposits. This is more than twice the number of lentils found at the site, even though lentils were a staple food in Egypt. Large amounts of charred peppercorns were found close to the Temple of Serapis in Berenice, the remains of a burnt offering to this Greek-Egyptian god. Foreign worshippers also buried two large Indian jars beneath the temple courtyard, each filled with black peppercorns.[106]

Martial attests to the popularity of pepper when he writes, 'often a cook will use wine and pepper so that tasteless beet, the food of working men, can acquire good flavours'.[107] A pound of pepper cost 4 denarii, which was about four days' pay for an ordinary labourer, but used sparingly this quantity of spice could improve the taste of dozens of meals.[108] Pepper was also used in medical concoctions including tonics believed to cure impotence and potions said to alleviate digestive problems.[109]

Pepper was added in small amounts to many Roman meals to enhance flavour and make perishable foods palatable for a longer period. Many of the urban poor in Rome lived in crowded multi-storey buildings that did not have interior kitchens. These city-dwellers depended on food outlets where they could buy cheap meals and many of these establishments spiced their foods to improve taste and increase sales.

Many richer households had their own kitchens stocked with various spices to add colour and flavour to Mediterranean dishes. Martial mentions a famous Roman named Apicius who was said to have spent 60 million sesterces on devising and preparing new recipes for extravagantly expensive feasts.[110] The name 'Apicius' probably became synonymous with fine dining and this explains why his name was attached to a collection of Roman recipes involving relatively ordinary foods. This cookbook has survived and mentions pepper in almost every recipe, including mundane everyday meals. Pepper was sprinkled on popular sea foods including sardines and added to sauces and salad dressings.[111] Apicius also suggests that common broths, such as barley soup, and meat dishes be thoroughly spiced with black pepper.[112] He recommends that lamb should be cooked with 'ordinary bean broth, pepper and laser, cumin, dumplings and a little olive oil'.[113] One recipe mentions 'Indian peas' enhanced by the flavour of black pepper, but this is probably a Mediterranean dish made from locally sourced black peas.[114] Pepper was also added to wine to preserve and enhance flavours. Apicius reports that 'long-lasting spiced honey wine is given to people on a journey' and he recommends four ounces of pepper (eight tablespoons) per two pints of wine.[115] Petronius suggests that forgetting to add a sprinkling of pepper was a minor error. He explains, 'suppose that a cook had just omitted a pinch of pepper, or a bit of cumin to the meal', then this could be quickly and easily fixed.[116]

Pepper was sold in cheap paper wrappings that the vender folded like a parcel around the product. Often old books and discarded papyrus scrolls were re-used as wrappings for spices. Statius complained that a book he received from his friend Grypus had its pages already disintegrating, so that it was 'like those papers that get soaked by Libyan olives, or are used to wrap up pepper, or incense'.[117] Horace muses that the fate of all 'impermanent writings' was to be torn apart by traders and 'conveyed to the street that sells frankincense, spices, and pepper'.[118] He went on to describe how the area was littered with the debris of discarded paper wrappings.

High-status Romans often had a network of clients who they supported in legal matters or financial business. In return the rich patron received social prestige and occasional gifts from his clients that included the best spiced foods to be enjoyed at feasts. Persius writes about prominent Romans, whose larders were overstocked with these gifts, including 'fees for defending your fat friends from Umbria, and the peppered hams from your Marsian client'.[119] Martial also mentions a lawyer named Sabellus who received a range of very modest gifts from his patrons during the Saturnalia festival. He describes how 'Sabellus swells with pride, excited by half a peck of gruel and dried beans; by three half pounds of frankincense and pepper; and by sausage from Lucania'.[120] Persius describes a 'miser' as someone who lived off dry salted vegetables and who shook pepper over his food once a year to celebrate his birthday.[121] This suggests that for most affluent Romans spiced foods were a commonplace enjoyment.

Martial was not keen on receiving perishables and felt cheated when his friend Sextus sent him a gift of pepper in place of silver. He complains, 'you used to send me silver, but now I get half a pound of pepper and nobody pays that much for this product'.[122] However, this had consequences when Martial was offered a giant boar as the centrepiece for a feast. He thought he could impress his guests by having the carcass stuffed with rich pepper sauce blended with an expensive wine, but his larder could not provide for his ambition. Martial was dismayed by the cost of buying the necessary ingredients on the open market and therefore abandoned the idea with the judgement, 'no great heap of pepper and Falernian wine in a secret sauce – return to your master you ruinous wild-boar, my kitchen fire is not for you. I will have less costly delicacies'.[123]

Martial recommended a recipe that had beccafico songbirds flavoured with pepper and Petronius describes a dish with small-birds cooked in peppered egg-yokes.[124] The feast of Trimalchio included a tray filled with a 'highly spiced sauce which flowed like a tide over the fish'.[125] Juvenal describes the owner of a mansion who was able to pay outside experts to prepare his feasts, including 'someone to skilfully arrange the courses and someone to spice the food'.[126] The character Trimalchio acquired the smallest ingredients from the furthest sources and 'even wrote to India to acquire mushroom spores' to flavour his food. [127] It was said that during his brief reign the Emperor Vitellius sometimes attended or organised several feasts in the same day and none of these banquets cost less than 400,000 sesterces.[128] Martial warned a man named Pomponius that when his large crowd of supporters publically praised him, 'it is not you Pomponius they are applauding, but the eloquence of your banquet'.[129]

Pepper was sent to all regions of the Roman Empire and enjoyed by many people with modest incomes. Pepper husks were found at the stone quarry of Mons Claudianus in the Eastern Desert of Egypt and peppercorns were excavated at a Roman army camp in Oberaden on the River Lippe in Germany.[130] Military writing tablets from Vindolanda Fort in northern Britain record an order for 2 denarii's worth pepper by a solider named Gambax, son of Tappo, while Roman pepper-pots have been excavated in Gaul.[131] A casket found in a Pompeian house contained over 100 pieces of silver-plate dining-ware, including cups, plates, bowls, spoons and two pepper-pots shaped like a perfume phial and a miniature amphora.[132] Archaeologists excavating houses near the gate of nearby Herculaneum have recovered fragments of pepper corns and cumin seeds that formed part of the town diet.[133] Excavations of the Herculaneum sewers located the remains of an enormous septic-tank made from cement and masonry that received waste from shops, kitchens, street-drains and a public exercise complex with pool facilities. The tank contained a large volume of waste from latrine-sewage, street-litter and food-scraps from the kitchens. From these desiccated remains, archaeologists have recovered shards of smashed pottery, small bronze artifacts, coins and gemstones lost from jewellry fittings. Organic remains included fish-bones and scales, eggshells, olive pits and plant seeds including pepper corns.[134]

Paint Pigments and Other Exports
The Tamil ports offered Roman traders further valuable goods including ivory and hawksbill turtle-shells. The local merchants acquired these shells from the Lakshadweep Islands which lie more than a hundred miles off the Malabar Coast.[135] Tamil ships also sailed around Cape Comorin on the southern tip of India to reach ports on the eastern seaboard of the subcontinent.[136] From there they acquired nard, cinnamon and diamonds from cities at the mouth of the Ganges, for shipment back to Nelcynda. Tamil merchants also crossed the Bay of Bengal on voyages to Burma and the Malay Peninsula returning with the best turtle-shell from a distant land that the Greeks called Chryse (*Golden*).[137] The Golden Land was probably Burma, the Malay Peninsula, or perhaps Sumatra (*Suvarnadvipa*). The Tamil ports also exported Chinese silk-cloth received via trade-stations in the Ganges or Chryse.

Indigo obtained from processed plant material was another valuable commodity imported at this time. The interior walls of many grand Roman houses were painted with realistic scenes from nature portrayed in vibrant colours. Pliny describes how Roman artisans used the Indian colorant indigo for outlines and the 'light and shade' decoration painted on to plaster walls. These paints could be applied as black, or watered down to produce a beautiful purplish-blue. Pliny describes how the cost of many murals had become more of a talking point than the actual artwork and 'nowadays, when purple is painted festively on walls, when India contributes pigments from the mud of her rivers and the gore of her snakes and elephants, there can be no such thing as high-class painting'. He adds, 'it used to be the genius of artisans that people valued, not the cost of their materials'.[138] Indigo was imported in such bulk that it undercut the price of the best Mediterranean paints which cost 10 denarii per pound. Pliny reports 'a short time ago Indian blue or indigo began to be imported at a price of 7 denarii'.[139]

The Romans imported other concentrated paint pigments from India including minerals and plant products that artists claimed were extracted from exotic animals. One of these mixtures was a black pigment said to be made from burnt ivory. Paints made from eastern colorants were added to the waxes that the Romans used to weatherproof timbers on their ships. This technique, known as encaustic or hot-wax painting, was used to paint distinctive decoration and emblems on timbers. Pliny reports that 'it is common for navy vessels to be painted and now many cargo ships follow this practice'. Surviving examples of this process can be seen on Egyptian coffin portraits from the Roman era and rich Romans were also known to 'decorate vehicles with paintings and paint the logs assembled for funeral pyres'.[140]

During the second century AD the government of Han China received reports concerning Tamil trade in the Bay of Bengal. The *Weilue* refers to Pandya as 'the Kingdom of Panyue' and reports that 'its inhabitants are small; they are the same height as the Chinese'. The *Weilue* also suggests that by this period traders from Yunnan in southwest China were reaching Pandya by way of Burma. It states that 'Traders from Shu (Western Sichuan) travel this far' and 'Panyue is in contact with the Yi Circuit (Yunnan)'.[141]

Roman Exports to the Tamil Kingdoms
Roman merchants offered the Tamils red coral, peridot, antimony sulphide and realgar. There was also a market for a substance called orpiment that the Tamils used for making clothing dyes and vivid yellow paints. Wine appears last on the list of Roman exports, but is well represented in the archaeological record. Fragments of Roman amphorae have been found at more than fifty sites in India including the Tamil lands. The *Periplus* specifies 'wine – in limited quantities, as much as goes to Barygaza'.[142] Wine heads the list of Roman exports to Barygaza, so perhaps the amount exported to the Tamil ports was only 'limited' compared with other cargo, especially base metals. When Roman writers refer to merchants from the Empire offering Italian products to Indian spice dealers, they are probably referring to wine. Persius mentions the appearance of 'someone who barters beneath the rising sun (distant east) and hands over the produce of Italy for wrinkled pepper and pale cumin seed'.[143]

Archaeological evidence suggests that the Indian kingdoms received relatively ordinary Mediterranean wines and most of the batches delivered to India were similar to wines enjoyed by Roman garrisons on the European frontiers.[144] These vintages tended to have a higher salt content and were less prone to spoiling on long journeys. The Tamils did not cultivate grape vines, but drank an alcoholic beverage known as 'toddy' produced from the fermented sap and fruit of palm trees. In India, ordinary Roman wines were therefore considered to be high-status commodities enjoyed by royal courts and Tamil poets describe how servants poured exotic foreign wines for the ruling elite. The *Purananuru* pictures how, 'with joy and pleasure the women, wearing shining bangles, pour into decorated gold-cups the sweet, cool wine brought by the superb *Yavana* ships'.[145]

Roman wine sent to Nelcynda was loaded aboard Tamil ships and taken to a trade-station on the east coast of India called Poduke (Arikamedu).[146] Hundreds of Roman pottery shards have been found at Arikamedu and about half of these finds are from Italian wine vessels. Many of the fragments have black volcanic grit in their ceramic composition, indicating that they were fired with clay from Campania in central Italy. When the volcano Vesuvius erupted in August AD 79, it destroyed the wine industry in Campania and this affected Roman exports to

India.[147] This crisis probably forced many Italian businessmen to increase their reliance on bullion for trade exchanges.

Pliny the Elder was in command of the Roman fleet at Naples during the devastating eruption of Vesuvius. While trying to evacuate civilians from the disaster zone he succumbed to the cloud of dust and ash, collapsed and died from asphyxiation.[148] Pliny's warning that Indo-Roman trade was draining bullion from the Empire therefore predates this volcanic disaster. Consequently, his esti-mate for bullion exports to India (50 million sesterces) refers to a time when Campanian wine was still a viable bulk cargo for eastern shipments.[149] Pliny's calculations therefore underestimate the long-term increase in bullion flow from the Empire to India.

The Tamils called Roman coins *cirupuram* which was their name for the nape of the neck. This was probably a reference to the image of the Emperor which appeared on Roman coins as a head-portrait in profile, detached at the neck.[150] Roman merchants also brought the Tamils plain clothing, multi-coloured textiles and large amounts of glass, copper, tin and lead. This trade was large-scale and Pliny believed that India relied on the Roman Empire for most of its base metals. He reports that 'India has no copper or lead, so the country procures these metals in exchange for pearls and precious stones'.[151]

The Tamils had a debased silver and copper currency so they used Roman money as gold and silver bullion. Roman coins were given a premium value in southern India because of their trusted metal content and distinctive designs. The sharp and detailed images struck on imperial money also gave Roman coins the decorative appeal of fine jewellery.

Roman hordes generally contain either gold or silver coins and rarely include issues from other Indian kingdoms.[152] There have been more than twenty Roman coin hoards found in southern India, nearly all from inland locations.[153] The money was stashed by local people in small clay pots, leather purses or cloth bags that have decomposed through time. The concentration of coins found near the Cheran capital Karuvur could be representative of a short period of unrest, perhaps during a war that encouraged many people to hide their wealth.[154] Many of the coins were buried years, or decades, after they first entered Tamil society and represent the available bullion circulating at the time they were hidden.

The Kottayam hoard found on the Malabar Coast is the only coin batch pos-sibly deposited by Roman subjects.[155] This find is the largest Roman coin hoard recovered from southern India and it was discovered in a sand-dune just north of ancient Nelcynda. The hoard could have been a coin consignment assembled for a single Roman trade venture. It contained over 8,000 gold aurei held in a large brass bowl. The latest coins in the find date to the reign of the Emperor Nero (AD 54–68) when there was an upsurge in Roman spending on eastern goods. The Kottayam hoard might have been stashed by a shipwrecked Roman crew who, for whatever reason, were unable to return to the site to recover their wealth.[156] This amount of gold represents 800,000 sesterces in imperial money and confirms that bullion exports were a serious issue for the Roman Empire.

If this represents a typical coin consignment for a voyage to southern India, then only sixty Roman ships could easily have exported more than 50 million sesterces of bullion from the Empire per annum.

This export figure seems plausible when ancient Chinese evidence is added to the debate. In AD 166 a Roman ship reached the Chinese Empire and the Han Court questioned the merchants who arrived aboard the vessel. Based on this information the *Hou Hanshu* reports 'the Romans conduct a sea trade with Parthia (Anxi) and India (Tianzhu) and their return gain is ten to one'.[157] This tenfold price gain between Egypt and India is confirmed by sixteenth century accounts that record how a quantity of pepper acquired in India for one gram of silver could be sold in Alexandria for about ten times that amount.[158] This means that a Roman ship would probably have had to export about a million sesterces of Mediterranean wealth to return with the type of Indian cargo documented in the *Muziris Papyrus* (worth 9.2 million sesterces).[159] The Kottayam hoard comes close to this figure with its monetary value of about 800,000 sesterces.

In most cases the date when a coin was issued in the Empire is not a good guide as to when it might have been exported to India. The Tamils preferred certain coin issues that had been minted by particular Emperors (mostly Augustus and Tiberius). Roman merchants secured better deals with these coins and special efforts were made to accumulate these particular coin types for export. A similar situation was occurring in northern Europe and Tacitus describes how German tribes living far from the frontier liked to receive 'trusted' Roman coin types in trade deals. They had a preference for 'the old and well-known money, preferring the coins that show a two-horse chariot'.[160] Writing in the sixth century, the Greek traveller Cosmas explains how Roman coins were chosen for eastern export on the basis of their design and quality with 'finely shaped pieces formed from bright metal being specially selected for export'.[161]

It seems that Roman merchants began sending coins to southern India during the reign of the Emperor Augustus (27 BC-AD 14). Also, as Roman hoards found in India generally contain more gold aurei from the reign of Tiberius than from the time of Augustus, this might indicate an increase in trade during this period (AD 14-37). The Tamils preferred silver Augustan denarii that depicted the imperial princes Gaius and Lucius, and large quantities of these coins were minted in Lyon from 2 BC to AD 14. The Tamils also valued a widely produced silver denarius issued by the Emperor Tiberius that portrayed his mother Livia.[162]

Almost all the silver denarii found in India are coins minted before the currency reforms instigated by the Emperor Nero in AD 64.[163] This was probably because Nero introduced base metal into new issues of denarii, so that more coins could be minted from existing government stocks of silver, thereby increasing cash for imperial spending. However, these debased silver coins could not be used as pure bullion in foreign markets. The reforms probably had little immediate impact on eastern trade because there were millions of pre-reform denarii still in circulation. These earlier coins did not disappear from the Roman economy until the second century AD and when this occurred, merchants visiting India simply switched to exporting silver bullion.

It made sense for Roman merchants to export older pre-reform coin in favour of newer issues. Most Julio-Claudian denarii contained 3.9 grams of pure silver, whereas newer coins had only 3.4 grams of silver. Both coins had the same monetary value in the Roman Empire, but in foreign trade the older denarii had a greater metal value.[164] This gave the older coins better exchange rates in the money markets of northern India which had their own debased currencies. Certain denarii found in southern India show evidence of heavy wear consistent with old coins that had circulated within the imperial economy for several decades. These were probably exported in the period between AD 70 and AD 100.[165] For example, a heavily worn Augustan denarius from the Budinatham hoard bore a countermark of the Emperor Vespasian (AD 69–79).[166]

Julio-Claudian denarii had a premium value in India because of its trusted silver content and decorative charm. But Roman merchants also exported bullion when sufficient amounts of coin were unavailable. The *Nicanor Archive* records that 3 talents-weight of silver bullion were sent to Myos Hormos in AD 62.[167] This quantity of silver was equivalent to more than 25,000 denarii and would have been worth over 100,000 sesterces in Roman markets. A papyrus letter dating to AD 117 indicates that silver bullion was routinely sold at Coptos and that the price continually fluctuated. The text reads, 'un-coined (silver) is now 362 (drachmas). As you know the best prices in Coptos change day by day.'[168]

About half of the gold hoards found in southern India contained aurei from later Emperors ranging from the reign of Vespasian to Marcus Aurelius (AD 161–180).[169] Although the currency reforms introduced by Nero reduced the weight of newly minted gold aurei, it did not change the purity of the metal. This meant that newer aurei were still valuable as bullion in foreign markets, but merchants preferred to export older coins because of their higher gold content (8 grams compared to only 7.3 grams). When the heavier Julio-Claudian aurei disappeared from circulation in the second century AD, Roman merchants switched to the newer issues, or simply used bullion.

Bullion Exports

Ancient evidence suggests that the Roman Empire was heavily reliant on bullion exports to sustain its international commerce. This topic became an important issue for the Roman regime in the decade after the civil war when Vespasian was declared Emperor (AD 69). Vespasian looked for new ways to increase long-term Roman revenues and secure the future of the imperial regime. Suetonius reports that 'he was driven by necessity to raise money by plunder because of the critical state of the treasury and the imperial accounts; this is evidenced by a statement at the start of his reign when he declared that 40 billion sesterces were required to set the State in order'.[170] The Emperor's long-term plans for the regime were not revealed to the Roman public, but Pliny was a member of Vespasian's advisory council and would have taken part in these discussions.[171]

Pliny gives estimates for the cost of eastern trade in his *Natural History*, including the value of bullion exported from Egypt to India through the Red Sea route. Pliny reports that 'reliable knowledge about the voyage from Egypt to India has become available for the first time. This is an important matter since India drains more than 50 million sesterces a year from our Empire.'[172] Most of this sum was probably gold and Tamil India was the main destination for Roman coin. The *Periplus* suggests that Roman ships sailing to southern India carried 'mainly a great amount of money' and the discovery of dozens of imperial coin hoards in this region provides support for this statement.[173]

Pliny also provides information about the total value of Rome's bullion exports to the distant East. The information appears when he discusses the widespread use of eastern aromatics in Roman society. He reports, 'by the smallest computation, India, the *Seres* (the Chinese) and the Arabian Peninsula take 100 million sesterces from our Empire every year – this is what our women and luxuries cost us'.[174] Rome was not trading directly with China, so this figure is probably included in the estimate for India (50 million sesterces). This means that southern Arabia was taking more than 50 million sesterces of bullion from the Empire every year. The figure is credible because there were over a million hectares of land with frankincense trees in Dhofar. This area produced at least 1,000 tons of frankincense with a market value worth more than 30 million sesterces.[175] The addition of myrrh crops, the development of further groves and the introduction of a second harvest, would have increased this figure to more than 50 million sesterces.[176]

Roman-Arabian trade is significant because the Arabs took a large part of their profits from the Empire as silver bullion. Strabo reports that the Nabataeans prized embossed silverware and the *Periplus* confirms that Roman ships sent these articles to the Saba-Himyarite Kingdom in southern Arabia.[177] The King of the neighbouring Hadramawt regime also received large quantities of silver denarii in return for his state-owned stocks of frankincense.[178] These silver exports to India and Arabia were probably greater than the amount of new bullion entering the Roman economy from its imperial mines. As a consequence, eastern trade drained silver resources from the Empire, thereby creating stress on the imperial currency system.

Roman Currency

The early Roman Empire was rich in silver and the regime released millions of silver denarii to circulate in the Mediterranean economy. Julius Caesar introduced the gold aureus for high-value purchases and the Emperor Augustus fixed its currency value in relation to silver denarii. The gold aurei was about half the size and weight of a silver denarius and this meant that 25 denarii were equal to 1 aureus. According to weight, Roman currency valued silver to gold at a ratio of about 12:1. This arrangement gave the Roman economy a very stable monetary system that inspired widespread confidence and encouraged deals using currency.

Both coins were useful units of exchange with a denarius equivalent to about a day's labour and an aureus worth a month's wage for a Roman solider.

Confirmation comes from the *New Testament* where the *Gospel of Matthew* cites a denarius as a typical day's wage.[179] The coin is also mentioned in connection to provincial poll-taxes. When Jesus was asked if it was right to pay tax to Roman authorities, he answered 'show me the coin used for the tax'. And when they brought him a denarius, Jesus said to them, 'Whose likeness and inscription is this?' They said, 'Caesar's', then he said to them, 'Therefore render to Caesar the things that are Caesar's, and to God the things that are God's'.[180]

Augustus probably fixed imperial currency at the 12:1 (silver to gold) ratio because of bullion prices in the Roman Empire. But these Roman rates did not reflect international values. Silver was comparatively rare in the Han Empire and market values near the Chinese frontier suggest a silver to gold value of about 10:1.[181] Indian Kingdoms also placed a relatively high value on silver and Saka inscriptions suggest a similar 10:1 (silver to gold) ratio in northern India.[182] This meant that merchants could often buy more products in eastern markets by exporting Roman silver instead of gold.

From the Augustan era onward, bullion wealth left the Roman economy in large quantities as a consequence of eastern commerce. The Roman economy probably experienced the early effects of this silver depletion by the mid-first century AD. In AD 64, Nero reformed Roman currency by introducing a small quantity of base-metal into newly issued silver denarii and by slightly reducing the size of freshly minted gold aurei. These measures were probably introduced to increase government funds, but the new currency also established a lower silver to gold ratio for Roman currency (11:1). This was closer to the bullion value represented by international trade (10:1). But silver exports continued after the debasement, since merchants could export bullion, ornaments and older coin that still had the higher, purer silver content.

The Emperor Trajan further debased the denarii so that silver to gold ratios in Roman currency fell to the rate of 10:1. These policies suggest that by the early second century AD, silver was becoming more scarce and valuable in the Roman Empire in relation to gold. Both Nero and Trajan were receiving large quantities of gold from lucrative new mines, but at the same time silver was leaving the Roman economy faster than it could be replaced. During this era, government supplies of silver were no longer sufficient to meet the required quotas of newly minted denarii. The solution was to maintain denarii production by debasing the standard of newly produced coins and by the end of the third century AD, the denarius was so debased that it had only a fiduciary value.[183]

Revenue in Cash and Goods

One of the biggest expenses for Roman merchants trading with India was the cost of paying the quarter-rate customs tax imposed on the imperial frontiers. Many traders had their capital invested in the return cargo and were unable to find the necessary cash funds. Roman officials therefore allowed merchants to pay their import taxes by handing over a quarter-share of their incoming cargoes.[184] Some of these goods could be auctioned in Alexandria to raise immediate cash revenues, but other commodities were shipped directly to warehouses in Rome. This meant that a large proportion of the revenue that Egypt sent to Rome took the form of eastern commodities. The Roman government could use these goods in State ceremonies, or sell them to consumers in the capital to raise further funds for the regime.

Clay seals found in Alexandria were stamped with the words 'The Spices of Caesar' and these labels confirm that imperial authorities controlled the shipment of eastern goods.[185] By the mid-first century AD, large government-owned stock-piles of eastern products in Rome were kept under imperial authority. The scale of the stores was demonstrated when Nero burnt great quantities of incense at the funeral of his wife Poppaea (AD 65). It was said that more incense was burnt in the ceremony than Arabia could produce in a year.[186] If the Roman Empire was taking quarter-shares of most eastern cargoes, then it would only take a few years to assemble more goods than a particular territory might produce annually.

The imperial government took a greater interest in eastern goods during the reign of Vespasian (AD 69–79). Roman authorities realised that eastern products would sell for higher prices in Rome than they did in Alexandria. It therefore made sense to ship more of the stock to the imperial capital where it could be stored and sold when prices were high and profits guaranteed. Suetonius is prob-ably referring to this practice when he reports, 'Vespasian openly engaged in business dealings which would have disgraced even a private citizen – such as cornering the stocks of certain commodities and then putting them back on the market at inflated prices'.[187] However, this policy required greater State invest-ment in storage and distribution. Vespasian therefore established a new treasury department called the *Fiscus Alexandrinus* to manage the increased resources coming from Alexandria. This department had its headquarters in Rome and small metal tags found in the centre of the city confirm that the organization was handling shipments of goods in place of cash revenues.[188]

Vespasian was succeeded by his son Domitian who oversaw the completion of large purpose-built spice warehouses in Rome known as the *Horrea Piperataria* (the Pepper Warehouses). The *Horrea Piperataria* was constructed on the Sacred Way which was one of the main thoroughfares through the monumental centre of Rome. The complex probably followed the storage practices of grain ware-houses and held over 9,000 tons of spice when fully stocked, at a time when 1,000 tons of relatively inexpensive black pepper would have cost 32 million sesterces in Roman markets.[189] The prices that Pliny provides for eastern goods are probably based on the state-owned products sold from the *Horrea Pipera-taria*.[190] The size and significance of the building is indicated by events in the later empire when the Emperor Maxentius built the Basilica Nova on the site in AD 308. The new Basilica was the one of the largest enclosed buildings in Rome and became the main administrative centre for the entire city.

The *Horrea Piperataria* also stored frankincense and myrrh and Dio describes the complex as a warehouse for 'Arabian products'.[191] Inside, the complex was divided into a maze of storerooms and high enclosed courtyards. Throughout the building there were numerous water troughs to dampen the oppressive atmo-sphere caused by the heavy, dry aroma of its precious stock.[192] Information about the people who worked in the *Horrea Piperataria* is revealed by a second century funerary inscription commissioned by a man named Publius Veracius Firmus. The inscription was made to honour his two brothers Proculus and Marcellus, who had been employed in the complex. The brothers were referred to as *Piperarii* which could be translated as Pepper Workers.[193] Some of the store-rooms in the *Horrea Piperataria* were hired out to professionals and wealthy businessmen who bought their products from the government. This included perfumer makers and doctors such as the renowned Greek physician Galen, who leased a room at the warehouse to store his medical treatments.[194]

The court poet Statius emphasises the importance of other eastern goods to the Roman system when he describes the income of the imperial treasury (the *fiscus*). He explains that Rome received 'riches from all populations and all revenues from the boundless earth'. These included newly mined bullion, wool from Greece to produce the finest togas, and grain from North Africa and Egypt. But Statius also mentions revenues received in the form of gemstones, pearls and ivory from beyond the Empire. During the reign of Domitian, Roman income included 'all that is extracted from Iberian gold mines, glittering metal received from Dalmatian hills, African harvests (grain) threshed on the floors of the sultry Nile, product gathered by the (pearl) divers who search the eastern seas; income from the flocks tended in Lacedaemonia, transparent crystals, citron wood from Massylia, and the glory of Indian tusks.'[195] The discovery of 675 cubic feet of ivory splinters at the *Horrea Galbae* confirms the significance of tusks imported from Africa.[196] The pearls received by the Roman treasury might have been from Red Sea fisheries under imperial control and the 'crystals' could be a reference to emeralds mined in the Eastern Desert of Egypt.[197] However, most of the precious gems and valuable pearls received by the treasury would have been the tax taken directly from eastern trade imports.

Return Voyage

During the Augustan era a few Roman captains explored the east coast of India, but Strabo reports 'only a small number have ever sailed as far as the Ganges'.[198] Roman ships were smaller in this era and found it easier to negotiate a dangerous line of reefs known as the Palk Straits which lie between India and Sri Lanka.[199] This sailing was not generally attempted as any Roman captains who sailed beyond the Straits risked missing their scheduled return on the winter monsoon winds. Once imperial businessmen began using larger ships, they could no longer sail safely through the Palk Straits.

By the time of the *Periplus*, most Roman captains ended their voyages on the southern coast of India. From there, Roman ships would begin their return sailings with the onset of the northeast monsoon in early November, but Pliny reports that many ships delayed their departure until January.[200] This was prob-ably to receive the extra stocks of black pepper produced in the late harvest season. Roman captains discovered that the best place to wait for the homeward monsoon was a large protected bay in the Mannar Gulf called 'the Strand'.[201]

Many merchants and passengers would remain at Muziris and Nelcynda while their vessels sailed onward to await the return journey at this final anchorage.

The sailing to the Strand took Roman ships past a village with a good harbour called Balita, then on toward the southern tip of India and a port named Comar. At Comar there was a religious community of people who had taken holy vows to honour an unnamed Indian goddess. The *Periplus* reports that 'men who wish to lead a holy life come there to perform oblations to their deity and live a celibate existence. Women also come here, for it is said that at one time the goddess stayed there and performed religious cleansings.'[202] This Indian goddess was possibly Manimekala whom Roman writers knew as the pearl-adorned 'daughter of Hercules'.[203] Confirmation of these practices comes from the Tamil *Manimekhalai* which describes how the pregnant wife of a Brahman teacher travelled to Kumari (Cape Comorin) because 'she wished to get rid of her sin by bathing in the sea'.[204]

Roman ships sailing around the tip of Cape Comorin reached the shallow Gulf of Mannar where the convict-worked pearl fisheries were located. The Strand was near the Palk Straits and the *Periplus* describes it as 'a bay connected with an inland region named Argaru (Uraiyur)'. Over a hundred Roman vessels would gather at the Strand to shelter from the ocean surf and the threat of tropical storms. As the crew waited, Indian merchants dealing with the inland Chola city of Uraiyur brought cotton garments down to the coast for further trade.[205]

When the time came to return, the Roman captains would sail their ships back to Nelcynda and Muziris. Once there, they would collect their passengers and any extra cargo that was available for loading. By this time some of these Roman travellers would have spent over four months in India.

Roman ships sailing back to Egypt would be joined by Indian vessels making the same crossings. Tamil literature describes the onset of the northeast monsoon when white clouds rolled across the sky and the roaring ocean became ominously dark. This was the signal for Tamil merchants to launch their vessels from the Malabar Coast and sail west with cargo holds full of spices, silk and aromatic woods. The *Silappatikaram* describes how 'when the broad-rayed sun ascends from the south and white clouds start to form in the early cool season, it is time to cross the dark, bellowing ocean. The rulers of Tyndis dispatch vessels loaded with eaglewood, silk, sandalwood, spices and all sorts of camphor.'[206] Passengers aboard Roman ships who returned safely to Alexandria would have spent almost nine months in distant lands beyond their Empire in pursuit of profit, or adventure.

CHAPTER FIFTEEN

The Anuradhapura Kingdom of Sri Lanka and the Far East

Roman mariners knew about the dangers of the Palk Strait which stretched from India to Sri Lanka. Pliny describes how this reef was 'shallow and not more than eighteen feet deep in most places, but in certain channels so deep that no anchors can hold at the bottom'. The shallow-hulled ships of the Tamils were able to glide over the Palk reefs to reach ports on the east coast of India. Pliny reports that these vessels could carry up to 150 tons of cargo, equivalent to 3,000 wine amphorae. The Indian ships also had a prow at each end so that they could be sailed backwards through tight channels where there was no space to turn.[1]

Tamil crews sailing through the Palk Straits transported Roman goods on-wards to cities and trade-stations on the eastern seaboard of India. The *Periplus* explains that 'there is a market on the east coast for all Roman goods and all year round these centres receive Roman cash and other products sent from Limyrike' (the Malabar Coast).[2] Tamil merchants also sailed to ports on the nearby island of Sri Lanka, which at that time was ruled by a powerful rival regime, the Anuradhapura Kingdom.

The Greeks and Romans called ancient Sri Lanka 'Taprobane', which was a version of the Sanskrit name 'Tamraparni' meaning 'Copper-coloured Leaf'. During the era of the *Periplus*, Roman merchants acquired Sinhalese goods from Tamil intermediaries. These goods included ivory, turtle-shell, pearls, gemstones and cotton clothes.[3] Strabo knew that Sri Lanka 'sends great amounts of ivory, tortoise-shell and other merchandise to the markets of India'.[4] Pliny was also informed that to, 'procure pearls Indians go to the islands, the most productive of which is Taprobane'.[5]

To protect this commerce, the Tamils probably discouraged Roman trade ventures to Sri Lanka. Strabo heard that Sri Lanka extended 500 miles in the direction of East Africa and the author of the *Periplus* was informed that 'only the northern parts are civilised and the island extends west almost to Azania (East Africa)'.[6] It is possible that some Roman traders had heard accounts of Mada-gascar and assumed that this African island might be connected to Sri Lanka. Millions of years ago the two islands were part of the same landmass and still share common features. This includes geology and the distinct species of fish that live in the rivers and brackish lagoons.

Direct Contact

Pliny reveals how this situation changed in AD 52 when a Roman revenue col-lector became lost at sea. The tax collector was the freed slave of a prominent

Roman businessman named Annius Ploclamus. Ploclamus had followed the wide-spread Roman practice of manumitting trusted slaves and making them his business associates. These freedmen acquired Roman citizenship from their former masters, received their family names and helped them to expand their business networks.

Ploclamus used slaves and freedmen to oversee his expeditions to India and one of his slaves carved Greek and Latin graffiti in a rock shelter on the desert road to Berenice. The Latin graffiti reads 'I, Lysas, slave of Publius Annius Plocamus, came here three days before the *nones* of July in the 35th year' (AD 9).[7] The early July date suggests that Lysas was probably involved in a trade venture to southern Arabia. Ploclamus also had slaves and freedmen operating his business interests in Rome where they collected items for export and acted as distribution agents by handling eastern imports. Inscriptions from the Italian port of Puteoli which served Rome mention a businessman named P. Annius Seleucius (AD 40), a town magistrate called Annius Maximus and a freedman of P. Annius Eros who was a partner in a business association.[8]

Annius Ploclamus and his business associates made further profit from buying contracts to collect Egyptian tax for the Roman government. These included operations in the Red Sea possibly involving the management of pearl fisheries, or the collection of peridot gemstones from Zabargad Island near Berenice. Around AD 50, one of the freedmen working for Ploclamus was sailing to southern Arabia when his ship was caught in a severe gale and swept out into the ocean. The captain was unable to alter course, so he decided to run before the storm hoping for landfall in southern India. But after a foureen day voyage the ship arrived in Sri Lanka.[9]

The Roman crew were brought to the court of the Anuradhapura King Bhatikabhaya where they learned the Sinhalese language. Amongst the ship's cargo was a trade consignment of Roman coin including denarii that impressed the king with its high-quality silver content. The silver content of Indian coins fluctuated according to the fortunes of the issuing kingdom and consequently their coins were rarely minted as pure bullion. By contrast all Roman denarii issued in this era were pure silver and this indicated to the Sinhalese that Rome was a stable and highly prosperous regime. Pliny explains, 'the king admired Roman integrity, because the denarii he took from the detainees were all minted according to an equal weight, though the various figures on the coins showed that they had been issued by several different emperors'.[10]

As a citizen and state-approved tax collector, the freedman presented himself as a representative of Roman government. When questioned by the Sinhalese court, he impressed them with stories of the wealth and power of the Roman Empire. In response King Bhatikabhaya (AD 35–63) sent an embassy to meet with the Emperor Claudius (AD 41–54) to instigate direct diplomatic relations between their two regimes.[11] Pliny explains, 'these facts strongly encouraged alliance and the King sent four envoys to Rome headed by a leader named Rachias'.[12]

Inscriptions found near the ancient Sinhalese capital Anuradhapura suggest that 'Rachias' was actually a nobleman named 'Raki' who had married into the royal household.[13] An early Sinhalese chronicle called the *Mahavamsa* offers further information about the possible composition of the embassies dispatched from ancient Sri Lanka to foreign courts. The *Mahavamsa* describes a four-party group of envoys sent to northern India which included a chief minister who was the king's nephew, a religious instructor, a treasurer and a further ministerial advisor. They travelled with a large group of retainers and brought precious stones and pearls as diplomatic gifts.[14] The Sinhalese envoys received by Claudius possibly included a similar representation of political and financial officials.

Pliny offers further information about the leading Sinhalese ambassador, the man named Rachia. Rachia's father had undertaken an expedition to the Seres (Silk-People) who lived north of the Himalayas. The Sinhalese traded with these 'Seres' who were not the Han Chinese, but part of a population of steppe nomads based in the Tarim kingdoms of Central Asia. These nomads brought silk from the Tarim territories down to the Ganges valley where it was received by Indian merchants.[15]

Brahmi inscriptions of this period mentioning Raki (Rachia) are found in ancient Buddhist monasteries near to the ancient Sinhalese capital Anuradhapura. At these sites rich donors paid for prayer-cells to be carved into caves and rock-faces. Several of these inscriptions name Raki, describing him as a 'Premier' and 'Lord' with one inscription reading, 'the cave of the Premier Raki, son of the Premier'.[16] This confirms Pliny's report that Rachia had an important father who also took part in distant diplomatic and trade missions. An inscription from another cell reads, 'the cave of Princess Anuradhi, daughter of the Great King Gamani Abhaya, the friend of the gods, and the wife of the Premier Raki'.[17] Gamani Abhaya is the dynastic name of King Bhatikabhaya, so it seems that this Raki was possibly the son-in-law of the Sinhalese monarch.

When the Sinhalese ambassadors reached the Roman court the freedman and his associates would have acted as translators. But they had difficulty translating certain Buddhist concepts into Latin, so the Roman record of this contact contains a confused description of Sinhalese society. Consequently, Roman senators opposed to the autocratic rule of the Emperors used this diplomatic contact to promote their own agenda. It was dangerous to openly criticise the Emperor, but Roman authors could introduce controversial ideas for alternative government in their discussions of foreign regimes. They suggested that the highly prosperous Anuradhapura Kingdom had accountable rulers who were selected on merit by the Sinhalese nobility. This implied that political reform was achievable in the Roman Empire where similar wealth maintained autocratic Emperors. Stories began to circulate that the ruler of Sri Lanka had to defer to the judgement of a ruling council and could be deposed from office for political or moral transgressions. These ideas promoted the hopes of those from the senatorial elite in Rome, who favoured a return to a Republican style government. State-spending was also discussed, since Pliny reports 'there are greater riches in Taprobane than in our country. But we make more use of our wealth'.[18]

The diplomatic contact between Sri Lanka and Rome is also referred to in early Buddhist annals composed in Pali script (a form of Sanskrit). These records refer to an extraordinary gift of red Mediterranean coral that the Emperor Claudius offered to King Bhatikabhaya. Bhatikabhaya donated the coral gift to a Buddhist temple called Mahathupa which was a dome-roofed *stupa* in his capital city. Royal artisans carved the coral into the lattice framework that decorated the relic-shrine of the Buddha at the ceremonial centre of the building (the *cetiya*). The *Mahavamsa* describes how the Sinhalese king 'had a priceless coral-net pre-pared and cast over the *cetiya*'.[19] The *Dipavamsa* confirms that Bhatikabhaya 'ordered a priceless lattice of corals to be made, covering the surface of the Mahathupa as if it were dressed in a garment'.[20]

The red coral *cetiya* continued to be celebrated a thousand years after the death of Claudius and Bhatikabhaya. The *Vamsathapakasini* explains that Bhatikabhaya 'sent someone to the overseas country named *Romanukha*. He had a very red coral brought back and made into a great flamed-coloured lattice.'[21] The country named *Romanukha* is probably a Sinhalese rendition of the Latin word *Romanus* meaning the Roman Empire.[22]

After this diplomatic contact, Roman ships began to make ocean crossings directly to Sri Lanka. On these voyages Roman pilots found and mapped the chain of islands that stretched from Lakshadweep to the Maldives.[23] The Roman geographer, Claudius Ptolemy, used data from second century trade *periploi* to map the distant east. Ptolemy records 1,378 islets in this sea, with nineteen atolls probably corresponding to the seventeen coral reefs recognised as islands in modern times.[24] Roman ships also sailed to Sri Lanka from the Tamil lands on a crossing that took four days. Pliny describes the voyage through coral reefs where 'the sea is a deep green colour and the rudders of passing vessels brush against underwater thickets'.[25]

By adopting direct sailings to Sri Lanka, Roman merchants had increased time to explore markets in eastern India before the onset of the return monsoon. Roman captains began to sail around Sri Lanka to reach the leading ports and cities on the east coast of India. Ptolemy's map records twelve cities and five harbours on the coast of the island and indicates that Roman merchants visited two trade centres (*emporia*) on the Sinhalese coast called Modurgi and Talacori. There they received rice, honey, ginger, beryls and purple amethyst gemstones. The Roman lookouts who sailed around the island gave Greek names to the prominent landmarks they sighted from their ships. These names were associated with figures from Greco-Roman religion, including Zeus, Helios and Dionysus. For example, there was a Jovis Promontory, a Solis Harbour and the 'city of the Dionysi or Bacchus City'.[26] Recently the remains of an ancient Roman shipwreck were found near Godavaya on the southern coast of Sri Lanka. The cargo is a mound of corroded metal including iron and copper bars, glass ingots and amphora fragments.[27]

Tamil trade business also increased during this period and when Ptolemy com-piled his geography, the Cheran port of Naura had become an emporium and Tyndis had developed into a coastal city. Muziris was still a leading trade centre, but the nearby Pandian port of Nelcynda had lost its status as an emporium. It seems the Pandian Kings re-directed Roman ships to an emporium called

Elancor which was closer to Cape Comorin. Elancor probably offered better cargo loading arrangements and was nearer to the north coast of Sri Lanka where the Romans were developing direct business interests. According to Ptolemy there was a further new emporium called Colchi near the Pandian pearl fisheries in the Gulf of Mannar. Ptolemy suggests that Indian pigeons were found at this port, which is probably a reference to the Roman trade in unusual pets.[28] Affluent Romans paid high prices for exotic Indian birds and clipped their wings before releasing them as living decorations into their formal gardens.[29]

The Chola Kingdom

The Tamil kingdom of Chola controlled several leading ports on the east coast of India including Kamara (Puhar), Poduke (Arikamedu), and Sopatma. The *Periplus* describes how these centres conducted trade with the west coast of India and were 'home ports for the local craft that sailed along the coast as far as Limyrike' (the Malabar seaboard). Large catamarans called *sangara* also operated from the Chola ports, along with the giant ocean-going vessels that sailed to the Ganges and Burma (the Golden Land). The *Periplus* reports that '*sangara* are very large dugout canoes held together by a yoke and the ports also accommodate very big *kolandiophonta* that sail across to Chryse and the Ganges'.[30]

Puhar, also known as Kaveripattinam (City of the Kaveri), was the main urban-centre in the Chola Kingdom. It was positioned on the Coromandel Coast near the mouth of the Kaveri River, which was the largest waterway in southern India and flowed into the ocean through a delta with several large outlets.[31] Tamil literature describes the city as a large urban-centre behind a substantial port complex. The *Pattinappalai* mentions early trade at the port which included 'agile jumping horses transported by sea; sacks of black pepper taken from carts; precious gems and gold produced in the northern mountain; sandalwood and akil from the western mountain; pearls from the southern seas; prosperity from the Ganges, the produce of the Kaveri River; Sri Lankan food-stuffs, artefacts of Kalakam and other rare and precious merchandise which are accumulated in the wide streets'.[32]

This business attracted foreign merchants to Puhar and some Roman business-men owned large buildings in the city-port. The *Silappatikaram* describes how 'the sun shines over open terraces and the warehouses near the harbour, over turrets with wide windows like the eyes of a deer, over the conspicuous buildings of the *Yavanas* whose prosperity is without limits. At the port there are sailors from distant lands who live as one community.'[33] The inner city was reserved for more distinguished members of Chola society and included temples, barracks and district palaces.[34]

The riverbank and seafront at Puhar were lined with quays and warehouses and the port had a customs station that bore the tiger emblem of the Chola Kingdom. There was also a lighthouse near the shore to guide ships approaching during the hours of darkness.[35] The Chola convened markets in the open ground between the port and the main city. Merchant deals were settled at this site and some of these markets were scheduled to be at night. On these occasions the stalls were lit by lamplight to enable business to be conducted beyond normal daylight hours.[36]

Tamil literature describes how the city of Puhar was cursed when a Chola prince defied an Indian goddess by refusing to perform her sacred rites. Puhar was subsequently destroyed when a great storm sent a vast tidal flood spilling over the port and permanently submerged the city.[37] This story is based on a genuine disaster as the remains of ancient buildings have been found underwater on this coast and storm tides still cast up ceramic remains from the sunken ruins.[38] On the 26th of December 2004, an earthquake beneath the Indian Ocean triggered a major tsunami in the Bay of Bengal. Witnesses on the beach near the modern town of Poompuhar watched as the sea retreated and for a few moments saw the remains of ancient sunken temples before the tsunami surged forward to engulf the beach.

North of Puhar was the Chola port of Poduke (Arikamedu) on the Ariyankup-pam River. Ancient Arikamedu was a trade port for Indian ships trafficking goods around Cape Comorin and it also accommodated larger vessels headed for the Ganges and Burma. The *Periplus* describes how large Indian catamarans were launched from Arikamedu on voyages across the ocean to Malaysia.[39] Excavations at Arikamedu have recovered hundreds of pottery shards from Roman wine amphorae made in Italy and the Aegean region. Some of the fragments belonged to olive oil containers and Roman amphorae that probably held garum fish sauce produced in Spain. Tamil poetry mentions attractive 'Yavana lamps' which could be a reference to imported olive oil used as a fuel source that burnt brightly without odour.[40] Shards of fine Roman tableware (*terra sigillata*) dating to the reign of Emperor Tiberius (AD 14–37) were also recovered at Arikamedu along with fragments of a storage vessel from southern Arabia.[41] Roman glassware was also present including pieces from a bulbous flask (an *unguentaria*) that possibly held ink, or perfumed oils.[42]

Some of the Tamil merchants operating at Arikamedu had business interests in Roman Egypt. The name 'Kanan' appears as a mark scratched on Indian pottery fragments found at Arikamedu and this name is also found on shards recovered from the Egyptian port of Myos Hormos. Kanan may have had agents or associates operating at both ports and used his name to mark the ownership of delivery batches. Other Tamil businessmen may have had even larger operations and another Arikamedu fragment bears the phrase *Kora Puman*, meaning 'Korran the Boss'.[43]

The East Coast of India

In the second century AD, a Greek businessman named Alexandros wrote a *periplus* that described Roman voyages to the Malay Peninsula.[44] The work does not survive, but data from the guide was used by Roman geographers, including Claudius Ptolemy. This information can be used to show how Roman trade operated during the epoch of the ancient economy. The *Periplus* mentions twenty prominent coastal sites between the Indus and the Ganges, but a century later Ptolemy lists almost sixty cities, ports and emporiums along this same coast.

During the time of Alexandros the Cholas had four commercial centres on the southeast coast of India. These were the city-port of Puhar and the emporiums of Salur, Sobura and Poduke (Arikamedu).[45] North of Chola territory was the eastern seaboard of the Satavahana Kingdom with four emporiums and a city-port called Palura.[46] Roman merchants used imperial currency to acquire goods at the Satavahana ports and more than ten hoards have been found in this part of eastern India. Some of these finds are located inland along the Krishna River valley where there were several important Buddhist temple centres. The large silver hoards at Akkanalle and Nasthullapur are close to the Buddhist sites of Amaravati and Nagarjunakonda which functioned as banking institutions accepting money from wealthy donors to lend out at profitable interest rates. The donors included merchant guilds that may have stored and transferred their wealth in foreign currency which included imperial coin.[47] More than half of the Roman hoards found in eastern India are composed of gold aurei with the majority containing coins issued by the Emperor Antoninus Pius (AD 138–161).[48]

Roman merchants were trading with the east coast of India at a time when Julio-Claudian denarii were becoming scarce in the Empire (AD 90–110). Since coins were considered to be more valuable than bullion, some Roman business-men began striking their own replica denarii based on the older issues. It was illegal to counterfeit Roman coins, but these replicas were made of pure silver and they were not created with the intention of defrauding anyone with a cheap copy. Vast quantities of these replica coins were produced for the eastern trade and some of the minting operations were transferred to India so that imperial autho-rities could not interfere with the process.

The Akenpalle hoard found in Andhra Pradesh (ancient Satavahana territory) contained 1,531 denarii with 55 of these silver coins identified as commercial replicas. The imitation coins were skilful die-struck copies of imperial issues and were only identified as counterfeit because of small mistakes in their legends (texts).[49] As there were no die linkages between the replicas, different counterfeit dies had been used to mint these coins. A single die can produce thousands of coins, so production of the counterfeits would have been on a large scale and operated by different trade firms. Confirmation comes from a Roman die for striking gold aurei that was found on the Amaravathi riverbed near the site of an ancient Buddhist Temple in Tamilnadu. It bears the portrait of the Emperor Hadrian and is exact enough to have been produced by the official Roman mint. Perhaps the die was covertly made, or was a genuine item stolen to order for a Roman businessman with operations in India.[50]

Some of the larger hoards of Roman aurei found in India contain defaced coins that were struck with a chisel to destroy the portrait of the Emperor.[51] These were possibly decommissioned coins intended for reminting within the Empire. But this process was interrupted when the old coins were offered wholesale to Roman traders amassing gold bullion for eastern export.[52]

Many Roman denarii found in eastern India bear the marks of money dealers from the Satavahana Realms who approved foreign currency by stamping it with tiny star symbols, swastikas and miniature Buddhist wheels. Some of these marks could also be devotional emblems stamped on to batches of foreign currency to be offered as donations to Buddhist temples by local merchants and business-men.[53] These coins never returned to the Empire as no denarii found in Roman territory have carried these distinctive symbols. This provides further evidence for the drain of bullion from the Empire in this period.

From the city-port of Paloura in Ganjam, Roman ships could launch into the open ocean and sail across the Bay of Bengal to a Burmese city called Sada. Ptolemy records, 'the sail across from Paloura to Sada is 13,000 *stades* in the direc-tion of the equatorial sunrise (due east).'[54] This voyage covered nearly 1,400 miles of ocean and would have taken ten days for the fastest ships to accomplish.

Other Roman ships could continue up the east coast of India to a Satavahana emporium called Alosygni. Alosygni was a trade-hub that received traffic from many parts of the Bay of Bengal and Ptolemy says that the port was 'used by those who sail and navigate the bay'.[55] Roman traders sailing further north could also visit cities and trade ports located along the Ganges Delta, a seacoast that was more than 200 miles long.

The Ganges and Burma
The Ganges was one of the richest and most densely populated parts of ancient India. The region was extensively urbanised by early Indian kingdoms including the Mauryan Empire which ruled most of the subcontinent from 322 to 185 BC. By the first century AD, the Ganges region was ruled by a number of royal city-states that were large and prosperous enough to avoid being coerced into any neighbouring kingdoms.

The author of the *Periplus* describes the northeast coast of India and reports that 'this region extends far inland and produces a great many cotton gar-ments'.[56] He also knew about a trade port on the Ganges which 'shipped out cinnamon, Gangetic nard, pearls and the very finest quality cotton garments – known as Gangetic cottons'. Roman merchants were told that there were gold mines in the area and there was an Indian regime that minted gold coins called *kaltis*.[57] Ptolemy records a group of five cities in the Ganges region that were visited by Roman traders.[58] These cities offered precious stones and Ptolemy notes that 'near the Ganges River are the Sabarae in whose region diamonds are found'. Ptolemy also records how large quantities of high-quality nard were produced in the eastern Himalayas and the region exported exotic birds including roosters with colourful plumes, white crows, and talking parrots. Roman traders visiting this region knew about an inland site called the 'Sardonyx Mountains' which sent red gemstones to the Ganges and other east coast ports.[59] Confirma-tion of these contacts comes from a Greek tutor named Dionysius Periegetes who wrote a brief account of world geography for his students. Dionysius describes the Indian Ocean but comments, 'I have not travelled these routes on black ships, because commerce is not my inherited livelihood. I have not visited the Ganges like those people who cross the ocean and risk their lives for enormous wealth'.[60]

Ships sailing further east reached Burma, known to the Romans as *India Trans Gangem* or 'India beyond the Ganges'.[61] In northern Burma the Brahmaputra

River led deep inland to Himalayan territories that produced the 'best cinnamon', known as malabathrum. The author of the *Periplus* believed that this region was on the frontier of *Thinae* (China) and describes how the cinnamon trade was conducted by an inland tribal people called the Sesatai or Besadae.[62] Ptolemy depicts these people as 'short, stooping, ignorant, uncultivated, with broad foreheads and pale skin'. They were nicknamed Besadae, the 'Sons of Bes', because they resembled the squat and broad-faced Egyptian god who was the protector of mothers and young children. Ptolemy mentions that Burma was the habitat of tigers and elephants and the region 'produced very much gold' and possessed 'well-guarded metal'.[63] Martial also describes how the Emperor Domitian had Bengal tigers displayed in the Roman arena.[64]

Indian merchants had extensive trade contacts with cities and trade-stations in Burma and ancient Sanskrit studies refer to this region as *Suvarnabhumi* or 'the Land of Gold'.[65] The Buddhist *Jatakas* mention a routine voyage from the Ganges to Burma when 'the merchants of Bharukaccha (Varanasi) were setting sail for the Golden Land'.[66] The *Arthasastra* lists the foreign merchandise valuable to an Indian kingdom including 'the products of the Gold-Land, resinous yellow sandalwood and reddish-yellow *auttaraparvataka* from the northern mountains'. These were aromatic woods considered to be 'fragrant substances of superior value'.[67]

The author of the *Periplus* knew that Indian ships were crossing the ocean to trade with a distant Gold-Land known in Greek as *Chryse* (Golden). However, the author believed that Chryse was an island and reports, 'at the furthest eastern extremity of the inhabited world is the island of Chryse, which lies beneath the rising sun and produces the finest turtle-shell of all places in the Erythraean Sea' (the Indian Ocean).[68] During most of this period Roman traders did not know what lay beyond the Gold-Land. It was believed that this was 'perhaps because of extreme storms, bitter cold and difficult terrain. Or perhaps these regions are not explored because some divine power of the gods has prevented it.'[69]

Writing in AD 90, Josephus indicates Jewish knowledge of trade voyages to the *Aurea Chersonesus*, described as the 'Golden-Peninsula, which belongs to India'.[70] This is probably Burma, or the Malay Peninsula which Roman traders had begun to explore on their most distant voyages. According to Ptolemy there were three emporia and two city-ports on the northern Burmese coast.[71] There were two further cities positioned near the Irrawaddy River which extended deep into Southeast Asia.[72] Ancient Indian texts suggest that merchants made voyages to these regions mainly to obtain diamonds, sandalwood and cinnamon.[73] Roman merchants probably used bullion to acquire these goods and would have sent slaves to the royal courts of Burmese kings.

The Chinese became aware of this commerce in AD 121 when a Burmese king from the State of Shan sent an overland embassy to the Han Emperor An. The embassy gave the Chinese Emperor diplomatic gifts that included exotic musicians and skilled conjurors. Among the party were a group of people who identified themselves as subjects of the Roman Empire. They told the Chinese they came from 'West of the Sea' and the Chinese concluded, 'this land must be the Roman Empire (*Da Qin*) and the State of Shan must communicate with Rome via a southwest route'.[74]

The 900 mile-long Malay Peninsula was the barrier that confined Roman trade voyages to the Indian Ocean. Ptolemy had some basic information about the shape of the Malay Peninsula, but he did not know about the narrow Malacca Straits that separate the headland from the island of Sumatra. Roman merchants had heard reports about three large islands near Indonesia, but nothing certain could be ascertained about their size, position or the inhabitants of these territories. Ptolemy mentions three islands populated by 'naked cannibals' and three Satyrorum islands inhabited by people 'said to have animal tails like Satyrs'.[75] Perhaps this is a reference to a species of Indonesian monkey, or Greek myths applied to populations believed to inhabit the edges of the known world.

Ptolemy seemed unaware of Sumatra, but he was able to record details about the neighbouring island of Java. Java was known to the Romans as Labadius, or 'Barley Island'. It was said to be highly fruitful and had a capital city on its eastern coast called Argentae Metropolis.[76] Roman traders probably received this information from early Indian settlers who called the island 'Java-Dvipa' meaning the 'Millet Island'. Perhaps the Roman traders wrongly assumed that Sumatra and Java were a single landmass. This would explain why Ptolemy claims Java produced a lot of gold when this is actually a feature of ancient Sumatra.[77]

Most Roman vessels ended their voyages at the Burmese city of Tamala on the northwest edge of the Malay Peninsula. Alexandros indicates that Indian merchants landing at Tamala made a land crossing of the Kra Isthmus. Ptolemy explains, 'they traverse from Tamala over the Golden Peninsula on a crossing that is 1,600 *stades* (176 miles) in the direction of the winter sunrise (southeast)'.[78] There was a trade-station on the far coast of the peninsula where merchants embarked on other vessels for their voyages across the Gulf of Thailand (known to Ptolemy as the Perimulic Gulf).

Alexandros heard about Thailand and Cambodia from Indian merchants who made the journey across the Kra Isthmus. Indian ships visited a commercial port in Thailand called Thipinobastae Emporium then followed the coast of Southeast Asia to a trade port called Zabia on the southern tip of Vietnam.[79] No Roman vessels had been able to measure the distances involved in this voyage, so Alexandros used sailing days to describe the route. He reported that 'the land curves south and those who sail along it reach the city of Zabai in twenty days'.[80] In Zabai visiting merchants were offered pearls, ivory, rhino-horn, turtle-shell and various fragrant woods.[81]

Indian ships that reached Zabia could sail out to sea on a voyage south to reach Borneo.[82] They made landfall on the north coast of the island and sailed to a trade outpost called Cattigara which is described as a 'roadstead for shipping'.[83] Alexandros was vague about the distances involved in this voyage, but he was clear about the directions. He reports that 'after sailing from Zabai in the direction of the south wind and travelling to the left for a number of days, they reach Cattigara'.[84] There were no cities or kingdoms in Borneo and the island contained an unexplored rainforest rich in natural resources, including scented camphor oil extracted from trees, which was used in various foods and medicines. Ptolemy imagined that the coast of Borneo was part of the Asian landmass as it curved southward from China to join with east Africa and encircle the entire Indian Ocean. He speculated that 'the encircling land connects to Rhaptum promontory and the southern parts of Azan (East Africa)'.[85]

As these journeys were powered by natural forces, all the expectant traveller had to do was invest his time in the journey and await eventual landfall. The Roman statesman Seneca asked: 'what is the space that lies between the furthest shores of Spain and India? Why, only a few days travel if a ship is blown by a favourable wind.'[86] Seneca was a tutor and advisor to the young Emperor Nero (AD 54–68), but he also wrote a book concerning India.[87] Unfortunately that study has not survived, but Seneca was unsure of what lay beyond the Indian frontiers and wrote about his fears in other works. He asked: 'what if some ruler of a great unknown nation was increased by good fortune? What if he had ambitions to expand the boundaries of his realm? What if he is at this very moment fitting out a fleet to send against us?'[88]

During the mid-second century AD Roman ships began sailing around the Malay Peninsula to reach markets in Thailand, and gold aurei minted by the Emperors Antoninus Pius (AD 138–161) and Marcus Aurelius (AD 161–180) have been found at Oc-eo in southern Vietnam.[89] During this period, reports reached Roman merchants that direct contact could be made with China by sailing north from Zabia into a sea called the Great Gulf (the South China Sea).[90] These accounts proved to be correct as the Chinese army had an important military base in the region called Rinan ('South of the Sun'). Rinan was on the northeast coast of Vietnam where the Red River flowed into the Gulf of Tonkin. From this place Roman subjects would have been able to meet state-agents of the Chinese Empire and in AD 166 direct contact was made.

CHAPTER SIXTEEN

The Antun Embassy to China and the Antonine Pandemic

By AD 160, the Chinese and Roman Empires were at their political and economic epoch, but devastating events were imminent. Chinese records reveal that the first direct engagement between representatives of the Roman regime and the Han Empire occurred at this time. However, the incident is not mentioned in Roman accounts probably because it took place at a period of extreme crisis for both ancient regimes.

The Han Empire was as large as its Roman counterpart with more than 50 million subjects and a similar sized domain. However, the Han military had a core professional army comprised of less than 40,000 permanent soldiers. Professional Roman troops fought with javelins and short-swords, while Chinese infantry had superior missile technology and carried sophisticated multi-shot crossbows with steel-tipped bolts. Frontline Chinese troops were equipped with spear-pointed halberds and the infantry were supported by substantial cavalry forces including allied steppe horsemen. The Han regime had access to an enormous reserve of peasant manpower that could be levied and trained as soldiers. Ancient documents recovered from the frontier region of Yinwan describe weaponry stored in the central state-armoury. On one occasion there were 23 million items of military equipment in the armoury, including 500,000 crossbows and over 11 million crossbow bolts.[1] The Chinese could therefore conduct wars on an enormous scale if the situation demanded.

The Romans became aware of the Chinese Empire from the reports of merchants and ambassadors who had contacts in Central Asia. The export of Mediterranean bullion to pay for Han silks made China an important issue for the Roman regime. The silk routes were also supplying the Parthians with high-grade steel that could produce superior lances, armour, and arrows. Plutarch describes Parthian arrows made from oriental steel as 'strange missiles that can pierce through every obstacle' and mailed steel armour as 'protection that cannot be penetrated'.[2] Chinese manufacturers could mass-produce this metal, but Roman workshops remained unfamiliar with the techniques. Juvenal mentions the Chinese in his satires, considering this to be one of the important topics being debated at the time. He ridiculed Roman women who involved themselves in politics by interrupting generals to ask 'what are the intentions of the Chinese?'[3]

In early AD 161 the Emperor Antoninus Pius died and was succeeded by Marcus Aurelius. That autumn the Parthian Empire challenged Roman interests in the east by invading the client kingdom of Armenia and installing their own candidate on the throne. The Roman governor of Cappadocia mobilised an army to confront the Parthians, but this expeditionary force was massacred near the frontier. After fifty years of peace and security, Persia and Rome once again prepared for full-scale war.

In summer AD 165 Marcus Aurelius sent envoys east aboard a Roman merchant ship with instructions to make direct contact with the Chinese Empire. This was not the first time that the Roman government had used merchants and trade ships to facilitate their distant diplomatic interests. A fragmentary inscription records how in AD 18 the imperial commander Germanicus used businessmen from the Syrian frontier-city of Palmyra to deliver a message to King Orabzes, who ruled the small Gulf Kingdom of Mesene. The Palymrenes had trade interests in Mesene, so they were able to deliver messages to the kingdom concerning Roman interests in Persia that could undermine Parthian rule.[4] When Rome and Parthia went to war over Armenia in AD 58, the imperial commander Corbulo received diplomats from the secessionist realm of Hyrcania which lay on the eastern shores of the Caspian Sea. Corbulo realised that these allies would be intercepted by hostile Parthian forces if they attempted to return to their homelands via Iran. He therefore placed them aboard a Roman ship bound for northwest India and the diplomats returned to their homeland via the Indus Region. Tacitus explains, 'Corbulo gave them an escort and conducted them down to the shores of the Red Sea and, by avoiding Parthian territory, they returned safely to their native lands'.[5] Whatever the route taken, the incident confirms that Roman Red Sea ships could be used to deliver envoys and messages to distant eastern regimes in order to undermine Parthian interests in Central Asia. This possibly explains the Roman voyage to China made in AD 165.

The crew that set out in AD 165 had to spend that winter in an Indian port before continuing around the Malay Peninsula to reach Vietnam in the summer of AD 166. Meanwhile the co-emperor Lucius Verus arrived in Syria to reclaim Armenia and prepare a full-scale attack on the Parthian Empire. The Romans possibly planned to conquer Persia and this explains why they sought new allies in the distant east, including China.

The Roman envoys who reached the Chinese outpost at Rinan were immediately dispatched under guard to the inland Han capital Luoyang along with part of their trade cargo. The journey to Luoyang was more than a thousand miles, but Chinese highways were double the size of most Roman roads and had a central lane reserved for official carriages and dispatch riders. State-run stables and way-stations were located at regular intervals to provide government agents with fresh horses, rest and provisions. But even with these advantages, the journey would have taken several weeks of fast-paced and relentless travel. The effort was justified since the Chinese had been trying to make contact with the Roman Empire since about AD 70, but their efforts were blocked by the Parthians. Chinese intelligence suggested that the Roman Empire (*Da Qin*) was a powerful political regime that matched the population, resources and military capacity of the Han Empire. This was an opportunity for the ancient world's two largest powers to form significant political and economic contacts.

At Luoyang the Roman delegates were granted an audience with the Han Emperor Huan and summoned to the inner court. They were asked a list of stock questions to confirm the scale and character of the Roman regime. Chinese reports claim the delegates represented 'Antun' which must be the Emperor Marcus Aurelius Antoninus and his co-ruler Lucius Verus. The delegates told the Chinese that the Roman regime had been trying to send representatives to China, but their efforts had been prevented by the Parthians who wanted to maintain control over the highly profitable silk route traffic in oriental fabrics.[6] Perhaps the delegates were on a fact-finding mission since they did not mention that the Roman army was preparing to invade Persia.

All responses given by the delegates were recorded in the Han court records along with comments made by senior members of the Chinese government. A few of these details were copied into a later historical work called the *Hou Hanshu* (*The Later Han Histories*) which offers a brief account of the distant west, including some facts known about *Da Qin* (Rome). This includes the surviving information about the meeting between the Han court and the *Antun* delegates.[7]

It was usual practice for embassies to offer costly diplomatic gifts to foreign rulers as tokens of respect and measures of prestige. However, the *Antun* delegates had no high-value offerings for the Han court and no costly Roman merchandise to present as gifts. In place of imperial gifts they offered the Han Emperor some of the cargo samples that had been removed from their ship at Rinan to be conveyed to the palace at Luoyang. These items were a collection of relatively ordinary eastern goods and Han officials were disappointed because they had expected to receive Roman jewellery, objects fashioned from delicate red coral and exquisite western fabrics dyed vibrant colours. The *Hou Hanshu* records: '*Antun* the ruler of *Da Qin*, sent envoys from beyond the frontiers to reach us through Rinan. They offered elephant tusks, rhinoceros horn, and turtle-shell. This was the very first time there was communication [between our countries].'

All foreign accounts suggested that Rome was immensely prosperous, so the lack of suitable diplomatic gifts was noted in the Han court records as being unusual. After receiving valuable gifts from the Han Emperor, the Romans delegates were escorted back to Rinan and their waiting ship. The delegates probably spent the summer of AD 168 in India with their return to Egypt planned for November of that year. Based on these schedules the Chinese expected to receive further contacts from the Romans in AD 170, but no one came, not even Roman merchants seeking lucrative new trade prospects.

Chinese officials looked for explanations in the court records and drew attention to the gifts offered by the *Antun* delegates. The *Hou Hanshu* reports 'the tribute they brought was neither precious nor rare, raising suspicion that the accounts of Rome might be exaggerated'.[8] In 1885 a German scholar named Friedrich Hirth translated this passage and assumed that the Chinese were 'suspicious' about the delegates.[9] He suggested that the delegates were fraudulent merchants, but the Chinese government had protocols for identifying and dealing with foreigners and the passage in the *Hou Hanshu* suggests the diplomats were genuine. An accurate reading of the ancient text suggests that when the Romans presented meagre gifts, the Chinese were suspicious of earlier reports describing the wealth and power of Rome. These doubts gained credibility when no further diplomats or merchants arrived from this distant western Empire. The Chinese did not realise that the Roman Empire was suffering from an unprecedented crisis and could no longer exploit the opportunities offered by distant exchanges.

The Antonine Pandemic
In ancient times some populations were carriers of lethal and highly infectious diseases. Over many generations of exposure, carrier populations developed a natural resistance to their local diseases, but foreign visitors did not have this advantage. During the mid-second century AD the expansion of ancient world commerce helped create the connections that released these diseases from their host peoples and allowed infections to spread to densely populated areas in foreign lands.

In AD 160, a virulent new disease was released into the ancient world trade routes, possibly by merchants returning from Borneo or some other previously remote region. The virus spread rapidly through Central Asia and in AD 162 an outbreak occurred among the Chinese army stationed on the northern frontiers of the Han Empire. In the space of a year the Han military lost a third of its operational army, with many more soldiers debilitated by the disease. Mounted steppe nomads immediately took advantage of the situation and overran the unprotected frontiers. The *Hou Hanshu* reports 'the roads came under attack and communications were broken. There was widespread sickness in the army and three or four out of every ten men died.'[10]

Casualty rates suggest that the Chinese had no previous exposure or natural resistance to this unamed disease. The epidemic was either an ancestral strain of smallpox or measles, or maybe a lethal combination of these two infections. Both diseases are highly infectious and before the advent of modern medicine frequently left survivors with severe long-term conditions. For example, measles triggers tissue inflammation that can cause permanent eyesight problems or brain damage, and smallpox leaves many survivors visually impaired or infertile.

The epidemic of AD 162 inflicted more damage to the Chinese military than any enemy force could achieve in years of conflict. It also limited Chinese prospects for recruiting new reserves of military manpower. As the disease spread through the countryside it infected the peasants usually called for service in the army. Fresh outbreaks occurred whenever new soldiers were mobilised or massed for action. In AD 166, when the Chinese Emperor Huan greeted the Roman delegates, he knew that the Han Empire was in no position to engage in ambitious military actions far from their currently threatened frontiers.

Meanwhile, in the Middle East, Roman armies regained possession of Armenia. The following year Roman forces began a campaign across the Euphrates Frontier to claim Babylonia from the Parthian Empire. By the end of AD 165 the Roman army occupied Iraq with plans to extend the invasion east into Parthian Iran. Suddenly, an unknown and lethal new disease broke out amongst the campaign troops. A variant of the disease that had crippled the Chinese army had reached the western world. Classical sources describe a virulent plague that is referred to in modern literature as the 'Antonine Pandemic'.

By AD 166 the disease had reached epidemic proportions in the densely populated cities of ancient Babylonia and the Roman army was ordered to withdraw from Iraq. War was suspended as Roman forces returned to camps and garrison posts in Syria and other frontier provinces. Dio reports that the co-emperor Lucius Verus 'lost a great many of his soldiers through supply shortages and disease, but he made it back to Syria with the survivors'.[11]

The returning troops rapidly spread the disease into the main cities of the Empire, including the imperial capital. The *Historia Augusta* claims that 'it was his fate that a disease seemed to follow Verus through whatever provinces he travelled on his return, until finally it reached Rome'.[12] Within a year, the disease was at epidemic proportions within the Empire and countless soldiers and civilians succumbed. Ammianus explains, 'this virulent and incurable disease burst forth and contaminated everywhere with illness and ruin from the frontiers of Persia all the way to the Rhine and Gaul'.[13] The pandemic also affected Britain and archaeologists excavating Wotton Cemetery in Gloucester (Glevum) uncovered a pit from this era filled with the remains of ninety-one men, women and children heaped into a mass grave. The bones showed no sign of trauma indicating that death was due to disease. Gloustershire had a population of about 10,000 people and this pit would have contained the death-toll incurred over several days.[14]

Casualty rates were highest in overcrowded cities, including Alexandria and Rome, which had prolonged warm temperatures during the summer months. The movement of army personnel was a key factor in the early spread of the disease, but maritime commerce also propagated and intensified the epidemic. People seemingly in good health at embarkation could develop full symptoms during sea voyages and infect other crew and passengers in the close confines of the ship. Crowded markets filled with people from distant regions also offered a chain of infection for renewed outbreaks.

Some communities suffered higher rates of infection due to their living arrangements or social practices. Roman soldiers who shared meals and accommodation probably incurred immediate losses as high as the one-third rate endured by Han troops on the Chinese frontier. Many who recovered were unfit for further service due to chronic disabilities that affected brain function, eyesight and mobility. Roman miners were also susceptible to the disease as they lived in large communal camps and worked in cramped enclosed conditions that readily transmitted infections. The disease therefore affected the output of mining operations.

One of the main factors that increased infection rates was that Roman society encouraged public bathing as a mass recreational activity and this practice continued after the first appearance of the disease.[15] Popular bath complexes known as *thermae* were monumental civic buildings fitted with different temperature pools, sauna-like steam-rooms and exercise yards. In large cities *thermae* were supplied by aqueducts and fitted with sophisticated hydraulic apparatuses to manage the flow of heated water between large bathing pools. The baths provided an environment that allowed people from all sections of Roman society to intermingle and most city *thermae* could accommodate hundreds of people. Bathing was recommended for good health, but the *thermae* were also highly popular centres for leisure activities, informal business and community networking. The baths of Caracalla, constructed during the early third century AD, covered fifty acres and could accommodate at least 1,600 bathers.[16] Even Roman forts on the frontiers contained bath houses as a necessary facility for the troops and in this period bathing facilities for a thousand soldiers were built in the newly captured city of Dura-Europos on the Euphrates frontier.[17] Emperors such as Hadrian encouraged sick and infirm people to bathe in the public baths in the early morning.[18] The Greek medical view that bathing could help recovery from illness therefore assisted the rapid and prolonged spread of the new infections throughout the Roman population.[19]

Aelius Aristides describes how he caught the disease in the early stages of the outbreak when he was living at Smyrna in Asia Minor. He explains that 'I was in the suburbs at the height of summer when the disease infected almost all my neighbours. First several of my servants grew sick in succession and the youngest to the oldest became bedridden. I was the last to be attacked.' Doctors summoned to the household were unable to cure the sickness and they informed a gravely-ill Aristides that he would die. However, contrary to expectations, 'slowly with trouble and difficulty, I recovered, but fever did not leave me completely until my favourite foster child died'.[20] Aristides worried that his patron goddess had taken the boy in his place, so when the daughter of his foster-sister became sick, he paid for doctors to treat the child. A doctor named Porphyrio advised that the little girl should bathe frequently to restore her heath and wash away the contagion.[21]

The Greek doctor Galen was living in Rome when the first outbreak began and left immediately for his home city of Pergamon.[22] In the densely populated centre of Rome the unchecked disease quickly reached epidemic proportions and the *Historia Augusta* describes how 'the corpses were removed in carts and wagons because of the unprecedented number of deaths'. No effective remedy could be found for the sickness and many of the nobility died during the outbreak.[23] If Roman delegates had returned from China, they would have found similar scenes in Alexandria at this time of unparalleled fear and prolonged crisis.

The Antonine disease remained at epidemic levels for over a decade (AD 165–175). Refugees fled regions threatened by the disease causing widespread panic and regional food shortages. Papyri tax records from Egypt show that some villages in the Egyptian delta were losing over 70 per cent of their adult male population as people fled agricultural estates threatened by the infection (AD 166–170).[24] After first exposure, new spates of infection occurred periodically and Egyptian records from the following decade indicate the casualty rates in rural communities that endured renewed outbreaks. Tax details for Socnopaiou Nesos record that between September AD 178 and February 179, a village with 244 male inhabitants lost 78 men due to the disease. This is almost one third of the male population in a six month period.[25] This supports Chinese accounts that the disease killed at least three out of every ten troops in their affected areas.

A papyrus from Egypt indicates that entire villages were being removed from the government tax records due to a combination of disease and attack by nomad shepherds engaged in banditry. After the village of Kerkenouphis was decimated by disease, 'most of the men were killed by the godless Nikochites who attacked and burnt the village. The remainder died of sickness and only a small number fled' (AD 168).[26]

Intensively managed agricultural estates in Italy would have endured similar losses during the height of the pandemic. Orosius describes how 'a disease spread through many provinces and laid waste to all Italy so that everywhere, country estates, fields and towns were left without cultivators and inhabitants'. Some regions never recovered their former productivity and Orosius claims that intense agriculture 'gave way to ruin and woodlands'.[27] But in the following decades there were fewer people to support, especially in the larger cities. Confirmation comes from a large villa complex excavated in Tuscany. During the late second century AD the slave-quarters at the Villa Settefinestre were abandoned and walled up. The complex was deserted shortly afterwards.[28]

The German populations who occupied lands beyond the Roman frontiers had no densely populated urban sites with social connections that easily propagated and spread diseases. Tacitus reports: 'it is well known that the German nations do not have cities, they do not even tolerate closely contiguous dwellings. They live scattered and apart, where a spring, a meadow, or wood has attracted them. Their villages are not arranged in our fashion with the buildings connected and joined together. Every person surrounds his dwelling with an open space.'[29] Furthermore, when the Germans met for communal meals, 'each person has a separate seat and table of his own'.[30] German communities were therefore not as severely affected by the new diseases as their urbanised Roman counterparts.

The Germans threatened war on the Rhine in AD 162, and in AD 166 the Roman army confronted German tribes attempting to cross the Danube frontier. But the Roman counter-attack was hindered as thousands of campaign soldiers succumbed to the Antonine pandemic. The rich gold-producing province of Dacia was overrun and occupied by German tribes and mounted Sarmation warriors from steppe lands near the Black Sea.

For the first time in more than two centuries it seemed possible that the frontier defences might fail and Italy could be overrun by foreign hordes. Rome had lost entire armies in previous battles, but it always had the manpower to quickly restore its losses and reconstitute its fighting forces. But the Antonine Pandemic threatened the long-term reserves of able-bodied manpower available to the Empire. It also crippled Roman finances which were reliant on mine production and the taxes imposed on international commerce.

An inscription from the gold-mining district of Dacia records that in AD 167, a company fund to arrange funerals for mine workers had to stop operating. The text reports that fifty-four men from the mining town of Laburnum paid regular sums into the funeral college to manage their burial rites, but within a year of the outbreak only seventeen of these individuals remained in the area. This means that nearly two-thirds of the workforce had succumbed to disease, or simply fled the region. The funeral association could not sustain its costs and closed its business after posting an inscription to memorialise its actions.[31] The mines were probably evacuated the following year when German tribes overran Dacia and plundered Pannonia.[32] Evidence suggests that the disease affected mining activities across the Empire and a series of dated lead ingots from mines in Roman Britain ends in AD 169.[33]

During this period Iberia was subject to raids from North Africa as Moors seized ships to attack overseas territories. Archaeology suggests that large-scale work at silver mines in southwest Iberia stopped during this decade.[34] Excavations at Corta Lago, one of largest mining settlements in Roman Spain, revealed a steep decline in the use of Samian ware during the 160s AD. Later pottery types do not appear in comparable quantities suggesting a serious and permanent decline in activity at the site.[35]

The evidence from Egypt also indicates a serious decline in the quantity of precious metal available to Roman government. During the imperial period Egypt had its own currency which consisted of large tetradrachma coins minted by the imperial authorities in Alexandria. By AD 150 tetradrachmas contained up to 18 per cent silver (2.3 grams) which was almost the same quantity of silver contained in a denarius and gave the two coins a similar monetary value.[36] But Egyptian currency was affected when diminishing silver supplies were diverted to other projects. In AD 167 the Alexandrian mint began producing tetradrachmas that contained half the normal silver content. Analysis of these coins shows greater impurities in the metal confirming that the usual silver supplies had been interrupted and the Alexandrian mint had begun recycling large amounts of older metalwork. In AD 170 the Alexandrian mint stopped producing new tetradrachma coins and apart from a limited issue in AD 177 did not resume full-scale minting until the end of the decade. In AD 185 the silver content of newly issued tetradrachma was again reduced so that it contained only a quarter of former silver content.[37] Faced with crisis and declining income the Roman State could no longer maintain the silver value of its Egyptian currency.

As for trade, even the wealthiest merchants were badly affected including those from the rich city of Tyre on the Phoenician coast. In AD 174 the Tyrian community trading at the Roman port of Puteoli wrote to the ruling council in their home city requesting immediate financial assistance to maintain their station. Many of their associates had died and the remaining traders could not meet operating costs.[38] That year the Emperor wrote to Athens giving a leading city council known as the Areopagus permission to relax its membership criteria. Previous membership of the Areopagus had been limited to Athenians with three generations of citizen ancestry, but Antoninus Pius advised they install any suitable citizen with freeborn parents. In the letter the Emperor acknowledged that 'many other cities have made special claims for relief', but Athens warranted special consideration due to its prestigious past.[39]

Evidence of continued outbreaks of the infection comes from the town of Virunum near the Danube frontier, where a bronze plaque gives a membership list for a local temple devoted to Mithras. In AD 183, the Mithraeum lost five of its ninety-eight members when there was a fresh outbreak of the disease.[40] Added to this were the people who recovered, but with serious disabilities that left them dependent on others, or vulnerable to further illnesses. There was a major recurrence of the disease in Rome during AD 189 when more than 2,000 people were reported to be dying every day.[41]

The Kingdom of Iron and Rust

The Roman military did not restore the Danube frontiers until AD 168. Led by the emperors Marcus Aurelius and Lucius Verus the Legions reclaimed the Danube region, but the mass movement of troops and supplies created new opportunities for the disease to spread. As winter approached, the Emperors returned to the city of Aquileia in northern Italy, the command centre for the frontier campaign.

That winter, the disease spread among troops confined to their barracks and doctors had to be summoned from Rome in an effort to alleviate and suppress the infection. Galen reports, 'when I reached Aquileia the infection was at a greater intensity than previous outbreaks. The Emperors immediately went back to Rome with a few soldiers, while the majority had difficulty surviving and most of us perished.'[42] On route to Rome, Verus suddenly fell sick and died. He may have become ill, or ingested a preventative remedy that had toxic effects. His death left Marcus Aurelius in sole charge of the Roman regime and burdened him with great responsibilities. The lone Emperor faced the challenge of how to defend an Empire depleted of troops and deprived of its organisational capacity by an unrelenting force of nature. Marcus Aurelius became famous for his personal writings on stoic philosophy, the *Meditations*, written during this period of crisis and exploring concepts of duty in response to extreme adversity.

Mainstream pagan religion expected divine favour to be granted in the physical world by material rewards, so it struggled to explain extreme and indiscriminate mass suffering. By contrast, Christianity had an explanation for the new horrors of disease, turmoil and war. The Christian theologian Cyprian explained 'the world is sentenced to death, for it is the law of God that everything that is born dies. Everything grows old, everything grows weak and everything declines.' He wrote about 'the scarred and exhausted mountains; the worked-out mines that provide fewer sources of silver and gold with meagre seams that diminish every day'.[43] As foretold in *Revelations*, the end of days was approaching and Christians could expect solace and reward in the afterlife.

A further serious outbreak of the new diseases occurred in AD 250 at a time when Christianity was gaining significant popularity in the Empire. Eusebius claims that Christians, 'heedless of the danger, took charge of the sick, attending to their every need and ministering to them in Christ'. By contrast, 'at the first onset of the diseases, the pagans pushed the sufferers away and fled from their dearest'. Cyprian reports that survivors suffered long-term weakness, including having their 'gait enfeebled, hearing obstructed, or eyesight darkened'.[44]

During this period, China faced similar challenges to state-endorsed religions and in AD 184 the Han Empire was seriously destabilised by a militia-based rebellion amongst the rural population. The rebellion was organised by a new Taoist sect called the 'Yellow Scarves' led by a cult of charismatic faith-healers who planned to seize governmental power from the Han. The movement declared that the Han regime had lost the Mandate of Heaven and the Yellow Scarves would return prosperity to a decaying world. The Yellow Scarves were defeated, but the Han regime was fatally compromised. The Emperor had to delegate important military and political powers to prominent generals and nobles who became provincial warlords. Buddhism also attracted numerous new Chinese converts during this period as the religion offered a persuasive pacifist philosophy. The first of the four guiding principles, or Noble Truths, of ancient Buddhism is that 'suffering exists'.

After AD 168 the Roman army endured severe losses during further outbreaks of the Antonine disease. Eutropius describes this period when he writes that 'whole armies were lost after the Parthian victory, because a devastating disease affected the greater part of the Roman population and all the troops in Rome, Italy and the provinces succumbed to the sickness.'[45] Most of the Roman population contracted the disease and those who recovered took weeks to return to health. Jerome sums up the overall effect of the pandemic when he reports 'there was such a sickness throughout the whole world that the Roman army was reduced almost to extinction'.[46]

These new outbreaks paralysed the Roman military and in AD 170, a Carpathian tribe called the Costoboci invaded the Balkan provinces and raided south into Central Greece. The northern frontiers collapsed as a coalition of German tribes led by the Marcomanni crossed the Danube, overran Pannonia and surged south towards the Italian Peninsula. There were fears that Italy would be overrun and according to the *Historia Augusta*, 'the Emperor declared that the Marcomannic War was a conflict that surpassed any war in human memory. Marcus Aurelius waged this war with valour and success at a time when many thousands of civilians and soldiers had succumbed to a terrible disease.'[47]

Roman state-income declined sharply as mine production failed along with revenues collected from taxing international commerce. Many regions probably struggled to meet their revenue targets as large parts of their population succumbed to the disease, or fled as refugees from their home territories. The *Historia Augusta* reports that 'with the treasury empty, Marcus Aurelius did not have the funds required for the soldiers and he did not wish to inflict new impositions on the provincials or Senate'.[48]

The Emperor therefore took over one of the main plazas in Rome known as Trajan's Forum. For two months, imperial agents set up stalls and staged continuous public auctions to sell all the most costly palace furnishings.[49] The auction items included 'crystalline and murrine goblets, gold-adorned silken dresses belonging to the Empress, and numerous gemstones, including items from a collection assembled by Hadrian'.[50] The sale of these heirloom imperial treasures generated large amounts of wealth for the State and 'such a store of gold was gathered that the Emperor could conduct the remainder of the Marcomannic War in full accordance with his plans'. The Emperor promised buyers that they could return the items for a full refund once victory was achieved and imperial wealth was restored.[51]

The Emperor instituted unprecedented measures to reconstitute the Roman army. During this period all available manpower was recruited into the military using measures that had not been necessary since the Punic Wars (264–146 BC). Previously, soldiers were not permitted to marry during military service and any children from unofficial partnerships were not eligible for citizenship entry into the legions. An inscription from Egypt dated to AD 168 reveals that this measure was temporarily rescinded to fast-track the sons of serving soldiers into legionary units.[52] The *Historia Augusta* reports that the Roman army also 'trained slaves for military service and called them "Volunteers"'. Gladiators were outfitted with military armour and 'even the bandits of Dalmatia and Dardania were recruited as soldiers'. Further recruits came from a force of patrol guards in Asia Minor known as the Diogmitae and 'payment was given to German tribes to fight as auxiliaries against their own countrymen'.[53] Orosius reports that military levies were imposed on the population of Dacia, but it took three years of selection to raise sufficient forces to stage a successful counter-offensive against the Germans.[54]

The manpower shortage forced the Emperor to adopt a risky new policy towards the German tribes. Marcus Aurelius granted land to German allies who were permitted to settle within the Empire as a reward for their military services. The pandemic had left large tracts of cultivated land deserted and this new policy offered the Empire a means to restore agricultural productivity and military manpower. Many of the frontier provinces were included in the scheme, but the Emperor made Italy exempt from foreign settlement after a group of Germans who were granted lands in northern Italy revolted and seized the city of Ravenna.[55]

Marcus Aurelius spent the remainder of his reign fighting on the frontiers to preserve the endangered Empire. But in AD 180 he contracted the disease on campaign and became gravely ill. Knowing he would not recover he asked his colleagues, 'why do you weep for me? Instead, think about the pestilence and death which we all share.' As Marcus Aurelius lay close to death one of his last acts was to send his son Commodus away from the military camp in case the imperial heir contracted the disease.[56]

After negotiating a peace settlement that required handing over large quantaties of cash to the leading enemy tribes, Commodus returned to Rome in the autumn of AD 180.[57] The Empire was exhausted and never recovered its former revenue wealth and splendour. Rome's abundant population was devastated by the lingering effects of the disease and agricultural prosperity was severely reduced. International seaborne commerce was in decline and the Roman regime was no longer producing a large surplus of bullion wealth. Dio explains that after the death of Marcus Aurelius the history of Rome 'descended from a kingdom of gold to one of iron and rust'.[58] The Golden Age of the Roman Empire was over and as long-term revenues faltered, imperial politics were increasingly decided by military contentions in a world of failing grandeur.

Conclusion: Assessing the
Roman Economy

The ancient sources suggest the authentic condition of the Roman Empire during the Imperial period. Augustus devised a large professional army to protect and administer the Empire, but this military system proved to be very expensive. Most Roman provinces produced little revenue profit that could be transferred to central government in Rome or sent to the militarised frontier regions. Certain frontier provinces were deficit regions that could not support their own defence costs, so central government paid money into these territories to ensure that the required military personnel were properly financed. Most of these deficit regions were in northern Europe and some were needed to safeguard the core Mediterranean provinces.[1] But others were conquered for reasons of pride, reputation, or ambition. Britain was in this category and was a deficit province that had minimal defensive value.

It is possible to estimate provincial tribute using Gaul as a basis for investigation. Modern scholars estimate that during the early Imperial period greater Gaul had a population of about 5 million people and ancient sources reveal that the region produced initial tribute worth 40 million sesterces (excluding Gallia Narbonensis).[2] This suggests a million provincials could produce at least 8 million sesterces of tax as tribute for Rome. The figure can be applied to population estimates from other regions to estimate possible provincial incomes. The approach is justified since Velleius states 'Caesar brought Gaul under Roman control and it now contributes the same tribute to the treasury as the rest of the Empire' (AD 29).[3] A further layer of detail can be added to the reconstruction by considering the position and cost of the Legions in different parts of the Empire. A map and a table of population estimates are included in this book for readers who would like to pursue this investigation (See Map 1 and Appendices B & C).[4] This map-based reconstruction can be used to conceptualise Western Europe, but the Greek East is a different matter because it had a higher number of well-established urban areas. The Roman geographer Claudius Ptolemy lists hundreds of cities in all parts of the Empire, so perhaps this detail could eventually be added to the model, along with figures for mine production and other regional resources.

Current estimates suggest that by the end of the first century AD the total expense-cost of the Roman Empire was about 1,000 million sesterces per annum with over 700 million sesterces spent on the military (thirty Legions).[5] The ancient evidence confirms that one of the biggest commitments for the Roman regime was the grain-dole offered to 200,000 citizens in the city of Rome. This bonus enabled citizens to spend a significant portion of their income on other goods, including imports from the distant east. As a consequence, Rome became the largest consumer-city in the ancient world. The grain dole was a major commitment for the Empire, representing 48 million sesterces worth of product shipped to Rome on private vessels contracted by the State. An estimated 16 million sesterces of this grain came from Egypt aboard a fleet comprising over a hundred ships. But this economic activity was exceeded by the large-scale commerce that developed between the Roman Empire and the distant east. By the first century AD, the value of Indian goods entering Roman Egypt was more than 1,000 million (1 billion) sesterces per annum.

The sources suggest that taxes imposed on trade within the Empire produced comparatively little revenue for the Roman State. By contrast, revenues gained from quarter-rate frontier taxes were highly lucrative and required minimal state-infrastructure to manage and collect. The evidence also suggests that Roman authorities were well-informed about the revenues of their Empire and had the means to estimate and assess the value of commerce occurring across their frontiers.

Pliny confirms that over 100 million sesterces of Roman bullion was exported from the Empire every year by businessmen involved in eastern trade.[6] This is equivalent to a tenth of the imperial budget and probably amounted to more silver bullion than the Empire was capable of annually producing from its mines. The result was a steady drain of precious metal wealth from the Roman economy that over time began to destabilise imperial currency. As mine production declined, the Roman regime had to find new ways to pay for the Empire, or lose its dominance over the western world.

The Problem for Empire
There was little that Roman government could do about bullion loss in international trade. A restriction on the export of precious metals was not an option because bullion was required to purchase eastern goods and the Roman government was dependent on the revenues produced by this commerce. The financial pressures on the Empire increased during the first century AD as the regime committed itself to higher army pay and was obligated to manage further high-deficit territories such as Britain. This situation was only sustainable while international trade produced such large and cost-effective revenues for the Roman State.

During its period of maximum prosperity the Empire received annually more than 380 million sesterces from the provinces and perhaps 300 million sesterces from the Egyptian economy.[7] But the main profits of Empire came from taxes on international trade that raised over 300 million sesterces per annum.[8] A quarter to a third of Roman income therefore came from customs taxes imposed at the Egyptian frontiers. With the development of international commerce, Rome could gather large revenues through the management of several key sites and their connecting routes (Berenice, Myos Hormos, Coptos and Alexandria). This involved a limited investment of troops in return for extraordinary profits.[9]

The Roman mines were another high-value source of income that required a comparatively small investment of manpower to sustain. Bullion from the mines generated over 120 million sesterces of gold and silver wealth per year during periods of high-level production.[10] This suggests that by the second century AD, the Roman Empire was operating on total revenues of about 1,100 million (1.1 billion) sesterces per year. These profits allowed the Empire to maintain armies in the deficit regions of northern Europe where large numbers of troops were needed to protect vulnerable frontiers. But over a third of this figure came from non-sustainable resources such as bullion and bullion-funded foreign commerce.

The early Roman system was successful because merchants involved in international business made such large profits that they could afford to pay the high-rate taxes imposed on the frontiers. The merchant community recouped these expenses by selling their eastern goods throughout the Empire to people with surplus money available to spend on exotic luxuries. The frontier tax was therefore an empire-wide tax on consumerism that made the businessmen do the work of finding and extracting money from Roman communities who possessed disposable wealth. The Roman government paid out the revenues collected from mines and trade-taxes to the frontier Legions and this wealth incentivised other merchants to supply the army for the sake of profit. Merchants were therefore performing the function of army quarter-masters and wealth-collecting tax officials. Other regimes, such as the Han Empire, delegated these same functions to costly civilian bureaucracies.

Imperial authorities could not restrict foreign trade since many eastern goods were considered essential to Mediterranean society. The eastern substances used in personal perfumes were the same ingredients used in religious ceremonies and important medical remedies.[11] Martial understood that spending on luxuries was based on competitive fashions and as a result the Roman elite could never be satisfied. He wrote about people 'who are fond of gold, purple, and jewels. Nothing is sufficient for them, neither the gold above, or below the earth, nor the produce of the Tyrian Sea (marine dyes), nor the freight that comes from India and Ethiopia.' Martial explains that in his era, 'not even a King Midas (who could turn his possessions into gold) would be satisfied'.[12]

The problem for the Empire was that any reduction in trade revenues required taxes to be raised from other sources. This meant higher provincial taxes and increased bureaucracy to manage and extract funds from less wealthy people. The Roman army could be adapted to take on a more bureaucratic role with increased personnel to manage new tax collections, but bureaucracy was expensive. It would require further finances from hard-pressed provinces with communities that could become antagonised by greater State demands.

The early imperial system was effective because it operated with minimal bureaucracy. Egypt produced half the revenues of the Roman Empire with the expense of just two Legions. This was because the fertilising Nile floods made the land highly productive, but also because Egypt had been subject to kingdom-based administrations for at least 3,000 years before the Roman conquest. Egypt therefore had infrastructures and tax systems that were better developed than anything that northern Europe could attain in a few decades of Roman rule.

The existence of large well-paid armies on the frontiers meant that Rome was diverting large quantities of wealth into northern Europe in the form of army pay. This wealth was disseminated by soldiers seeking supplies and services from the local population, or dealing directly with merchants looking for profit by supplying market goods. The resultant investment transformed Britain and Gaul and helped establish the first urban civilisations experienced in these regions. The Roman regime therefore ensured that money from bullion and business was redirected into underdeveloped resource-rich territories. But without international commerce, these finances would fail and northern Europe was destined to revert back into a condition of inter-tribal violence in a largely de-urbanised landscape. As Tacitus explains, 'if the Romans should be driven out of Gaul the result would be wars between all these nations' (Gauls, Britons and Germans).[13] This outcome could be expected when the Roman revenues faltered and the provision of military funds to maintain the *Pax Romana* failed.

Confronting the Problem

The Roman ruling class assessed their Empire by a mixture of practical and moral principles. Many members of the governing class came from the traditional landholding elite who were responsible for managing large family estates worth millions of sesterces. These familial obligations gave Roman officials a model for understanding the economic operation of their Empire and assessing trade beyond the frontiers.

Among the Roman governing class there was a strong tradition that powerful estates should aim for self-sufficiency, but within this context it was acceptable for an estate to export its surplus produce for market sale, or trade.[14] Conversely, the expenditure of large sums of money, or bullion, to acquire outside resources was considered to be an 'inefficient' and detrimental practice. Cato the Elder advised 'sell your oil if the price is satisfactory and sell your surplus wine and grain ... but the master of a household should be a seller, not a buyer'.[15] Roman dealings with the distant East contravened this practice with the mass export of cash and bullion. Eastern trade was therefore forcing the Empire to operate like a 'badly managed estate' and this explains why Pliny offers figures for bullion exports when he quantifies this commerce.

Eastern trade was also contravening Roman ideas about 'proper' tribute relations between the Empire and 'outsiders'. It was expected that foreign people should pay tribute to Rome as the dominant power. Yet eastern commerce created a system whereby Romans sent wealth out of their domain to acquire exotic goods from overseas countries. This commerce enriched foreign nations at the expense of Roman territories and that was why Dio Chrysostom condemned 'Celts, Indians, Iberians (from the Caucases), Arabs and Babylonians, who all extract tribute from us'. Roman wealth was being taken abroad by merchants 'who ensure that silver is willingly sent out over long roads and across a vast expanse of sea to distant people who cannot easily even set foot upon our territory'.[16] The real problem was not the greed of these merchants, but the Roman market demand for foreign goods and the lack of any Mediterranean commodity that could replace bullion as a convenient and sustainable exchange export.

Other Roman criticisms of eastern trade involved popular misconceptions about transport costs and merchant profits. Many elite Romans resented how people of low social standing could become prosperous from their successful business ventures and thereby gain fortunes that rivalled the inherited wealth of the aristocratic class. One criticism that ancient authors directed at merchants was that they deliberately misrepresented the 'true value' of their goods, by selling imports in Roman markets at prices that were many times higher than the original cost of the item in foreign regions. Some people felt that they were over-paying for foreign goods and their money was enriching unworthy opportunists. The Roman statesman Cicero represents these ideas when he writes that regional commerce 'would not be greatly criticised if it was large-scale and extensive, importing much from all over and distributing it to many without misrepre-sentation'.[17] The key concept is 'misrepresentation' and for many Romans, eastern trade deserved criticism for not preserving the 'true' value of foreign imports. This is why Pliny complains about India goods being sold in Roman markets 'at 100 times their prime cost'.[18]

A further Roman criticism of eastern trade was that it created a consumer market for expensive foreign goods that were wastefully extravagant and ulti-mately unnecessary. Traditionalists who held these opinions had an idealised view of their distant past when foreign imports had little impact on Roman society. For these critics, foreign luxuries, especially in female fashions, were a measure of how far Rome had departed from its traditional values of austerity, military endeavour and respect for aristocratic ancestry.

Eastern trade produced other stresses in Roman society and this created pres-sure for economic reforms. During the Julio-Claudian era aristocratic families competed for political status and prestige through the ostentatious display of wealth. This involved vast sums spent on furnishing mansions and staging costly banquets to impress influential guests. Tacitus explains that in this era 'fortunes and the contents of mansions decided the number of a man's dependent followers and the scale of his reputation'.[19] Cash spent on exotic and expensive com-modities therefore brought influence and increased reputations that could guarantee greater opportunities for political advancement.

Some of the less affluent senatorial families found their personal fortunes exhausted by this competition for status and high office. To maintain their own political survival, these men tried to restrict the ways that wealth could be used to determine elite social position. There was a call for new sumptuary laws to restrict excessive spending at banquets and limit costly consumerism amongst the nobility, including the wearing of silk. These 'moderate' senators wanted social position to be determined by the prestige of family and ancestors, rather than by costly consumer-driven display. Their practical motives were given greater authority by moral appeals to traditional values that prompted austerity and condemned luxury.[20]

The situation became critical in AD 22 when the competitive demand for expensive display began to cause wider price inflation in Rome. Tacitus describes how 'there was uneasiness in Rome at the prospect of stern measures against luxury which had broken all bounds and extended to every object on which money could be squandered'. Action had to be taken when 'prices for food began to increase beyond lawful levels and it was thought that this process could not be checked by lenient intervention'.[21]

Demands were made for the Emperor Tiberius to impose firm restrictions on elite consumerism and to set maximum prices on basic commodities so that essential goods would be affordable for the general multitude. Tiberius did not submit to this political pressure, probably because he understood that higher prices incentivised traders to convey their produce to Rome. If prices were fixed at an artificially low level, then fewer merchants would be prepared to undergo the expense and risk involved in bringing their goods to the capital. If this were to happen, then the supply of commodities would falter and there would be a food and resource crisis at the centre of the Empire.

Tiberius addressed the Senate at the height of the crisis. He explained: 'Italy is dependent on external supply and without provincial resources to supplement our agriculture, woodlands and estates, we would not have sufficient food. Senators, this is the anxiety of the Empire. The neglect of this concern would mean national ruin.'[22] By this era, Mediterranean trade was a key part of the world economy, and the supply of essentials to Rome was inseparable from the shipment of eastern goods. Egyptian merchants who supplied Rome with grain also profited from sales of spices and silk to rich Romans who were prepared to pay inflated prices for these exotic goods. If the Emperor restricted the luxury market, or imposed regulations on elite spending, this would reduce merchant profits and de-incentivise trade to the extent that essential supplies might no longer reach the capital. Tiberius chose an appropriate response to the crisis and imposed no further measures to restrict elite consumerism. But in his speech to the Senate he made it apparent that he understood that a long-term issue had been raised by the crisis. His concern was that 'our wealth is transported to alien and hostile countries'.[23]

The Emperor also dealt with the issue of senatorial families being exhausted by consumer competition. He offered large grants of State money to members of the old aristocracy who required financial support. This policy lessened the political pressure placed on Emperors to enforce controls on elite spending.[24] The crisis of AD 22 abated because escalating prices attracted further merchants to Rome and the guarantee of profit led these businessmen to increase the provincial merchandise they shipped to the capital. Inflation was curtailed by increased supplies and prices fell back to affordable levels due to the additional imports.

Inevitable Decline
The Roman Empire was dependent on international trade for the revenues needed to maintain its Empire, but this system was finite. Throughout the Imperial period Roman merchants exported large quantities of bullion to pay for

perishable incense, spices, pearls and silk. The problem for Rome was that many eastern goods were a renewable commodity in the regions that profited from their production. These included incense and spices which were natural resources that were replenished every year. By contrast Roman wealth, in the form of gold and silver, coins and bullion, was a finite resource. International trade steadily drained precious metal from the Roman economy and this process was only sustainable as long as the imperial mines continued to provide large enough volumes of fresh bullion. But when the mines were no longer productive, then the Roman Empire was destined to de-stabilise as other sources of government income failed to meet the cost of essential expenses, especially those needed to sustain its professional armies.

The system that ran the Empire was unsustainable, but decline was far beyond the immediate concerns of the early Emperors. When the Emperor Antoninus Pius died in AD 161, he left his successor Marcus Aurelius with 2,700 million (2.7 billion) sesterces in the Roman treasury.[25] By this period the Roman Regime was arguably the most prosperous Empire in the entire ancient world, but its economy was not set up for long term endurance and a crisis was inevitable. This crisis was hastened by the appearance of the Antonine Pandemic which devastated the Roman Empire and permanently altered its prospects against the northern peoples, especially the Germans.

Modern scholars often refer to the 'Five Good Emperors' of Rome, who ruled from AD 96 to AD 180 (Nerva, Trajan, Hadrian, Antoninus Pius and Marcus Aurelius). But the success of a regime is not simply a consequence of having 'good rulers' preside over government affairs. By the time Commodus became Emperor in AD 180 the Roman population had been ravaged by the Antonine Pandemic. The Roman army was severely reduced by disease and the revenues from mines and international trade had seriously declined. This is confirmed by a reduction in mine activity in Roman Iberia and the declining silver content in imperial coinage minted at Alexandria.

By the second century AD, the main regimes of the ancient world were so economically interdependent that the fate of one major economy was capable of providing the trigger for world-wide financial collapse and decline. In China, when the Han Emperor Ling died in AD 189, Chinese warlords fought to control the imperial heirs and establish their own self-governing domains. By AD 220 the Han Empire was destroyed by civil war and in Persia the Parthian Empire was overthrown in AD 224. The Satavahana Kingdom disintegrated in the 220s AD and the Kushan Empire of Central Asia collapsed in AD 230. Southern India was also in economic and political turmoil and the Cheran and Pandian dynasties that ruled Tamil India were destroyed by conflict in this same period.

Between AD 235 and 284, the Roman Empire entered an era known to modern historians as the 'Crisis of the Third Century', the 'Military Anarchy', or the 'Imperial Crisis'. In a fifty-year period there were over twenty-five claimants to the title of Emperor and the Roman army fought repeated civil wars that devastated the Legions and diminished their long-established military expertise. When the available income of the Roman government was unable to meet its military costs the silver coinage was debased. By the end of the third century AD the denarius contained only minute quantities of silver and serious price inflation took hold in Roman markets. The Roman State was forced to develop a larger bureaucratic tax-system to extract essential resources from its subject populations. But the growth in bureaucracy increased imperial costs and the Roman State became too large and complex to be administered by a single government. During the fourth century the Roman Empire split into two separate regimes, one authority overseeing the vulnerable Latin West and the other governing the wealthy Greek East from a new imperial capital at Byzantium called Constantinople.[26]

The evidence therefore suggests that Imperial Rome was financially dependent on a world economy and international trade was one of the main mechanisms that supported the Empire during its period of greatest prosperity. The Roman regime may have had a limited span of existence, but it provided northern Europe with its first urbanised civilisation. Rome extended the commercial prospects of its subjects across the known world and Roman commerce reached lands far beyond the limits of imperial ambition. Roman merchants left their imprint in distant kingdoms attested by the evidence of Augustan Temples from Babylonia to Tamil India.[27] Through trade, Rome acquired and controlled a greater range of world resources than could ever have been achieved through military coercion alone.

Seneca concluded: 'we have been given winds so that the wealth of each region might become common. These winds should not convey legions and cavalry, or bring harmful intent to foreign peoples.'[28] The forces that destabilised the ancient world economy are still in effect, including the reliance on finite resources for trade wealth and essential revenues. Mass population movements, natural disasters, wars and the threat of global pandemics still have the potential to diminish human progress. Ultimately, this is the significance of distant trade and the ancient world economy.

The Roman Economy

Revenues (per annum)
- Revenues of the Ptolemaic Kingdom of Egypt (mid-first century BC): 300 million sesterces.[1]
- Revenues of the Roman Republic (61 BC): 340 million sesterces.[2]
- Revenues of Roman Egypt (AD 66): 570+ million sesterces.[3]
- Revenues of the Roman Empire including mined bullion: 1,100 million sesterces.

Balsam Production
- Main balsam grove at Jericho: 5 hectares (12 acres) with each tree producing 6 pints of sap.[4] Modern estimates: myrrh grove 560+ trees per hectare.[5] Therefore 2,800 trees producing 16,800 pints (at 300 denarii per pint) = 20 million sesterces per year.
- The smaller grove at En Gedi produced one-third the balsam of the larger grove in the time of Alexander (323 BC).[6] So perhaps 6 million sesterces in the Roman era.
- Balsam production: 26+ million sesterces.

Arabian Incense
- Size of Arabian forests in Yemen-Dhofar: 1.3 million hectares.[7] Modern estimates: 30+ frankincense trees per hectare (Somaliland) with 0.5 pounds of gum per tree per season.[8] Therefore at least 1,000 tons of frankincense per harvest or 2,000 tons per annum (two harvests).[9]
- Production ratio, frankincense to myrrh = 5:1. Alexander took 500 talents-weight of frankincense and 100 talents-weight of myrrh from Gaza.[10] Gerrhaean tribute to Antiochus II (205 BC) = 1,000 talents of frankincense and 200 talents of myrrh.[11]
- Pliny: 50 million sesterces of Roman bullion exported to Arabia per annum.[12] In Rome frankincense was valued at 6 denarii per pound and myrrh at 16 denarii per pound.[13]
- In the third century AD, the Persian prophet Mani crossed the Arabian Sea aboard an eastern merchant ship. His parables suggest that merchants could double their investments on a successful trade run.[14] So Roman bullion exports worth 50 million sesterces might buy 1,400 tons of frankincense (at 3 denarii per pound) and 280 tons of myrrh (at 8 denarii per pound).

Roman Bullion Revenues (per annum)
- Spanish silver mines: less than 39 tons of silver, worth 36 million sesterces.[15]
- Iberian gold mines (AD 73): 7+ tons of gold, worth 80 million sesterces.
- Gold mine in Dalmatia (Croatia) (AD 55): 70 million sesterces worth of gold.[16]

Annual Cost of Eastern Trade – Exports
- Roman bullion exports to Southern Arabia, India and China (AD 77): 100 million sesterces.[17]
- Roman bullion exports to Southern Arabia: 50 million sesterces (mostly in silver).[18]
- Bullion exports to India: 50 million sesterces (gold and silver).

- Exports to India (goods and bullion): 100 million sesterces.[19]
- Number of Roman ships sailing from Egypt to India in 26 BC: 120 vessels.[20]

Evidence for Eastern Trade (*Muziris Papyrus*, second century AD)
- Indian cargo carried aboard a Roman merchant ship: 220+ tons.
- Value of Indian cargo carried aboard the vessel: 9.2 million sesterces.
- Customs tax collected on this single cargo: 2.3 million sesterces.

Annual Scale and Value of Eastern Trade
- Possible scale of Indian imports entering the Roman Empire: 26,000 tons.
- Value of Indian imports: 1,000 million (a billion) sesterces.
- Amount of revenue raised by the quarter-rate customs tax (the *tetarte*): 250+ million sesterces.

Reconstructing Roman Revenues

Modern Population Estimates

Region	AD 14 (millions)	AD 164 (millions)
Italy	7.0	7.6
Sicily	0.6	0.6
Sardinia/Corsica	0.5	0.5
Iberia (Spain and Portugal)	5.0	7.5
Annexations including Britain and Dacia	–	2.5
Gaul/Germany	5.8	9.0
Danube Region	2.7	4.0
Greek Peninsula	2.8	3.0
Asia Minor (Anatolia)	8.2	9.2
Greater Syria including Lebanon and Palestine	4.3	4.8
Annexations including Nabataea	–	0.2
Cyprus	0.2	0.2
Egypt	4.5	5.0
Libya (N. Africa)	0.4	0.6
Maghreb (N.W. Africa)	3.5	6.5
Population Total for the Empire	45.5	61.4

Source: Frier, 'Population' in *Cambridge Ancient History*, *volume 11*, *The High Empire* (1996), 812–14.

Populations
- Italy = 7 million (rising to 7.6 million).
- Western provinces plus North Africa = 18 million (rising to 31 million).
- The Greek East of Empire excluding Egypt = 16 million (rising to 17 million).
- Egypt = 4.5 (rising to 5 million).

Evidence for provincial Roman revenues (suggesting 8–10 million sesterces raised per million people)
- Funds offered by central and southern Iberia during Roman Civil War (49 BC): 18 million sesterces.[1]
- Tribute from Greater Gaul (newly conquered in 50 BC): 40 million sesterces.[2]
- Roman revenues before Pompey's Eastern Conquests (65 BC): 200 million sesterces.
- Revenues from Greater Anatolia plus Syria (61 BC): 140 million sesterces.[3]
- Possible revenues from Anatolia (Asia Minor): 60+ million sesterces.[4]
- Revenues from the main territories of Herod's Kingdom in Palestine (4 BC): 22 million sesterces.[5]
- Revenues from Palestine including balsam (AD 44): 48 million sesterces.[6]

- Annual revenues from the Kingdom of Commagene in Anatolia (AD 18–38): 5 million sesterces.[7]
- Annual tribute from the province of Asia (500 cities in western Anatolia) (AD 125): 28 million sesterces.[8]

Possible revenues (based on population estimates and revenues of 10 million sesterces per million people)

- Western provinces plus North Africa = up to 180 million sesterces
  (Perhaps increasing to 310 million sesterces by the mid-second century AD)
- The Greek East of Empire excluding Egypt = 160 million sesterces
  (Perhaps increasing to 170 million sesterces by the mid-second century AD)
- Ancient evidence for Egyptian revenues = 300 million sesterces increasing to 576 million sesterces.[9]
- The Greek East including Egypt = 460 million sesterces increasing to 746 million sesterces.

The Expense of Roman Legions

AD 14. Cost estimate: 11 million sesterces per Legion including Auxiliary support[1]

Region	No. of Legions	Military Cost (sesterces)
Spain	3	33 million
Rhine	8	88 million
Pannonia-Dalmatia (Western Danube)	5	55 million
Balkans (Eastern Danube)	2	22 million
Syria*	4	44 million
Egypt**	2	22 million
North Africa	1	11 million
Total	25 (3 lost in Germany)	275 million

* Syria: soldiers perhaps in understrength units and characterised by Tacitus as 'men without helmets or breastplates, sleek money-makers, who had served all their time in towns'. They had to be reinforced and drilled to fight in Armenia (AD 56).[2]
** Egypt: large pay deductions for provisions (AD 81).[3]

- Military cost: Western Empire plus North Africa = 187 million sesterces.
- Military cost: Eastern Empire = 88 million sesterces.

Late First Century AD. Cost estimate: 14 million sesterces per Legion after Domitian's pay increase[4]

Region	No. of Legions	Military Cost (sesterces)
Britain	4	56 million
Spain	3	42 million
Rhine	8	112 million
Pannonia-Dalmatia (Western Danube)	4	56 million
Balkans (Eastern Danube)	4	56 million
Asia Minor (Euphrates)	2	28 million
Syria	2	28 million
Palestine	1	14 million
Egypt	2	28 million
North Africa	1	14 million
Total	31	434 million

- Military cost: Western Empire plus North Africa = 280 million sesterces.
- Military cost: Eastern Empire = 154 million sesterces.

Mid-Second Century AD[5]

Region	No. of Legions	Combined Military Costs (sesterces)
Britain	3	42 million
Iberia (Spain and Portugal)	1	14 million
Rhine	5	70 million
Pannonia-Dalmatia (Western Danube)	6	84 million
Balkans (Eastern Danube)	3	42 million
Dacia	1	14 million
Asia Minor (Euphrates)	3	42 million
Syria	3	42 million
Palestine	1	14 million
Arabia	1	14 million
Egypt	2	28 million
North Africa	1	14 million
Total	30	420 million

- Military cost: Western Empire plus North Africa = 224 million sesterces.
- Military cost: Eastern Empire = 196 million sesterces.

Surplus and deficit regions based on population estimates, revenue calculations (10 million sesterces per million people) and military costs (Bullion production has not been included)[6]

Region	AD 14 (sesterces)	Late First Century (sesterces)	Mid-Second Century (sesterces)
Danube	−50 million	−85 million	−100 million
Gaul/Germany (Rhine)	−30 million	−64 million	−20 million
Britain	+11 million (frontier trade-taxes)[7]	−31 million	−17 million
North Africa	+29 million	+36 million	+54 million
Asia Minor	+82 million	+54 million	+50 million
Egypt	+300 million[8]	+576 million	+576 million[9]

Regional financial status can be depicted on modern maps of the Empire (Green: revenue surplus; Yellow: financial balance; Red: deficit). Note the contrast between the Greek East of the Empire and the Latin West.

Notes

Ancient Figures and Modern Estimates
1. *Res Gestae*, 15.
2. Hopkins, 'Models, Ships and Staples' (1983), 86.
3. Josephus, *Jewish War*, 2.16.4.
4. Full strength Legion: 5,500 legionaries. Campbell, *The Emperor and the Roman Army* (1984), 162–3. Pay deductions and understrength units: *The Roman Army* (1994), 84.
5. Tacitus, *Annals*, 4.5.
6. Herz, 'Finances and Costs of the Roman Army' (2010), 308–11.
7. Tacitus, *Annals*, 1.17 (complaints about land-grants in place of cash bonuses). *I.L.S.* 2302; *C.I.L.* 3.6580 (discharge numbers).
8. *Roman Military Records on Papyrus*, 83 (deposit price for horse).
9. Tacitus, *Agricola*, 19–20.
10. *Papyrus Geneve Latin*, 1 (AD 81). Situation in Egypt where State received large-scale grain revenues.
11. Suetonius, *Domitian*, 7 (northern Europe).
12. Dio, 55.23.
13. Dio, 55.24. *Historia Augusta, Hadrian*, 15.
14. Duncan-Jones, *Money and Government* (1994), 33–45. Hopkins, 'Rome Taxes Rents and Trade' (2002), 200.

Introduction: The Ancient Economy
1. Virgil, *Aeneid*, 1.1.279.
2. *Hou Hanshu*, 88.12.
3. Strabo, 2.5.12; Pliny, 9.59.
4. McLaughlin, *Rome and the Distant East* (2010), 160–8.
5. Suetonius, *Augustus*, 49.2; *Res Gestae*, 17; Dio, 54.25.

Chapter 1: Revenue and the Roman Economy
1. Cicero, *De legibus*, 3.41 (52–45 BC).
2. Appian, *History*, preface, 15.
3. *Historia Augusta, Antoninus Pius*, 7.8.
4. Dio 53.30.1–2.
5. Statius, *Silvae*, 3.3.101–2.
6. Pliny the Younger, *Letters*, 3.5.
7. Tacitus, *Annals*, 1.11.
8. Suetonius, *Augustus*, 101.
9. Suetonius, *Caligula*, 16.
10. Tacitus, *Annals*, 13.51.
11. *The Berenice Ostraca*.
12. Strabo, 7.1.45.
13. *Periplus*, 14 (July: Somalia); 39; 49; 56 (July: India). 6; 24 (September: Arabia, East Africa).
14. *Periplus*, 19. *P. Vindob. G.* 40822.
15. Pliny, 6.24.
16. *C.I.L.* 10.1782, 1784.

17. Josephus, *Antiquities*, 18.8.1; 20.5.2; *Jewish War*, 5.8.5.
18. *Acts*, 4.6.
19. Josephus, *Jewish War*, 5.5.3.
20. Josephus, *Antiquities*, 18.6.3.
21. *Ibid.* 19.5.1.
22. Philo, *Embassy to Gaius*, 46; Josephus, *Antiquities*, 18.8.1; 19.5.1.
23. *Ibid.*
24. *Ostraca Petrie*, 252 (AD 37); 266; 267; 268; 271; 282 (AD 43/44).
25. Thebaid office: *Corpus Papyrorum Judaicarum*, 2.419. Procurator Judea: Josephus, *Antiquities*, 20.5.2. Parthian war: Tacitus, *Annals*, 15.28.
26. Josephus, *Antiquities*, 19.5.1.
27. Josephus, *Jewish War*, 4.10.5; Tacitus, *History*, 2.7.9; Suetonius, *Vespasian*, 6.3.
28. Josephus, *Jewish War*, 5.1.6; Juvenal, 1.127–46.
29. Arrian, *Periplus of the Black Sea* (written for the Emperor Hadrian).
30. Strabo, 2.5.12.
31. *Periplus*, 19.
32. Pliny, 12.32.
33. Pliny: 'The remainder of the envoys' account agreed with the reports of our traders' (6.24) and 'those who are most knowledgeable in this matter assert that Arabia does not produce in a whole year ...' (12.41).
34. Pliny, 12.35 (Gebbanite = Qataban).
35. *Periplus*, 23. Pliny, 6.31: 'Arab envoys and our own traders who have come from Charax report its present distance from the coast to be ...'.
36. Pliny, 14.1–9.
37. Pliny, 12.30.
38. Plutarch, *Pompey*, 45.
39. Strabo, 17.1.13.
40. Suetonius, *Julius Caesar*, 25.
41. Cicero, *For Manilia*, 14.
42. Cicero, *De Lege Agraria contra Rullum*, 2.80.
43. Dio, 51.18; Suetonius, *Augustus*, 18.
44. Velleius, 2.39.
45. Dio, 52.6.
46. Planned Parthian conquests: Isidore, *Parthian Stations*.
47. Appendix A.
48. Strabo, 16.4.22.
49. *Ancient Figures and Modern Estimates.*
50. Plutarch, *Aemilius Paulus*, 28.3.
51. Tacitus, *Annals*, 2.56.4.
52. Strabo, 3.4.13; Caesar, *Civil War*, 3.4.
53. Livy, *Periochae*, 134.2; Dio, 53.22.5 (27 BC); Tacitus, *Annals*, 1.31.2 (AD 14).
54. Livy, *Periochae*, 139.1.
55. First and Second Satrapies (including Ionia and Lydia). Herodotus, 3.90.
56. Philostratus, *Lives of the Sophists*, 548.
57. Cicero, *For Manilia*, 14.
58. Plutarch, *Brutus*, 25 (Antistius = Appuleius).
59. Seneca, *De Consolatione ad Helviam Matrem*, 10.4.
60. Suetonius, *Caligula*, 16.
61. *I.L.S.* 8794.
62. Philostratus, *Lives of the Sophists*, 548.
63. Cicero, *Against Piso*, 86.
64. Appian, *History*, preface, 7.
65. Plutarch, *Marius*, 27.
66. Caesar, *Gallic Wars*, 1.33.

67. Suetonius, *Augustus*, 25.
68. Dio, 56.33; Tacitus, *Annals*, 1.11.
69. Tacitus, *Annals*, 1.16–17, 31.
70. *Ancient Figures and Modern Estimates.*
71. Tacitus, *Histories*, 4.74.
72. Josephus, *Jewish War*, 2.16.4.
73. *Cambridge Ancient History*, volume 11 (2000), 738.
74. Strabo, 4.5.3.
75. Strabo: 'At least one legion and some cavalry would be required to extract tribute' *ibid.*
76. Strabo, 2.5.8.
77. Suetonius, *Claudius*, 17.
78. Appian, *Preface*, 5.
79. Suetonius, *Nero*, 18.
80. Diodorus, 17.52.
81. Expense of Legions offset by local extractions: Tacitus, *Agricola*, 19–20.
82. *Ancient Figures and Modern Estimates.*
83. Pliny the Younger, *Letters*, 3.5.17.
84. Pliny, 33.31. Roman mint: 84 denarii per Roman pound (pre-reform) and 96 denarii per pound after AD 64.
85. Strabo, 3.2.10.
86. Roman mint: 40 aurei per Roman pound (pre-reform) and 45 aurei per pound after AD 64.
87. Pliny, 33.21.
88. *Ibid.*
89. Tacitus, *Annals*, 15.18 (AD 62). Nero gave 40 million sesterces to the state-treasury in AD 57 (*Ibid.* 13.31).
90. Statius, *Silvae*, 3.3.92.
91. Duncan-Jones, *Money and Government* (1994) 111; 164–5. Denarii: 8,000 coins per reverse die; average of 2,000 dies per year. Aurei: 43,000 coins per reverse die; 25–50 dies operative per year.
92. Indian cargo = 9 million sesterces (*Muziris Papyrus*) × 120 Roman ships sailing to India (Strabo, 2.5.12). Value of imports: 1,080 million sesterces.
93. Pliny, 13.2.
94. Pliny, 16.59.
95. Pliny, 13.2.
96. Dio, 52.27.
97. *Ibid.*
98. Dio, 54.7.
99. *Res Gestae*, 3.
100. Justinian, *Digest*, 50.16.27.
101. *Ancient Figures and Modern Estimates.*
102. Pliny, 12.42.

Chapter 2: Roman Prosperity
1. Dio, 51.17.
2. Dio, 51.21.
3. Paulus Orosius, 6.19.
4. Suetonius, *Augustus*, 41.
5. Dio, 51.21.
6. Strabo, 2.5.12.
7. Plutarch, *Pompey*, 45.
8. Confirmed by greater Gaul and the Rhineland: 5 provinces producing at least 40 million sesterces of revenue per annum (Suetonius, *Julius Caesar*, 25).
9. Seneca, *De Consolatione ad Helviam Matrem*, 10.4.
10. *P. Vindob. G.* 40822.
11. Strabo, 2.5.12.

12. Indian imports worth 1,080 million sesterces divided by 40 (the *portoria*) = 27 million sesterces.
13. Strabo, 17.1.13.
14. Imports worth 1,080 million sesterces subject to *tetarte* (one-quarter) and *portoria* (one-fortieth) = 270 million and 27 million = 297 million sesterces revenue.
15. Pliny, 12.21.
16. *Hou Hanshu*, 88.12.
17. Strabo, 17.1.13.
18. Plutarch, *Pompey*, 45; Suetonius, *Julius Caesar*, 25.
19. Internal Mediterranean economy: 300 million; exports to India: 25 million, imports from India: 270 million; *portoria* at Alexandria: 27 million.
20. Josephus, *Jewish War*, 2.16.4.
21. Josephus, *Antiquities*, 19.8.2.
22. Suetonius, *Caligula*, 16. Different figure: Dio, 59.2.
23. AD 14–37 (23 years) = 2,700 million sesterces. Increased by mine seizure and reduced court spending as the Emperor became reclusive (AD 31–7). Suetonius, *Tiberius*, 48; Tacitus, *Annals*, 6.19.
24. Dio, 56.33; Tacitus, *Annals*, 1.11.
25. Suetonius, *Domitian*, 7; Dio, 67.3.5.
26. Cost of two legions = 22 million sesterces.
27. Strabo, 17.1.7.
28. Suetonius, *Augustus*, 98.
29. Dio, 51.17.
30. Tacitus, *Histories*, 3.8.
31. *Ibid.* 2.84.
32. Florus, 2.1.
33. *Res Gestae*, 15.4.
34. Hopkins, 'The Political Economy of the Roman Empire' (2010), 191.
35. Juvenal, 10.77–81.
36. Suetonius, *Vespasian*, 18.
37. Philostratus, *Life of Apollonius of Tyana*, 4.32.
38. Schinz, *The Magic Square: Cities in Ancient China* (1996), 134.
39. Hopkins, 'Rome, Taxes, Rents and Trade' (2002), 220.
40. Aldrete and Mattingly, 'Feeding the City' (1999), 178.
41. *Ibid.*
42. Tiberius increased grain shipments: Tacitus, *Annals*, 6.13.
43. Josephus, *Jewish War*, 2.16.4.
44. Egypt: 2 sesterces per *modius* (6.55 kilograms or 14.4 pounds). Rome: 4 sesterces per *modius*. Medium price: 3 sesterces per *modius* = 417 sesterces per ton. Hopkins, 'Models, Ships and Staples' (1983), 88. High-price recorded in Pompeii: 7.5 sesterces per *modius* (*C.I.L.* 4.4811).
45. Plutarch, *Cato*, 27.
46. Alexandria to Rome about 40 days outbound; return voyage 14 days. Sailing season: April–September. Casson, *Ships and Seamanship* (1971), 297–9.
47. *Acts*, 27.10.
48. Gaius, *Institutes*, 1.32c; Justinian, *Digest*, 50.6.6.2–5; Ulpian, *Edict*, 3.6.
49. Justinian, *Digest*, 50.5.3.
50. Suetonius, *Claudius*, 18–19 (AD 51).
51. Stevedores in Ostia (*C.I.L.* 14.448); Sand-diggers (*Corpus Saburrariorum*, 156; 210).
52. Tacitus, *History*, 4.38.
53. Pliny, *Pangyric*, 29.3–5.
54. Tacitus, *Annals*, 2.87.
55. *Ibid.* 15.39.
56. Justinian, *Digest*, 50.5.3; Gaius, *Institutes*, 1.32c.
57. *Fayyum Papyrus Bingen*, 77.
58. Lucian, *The Ship*, 5. Casson, *Ships and Seamanship* (1971), 188.

59. *The Cambridge Ancient History*, volume 11 (2000), 738.
60. Tacitus, *Annals*, 3.55.
61. Pliny, 9.59.
62. Diocletian, *Price Edict*, 17; 35. Greene, *Archaeology of the Roman Economy* (1983), 40.
63. Pliny, 1.77.
64. Pliny, 18.49.
65. Aristides, *Orations*, 26.7.
66. *Ibid.* 26.11–12.
67. *Revelations*, 18:19.
68. Estimates: 237,000 tons of grain for Rome = 948 shiploads (cargo ships carrying 250 tons); 26,000 tons of olive oil = 104 shiploads; 160,000 tons wine = 640 shiploads. Aldrete and Mattingly, 'Feeding the City' (1999), 193–6.
69. Tacitus, *Annals*, 15.18.
70. Seneca, *Natural Questions*, 6.
71. Pliny, 12.14. Sack: 50 pounds.
72. Aristides, *Oration*, 26.11–12.
73. *Revelations*, 18:23.
74. *Revelations*, 18:12.
75. *Revelations*, 18:18.

Chapter 3 – Incense: A Unique Product
1. Pliny, 12.32.
2. *Matthew*, 20.2.
3. Strabo, 16.4.22.
4. Pliny, 12.30.
5. *Egyptian Book of the Dead*, plates 5–6 (censer-burner and offerings to the dead) 11–12, 17 (incense burner) 22, 27 (text 79) 29–30 (text 75) 33, 34.
6. Herodotus, 2.40.
7. *Exodus*, 30.
8. *Ibid.*
9. 1 *Chronicles*, 28:18; 2 *Chronicles*, 2:4; *Leviticus*, 16:12–13.
10. Talmud, *Keritot*, 6a.
11. *Matthew*, 2.11.
12. Herodotus, 1.183.
13. Herodotus, 1.198.
14. Herodotus, 4.71.
15. Sappho, *Fragment*, 44.
16. Diogenes Laertius, *Life of Pythagoras*, 8.
17. Ovid, *Fasti*, 1 January 9.
18. Suetonius, *Augustus*, 35.
19. Roman relief sculptures including Trajan's Column.
20. Arrian, *Periplus of the Black Sea*, 1–2.
21. Heliodorus, *Aethiopica*, 4.16.6.
22. Propertius, 2.19.1–32.
23. Martial, 7.54.
24. Ovid, *Fasti*, 4. May 2.
25. *Ibid.* April 24.
26. Cato, *On Agriculture*, 134:
27. Ovid, *Fasti*, 2.
28. *Ibid.* 4.
29. *Feriale Duranum.*
30. Persius, *Satires*, 3.103–5.
31. Propertius, 2.13.
32. Martial, 11.54.

33. *John*, 19:40.
34. Bird, 'Incense in Mithraic Ritual' (2006), 127.
35. Tacitus, *Germania*, 27.
36. Pliny, 13.2.
37. Persius, 6.31–7.
38. Propertius, 4.7.
39. Propertius, 2.13.
40. Statius, *Silvae*, 2.4.
41. Pliny, 21.8.
42. Pliny, 12.42.
43. Tibullus, 2.2.
44. Propertius, 2.10.13–18.
45. Pliny, preface, 11.
46. Martial, 13.4.
47. Perhaps a list of goods sold from the residence. Etienne, *Pompeii* (1992), 184–5.
48. Pliny, 12.41.
49. Tacitus, *Annals*, 16.6.
50. Pliny, 12.41.
51. Pliny, 7.53.
52. Pliny, 33.47.
53. Suetonius, *Vespasian*, 2.
54. Butterworth and Laurence, *Pompeii* (2005), 16.
55. Hopkins, *Death and Renewal* (1983), 211.
56. Celsus, *On Medicines*, 5.2.1.
57. *Mark*, 15.23.
58. Celsus, *On Medicines*, 5.18.6–7.
59. Pliny, 15.31.
60. *Papyrus Geneve Latin, 1 recto I* (AD 81).
61. Pliny, 13.4.
62. Suetonius, *Vespasian*, 8.
63. Pliny, 12.35.
64. Aelian, *Animals*, 4.36.
65. Pliny, 24.2.
66. Pliny, 12.32.
67. Pliny, 24.77.
68. Pliny, 27.14–22; Dioscorides, 3.22.1–5.
69. Celsus, *On Medicines*, 5.18.6–7 (muscle pain); 5.25.3 (menstrual pains). Galen, *On Antidotes*, 2.10 (myrrh to heal wounds).
70. *Oxyrhynchus Papyri*, 8.113; Dioscurides, 1.24.
71. Celsus, *On Medicines*, 6.6.24.
72. Pliny, 35.46.
73. Pliny, 22.56.
74. Celsus, *On Medicines*, 5.
75. Galen, *On Antidotes*, 1.13–14; *Avoidance of Grief*, 5–6.
76. Pliny, 15.31.
77. Virgil, *Georgics*, 2.466; Martial, 4.13.
78. Persius, *Satires*, 2.61–72.
79. Pliny, 12.59.
80. Pliny, 14.1.
81. Martial, 4.13.
82. Pliny, 32.63 (clam weight: 500 pounds).
83. Butterworth and Laurence, *Pompeii* (2005), 62.
84. Apicius, *On the Subject of Cooking*, 9.1.7.
85. Pliny, 12.26.

86. Juvenal, 6.286–313.
87. Strauss, *Roman Cargoes* (2007), 247.
88. Pliny, 18.29.
89. Walker, *Ancient Faces: Mummy Portraits in Roman Egypt* (2000), 60.
90. Pliny, 13.2.
91. Pliny, 12.32.
92. Pliny, 13.2.
93. Seneca, *Epistles*, 108.4.
94. Pliny, 13.2–3.
95. Persius, *Satires*, 2.61–72.
96. Pliny, 36.12–13.
97. *John*, 11:1–2, 12:1–8, *Luke*, 7:36–50.
98. *Mark*, 14:3, *Matthew*, 26:6–13.
99. Pliny, 12.26.
100. *P. Vindob. G.* 40822. Pliny, 12.26.
101. Juvenal, 6.457–507.
102. Pliny, 13.2.
103. Pliny, 13.4.
104. Pliny the Younger, *Letters*, 2.11.23.
105. Seneca, *Epistles*, 86.
106. Juvenal, 4.105–10.
107. Athenaeus, 15.38.688.
108. Martial, 11.15.
109. Seneca, *On the Happy Life*, 1.4.
110. Juvenal, 9.128.
111. Petronius, *Satyricon*, 31.
112. Martial, 3.82.
113. Martial, 3.12.
114. Martial, 2.29.
115. Ovid, *Art of Love*, 3.10.
116. Pliny, 13.4.
117. Theophrastus, *On Odours*, 57–8.
118. Pliny, 13.3; 23.48.
119. Pliny, 13.5.
120. Martial, 14.110.
121. Martial, 11.18.
122. Martial, 1.87.
123. Martial, 6.55.
124. Pliny, 23.48.
125. Propertius, 2.29.
126. Martial, 11.8.
127. Martial, 3.63.
128. Martial, 3.55.
129. Martial, 12.65.
130. Martial, 12.55.
131. Ovid, *The Loves*, 3.15.83–98.
132. Ovid, *Cosmetics for Ladies*, 83–4.
133. Pseudo-Lucian, *The Loves*, 39.
134. Juvenal, 6.457–507.
135. *Ibid.*
136. Pseudo-Lucian, *The Loves*, 39.
137. Martial, *Epigrams*, 14.24.
138. Juvenal, 6.457–507.
139. Dio Chrysostom, 7.117.

140. Justinian, *Digest*, 39.4.16.7.
141. Pliny, 12.54; 16.59. Diodorus, 2.48; 19.98.
142. Safrai, *The Economy of Roman Palestine* (1993), 147.
143. *Genesis*, 37:25–8.
144. *Genesis*, 43:11.
145. Josephus, *Antiquities*, 8.6.5.
146. *Song of Solomon*, 5:13; 6:2.
147. *Babylonian Talmud*, 5.2.
148. *Jeremiah*, 8:22; 46:11; 51:8.
149. *Ezekial*, 27:17.
150. Josephus, *Jewish War*, 4.8.3.
151. Pliny, 12.54.
152. Theophrastus, *Historia Plantarum*, 4.4.14; 9.1.6.
153. Josephus, *Jewish War*, 4.8.2–3; *Antiquities*, 15.4.2.
154. Strabo, 16.2.41.
155. *Luke*, 23:43.
156. Strabo, 16.2.41.
157. Pliny, 12.54.
158. Strabo, 16.2.41.
159. Josephus, *Antiquities*, 14.4.1.
160. Josephus, *Jewish War*, 1.18.5.
161. Josephus, *Antiquities*, 15.4.2.
162. *Ibid.* 17.11.4.
163. Tacitus, *Histories*, 5.6.
164. Galen, *On Antadotes*, 1.4.
165. Dioscorides, 1.18.
166. Strabo, 16.2.41; Josephus, *Antiquities*, 15.4.2.
167. The Roman State and client Kings could share resource revenues. Augustus gave Herod management responsibility for copper mines on Cyprus and a half-share of profits (12 BC) (Josephus, *Antiquities*, 16.4.5).
168. Pliny, 12.54.
169. *Ibid.*
170. *Ibid.*
171. Estimate: 215 trees per acre. Appendix A.
172. Pliny, 12.54.
173. *Ibid.*
174. Martial, 14.59.
175. Pliny, 12.54.
176. Josephus, *Jewish War*, 4.7.2.
177. Pliny, 5.15.
178. Pliny, 12.54.
179. Solinus, *Collection of Curiosities*, 34–5.
180. Conan, *Botanical Progress* (2004), 111.
181. Masada: Inventory Number: 1039–122/1.
182. *Babylonian Talmud, Berachot*, 43a.
183. *Babylonian Talmud, Avodah Zarah*, 10a–b.
184. Eusebius, *Onomasticon*, 86.18.
185. Jerome, *Letter*, 108: *To Eustochium*, 11.5.
186. Taylor, *The Essenes* (2012), 313.
187. Qumran, Cave 13. Conan, *Botanical Progress* (2004), 110.

Chapter 4 – The Intermediaries: Petra and the Nabataeans

1. Diodorus, 19.97.
2. Diodorus, 19.95.

3. *Ibid.*
4. Diodorus, 19.96–7.
5. Diodorus, 19.97.
6. Diodorus, 19.98–100.
7. Strabo, 16.4.18.
8. Diodorus, 3.42.
9. Strabo, 16.4.19.
10. Strabo, 16.4.18.
11. Strabo, 16.4.19.
12. *R.E.M.* 3429 (coffin) 3570 (Delos: bilingual Minaean–Greek).
13. *R.E.S.* 2771; 3022. Sidebotham, *Roman Economic Policy* (1986), 98–9.
14. Strabo, 16.4.19; Pliny, 6.32.
15. Pliny, 12.30.
16. Strabo, 16.4.22.
17. Pliny, 12.33 (information possibly from Juba, 48 BC–AD 23).
18. Strabo, 16.4.18.
19. Strabo, 16.4.22–3.
20. *Ibid.*
21. Strabo, 16.4.23.
22. Horace, *Odes*, 1.29.
23. Strabo, 16.4.24.
24. Strabo, 16.4.19; Pliny, 6.32.
25. Taylor, *Petra* (2011), 61–2.
26. Strabo, 17.1.53.
27. Strabo, 16.4.24.
28. Strabo, 16.4.21.
29. *Periplus*, 23.
30. Strabo, 16.4.21.
31. *Ibid.*
32. Taylor, *Petra* (2011), 79–121.
33. Strabo, 16.4.26.
34. Pliny, 12.38.
35. Pliny, 6.32.
36. Parker, *The Great Trade Routes* (2012), 136–7.
37. Procopius, *Persian Wars*, 1.19.23–4 (6th century AD).
38. Strabo, 16.4.4. Information from Eratosthenes (275–194 BC).
39. Strabo, 17.1.45.
40. Hill, *Weilue*, 16 (Silk Road Seattle, 2004).
41. Strabo, 16.4.23–4.
42. *Periplus*, 19.
43. Strabo, 16.4.23.
44. *Periplus*, 19.
45. *Ibid.*
46. Sidebotham, *Berenike* (2011), 185.
47. Pliny, 6.26; 12.41.
48. Bowersock, *Roman Arabia* (1983), 76–89.

Chapter 5 – Beyond Egypt: The Nile Route and the African Kingdom of Meroe
1. Pliny, 5.10.
2. Mieroop, *A History of Ancient Egypt* (2011), 289 (Psammetichus = Psamtek).
3. Diodorus, 3.3.
4. Herodotus, 7.69.
5. Diodorus, 3.8.
6. Herodotus, 3.26.

7. Herodotus, 3.97.
8. Herodotus, 7.69.
9. Diodorus, 3.6. *The Cambridge History of Africa*, volume 2 (1979), 228.
10. Pliny, 6.35.
11. *F.H.N.* 2.135.
12. Ovid, *Amores*, 4. Servius, *On Virgil, Eclogue*, 10.46.
13. Strabo, 17.1.53.
14. *F.H.N.* 2.163.
15. Torok, *The Kingdom of Kush* (1998), 450.
16. Dio, 53.23.
17. Strabo, 17.1.54.
18. *F.H.N.* 2.174.
19. Strabo, 17.1.54.
20. *Ibid.*
21. *Ibid.*
22. Dio, 53.28.1.
23. Torok, *The Kingdom of Kush* (1998), 455.
24. Strabo, 17.1.54.
25. Pliny, 6.35.
26. Strabo, 17.1.54.
27. *Res Gestae*, 26.
28. Pliny, 6.35 (570 Roman miles) Roman mile = 4,851 feet.
29. Strabo, 17.1.54.
30. Dio, 54.5.
31. Dio, 53.28.
32. Strabo, 17.1.54.
33. *Ibid.*
34. Strabo, 2.5.8; 4.5.3.
35. Procopius, *Persian Wars*, 1.19.28–9.
36. Torok, *The Kingdom of Kush* (1998), 452 (Prima Porta-type statue).
37. *F.H.N.* 2.176; Torok, *The Kingdom of Kush* (1998), 456.
38. Shinnie and Bradley, 'The Murals from the Augustus Temple, Meroe' (1981), 167–72.
39. Jackson, *At Empire's Edge* (2002), 144–5.
40. *The Gallus Fragment*, 2–5.
41. Strabo, 17.1.53.
42. Strabo, 17.1.2.
43. Strabo, 17.1.49–50.
44. Jackson, *At Empire's Edge* (2002), 118–19.
45. *Ibid.* 135.
46. *Ibid.* 142.
47. Torok, *Between Two Worlds* (2009), 444–5.
48. Pliny, 5.10.
49. Philostratus, *Life of Apollonius of Tyana*, 6.2.
50. *Prices Edict*, 32.1a. A labourer could earn 25 debased denarii per day (*Edict*, 7).
51. Philostratus, *Life of Apollonius of Tyana*, 6.2.
52. Pliny, 36.25 (magnets); 37.60, 67.
53. Pliny, 37.50.
54. Heliodorus, *Aethiopica*, 2.30.
55. *Corpus Inscriptionum Graecarum*, 5075. Warmington, *The Commerce between the Roman Empire and India* (1928), 308.
56. Pliny, 5.10.
57. Juvenal, 11.126–7.
58. Pliny, 33.152.
59. *P. Vindob. G.* 40822. Ivory: 48 Egyptian drachmas per mina (434 grams). Tusk: 30 kilograms.

60. Statius, *Silvae*, 3.3.101–2.
61. Dio, 61.9.
62. Loane, *Industry and Commerce* (1938), 50.
63. Brosius, *The Persians* (2006), 59; 71.
64. *Acts*, 8:27.

Chapter 6 – The Red Sea Route
1. Avakov, *Two Thousand Years of Economic Statistics* (2010), 4.
2. Pliny, 6.21.
3. Mortuary Temple of Hatshepsut at Deir el-Bahari. See Parker, *The Great Trade Routes* (2012), 29.
4. Herodotus, 3.89–96.
5. Herodotus, 4.44.
6. Aristole, *Polotics* 7.13.2; Plutarch, *Alexander*, 7.
7. Arrian, *Alexander*, 5.
8. Curtius Rufus, 8.14; Arrian, *Alexander*, 5.17–18.
9. Sidebotham, *Berenike* (2011), 39.
10. Plutarch, *Alexander*, 62.
11. Arrian, *Alexander*, 6.2–3, 21; *Indica*, 18–42.
12. Engels, *Alexander the Great and the Logistics of the Macedonian Army* (1978), 155–6.
13. Arrian, *Alexander*, 7.20.
14. Kistler & Lair, *War Elephants* (2007), 10, 20, 34, 73, 101, 136.
15. *Pithom Stele* (264 BC).
16. Arsinoe also known as Cleopatris or Clysma.
17. Sidebotham, *Berenike* (2011), 48–52.
18. *Ibid.* 117.
19. Strabo, 17.1.45.
20. Sidebotham, *Berenike* (2011), 41–2.
21. Sidebotham, *Roman Economic Policy* (1986), 100–1.
22. Polybius, 5.84–5.
23. *Sammelbuch*, 3.7169 (150 BC).
24. Diodorus, 3.43.5.
25. Strabo, 16.4.4.
26. Strabo, 2.3.4.
27. *P. Vindob. G.* 40822. India: *Arthasastra*, 2.22.
28. Agatharchides, 5.105; Diodorus, 3.47.
29. *Periplus*, 26.
30. Strabo, 17.1.13.
31. Dio, 51.7; Plutarch, *Antony*, 69.
32. Suetonius, *Julius Caesar*, 52; *Augustus*, 17.
33. Plutarch, *Antony*, 81.
34. *Ibid.*
35. Appendix B.
36. Strabo, 17.1.12–3.
37. Strabo, 16.4.23.
38. *Periplus*, 26.
39. Strabo, 2.5.12.
40. Strabo, 17.1.45.
41. Pliny, 5.11.
42. Pliny, 6.26.
43. Strabo, 17.1.45.
44. Pliny, 6.26.
45. Strabo, 17.1.45. *P. Vindob. G.* 40822 (second century AD).
46. The Apollonis Station accommodated perhaps 215 soldiers. Adams, *Land Transport in Roman Egypt* (2007), 39.

47. Mons Porphyrites (Gebel Abu Dukhan) and Mons Claudianus (Gebel Abu Hamr).
48. Sidebotham, *The Red Land* (2008), 70–93 (pillar: 78).
49. Gold mines at Barramiya. Emerald mines at Mons Smaragdus (near Wadi Nuqrus).
50. Jackson, *At Empire's Edge* (2002), 105.
51. Adams, *Land Transport in Roman Egypt* (2007), 209, 222–5, 231.
52. *Nicanor Archive.*
53. *Ostraka Petrie*, 245.
54. *Inscriptiones Graecae ad Res Romanas*, 1.1172 (dated AD 32). Nicanor Archive: *Ostraka Petrie*, 228–9 (Myos Hormos); 231 (Berenice).
55. Sidebotham, *Roman Economic Policy* (1986), 99 (AD 70). Hermeros in the *Nicanor Archive* (*Ostraka Petrie*, 287).
56. *Papyrus London* (British Museum) 2.260.1.42 (AD 72).
57. Roman citizens: Tiberius Claudius Agathocles (*Ostraka Petrie*, 275, 276), Gaius Julius Bacchylus (228; 291) Gaius Norbanus (244, 257). Roman citizens who possibly owned firms: Popilius Mamilius Andromachus (271), Tiberius Claudius Castor (275), Claudius Demetrius (275) and Tiberius Claudius Theodorus (276).
58. Plaster plugs with the names: L. Titus Primus, L. Piso and Ti. Cl. Serenus.
59. *Ostraka Petrie*, 244, 257. Sidebotham, *Roman Economic Policy* (1986), 86; 89.
60. Bagnall, *Documents from Berenike* (2000), *BE* 71.
61. Judd, 'The trade with India through the Eastern Desert of Egypt' (2007), 2–3.
62. De Romanis, *Cassia, Cinnamomo, Ossidiana* (1996), 253.
63. *C.I.L.* 10.1797.
64. *Sammelbuch*, 7539.
65. Young, *Rome's Eastern Trade* (2001), 52–3.
66. Strabo, 17.1.45.
67. Pliny, 6.26.
68. Not all halts in use during the same period. Sidebotham, *Berenike* (2011), 156–61.
69. *Coptos Tariff: O.G.I.S.* 674.
70. Sidebotham, *Roman Economic Policy* (1986), 69.
71. *Acts of Thomas* (written third century AD).
72. Philo, *On Flaccus*, 92.
73. *Ibid.*
74. *Griechische Papyri*, 47 (AD 117). Frank, *An Economic Survey of Ancient Rome* (1959), 444–5.
75. Strabo, 7.1.45.
76. Strabo, 16.4.5.
77. Strabo, 17.1.45. Perhaps an association of ship-owners (Justinian, *Digest*, 50.6.6.6).
78. Original fleet: 130 transport ships, but many were damaged or destroyed. Strabo, 16.4.23–4.
79. Strabo, 2.5.12.
80. Sidebotham, *Berenike* (2011), 197.
81. *Ibid.* 184–6.
82. *Ibid.* 85–6.
83. *Ibid.* 62.
84. Berenice-Coptos road: three graffiti from the Augustan era (30 BC–AD 14), compared with seventeen dated to the Tiberian period (AD 14–37). Sidebotham, *Roman Economic Policy* (1986), 54; 81.
85. Beets (*Berenike*, 87); onions (*BE* 78); *pharmakoi* (*Ostraka Petrie*, 275, 283).
86. Quince (*Berenike*, 4).
87. *Ostraka Petrie*, 245.
88. Myos Hormos (*Ostraka Petrie*, 228–9) Berenice (231, 240, 265). Sidebotham, *Roman Economic Policy* (1986), 49–51; 59; 84.
89. Cappers, 'Archaeobotanical Evidence of Roman trade with India' (1999), 56–7.
90. Sidebotham, *Berenike* (2011), 196.
91. Bagnall, *Documents from Berenike 1* (2000), 1–10.
92. *Ibid. BE* 39.
93. *Berenike Ostraka*, 159–85 ('Dossier of Sarapion'). Dossier includes mention of 'double bags'.

94. Epiphanius, *De Mensuris et Ponderibus*, 53. Tesoretto Rimigliano (shipwreck find): a basket holding 3,600 coins in 18 pouches. Each pouch containing 200 coins (20 stacks of 10 wrapped coins). Transport of coin-baskets by Nicanor Firm: '1 basket of silver tetradrachms' (*Ostraka Petrie*, 240).
95. Pliny, 12.14.
96. *Periplus*, 24; 28.
97. Pliny, 6.24.
98. *Ostraka Petrie*, 290 (22 July AD 62).
99. *Periplus*, 49.
100. *Periplus*, 6; 8.
101. Turner, *Roman Coins from India* (1989), 47; 50.
102. Herodotus, 2.158; Diodorus, 1.33.9.
103. Pliny, 6.33; Strabo, 17.1.25–6.
104. Ptolemy, *Geography*, 4.5. Silting a recurrent problem: the ninth century Arab writer Al-Maqrizi reports that the Emperor Hadrian had to dredge the canal. Details: Sidebotham, *Berenike* (2011), 181.
105. Greene, *Archaeology of the Roman Economy* (1983), 40.
106. Sidebotham, *Berenike* (2011), 181.
107. Lucian, *Alexander the False Prophet*, 44.
108. *Ibid.* 59.

Chapter 7 – The Scale and Significance of Indian Ocean Trade

1. Pliny, 19.19.
2. Dio Chrysostom, 32.36.
3. Strabo, 17.1.13.
4. Justinian, *Digest*, 39.4.16.7.
5. Appendix B.
6. Pliny, 14.1.
7. Seneca, *On Tranquility of Mind*, 4.4.
8. Pliny, 12.14.
9. Pliny, 37.78.
10. *P. Vindob. G.* 40822. Cargo = pepper (135 tons), malabathrum (83.9 tons), nard (1.3–3.4 tons), ivory (4.8 tons) and turtle-shell (2.3 tons).
11. For text and translation: Casson, 'New Light on Maritime Loans: P. Vindob. G 40822' (1990), 195–206; Rathbone, 'The 'Muziris' Papyrus' (2001), 39–50; De Romanis, 'Playing Sudoku on the Verso of the '*Muziris* Papyrus'' (2012), 75–101.
12. *P. Vindob. G.* 40822.
13. Casson, 'New Light on Maritime Loans' (1990), 195.
14. *P. Vindob. G.* 40822.
15. *Ibid.* A camel can carry 400 pounds (long-distance load).
16. A driver can manage 6 camels in tandem.
17. *Coptos Tariff*, 674.
18. Return voyage (with delays): two weeks ocean crossing; four weeks sailing through the Gulf of Aden and the Red Sea; two weeks offloading cargo and crossing the Eastern Desert; two weeks travel down the Nile from Coptos to Alexandria.
19. *P. Vindob. G.* 40822.
20. *Ibid.*
21. Lucan, *Pharsalia*, 10.169–71.
22. Pliny, 12.32.
23. Pliny, 12.54.
24. *Price Edict*, 23.1.1; 24.1.1.
25. Strabo, 17.1.13.
26. Dio Chrysostom, 32.36.
27. Pliny, 33.57.
28. Justinian, *Digest*, 35.2.63.2.

29. *P. Vindob. G.* 40822.
30. *Periplus*, 56.
31. Price ivory: 48 drachmas per mina (*Muziis Papyrus*); 9 denarii (36 sesterces) per pound at Rome in AD 48 (*Tabulae Pompeianae Sulpiciorum*, 101). Diocletian's *Price Edict* does not take into account regional price differences.
32. *Periplus*, 56.
33. Pliny, 12.14 (Roman pound = about 12 ounces). Greek talent-weight = 30.666 kilograms (95 Roman pounds). There were 60 mina in a talent-weight.
34. Pliny, 12.42–3.
35. *Price Edict*, 16.10–11 (turtle-shell price). De Romanis, 'Playing Sudoku on the Verso of the 'Muziris Papyrus' (2012), 75–101.
36. *Price Edict*, 25.5; 32.32 (25 debased denarii = a day's labour).
37. *P. Vindob. G.* 40822. The Asian elephant population was over 200,000 at the start of the eighteenth century (World Wildlife Fund).
38. Braudel, *Civilization and Capitalism*, 2 (1981), 405.
39. Prakash, *European Commercial Enterprise in Pre-Colonial India* (1998) 40–2. Weights: Lisbon quintal = 51.4 kilograms (1,000 Lisbon quintals = 56 tons).
40. Findlay & O'Rourke, *Power and Plenty* (2009), 203.
41. *P. Vindob. G.* 40822.
42. Pseudo-Lucian, *The Loves*, 41 (pearl worth 6,000 sesterces); Juvenal, 7.139–40 (200 sesterces for a gemstone ring).
43. Some figures based on cargo value after tax deduction.
44. *Hermapollon*'s cargo valuation before tax: 1,154 talents and 2,852 drachmas (equivalent to 9.2 million sesterces). Fleet size: Strabo, 2.5.12.
45. *Ancient Figures and Modern Estimates.*
46. *Hermapollon*'s cargo more than 220 tons. *P. Vindob. G.* 40822.

Chapter 8 – International Business

1. Sidebotham, *Berenike* (2011), 195.
2. Casson, *The Periplus* (1989), 35.
3. Philostratus, *Life of Apollonius of Tyana*, 3.35.
4. Narbonne Relief; Isis Geminiana Painting (Ostia); Tabularii Relief (Portus). Vitruvius, 10.2.10 (rotatory-cranes).
5. Sidebotham, *Berenike* (2011), 198–200.
6. *Coptos Tariff*, 674.
7. Sidebotham, *Berenike* (2011), 201.
8. Procopius, *Persian Wars*, 1.19.23–4 (6th century AD).
9. *Periplus*, 36.
10. Sidebotham, *Berenike* (2011), 204–5, 239–40, 243.
11. Philostratus, *Life of Apollonius of Tyana*, 3.35.
12. Achilles Tatius, 5.15.
13. Petronius, *Satyricon*, 102.5.
14. *Acts*, 27.16.
15. Philostratus, *Life of Apollonius of Tyana*, 3.35.
16. Pliny, 19.1.
17. Seneca, *Epistles*, 77.1–2.
18. Athenaeus, *The Deipnosophists*, 43.
19. Sidebotham, *Berenike* (2011), 202.
20. Ship-to-shore craft: Plutarch, *Pompey*, 73.
21. Greene, *Archaeology of the Roman Economy* (1983), 27.
22. *Torlonia Relief* (Portos).
23. Lucian, *The Ship*, 5.
24. Vegetius, 4.37.
25. Pliny, 19.5.

26. Vitruvius, 10.3.5.
27. Lucian, *The Ship*, 6.
28. Lucian, *Lexiphanes*, 15.
29. Apian, *Civil Wars*, 2.89; Dio, 49.17.2.
30. Lucian, *The Ship*, 5.
31. *Perumpanarruppatai*, 316–8.
32. Spargi Wreck.
33. Petronius, *Satyricon*, 108.
34. Seneca, *Epistles*, 76.13.
35. Capitoline Museum Rome.
36. Ovid, *Tristia*, 1.10.1–2. Apuleius, *Metamorphosis*, 11.16.
37. *Digest*, 19.2.31.
38. *Septuagint, Maccabees*, 3.4.10.
39. Athenaeus, *The Deipnosophists*, 42.
40. *Syracusia*, Athenaeus, 5.208a.
41. Caesar, *Civil Wars*, 3.15.
42. Athenaeus, *The Deipnosophists*, 42.
43. Pausanias, 8.12.1.
44. Lucian, *Toxaris*, 20.
45. Athenaeus, *The Deipnosophists*, 43.
46. Thucydides, 7.25.6.
47. *Sivakasindamani*, 1.101–4.
48. Athenaeus, *The Deipnosophists*, 43.
49. Thucydides, 41.2. Athenaeus, *The Deipnosophists*, 43. Casson, *Ships and Seamanship* (1971), 239.
50. *P. Vindob. G.* 40822.
51. Sidebotham, *The Red Land* (2008), 195.
52. *Michigan Papyri*, 4703 (fleet: Classis Alexandrina). Gardner, *Women in Roman Law and Society* (1986), 41.
53. *Draco* (CPL 210), *Fides* (CPL 191), *Lupa* (BGU 741.7–8), *Taurus* (CPL 223,) *Neptunus* (CPL 250), *Mercurius* (CPL 125), *Sol* (BGU 455). CPL – *Corpus Papyrorum Latinarum*. BGU = *Berliner Griechische Urkunden*.
54. Blue, 'New Light on the Nature of Indo-Roman Trade' (2012), 91–100.
55. *Ibid.*
56. *Ibid.* 96. Sidebotham, *Berenike* (2011), 199.
57. *Inscription Pan-Grotto*, 57.
58. *Sammelbuch*, 7539.
59. Philostratus, *Life of Apollonius of Tyana*, 6.12.
60. Strabo, 2.99.
61. Philostratus, *Life of Apollonius of Tyana*, 3.35.
62. *Coptos Tariff*, 674.
63. Philostratus, *Life of Apollonius of Tyana*, 3.35.
64. Lucian, *Toxaris*, 33–4.
65. Plutarch, *Moralia*, 1.
66. *Ibid.* 21.
67. Philostratus, *Life of Apollonius of Tyana*, 3.35.
68. Pliny, 6.26.
69. *Michigan Papyri*, 8. 467.19–21; 468.24–25.
70. Statius, *Silvae*, 3.2.24–30.
71. Philostratus, *Life of Apollonius of Tyana*, 4.9.
72. Pliny, 6.24. De'Arms, *Commerce and Social Standing in Ancient Rome* (1981), 166.
73. Cicero, *Against Verres*, 2.5.29.
74. Plutarch, *Pompey*, 73.
75. Diodorus, 4.4.3. *Dionysus Sarcophagus*.
76. Tchernta, 'The Dromentary of the Peticii' (1997), 241–3.

77. *Ibid.*
78. *Ibid.* 139.
79. *C.I.L.* 2.1.157–8.
80. *Inscriptiones Graecae*, 14.842a.
81. Hopkins, 'Taxes and Trade in the Roman Empire' (1980), 105–6.
82. Pliny, 12.14.
83. Thucydides, 1.96. Andocides, 3.9.
84. North Africa (second century AD). Two temples of Concord constructed at a cost of 50,000 sesterces (*C.I.L.* 8.26467–70). A Temple of Fortuna: 70,000 sesterces (*C.I.L.* 8.26471). Library: 400,000 sesterces (*I.L.S.* 9362).
85. Petronius, *Satyricon*, 76.
86. *Ibid.*
87. Bagnall, *Documents from Berenike* (2000) *BE* 71; *Sammelbuch*, 7539.
88. Juvenal, 14.256–302.
89. Philostratos, *Lives of the Sophists*, 21.603.
90. Petronius, *Satyricon*, 76; Lucian, *The Ship*, 14.
91. *Oxyrhynchus Papyri*, 10.1259; 17.2125 (third century AD).
92. Philostratus, *Life of Apollonius of Tyana*, 3.24.
93. *P. Vindob. G.* 19792 (Bank of Marcus Claudius Sabinus, AD 149). Casson, 'New Light on Maritime Loans' (1986), 11–17.
94. A five person venture to Somalia is described in the papyrus *Sammelbuch*, 3.7169 (150 BC).
95. Low price: Egypt 2 sesterces; Rome 4 sesterces per modius (6.55 kilograms or 14.4 pounds). Duncan-Jones, *The Economy of the Roman Empire*, (1974) 145–6.
96. Hopkins, 'Models, Ships and Staples' (1983), 101.
97. Juvenal, 14.256–302.
98. Juvenal, 14.189–255.
99. Plutarch, *Elder Cato*, 21.
100. Sidebotham, *Berenike* (2011), 185.
101. Sidebotham, *Roman Economic Policy* (1986), 86–8.
102. Sidebotham, *Berenike* (2011), 185.
103. Parker, *The Making of Roman India* (2008), 174.
104. Sidebotham, *Berenike* (2011), 75.
105. Salomon, R., 'Epigraphic Remains of Indian Traders in Egypt' (1991), 731–6.
106. Dio Chrysostom, 32.40.
107. Xenophon of Ephesus, *Ephesian Tale*, 3.11.4.3.
108. Martial, 7.30.
109. Tibullis, 2.58.
110. Petronius, *Satyricon*, 34.
111. Juvenal, 5.59.
112. Philostratus, *Lives of the Sophists*, 552–3.
113. Juvenal, 6.585.
114. Petronius, *Satyricon*, 34.
115. Martial, 3.82.
116. Justinian, *Digest*, 39.4.16.7.
117. Pliny, 7.39; Martial, 3.62; 11.70.
118. Tacitus, *Annals*, 3.53.
119. Vergil, *Moretum*, 32–5.
120. Schmitthenner, 'Rome and India' (1979), 96.
121. *Oxyrhynchus Papyri*, 2.300. Warmington, *The Commerce between the Roman Empire and India* (1928), 67–8.
122. *C.I.L.* 6.21650: Parents: Zeuxis and Areskousa.
123. *C.I.L.* 6.38159; 6.22628. Raschke, 'New studies in Roman commerce with the East' (1978), 241.
124. Archaeology Department, McMaster University.

125. Suetonius, *Augustus*, 28.
126. Pliny, 36.9.
127. McCloud, 'The Romance of Marble Cutting' (1927), 226–30.
128. Pliny, 36.9.
129. *Ibid.*
130. Casson, *The Periplus* (1989), 8.
131. *Periplus*, 20.
132. *Periplus*, 19. Casson, *The Periplus* (1989), 8; 144.
133. *Periplus*, 41. Casson, *The Periplus* (1989), 198.
134. *Periplus*, 61.
135. Pliny, 6.26.
136. Tchernia, 'Winds and Coins' (1997), 252.

Chapter 9 – East Africa and the Aksumite Kingdom
1. Strabo, 16.4.24.
2. Greene, *Archaeology of the Roman Economy* (1983), 40.
3. Pliny, 12.14.
4. Strabo, 17.1.13.
5. *Periplus*, 26.
6. *Periplus*, 2.
7. Ptolemais Theron situated near the border between modern Sudan and Eritrea.
8. Strabo, 16.4.7.
9. *Periplus*, 3.
10. Pliny, 6.39.
11. *Periplus*, 5.
12. *Periplus*, 4.
13. Pliny, 6.34.
14. Seland, *Ports and Political Power* (2010), 35.
15. Pliny, 6.34.
16. Strabo, 16.4.14–15.
17. *Periplus*, 4.
18. *Periplus*, 24.
19. Procopius, *Persian Wars*, 1.19.22.
20. *Periplus*, 4.
21. *Periplus*, 5–6.
22. Pliny, 36.67.
23. Pliny, 37.76.
24. *Periplus*, 4.
25. Seland, *Ports and Political Power* (2010), 35.
26. Livy, 41.20.1; Ovid, *Fasti*, January 1.
27. Martial, 12.66.
28. Plutarch, *Morals*, 7.9.
29. Ovid, *Metamorphosis*, 2.737.
30. Virgil, *Georgics*, 2.463–6.
31. Horace, *Odes*, 2.18.
32. Propertius, 3.2.
33. Martial, 3.62.
34. Pliny, 9.13.
35. Juvenal, 11.121.
36. Varro, *The Latin Language*, 9.33.47.
37. *Tabulae Pompeianae Sulpiciorum*, 101. Diocletian, *Price Edict*, 16.10–11 (turtle-shell is two-thirds the price ivory).
38. *P. Vindob. G.* 40822.
39. Seneca, *On Benefits*, 7.9.

40. Pliny, 9.65; 16.8.
41. Juvenal, 6.80.
42. Martial, 2.43 (ivory table legs); 9.59 (Manurra).
43. Martial, 14.87.
44. Martial, 14.88.
45. Seneca, *On Benefits*, 7.9.
46. Pliny, 12.9.
47. Juvenal, 14.303–31.
48. Juvenal, 11.120–4.
49. Philo, *On Dreams*, 2.57.
50. Clement, *The Instructor*, 2.3.
51. Statius, *Silvae*, 4.2.38–40.
52. Apuleius, *Metamorphesus*, 2.76–8.
53. Propertius, 2.13.
54. Wallace-Hadrill, *Rome's Cultural Revolution* (2008), 429–31.
55. Propertius, 4.6.
56. Virgil, 2.193.
57. Petronius, *Satryicon*, 135.
58. Lucian, *Zues Tragoedus*, 7–8.
59. Propertius, 4.2.
60. Apuleius, *Metamorphesus*, 11.552–5 (ivory comb).
61. Martial, 14.83.
62. Martial, 14.5.
63. Martial, 14.14.
64. Martial, 14.12; 14.78.
65. Ovid, *Fasti*, June 21; Ovid, *The Art of Beauty*, 2.22.
66. Propertius, 3.3; 2.24.
67. Martial, 1.72.
68. Juvenal, 11.120–4.
69. Pliny, 8.4.
70. Pliny, 33.54.
71. Juvenal, 7.98–149.
72. Martial, 14.53.
73. Peachin, *The Oxford Handbook of Social Relations in the Roman World* (2011), 78–9.
74. Juvenal, 7.192.
75. Petronius, *Satyricon*, 32.
76. *Periplus*, 4.
77. *Ibid.*
78. *Periplus*, 5.
79. *Periplus*, 6.
80. *Ibid.*
81. *Periplus*, 14.
82. Philostratus, *Life of Apollonius of Tyana*, 6.12.
83. *Periplus*, 14.
84. Seland, *Ports and Political Power* (2010), 41–2.
85. Pliny, 12.35.
86. Pliny, 12.43.
87. Pliny, 12.42.
88. *Periplus*, 7.
89. *Ibid.*
90. Pliny, 2.42.
91. *Periplus*, 8.
92. *Ibid.*
93. Seland, *Ports and Political Power* (2010), 40.

94. *Periplus*, 8.
95. *Periplus*, 10.
96. *Ibid.*
97. *Periplus*, 11.
98. *Periplus*, 30. Strabo, 16.4.14; Ptolemy, *Geography*, 1.9 ('Aromatic Lands').
99. *Periplus*, 12.
100. *Periplus*, 57.
101. *Periplus*, 13.
102. *Periplus*, 6, 31.
103. *Periplus*, 14.
104. Pliny, 8.4.
105. *Periplus*, 15.
106. Casson, *The Periplus* (1989), 139–40.
107. *Ibid.*
108. *Periplus*, 15.
109. Rhapta perhaps at the Rufiji River delta. Seland, *Ports and Political Power* (2010), 42–4.
110. *Periplus*, 16.
111. *Ibid.*
112. *Periplus*, 17.
113. *Ibid.*
114. Ptolemy, *Geography*, 1.9.
115. *Ibid.* 4.7.
116. Peppard, 'A Letter concerning Boats in Berenike and Trade on the Red Sea' (2009), 193–8.
117. *P.CtYBR Inv.* 624 (Beinecke Rare Book and Manuscript Library, Yale University).
118. Sailing runs: *Periplus*, 15–16. Casson, *The Periplus* (1989), 281.
119. *Periplus*, 18.

Chapter 10 – Southern Arabia and the Saba-Himyarites
1. Strabo, 16.4.2.
2. Strabo, 16.4.18.
3. *Periplus*, 23. Pliny, 6.31.
4. Appendix A.
5. Suetonius, *Julius Caesar*, 25.
6. Strabo, 16.4.22.
7. Pliny, 37.23–4, 28, 42, 45, 60, 65.
8. Pliny, 37.24, 40.
9. Pliny, 12.30.
10. Pliny, 12.41.
11. 1 *Kings*, 10.
12. *Ibid.*
13. Herodotus, 1.183. Pliny, 12.80.
14. Pliny, 12.32.
15. Plutarch, *Alexander*, 29.
16. Strabo, 16.4.17.
17. *Periplus*, 20.
18. *Ibid.*
19. Pliny, 6.34.
20. *Periplus*, 20.
21. Sidebotham, *Berenike* (2011), 188.
22. Ptolemy, *Geography*, 4.5; Eutropius, 8.3.
23. Arrian, *Alexander*, 7.20.
24. *Periplus*, 16.
25. *Periplus*, 31.
26. *Inventaire des Inscriptions de Palmyre*, 10.38, 112. Young, *Rome's Eastern Trade* (2001), 130.

27. Phillips, 'A Latin Inscription from South Arabia' (2004), 244.
28. *Periplus*, 23.
29. *Periplus*, 16, 31.
30. *Periplus*, 19.
31. Statius, *Silvae*, 3.3.89 (AD 93).
32. Pliny, 6.26.
33. Pliny, 9.54–6.
34. Pliny, 12.44.
35. Pliny, 12.42.
36. Naval station: Strabo, 17.1.45.
37. Sidebotham, *Berenike* (2011), 188.
38. Phillips, 'A Latin Inscription from South Arabia' (2004), 245.
39. Pliny, 6.34. Ptolemy, *Geography*, 1.17.9.
40. *Weilue*, 11. Hill, *Weilue*, (Silk Road Seattle, 2004).
41. *Hou Hanshu*, 88.12.
42. *Weilue*, 15.
43. *Periplus*, 24.
44. *Periplus*, 21. Casson, *The Periplus* (1989), 148.
45. *Periplus*, 24.
46. *Periplus*, 7, 8, 16 (Africa); 21 (India).
47. Himyarites: known as 'Homeritai' in Greek and 'Homeritae' in Latin (Pliny, 6.32).
48. Pliny, 12.35.
49. Pliny, 6.26.
50. *Periplus*, 24.
51. *Ibid.*
52. Pliny, 12.35.
53. *Periplus*, 7, 8, 16.
54. *Periplus*, 7.
55. *Periplus*, 24.
56. *Ibid.*
57. Pliny, 36.41; 37.54.
58. *Periplus*, 24.
59. Casson, *The Periplus* (1989), 53.
60. *Periplus*, 24.
61. *Ibid.*
62. Pliny, 14.19.
63. *Periplus*, 24. Seland, *Ports and Political Power* (2010), 18–19.
64. *Periplus*, 16.
65. *Periplus*, 23.
66. Pliny, 12.31.
67. Bowersock, *Roman Arabia* (1994), 148–53.
68. Galen, *De Libris Propriis*, 11; *Avoidance of Grief*, 20.
69. Pliny, 7.16.
70. *Periplus*, 24.
71. *Periplus*, 28.
72. Pliny, 6.24.
73. Pliny, 12.32.
74. Pliny, 6.26.
75. *Periplus*, 25.
76. Pliny, 6.26.
77. Ptolemy, *Geography*, 6.7.
78. *Periplus*, 25.
79. Seland, *Ports and Political Power* (2010), 19–22.
80. Pliny, 6.32.

81. *Periplus*, 26.
82. Pliny, 6.32.
83. Gebbanitaes (Qataban) farming the Somali coast. Pliny, 6.42.
84. Sidebotham, *Roman Economic Policy* (1986), 99.
85. Ptolemy, *Geography*, 26.8.23.
86. Pliny, 6.42.
87. Pliny, 12.42.
88. Seland, *Ports and Political Power* (2010), 24.
89. *Mercantile Code of Qataban*: R.E.M. 4337c.11–14.
90. Pliny, 12.42.

Chapter 11 – Arabia Felix and the Hadramawt Kingdom
1. *Periplus*, 27.
 2. Seland, *Ports and Political Power* (2010), 26.
 3. *Periplus*, 27.
 4. Pliny, 6.26.
 5. *Periplus*, 27.
 6. Seland, *Ports and Political Power* (2010), 27–8.
 7. *Periplus*, 27.
 8. Husn al-Ghurab ('Fortress of the Crows').
 9. Sedov, 'The Port of Qana and the Incense Trade' (2007), 71; 101 (storerooms: 79, 90).
10. Appendix A.
11. Tomber, *Indo-Roman Trade* (2008), 103.
12. Sedov, 'The Port of Qana and the Incense Trade' (2007), 91–2.
13. *Ibid.* 74; 76; 90–1.
14. Seland, *Ports and Political Power* (2010), 27–8.
15. *Periplus*, 27.
16. *Periplus*, 24. Pliny, 6.26.
17. Sedov, 'The Port of Qana and the Incense Trade' (2007), 78.
18. *Periplus*, 24.
19. Pliny, 12.32.
20. Tomber, *Indo-Roman Trade* (2008), 105–8.
21. Sedov, 'The Port of Qana and the Incense Trade' (2007), 76; 78; 101.
22. Sedov, 'Qana (Yemen) and the Indian Ocean' (1996), 15; 60.
23. Sidebotham, *Berenike* (2011), 88–9.
24. *Periplus*, 28.
25. *Periplus*, 27.
26. *Periplus*, 28.
27. Dioscorides, 3.22.1–5; Pliny, 27.5.
28. *Periplus*, 27–8.
29. *Periplus*, 49.
30. Sedov, 'The Port of Qana and the Incense Trade' (2007), 76; 102.
31. Peacock, 'Ballast as Ships' Ballast' (2006), 29–31; 59; 62.
32. *Periplus*, 30. Pliny, 6.32.
33. *Periplus*, 31.
34. Pliny, 13.2; 29.8; 29.18; 33.39–40. Dioscorides, 5.94.
35. *Periplus*, 30.
36. *Ibid.*
37. *Periplus*, 31.
38. Seland, *Ports and Political Power* (2010), 44.
39. *Periplus*, 31.
40. Sedov, 'The Port of Qana and the Incense Trade' (2007), 100.
41. Seland, *Ports and Political Power* (2010), 45.

42. Bukharin and Strauch, 'Indian Inscriptions from the Cave Hoq on Suqutra (Yemen)' (2004), 121–38.
43. *Periplus*, 24.
44. *Periplus*, 30.
45. Strabo, 15.2.13.
46. Philostratus, *Life of Apollonius of Tyana*, 3.57.
47. Dioscorides, 1.68.
48. Pliny, 12.30.
49. Herodotus, 3.109.
50. Pliny, 6.42.
51. Pliny, 12.32.
52. *Periplus*, 29.
53. Appendix A.
54. Pliny, 6.30.
55. *Periplus*, 29.
56. *Periplus*, 32. Coastline: 1100 *stades*.
57. *Ibid.*
58. Pliny, 12.32.
59. Seland, *Ports and Political Power* (2010), 29.
60. Sedov, 'Qana (Yemen) and the Indian Ocean' (1996), 24.
61. *Khor Rori*, 2; 4. Seland, *Ports and Political Power* (2010), 29–30.
62. Seland, *Ports and Political Power* (2010), 30.
63. *Periplus*, 32.
64. Sidebotham, *Berenike* (2011), 188–9.
65. *Periplus*, 32.
66. *Periplus*, 33.
67. There are now five Khuriya Muriya islands. Casson, *The Periplus* (1989), 174.
68. World Wildlife Fund.
69. *Periplus*, 33.
70. Ptolemy, *Geography*, 6.7.

Chapter 12 – The Indo-Parthians

1. Sailing speeds: *Periplus*, 4; 21.
2. *Periplus*, 57.
3. Pliny, 6.26. Tchernia, 'Winds and Coins' (1997), 252.
4. Pliny, 6.26.
5. *Periplus*, 57.
6. Pliny, 6.26.
7. *Periplus*, 39.
8. *Periplus*, 38.
9. *Acts of Thomas*, 3. 'Gudnapharor' = Gondophares (possible Indo-Iranian royal title).
10. *Acts of Thomas*, 17. Parker, *The Making of Roman India* (2008), 297–301.
11. *Takht-i Bahi Inscription* (AD 45).
12. *Periplus*, 38.
13. *Periplus*, 39.
14. Sections of the *Arthasastra* date to the second century AD. The work is attributed to Kautilya the mentor of the Mauryan Emperor Chandragupta (320 BC). The *Arthasastra* represents long-standing knowledge and practice. Seland, *Ports and Political Power* (2010), 50.
15. Arthasastra, 2.16.
16. Arthasastra, 2.21.
17. Arthasastra, 2.22.
18. Arthasastra, 2.21.
19. *Ibid.*
20. *Ibid.*

21. Arthasastra, 2.16.
22. *Periplus*, 39.
23. Ovid, *Metamorphosis*, 4.835–43.
24. Pliny, 32.11.
25. *Arthasastra*, 2.11.
26. Bhartrhari, *Vakyapadiya*, 2.1.1.42 (fifth century text).
27. Pliny, 32.11.
28. *Arthasastra*, 2.11.
29. Pliny, 32.11.
30. *Garuda Puranam*, 68.
31. *Ibid.* 80.
32. *Ibid.*
33. *Ratnapariksa*, 250–2.
34. *Arthasastra*, 2.6.
35. Pliny, 32.11.
36. *Periplus*, 39.
37. *Periplus*, 47.
38. Tomber, *Indo-Roman Trade* (2008), 122–4.
39. Hiebert & Cambon, *Afghanistan* (2011), 131–209 (Begram), 211–93 (Tillya Tepe).
40. *Hou Hanshu*, 88.15.
41. Ptolemy, *Geography*, 7.1. Roman naval station at Myos Hormos: Strabo, 17.1.45.

Chapter 13 – The Saka and Satavahana Kingdoms
 1. *Periplus*, 40.
 2. *Ibid.*
 3. Catsambis, *The Oxford Handbook of Maritime Archaeology* (2012), 518–19.
 4. *Periplus*, 40.
 5. Suetonius, *Augustus*, 21.
 6. Paulus Orosius, 6.21.19.
 7. Higham, *Encyclopedia of Ancient Asian Civilizations* (2004), 82.
 8. Strabo, 15.1.73.
 9. *Ibid.*
10. Dio, 54.9.
11. Strabo, 15.1.73.
12. Pliny, 12.42.
13. Dio, 54.9.
14. Strabo, 15.1.73.
15. Dio, 54.9.
16. Plutarch, *Alexander*, 69.
17. Strabo, 15.1.4.
18. Plutarch, *Alexander*, 69.
19. *Res Gestae*, 31.
20. *Periplus*, 41.
21. *Ibid.*
22. Pliny, 18.10.
23. *Periplus*, 44.
24. *Periplus*, 43.
25. *Periplus*, 44.
26. *Arthasastra*, 2.16. Seland, *Ports and Political Power* (2010), 54.
27. Pliny, 37.76.
28. Pliny, 37.
29. Propertius, 2.22.
30. Pseudo-Lucian, *The Loves*, 41.
31. Tertuillian, *On the Apparel of Women*, 1.6.

32. Juvenal, 6.136–60.
33. Martial, 11.50.
34. Martial, 4.28.
35. Ovid, *Cosmetics for Ladies*, 19–23.
36. Pliny, 33.6.
37. Pliny, 37.76.
38. Solinus, 30.33.
39. Pliny, 33.6.
40. Martial, 5.11.
41. Pliny, 37.23.
42. Martial, 11.27.
43. Juvenal, 6.380–2.
44. Juvenal, 13.139.
45. Pliny, 37.23.
46. Martial, 2.37.
47. Martial, 9.59.
48. Juvenal, 7.149.
49. Juvenal, 7.139–40.
50. Martial, 11.59.
51. Philostratus, *Life of Apollonius of Tyana*, 1.10.
52. Pliny, 37.6.
53. Martial, 14.109.
54. Juvenal, 5.25–65.
55. Petronius, *Satryicon*, 33.
56. Pliny, 37.45.
57. Barygaza traded with: Arabian kingdoms (*Periplus*, 21, 27, 32), Socotra Island (31), Aksum in Eritrea (6), Somalia (14), Persian Gulf and Parthia (36).
58. Tomber, *Indo-Roman Trade* (2008), 125.
59. *Periplus*, 41.
60. Isidore, *Parthian Stations*, 18.
61. Seland, *Ports and Political Power* (2010), 49.
62. *Periplus*, 41.
63. Arthasastra, 6–8; 11.
64. *Periplus*, 48.
65. Pliny, 37.5.
66. *Periplus*, 48.
67. Pliny, 12.28–9.
68. *Periplus*, 49.
69. Goods produced in India (*Periplus*, 41). Shipped to Socotra (31), Somalia (14) and Southern Arabia (32).
70. Ovid, *Cosmetics for Ladies*, 10.
71. Butterworth and Laurence, *Pompeii* (2005), 16.
72. *Periplus*, 49.
73. *Periplus*, 36.
74. *Periplus*, 49.
75. Sousse Museum (Tunisia).
76. Lucian, *Nigrinus*, 5.
77. *Periplus*, 49.
78. Shipwreck: Bet Dwarka Island on the Gulf of Kutch. Catsambis, *The Oxford Handbook of Maritime Archaeology* (2012), 518–9.
79. Pliny, 34.55.
80. *Arthasastra*, 2.16.
81. Seland, *Ports and Political Power* (2010), 54.
82. *Periplus*, 49.

83. Macdowell, 'Finds of Roman Coins in Southern Asia' (1990) 61; Macdowell, 'Indian Imports of Roman Silver Coins' (1991), 151–2.
84. *Epigraphia Indica*, 8 (Nasik Caves) (year 42).
85. One aureus (8 grams of gold) = 25 denarii (97.5 grams of silver).
86. Turner & Cribb, 'Numismatic Evidence for the Roman Trade with Ancient India' (1996), 312–13.
87. *Periplus*, 47.
88. Turner, *Roman Coins from India* (1989), 17–8.
89. Tomber, *Indo-Roman Trade* (2008), 37.
90. *Periplus*, 49.
91. Kalidasa, *Vikramorvasiyam*, 5.
92. *Acts of Thomas*, 8–9.
93. *Oxyrhychus Papyrus*, 3.413.
94. *Periplus*, 49.
95. Paithana: a royal residence in Ptolemy, *Geography*, 7.1.
96. *Periplus*, 51.
97. Apannaka-Jataka, 1 (500 carts = 250 tons).
98. *Periplus*, 45.
99. *Ibid.*
100. *Periplus*, 46.
101. Ptolemy, *Geography*, 7.1.
102. The Satavahanas are also known as the 'Andhras'. Andhra was the name of a *Jati* (caste-group) of the Satavahana dynasty.
103. *Periplus*, 50.
104. Ajunta, Cave 2 (interior, right wall).
105. Sidebotham, *Berenike* (2011), 202.
106. Tomber, *Indo-Roman Trade* (2008), 130–2.
107. *Periplus*, 52. Casson, *The Periplus* (1989), 215.
108. *Periplus*, 52.
109. Cribb, 'Western Satraps and Satavahanas' (1998), 177.
110. *Periplus*, 50.
111. Ptolemy, *Geography*, 7.1.
112. *Periplus*, 48; 51.
113. Nasik Cave: 17 (AD 110). Thapar, *Early India* (2004), 260.
114. Warmington, *The Commerce between the Roman Empire and India* (1928), 112. Ball, *Rome in the East* (2000), 126.
115. Junnar: 5 (cisterns), 16 (hall façade), 8 (refectory).
116. Thapar, *Cultural Pasts* (2000), 547.
117. Karle Pillars: 7; 10; 17; 24.
118. Karle, Caitya, right pillar 11. Thapar, 'Early Mediterranean contacts with India' (1997), 34–5.
119. Karle, Caitya, right pillar 5.
120. Reading 'Milinda' in place of 'Mitidasa'.
121. Ray, 'A Resurvey of 'Roman' Contacts with the East' (1995), 80–1.
122. Karle, Caitya, right pillar 17. Milinda's wife was named Jayamita, two sons Bhayabhuti and Nabubhuti, and daughter Vasumita.
123. Varahamihira, *Pancasiddhantika*, 1.3.
124. *Ibid.* 1.4.
125. Varahamihira, *Brihat-Samhita*, 2.15.
126. Parker, *The Making of Roman India* (2008), 128–9.

Chapter 14 – The Tamil Kingdoms of Southern India
1. From Barygaza, 'most vessels continue on to the Strand' (*Periplus*, 51).
2. *Periplus*, 56.
3. *Periplus*: 'The voyage as far as Limyrike [Malabar Coast] is 7,000 *stades* [770 miles]' (*Periplus*, 51).

4. *Periplus*, 53.
5. *Peutinger Table*, 11.
6. *Periplus*, 52.
7. *Patirruppattu*, 2.4–10.
8. *Periplus*, 53.
9. Pliny, 6.26.
10. *Periplus*, 55.
11. *Periplus*, 54.
12. Pliny, 6.26.
13. *Akananuru*, 149.7–11.
14. *Periplus*, 54.
15. *Purananuru*, 343.1–10. De Romanis, 'Rome and the Notia of India' (1997), 94–5; 136–7.
16. Sidebotham, *Berenike* (2011), 190–1.
17. *Peutinger Table*, 11.
18. Palmyra: *C.I.S.* 2.3917.
19. Philo, *Embassy to Gaius*, 22.150.
20. *Periplus*, 56. Casson, *The Periplus* (1989), 85, 221.
21. Perhaps 50 crew and passengers per ship and 120 ships in the merchant fleet (Strabo, 2.5.12).
22. Eusebius, *Church History*, 5.10 (events before AD 200). Parker, *The Making of Roman India* (2008), 299–300.
23. *Acts*, 4:6. *Ostraca Petrie*, 266–8; 271.
24. Cochin Jews: Warmington, *The Commerce between the Roman Empire and India* (1928), 59.
25. Karuvur (Vanji) possibly modern Karur on the Amaravati River. Ptolemy, *Geography*, 7.1.
26. Turner, *Roman Coins from India* (1989), 5–6.
27. *Periplus*, 56.
28. *Garuda Puranam*, 68–80.
29. *Arthasastra*, 6, 11.
30. Pliny, 37.20.
31. Martial, 1.109.
32. Propertius, 4.7.18–19.
33. Pliny, 6.24. Tchernia, 'Winds and Coins' (1997), 252.
34. Pliny, 6.24.
35. *P. Vindob. G.* 40822.
36. *Periplus*, 54.
37. *Periplus*, 56.
38. Pliny, 6.23; Arrian, *Indika*, 8–9.
39. Arrian, *Alexander*, 8.8.
40. *Periplus*, 59.
41. *Arthasastra*, 6; 12.
42. Pliny, 9.65.
43. *Garuda Puranam*, 68–80.
44. *Arthasastra*, 2.11.
45. Florus, 2.34–62.
46. Suetonius, *Augusus*, 30.
47. Revenues Palestine: 48 million sesterces (Josephus, *Antiquities*, 19.8.2). Revenues Gaul: 40 million sesterces (Suetonius, *Julius Caesar*, 25). Cost of a Roman Legion: 11 million sesterces.
48. Horace, *Epistles*, 2.1.196.
49. Jennison, *Animals for Show and Pleasure in Ancient Rome* (1937), 66.
50. Florus, 2.34–62. Warmington, *The Commerce between the Roman Empire and India* (1928), 36–7.
51. Pliny, 9.54.
52. *Matthew*, 13:45–6.
53. Petronius, *Satyricon*, 76.
54. Pliny, 9.56.
55. Arrian, *Indica*, 8.9.

56. Propertius, *Eulogies*, 1.8.27–46.
57. Pliny, 33.12.
58. Martial, 8.81.
59. Martial, 8.45.
60. Martial, 10.38.
61. Martial, 5.37.
62. Walker, *Ancient Faces: Mummy Portraits in Roman Egypt* (2000).
63. Sidebotham, *Berenike* (2011), 237.
64. *Historia Augusta, Aurelian*, 45.2; Clement, *The Instructor*, 2.11.
65. Horace, *Satires*, 1.2.80.
66. Pseudo-Lucian, *The Loves*, 41.
67. Pliny, 9.56.
68. Pliny, 9.58.
69. Seneca, *On Benifits*, 7.9.5.
70. Juvenal, 6.457–507.
71. Ovid, *Cures for Love*, 5.53–4.
72. Pliny the Younger, *Letters*, 5.16.
73. Martial, 9.2.
74. Seneca, *On Consolation*, 16.50.
75. Seneca, *Tragedies*, 1.387–91.
76. Petronius, *Satyricon*, 55.
77. Horace, *Satires*, 1.2.79–80.
78. Pliny, 37.6.
79. Pliny, 9.56.
80. *Matthew*, 7:6.
81. I *Timothy*, 2:9.
82. Clement, *The Instructor*, 2.13.
83. Pliny, 12.41.
84. Nellin ur (city of Nell). *Maturaikkanci*, 75–88. De Romanis, 'Rome and the Notia of India' (1997), 143–4.
85. *Periplus*, 54–5.
86. Pliny, 6.26.
87. *Ibid.* Confirmed by *Periplus*, 55: 'the kings of both these trade ports (Muziris and Nelcynda) dwell inland'.
88. *Akananuru*, 57.14–7. Celiyan is a royal epithet of the Pandian King.
89. *Akananuru*, 149.7–13. De Romanis, 'Rome and the Notia of India' (1997), 108.
90. Modura Regia: Ptolemy, *Geography*, 7.1.
91. *Maturaikkanci*, 331–669.
92. Dio Chrysostom, 35.22.
93. *Manimekalai*, 19.1.45. *Perungadai*, 1.17.15.
94. Ball, *Rome in the East* (2000), 141.
95. *Silappatikaram*, 14.66–7. Surviving verses composed fifth century AD. Seland, *Ports and Political Power* (2010), 59.
96. Tradition dated first-second century AD.
97. *Mullaippattu*, 59–62.
98. Zvelebil, 'The *Yavanas* in Old Tamil Literature' (1956), 405.
99. *Sivakasindamani*, 1.101–4.
100. *Periplus*, 56.
101. De Romanis, 'Rome and the Notia of India' (1997), 100.
102. Pliny, 12.14.
103. *Periplus*, 56.
104. *Piper nigrum* (black pepper) grown in the Southern Ghats (modern Kerala and Tamil Nadu).

105. Black pepper flowers May–June. The crop takes six to eight months from flowering to harvest. The harvest season extends from November–January in the plains and January–March in the hills.
106. Sidebotham, *Berenike* (2011), 79; 268.
107. Martial, 13.13.
108. Pliny, 12.14; *Matthew*, 20:2–10.
109. Petronius, *Satyricon*, 2.74. Galen, *On Compounding*, 13.153. Celsus, *On Medicines*, 4.22.
110. Martial, 3.22.
111. Apicius, *On the Subject of Cooking*, 4.4.1.
112. *Ibid.* 4.5.2.
113. *Ibid.* 8.6.355.
114. *Ibid.* 5.3.187.
115. *Ibid.* 1.1–2.
116. Petronius, *Satyricon*, 2.49.
117. Statius, *Silvae*, 4.9.12.
118. Horace, *Epistles*, 2.1.270.
119. Persius, *Satires*, 3.75
120. Martial, 4.46.
121. Persius, *Satires*, 6.21.
122. Martial, 10.57.
123. Martial, 7.27.
124. Martial, 13.5; Petronius, *Satyricon*, 33.
125. Petronius, *Satyricon*, 36.
126. Juvenal, 7.184–5.
127. Petronius, *Satyricon*, 38.
128. Suetonius, *Vitellius*, 13.
129. Martial, 6.48.
130. Mons Claudianus: Veen, 'A life of luxury in the desert?' (1998), 101–5. Oberaden: De Romanis, 'Rome and the Notia of India' (1997), 100.
131. *Vindolanda Tablet*, 184. Pepper pots: Warmington, *The Commerce between the Roman Empire and India* (1928), 183–4.
132. House of Menander.
133. Beard, *Pompeii* (2008), 37.
134. Herculaneum Conservation Project.
135. *Periplus*, 56.
136. *Periplus*, 60.
137. *Periplus*, 56, 63.
138. Pliny, 35.32.
139. Pliny, 33.57.
140. Pliny, 35.32.
141. *Weilue*, 8 (Silk Road Seattle, 2004).
142. *Periplus*, 56.
143. Persius, *Satires*, 5.53–5.
144. Rauh, *Merchants, Sailors and Pirates in the Roman World* (2003), 98–9.
145. *Purananuru*, 56.18–21.
146. *Periplus*, 60.
147. Williams, 'The Eruption of Vesuvius and its Implications for the Early Roman Amphora Trade with India' (2004), 441–50.
148. Pliny the Younger, *Letters*, 6.16, 20.
149. Pliny, 6.26.
150. De Romanis, 'Rome and the Notia of India' (1997), 139–40.
151. Pliny, 34.48.
152. The Iyyal hoard contained both gold and silver coin (twelve aurei, seventy-one denarii, and thirty-four Indian punch-marked coins). Turner, *Roman Coins from India* (1989), 55–6.

153. From the Roman coins found in India about 5,400 denarii and 800 aurei are held in modern collections. Ball, *Rome in the East* (2000), 132.
154. Seland, *Ports and Political Power* (2010), 64–6.
155. Dio Chrysostom, 35.22.
156. Turner, *Roman Coins from India* (1989), 8–9; 62–3.
157. *Hou Hanshu*, 88.12.
158. Braudel, *Civilization and Capitalism*, 2 (1992), 405.
159. *P. Vindob. G.* 40822.
160. Tacitus, *Germania*, 1.5.
161. Cosmas Indiopleustes, *Christian Topography*, 11.441.
162. Turner, Roman Coins from India (1989), 20–24.
163. Tchernia, 'Winds and Coins' (1997), 264–5.
164. Turner, *Roman Coins from India* (1989), 24–7.
165. Macdowell, 'Finds of Roman coins in Southern Asia' (1990), 49–73.
166. Tchernia, 'Winds and Coins' (1997), 265–6.
167. *Ostraka Petrie*, 290 (22 July AD 62).
168. *Papyrus Giessen*, 2.47. Young, *Rome's Eastern Trade* (2001), 50–1.
169. Turner, *Roman Coins from India* (1989), 122–6.
170. Suetonius, *Vespasian*, 16.
171. Pliny the Younger, *Letters*, 3.5.7; 6.16.4.
172. Pliny, 6.26.
173. *Periplus*, 56.
174. Pliny, 12.41.
175. Appendix A.
176. Pliny, 12.32.
177. Strabo, 16.1.26. *Periplus*, 24.
178. *Periplus*, 28. Pliny, 6.24 (denarii as cargo).
179. *Matthew*, 20:2–10.
180. *Matthew*, 22:15–22.
181. One *Liu* (125 grams) of silver = 1,000 cash (AD 9) (*Hanshu*, 24B: 20b); Gold values: bamboo strips found near the Chinese frontier, one *Liang* (15.25 grams) of gold = 1,327 cash (12 BC) (*Juyan Hanjian Shiwen Hexiao*, 506:27) Further examples: 504:13; 505:20; 506:11.
182. *Epigraphia Indica*, 8 (Nasik Caves). Macdowell, 'Indian Imports of Roman Silver Coins' (1991), 151–2.
183. Duncan-Jones, *Money and Government* (1994), 215–32.
184. *P. Vindob. G.* 40822.
185. Loane, *Industry and Commerce* (1938), 139.
186. Pliny, 12.41.
187. Suetonius, *Vespasian*, 16.
188. Loane, *Industry and Commerce* (1938), 143.
189. *Horrea Galbae*: 15,000 square metres storage space excluding courtyards. Assuming grain stacked 2 metres depth = 22,500 tons (Rickman, *Roman Granaries and Store Buildings* (1971), 104–6). *Horrea Piperataria*: concrete foundations 100 metres × 65 metres = 6,500 square metres (70,000 square feet) = over 9,000 tons.
190. Pliny, 12.14.
191. Dio, 73.24.
192. Rickman, *Roman Granaries and Store Buildings* (1971), 106.
193. *L'année épigraphique*, 1994, 297.
194. Galen, *Avoidance of Grief*, 8–9.
195. Statius, *Silvae*, 3.3.89–98. Mattern, *Rome and the Enemy* (1999), 129.
196. Loane, *Industry and Commerce* (1938), 50.
197. Possible Red Sea pearl-fisheries: Pliny, 6.24.
198. Strabo, 15.1.4.
199. *Periplus*, 57.

200. Pliny, 6.26.
201. *Periplus*, 51, 59.
202. *Periplus*, 58.
203. Pliny, 6.23; Arrian, *Indika*, 8–9.
204. *Manimekhalai*, 13.1.
205. *Periplus*, 59.
206. *Silappatikaram*, 14.104–12.

Chapter 15 – The Anuradhapura Kingdom of Sri Lanka and the Far East

1. Pliny, 6.24.
2. *Periplus*, 60.
3. *Periplus*, 61.
4. Strabo, 2.1.14.
5. Pliny, 9.54.
6. Strabo, 2.1.14 (5,000 *stades* = 550 miles). *Periplus*, 61.
7. West rock-face of Wadi Menih, inscription: 2 (Greek: dated 2nd July) and 5 (Latin: dated 5th July). Lysas was probably there on a single day, but made a mistake on one of the calendar systems he was using (Roman or Greek-Egyptian). Sidebotham, *Berenike* (2011), 72, 197.
8. De'Arms, *Commerce and Social Standing* (1981), 166.
9. Pliny, 6.24.
10. *Ibid.*
11. Sources: 'the Prince named [Bhatika] Abhaya, the son of Kutakanna reigned twenty-eight years' (*Dipavamsa*, 21.1–30) or 'the Prince named Bhatikabhaya, reigned twenty-two years' (*Mahavamsa*, 34.37). De Romanis, 'Romanukharattha and Taprobane' (1997), 192–3.
12. Pliny, 6.24.
13. Abeydeera, 'Raki's Mission to Romanukharattha' (2009), 146–65.
14. *Mahavamsa*, 11.20–22 (written in Pali script). Weerakkody, *Taprobane* (1997), 57–8.
15. Pliny, 24.88.
16. Titles: *parumaka* (Eminence or Premier) and *bata* (Lord). Inscription 399 at Niyandavaragala in Batticaloa. Inscription 1000 at Sasseruva near Anuradhapura District ('son of the Premier').
17. Inscription 994 at Sasseruva. Abeydeera, 'Raki's Mission to Romanukharattha' (2009), 153–4.
18. Pliny, 6.24.
19. *Mahavamsa* (*The Great Chronicle*), 34.47.
20. *Dipavamsa*, 21.13.
21. *Vamsathapakasini* commentating on *Mahavamsa*, 34.47. The *Vamsathapakasini* was written between the tenth and thirteen centuries AD.
22. De Romanis, 'Romanukharattha and Taprobane' (1997), 188–91.
23. Warmington, *The Commerce between the Roman Empire and India* (1928), 25.
24. Ptolemy, *Geography*, 7.4.
25. Pliny, 6.24.
26. Ptolemy, *Geography*, 7.4.
27. Institute of Nautical Archaeology at Texas A&M University.
28. Ptolemy, *Geography*, 7.1.
29. Aelian, *Nature of Animals*, 16.2; Ovid, *The Loves*, 2.6.
30. *Periplus*, 60.
31. Kaveripattinam (modern Poompuhar). Seland, *Ports and Political Power* (2010), 59.
32. *Pattinapalai*, 184–93. Composed about AD 190 (reign of King Karikala Cholan). De Romanis, 'Rome and the Notia of India' (1997), 114–15.
33. *Silappatikaram*, 5.9–12.
34. *Manimekalai*, 1.72; 3.45; 19.54; *Silappatikaram*, 5.117; 5.213; 6.127; 10.31.
35. *Perumpanarruppatai*, 349–51.
36. *Akananuru*, 73.10; *Silappadikaram*, 5.63.
37. *Manimekhalai*, 24.177. Tomber, *Indo-Roman Trade* (2008), 138.

38. Gaur, 'Underwater Exploration off Poompuhar and Possible Causes of its Submergence' (1998), 84–90.
39. *Periplus*, 60.
40. *Perungadai*, 1.17.15.
41. Sidebotham, *Berenike* (2011), 191.
42. Tomber, *Indo-Roman Trade* (2008), 132–7.
43. Sidebotham, *Berenike* (2011), 75.
44. Ptolemy, *Geography*, 1.14.
45. Chaberis (Puhar). Ptolemy, *Geography*, 7.1.
46. East Coast Satavahana: emporiums of Melanga, Maliarpha, Contacossyla, Alosygni and the city-port of Palura. Ptolemy, *Geography*, 7.1.
47. Turner, *Roman Coins from India* (1989), 43–44, 119.
48. *Ibid.* 46–119.
49. *Ibid.* 37–40, 47.
50. Krishnamurthy, 'Imitation Roman Gold Coins from Tirukoilur Hoard, Tamilnadu' (1998), 147.
51. Turner, *Roman Coins from India* (1989), 29–33.
52. Macdowell, 'The Defacement of Roman Aurei Exported to India' (1998), 139.
53. Turner, *Roman Coins from India* (1989), 34–6.
54. Ptolemy, *Geography*, 1.13.
55. *Ibid.* 7.1.
56. *Periplus*, 61.
57. *Periplus*, 62.
58. Ptolemy, *Geography*, 7.2 (Pentapolis: 'Five-cities').
59. *Ibid.* 7.1.
60. Dionysius Periegetes, 707–12.
61. Ptolemy, *Geography*, 7.2.
62. *Periplus*, 64.
63. Ptolemy, *Geography*, 7.2.
64. Martial, *Spectacles*, 8.26.
65. *Suvarnabhumi*: 'Golden-Land' or *Suvarnadvipa*: 'Golden-Island'.
66. *Jatakas*, 3.360.
67. *Arthasastra*, 2.11.59.
68. *Periplus*, 63. *Suvarnadvipa*: 'Golden-Island' (Sumatra).
69. *Periplus*, 66.
70. Josephus, *Antiquities*, 8.6.4.
71. Bangladesh and Burma: Baracura Emporium (near Chittagong?), Samba City, Sada City, Barabonna Emporium, Sabara City, Bsyga Emporium, Berobae City (Ptolemy, *Geography*, 7.1).
72. Tacola Emporium (Yangon?) and Sabana Emporium (Ptolemy, *Geography*, 7.2). Warmington, *The Commerce between the Roman Empire and India* (1928), 127.
73. *Arthasastra*, 2.11.59; *Silappatikaram*, 14.104–12.
74. *Hou Hanshu*, 5. Leslie & Gardiner, *The Roman Empire in Chinese Sources* (1996), 150–1.
75. Ptolemy, *Geography*, 7.2.
76. *Ibid.*
77. Warmington, *The Commerce between the Roman Empire and India* (1928), 128.
78. Ptolemy, *Geography*, 1.13. Berggren & Jones, *Ptolemy's Geography* (2000), 75.
79. Thailand: Thipinobastae Emporium (near Bangkok?). Ptolemy, *Geography*, 7.2.
80. Ptolemy, *Geography*, 1.14.
81. *Hou Hanshu*, 88.12; *Huai-nan Tzu*, 18.21. Yu, *Trade and Expansion in Han China* (1967), 182.
82. Ptolemy, *Geography*, 1.14. Berggren & Jones, *Ptolemy's Geography* (2000), 155–6.
83. Ptolemy, *Geography*, 7.3.
84. *Ibid.* 1.14.
85. *Ibid.* 7.3.
86. Seneca, *Natural Questions*, preface, 1.11.
87. Pliny, 6.21; Servius, *Commentary on Virgil*, 1.9.30.

88. Seneca, *Natural Questions*, 5.18.11.
89. Oc-eo near Ho Chi Minh City. Young, *Rome's Eastern Trade* (2001), 29.
90. Sinae (China). Ptolemy, *Geography*, 7.3.

Chapter 16 – The Antun Embassy to China and the Antonine Pandemic

1. Loewe, *The Men who Governed Han China* (2004), 77–8.
2. Plutarch, *Crassus*, 18; 24–5; 27.
3. Juvenal, 6.400–3.
4. Text: 'Alexandros . . . [the] Palmyrene . . . performed . . . and Germanicus sent him to . . . of Mesene and to Orabzes . . . Samsigeram, the Supreme King'. *Palmyrene Aramaic Texts*, 2754.
5. Tacitus, *Annals*, 14.25.
6. *Hou Hanshu*, 88.12.
7. Hill, *Through the Jade Gate to Rome* (2009), v–xvi.
8. *Hou Hanshu*, 88.12.
9. Hirth, *China and the Roman Orient* (1885), 173–8.
10. *Hou Hanshu*, 65/55.2133 (4a-b).
11. Dio, 71.2.
12. *Historia Augusta, Lucius Verus*, 8.1–4.
13. Ammianus Marcellinus, 23.6.24.
14. Oxford Archaeology Department.
15. Fagan, *Bathing in Public in the Roman World* (1999).
16. Castex, *Architecture of Italy* (2008), 4–7.
17. Pollard, *Soldiers, Cities, and Civilians in Roman Syria* (2000), 52.
18. *Historia Augusta, Hadrian*, 22.
19. Celsus, *On Medicines*, 4.2–28.
20. Aelius Aristides, 48.38–44.
21. *Ibid.* 51.24–5.
22. Galen, *Opera Omnia*, 19.15.
23. *Historia Augusta, Marcus Aurelius*, 13.
24. Duncan-Jones, 'The Impact of the Antonine Plague' (1996), 120–1.
25. *Sammelbuch*, 16.12816.
26. *Papyrus Thmouis*, 1.104.10–18 (AD 173).
27. Orosius, 7.15.5–6.
28. Duncan-Jones, 'The Impact of the Antonine Plague' (1996), 121.
29. Tacitus, *Germania*, 16.
30. *Ibid.* 22.
31. *I.L.S.* 7215a.
32. MacKendrick, *The Dacian Stones Speak* (1975), 206–7.
33. Duncan-Jones, 'The Impact of the Antonine Plague' (1996), 121.
34. *Historia Augusta, Marcus Aurelius*, 21. Haley, *Baetica Felix* (2003), 70; 184; 190.
35. Jones, G. (1980), 'The Roman Mines at Rio Tinto' in *J.R.S.* 70 (1980), 161.
36. AD 150: Tetradrachm, weight: 12.9 grams, silver content: 2.3 grams. Denarius, weight: 3.4 grams, silver content 2.4 grams.
37. Howgego & Butcher, 'Coinage and the Roman Economy in the Antonine Period' (2013), 13–15.
38. *O.G.I.S.* 595.
39. *Marcus Aurelius to the Athenians on Appeals, Trigonia, and Herodes Atticus* (AD 174/5).
40. *C.I.L.* 3.5567.
41. Dio, 72.14.2–4; Eusebius, 7.22.
42. Galen, *Opera Omnia*, 19.17–18.
43. Cyprian, *To Demetrius*, 3.
44. Cyprian, *On the Mortality*, 14.
45. Eutropius, 8.12.
46. Jerome, *Chronicle*, 172.
47. *Historia Augusta, Marcus Aurelius*, 17.2.

48. *Ibid.* 17.4.
49. *Ibid.* 21.2.
50. *Ibid.* 17.4.
51. *Ibid.* 21.2.
52. *I.L.S.* 2304.
53. *Historia Augusta, Marcus Aurelius*, 21.6.
54. Orosius, 7.15.5–6.
55. Dio, 71.11.
56. *Historia Augusta, Marcus Aurelius*, 28.
57. Dio, 74.6.
58. Dio, 72.35.

Conclusion: Assessing the Roman Economy
1. Concept of bulwark territory: Dio, 75.3.2.
2. Appendix B.
3. Velleius, 2.39.
4. Map 1 and Appendices B & C.
5. *Ancient Figures and Modern Estimates*.
6. Pliny, 12.41.
7. Plutarch, *Pompey*, 45 (Republic: 340 million); Suetonius, *Julius Caesar*, 25 (Gaul: 40 million); Strabo, 2.5.12 (Egypt: 300 million sesterces). Total: 680 million sesterces, but see Appendix B for population increases.
8. Josephus, *Jewish War*, 2.16.4 (Egyptian revenue per month = annual revenues from Palestine); Josephus, *Antiquities*, 19.8.2 (Palestine revenue: 48 million sesterces per annum). Therefore: Egyptian revenues worth at least 576 million sesterces per year by the late first century AD.
9. There was a garrison of only three cohorts at Syene (perhaps 1,500 men: Egypt-Ethiopia frontier). Strabo, 17.1.53: Leuke Kome, a Nabataean port imposing the quarter rate *tetarte* tax was managed by 'a detachment of soldiers' (*Periplus*, 19).
10. Pliny, 33.21.
11. Ovid, *Cosmetics for Ladies*, 83–4; Juvenal, 6.457–507.
12. Martial, 2.22.
13. Tacitus, *Histories*, 4.74.
14. Mattern, *Rome and the Enemy* (1999), 123–6.
15. Cato, *On Agriculture*, 2 (160 BC).
16. Dio Chrysostom, *On Wealth*, 79.5.
17. Cicero, *On Duties*, 1.151.
18. Pliny, 6.26. Tenfold gain on Indo-Roman voyages (*Hou Hanshu*, 88.12) and tenfold cost increases on the most expensive processed goods (*Price Edict*, 23.1.1; 24.1.1) = hundredfold price increase between India and Rome.
19. Tacitus, *Annals*, 3.55.
20. De Romanis, 'Rome and the Notia of India' (1997), 124–6; 158.
21. Tacitus, *Annals*, 3.52.
22. *Ibid.*
23. Ibid. 3.53.
24. *Ibid.* 2.37–8 (Tiberius financially assists the nobility); 48 (aristocrats in financial difficulty due to excessive spending); Dio, 57.10 (Tiberius offers financial assistance to impoverished senators); Tacitus, *Annals*, 13.34 (Nero offers financial support to members of the nobility who had 'squandered their ancestral wealth on extravagances').
25. Dio, 74.8.
26. Compare the revenues between east and west: Appendixes A–C.
27. *Peutinger Table*, 11. Palmyra: *C.I.S.* 2.3917.
28. Seneca, *Natural Questions*, 5.18.4.

Appendix A: The Roman Economy
1. Strabo, 17.1.13.
2. Plutarch, *Pompey*, 45.
3. Josephus, *Jewish War*, 2.16.4; *Antiquities*, 19.8.2.
4. Pliny, 12.54. One *iugera* = 0.25 hectare.
5. Lemenih, 'Opportunities and Challenges for Sustainable Production' (2011), 22.
6. Pliny, 12.54.
7. Pliny, 12.30. Persian *schoeni* = 3.5 miles.
8. Lemenih, 'Management Guide for Sustainable Production of Frankincense' (2011), 20–4. In 1835 over 450 tons of frankincense was being shipped from Aden to Bombay (Groom, *Frankincense and Myrrh*, (1981), 135).
9. Pliny, 12.32.
10. Plutarch, *Alexander*, 29.
11. Polybius, 13.9.
12. Pliny, 6.26; 12.41.
13. Pliny, 12.32; 35.
14. *Kephalaia*, 1.11: 'like the merchant who shall return from a country with the doubling of his great cargo and the riches of his trading'.
15. Strabo, 3.2.10.
16. Pliny, 33.21. Roman pound (*libra*) = about 329 grams.
17. Pliny, 12.41.
18. Pliny, 6.26.
19. *Hou Hanshu*, 88.12 (ten-fold gain).
20. Strabo, 2.5.12.

Appendix B: Reconstructing Roman Revenues
1. Caesar, *Civil War*, 3.4.
2. Suetonius, *Julius Caesar*, 25.
3. Plutarch, *Pompey*, 45.
4. Revenues of the Roman province of Asia (28 million sesterces). Greater Anatolia perhaps double this figure based on territorial size and tribute figures from fifth century Persian Empire (Ionia: 520 Attic talents; Lydia: 650 talents; Pyrgia-Cappadocia: 468 talents; Cilicia: 468 talents). *Herodotus*, 3.90.
5. Ethnarchy of Archelaus; Tetrarchies of Antipas and Philip (600; 200; 100 talents). Josephus, *Antiquities*, 17.11.4.
6. *Ibid.* 19.8.2.
7. Suetonius, *Caligula*, 16 (100 million sesterces over twenty years).
8. Philostratus, *Lives of the Sophists*, 548.
9. Strabo, 17.1.13; Josephus, *Jewish War*, 2.16.4.

Appendix C: The Expense of Roman Legions
1. Location of Legions: Dio, 55.23–4. Cost: *Ancient Figures and Modern Estimates*.
2. Tacitus, *Annals*, 13.35.
3. *Papyrus Geneve Latin*, 1. Egyptian payment in grain for garrisons a feature of the monetised Persian Empire (Herodotus, 30.91).
4. Suetonius, *Domitian*, 7; Dio, 67.3.5.
5. *C.I.L.* 6.3492 (AD 165).
6. Assuming the figure of 8 million sesterces per million people produces estimates that display greater deficits and reduced surplus.
7. Strabo, 4.5.3.
8. Strabo, 17.1.13.
9. Josephus, *Jewish War*, 2.16.4.

Bibliography

Abeydeera, A., 'Raki's Mission to Romanukharattha' in *Habis* 40 (2009), 145–65.

Adams, C., *Land Transport in Roman Egypt* (OUP, 2007).

Aldrete, G. and Mattingly, D., 'Feeding the City' in Potter, D. (ed.), *Life, Death, and Entertainment* (Michigan University, 2010), 171–204.

Avakov, A., *Two Thousand Years of Economic Statistics* (Algora Publishing, 2010).

Bagnall, R., *Documents from Berenike. Volumes 1 and 2* (Fondation Égyptologique Reine Élisabeth, 2000/2005).

Ball, W., *Rome in the East: the Transformation of an Empire* (Routledge, 2000).

Berggren, J. and Jones, A., *Ptolemy's Geography* (Princeton University Press, 2000).

Beard, M., *Pompeii: Life of a Roman Town* (Profile Books, 2008).

Bird, J., 'Incense in Mithraic Ritual' in Peacock, D. (ed.), *Food for the Gods* (Oxbow Books, 2006), 122–34.

Blue, L., 'New Light on the Nature of Indo-Roman Trade' in Agius, D. (ed.), *Navigated Spaces, Connected Places* (Archaeopress, 2012), 91–100.

Bowersock, G., *Roman Arabia* (Harvard University Press, 1983).

Braudel, F., *Civilization and Capitalism 15th–18th Century. Volume 2* (Collins, 1981).

Brosius, M., *The Persians* (Routledge, 2006).

Butterworth, A. and Laurence, R., *Pompeii: The Living City* (Phoenix, 2005).

Bukharin, M. and Strauch, J., 'Indian Inscriptions from the Cave Hoq on Suqutra (Yemen)'. *Annali Istituto Universitario Orientale*, 64 (2004), 121–38.

Campbell, B., *The Emperor and the Roman Army* (OUP, 1984).

Campbell, B., *The Roman Army* (Rutledge, 1994).

Cappers, R., 'Archaeobotanical Evidence of Roman Trade with India' in Ray, H. (ed.), *Archaeology of Seafaring* (Indian Council of Historical Research, 1999), 51–69.

Casson, L., *The Ancient Mariners* (Princeton University Press, 1959).

Casson, L., *Ships and Seamanship in the Ancient World* (Princeton University Press, 1971).

Casson, L., 'New Light on Maritime Loans: P. Vindob. G 19792' in Bagnall, R., *Studies in Roman Law* (1986), 11–7.

Casson, L., *The Periplus Maris Erythraei: Text, Translation, and Commentary* (Princeton University Press, 1989).

Casson, L., 'New Light on Maritime Loans: P. Vindob. G 40822' in *Zeitschrift für Papyrologie und Epigraphik*, 84 (1990), 195–206.

Castex, J., *Architecture of Italy* (Greenwood, 2008).

Catsambis, D., *The Oxford Handbook of Maritime Archaeology* (OUP, 2012).

Conan, M. and Kress, W., *Botanical Progress, Horticultural Innovation and Cultural Changes* (Harvard University Press, 2007).

Cribb, J., 'Western Satraps and Satavahanas' in Jha, A. (ed.), *Ex Moneta* (Harman Publishing House, 1998).

De Romanis, F., *Cassia, Cinnamomo, Ossidiana* (L'Erma di Bretschneider, 1996).

De Romanis, F., 'Rome and the Notia of India' in De Romanis, F. (ed.), *Crossings: Early Mediterranean Contacts with India* (Manohar Publishers, 1997), 80–160.

De Romanis, F., 'Playing Sudoku on the Verso of the "Muziris Papyrus"' in *Journal of the Ancient Indian History* (2012), 75–101.

De'Arms, J., *Commerce and Social Standing in Ancient Rome* (Harvard University Press, 1981).

Duncan-Jones, R., *Money and Government in the Roman Empire* (Cambridge University Press, 1990).

Duncan-Jones, R., *Structure and Scale in the Roman Economy* (Cambridge University Press, 1994).

Duncan-Jones, R., 'The Impact of the Antonine Plague' in *Journal of Roman Archaeology*, 9 (1996), 108–36.

Engels, D., *Alexander the Great and the Logistics of the Macedonian Army* (California University Press, 1978).

Etienne, R., *Pompeii: The Day a City Died* (Thames and Hudson, 1992).

Fagan, G., *Bathing in Public in the Roman World* (Michigan University Press, 1999).

Fage, D. (ed.), *The Cambridge History of Africa. Volume 2: From c.500 BC to AD 1050* (Cambridge University Press, 1979).

Findlay, R. and O'Rourke, K., *Power and Plenty: Trade, War, and the World Economy in the Second Millennium* (Princeton University Press, 2009).

Frank, T., *An Economic Survey of Ancient Rome* (Pageant Books, 1959).

Frier, B., 'Population' in *Cambridge Ancient History, volume 11: The High Empire, AD 70–192* (Cambridge University Press, 2000), 811–6.

Gardner, J., *Women in Roman Law and Society* (Indiana University Press, 1986).

Gaur, A., 'Underwater Exploration off Poompuhar and Possible Causes of its Submergence' in *Bulletin of the Indian Archeological Society*, 28 (1998), 84–90.

Graf, D., *Rome and the Arabian Frontier: From the Nabataeans to the Saracens* (Ashgate, 1997).

Greene, K., *Archaeology of the Roman Economy* (Batsford, 1983).

Groom, N., *Frankincense and Myrrh: A Study of the Arabian Incense Trade* (Longman, 1981).

Haley, W., *Baetica Felix: People and Prosperity in Southern Spain from Caesar to Septimius Severus* (Texas University Press, 2003).

Herz, P., 'Finances and Costs of the Roman Army' in Erdkamp, P., *A Companion to the Roman Army* (Wiley-Blackwell, 2010), 306–22.

Hiebert, F. and Cambon, P., *Afghanistan: Crossroads of the Ancient World* (British Museum Press, 2011).

Higham, C., *Encyclopaedia of Ancient Asian Civilizations* (Facts on File, 2004).

Hill, J., *Weilue* (Silk Road Seattle, 2004).

Hill, J., *Through the Jade Gate to Rome* (BookSurge Publishing, 2009).

Hopkins, K., 'Taxes and Trade in the Roman Empire' in *J.R.S.* 70 (1980), 101–25.

Hopkins, K., 'Models, Ships and Staples' in Garnsey, P. (ed.), *Trade and Famine in Classical Antiquity* (Cambridge Philological Society, 1983), 84–109.

Hopkins, K., *Death and Renewal: 2* (Cambridge University Press, 1985).

Hopkins, K., 'Rome, Taxes, Rents and Trade' in Scheidel, W. (ed.), *The Ancient Economy* (Edinburgh University Press, 2002), 190–232.

Hopkins, K., 'The Political Economy of the Roman Empire' in Morris, I. (ed.), *The Dynamics of Ancient Empires* (OUP, 2010).

Howgego, C. and Butcher, K., 'Coinage and the Roman Economy in the Antonine Period: the view from Egypt' (Online, 2013).

Jackson, J., *At Empire's Edge: Exploring Rome's Egyptian Frontier* (Yale University Press, 2002).

Jennison, G., *Animals for Show and Pleasure in Ancient Rome* (Manchester University Press, 1937).

Jones, G., 'The Roman Mines at Rio Tinto' in *J.R.S.* 70 (1980) 146–65.

Judd, T., 'The Trade with India through the Eastern Desert of Egypt under the Roman Empire' (Liverpool University, 2007).

Kistler, J. and Lair, R., *War Elephants* (Praeger, 2007).

Krishnamurthy, R., 'Imitation Roman Gold Coins from Tirukoilur Hoard, Tamilnadu' in Jha, A. (ed.), *Ex Moneta* (Harman Publishing House, 1998), 131–6.

Lemenih, M., 'Management Guide for Sustainable Production of Frankincense' (Online, 2011).

Lemenih, M., 'Opportunities and Challenges for Sustainable Production and Marketing of Gums and Resins in Ethiopia' (Online, 2011).

Leslie D. and Gardiner, K., *The Roman Empire in Chinese Sources* (Bardi, 1996).

Loane, H., *Industry and Commerce of the City of Rome* (Johns Hopkins Press, 1938).

Loewe, M., *The Men who Governed Han China* (Brill, 2004).

Macdowell, A., 'Finds of Roman Coins in Southern Asia' in *Ancient Ceylon*, 9 (1990), 49–73.

Macdowell, A., 'Indian Imports of Roman Silver Coins' in Jha, A. (ed.) *Coinage Trade and Economy* (India Institute for Research in Numismatic Studies, 1991), 145–63.

Macdowell, H., 'The Defacement of Roman Aurei Exported to India' in Jha, A. (ed.) *Ex Moneta* (Harman Pubishing House 1998), 129–44.

MacKendrick, P., *The Dacian Stones Speak* (North Carolina University Press, 1975).

Mattern, S., *Rome and the Enemy: Imperial Strategy in the Principate* (California University Press, 1999).

McCloud, N., 'The Romance of Marble Cutting' in *Popular Mechanics Magazine* 48 (August 1927), 226–30.

McLaughlin, R., *Rome and the Distant East: Trade Routes to the Ancient Lands of Arabia, India and China* (Bloomsbury-Continuum, 2010).

Mieroop, M., *A History of Ancient Egypt* (Wiley-Blackwell, 2011).

Millar, F., 'Caravan Cities' in Austin, M. (ed.), *Modus Operandi* (Institute of Classical Studies, 1997), 122–37.

Parker, G., *The Making of Roman India* (Cambridge University Press, 2008).

Parker, P., *The Great Trade Routes* (Conway, 2012).

Peachin, M., *The Oxford Handbook of Social Relations in the Roman World* (O.U.P. 2011).

Peacock, D., 'Ballast as Ships' Ballast' in Peacock (ed.), *Food for the Gods* (Oxbow Books, 2006), 28–70.

Phillips, C., 'A Latin Inscription from South Arabia' in *Proceedings of the Seminar for Arabian Studies* 34 (2004), 239–50.

Pollard, N., *Soldiers, Cities, and Civilians in Roman Syria* (Michigan University Press, 2000).

Prakash, O., *European Commercial Enterprise in Pre-Colonial India, volume 2* (Cambridge University Press, 1998).

Raschke, M., 'New Studies in Roman Commerce with the East' in *Aufstieg und Niedergang der Römischen Welt*, 2:9.2 (1978), 604–1378.

Rathbone, D., 'The 'Muziris' papyrus (SB XVIII 13167)' in *Alexandrian Studies II* (Bulletin de la Société d'Archéologie d'Alexandrie, 2001), 39–50.

Rauh, N., *Merchants, Sailors and Pirates in the Roman World* (Tempus, 2003).

Ray, H., 'A Resurvey of 'Roman' Contacts with the East' in Boussac, M. (ed.), *Athens, Aden, Arikamedu* (Centre de Sciences, 1995), 97–114.

Reid, S., *The Silk and Spice Routes: Exploration by Sea* (Belitha, 1994).

Rickman, G., *Roman Granaries and Store Buildings* (Cambridge University Press, 1971).

Safrai, Z., *The Economy of Roman Palestine* (Routledge, 1993).

Salomon, R., 'Epigraphic Remains of Indian Traders in Egypt' in *Journal of the American Oriental Society* 3 (1991), 731–6.

Schinz, A., *The Magic Square: Cities in Ancient China* (Axel Menges, 1996).

Schmitthenner, W., 'Rome and India' in *J.R.S.* 69 (1979), 90–106.

Sedov, A. 'Qana (Yemen) and the Indian Ocean' in Ray, H. (ed.), *Tradition and Archaeology* (Manohar Publishers and Distributors, 1996), 128–80.

Sedov, A., 'The Port of Qana and the Incense Trade' in Peacock, D. (ed.), *Food for the Gods* (Oxbow, 2007), 71–111.

Seland, E., *Ports and Political Power in the Periplus: Complex Societies and Maritime Trade on the Indian Ocean in the First Century AD* (Archaeopress, 2010).

Shinnie, P. and Bradley, R., 'The Murals from the Augustus Temple, Meroe' in Kelly, W. (ed.), *Studies in Ancient Egypt* (Museum of Fine Arts, 1981), 167–72.

Sidebotham, S., *Roman Economic Policy in the Erythra Thalassa* (E.J. Brill, 1986).

Sidebotham, S., *The Red Land: The Illustrated Archaeology of Egypt's Eastern Desert* (American University in Cairo Press, 2008).

Sidebotham, S., *Berenike and the Ancient Maritime Spice Route* (University of California Press, 2011).

Singer, C., 'The Incense Kingdoms' in Peacock, D. (ed.), *Food for the Gods* (Oxbow Books, 2006), 4–27.

Strauss, J., *Roman Cargoes* (PhD Thesis London University, 2007).

Taylor, J., *Petra and the Lost Kingdom of the Nabataeans* (I. B. Tauris, 2011).

Taylor, J., *The Essenes, the Scrolls, and the Dead Sea* (O.U.P. 2012).

Tchernta, A., 'The Dromentary of the Peticii and Trade with the East' in De Romanis, F. (ed.), *Crossings* (Manohar Publishers, 1997), 238–49.

Tchernia, A., 'Winds and Coins' in De Romanis, F. (ed.), *Crossings* (Manohar Publishers, 1997), 250–76.

Thapar, R., 'Early Mediterranean Contacts with India: an Overview' in De Romanis, F. (ed.), *Crossings* (Manohar Publishers, 1997), 11–40.

Thapar, R., *Cultural Pasts: Essays in Early Indian History* (OUP, 2000).

Tomber, R., *Indo-Roman Trade: From Pots to Pepper* (Duckworth, 2008).

Török, L., *The Kingdom of Kush* (Brill, 1998).

Török, L., *Between Two Worlds: The Frontier Region between Ancient Nubia and Egypt* (Brill, 2009).

Turner, P., *Roman Coins from India* (Royal Numismatic Society, 1989).

Turner, P. and Cribb, J., 'Numismatic Evidence for the Roman Trade with Ancient India' in Reade, J. (ed.), *The Indian Ocean in Antiquity* (Kegan Paul International, 1996), 309–19.

Veen, V., 'A Life of Luxury in the Desert?' in *Journal of Roman Archaeology* 11 (1998), 101–16.

Walker, S., *Ancient Faces: Mummy Portraits in Roman Egypt* (British Museum Press, 2000).

Wallace-Hadrill, A., *Rome's Cultural Revolution* (Cambridge University Press, 2008).

Wallech, S., *World History: A Concise Thematic Analysis* (Wiley-Blackwell, 2012).

Warmington, E., *The Commerce between the Roman Empire and India* (Curson Press, 1928).

Weerakkody, D., *Taprobane: Ancient Sri Lanka as known to Greeks and Romans* (Brepols, 1997).

Williams, D., 'The Eruption of Vesuvius and its Implications for the Early Roman Amphora Trade with India' in Eiring, J. (ed.), *Transport Amphorae and Trade in the Eastern Mediterranean* (Aarhus University Press, 2004), 441–50.

Young, G., *Rome's Eastern Trade: International Commerce and Imperial Policy* (Routledge, 2001).

Yu, Y. *Trade and Expansion in Han China* (Cambridge University Press, 1967).

Zvelebil, K., 'The *Yavanas* in Old Tamil Literature' in *Charisteria Orientalia* (Nakladatelství Ceskoslovenské Akademie, 1956).

Index